ENTANGLING THE QUEBEC ACT

MCGILL-QUEEN'S STUDIES IN EARLY CANADA / AVANT LE CANADA

Series Editors / Directeurs de la collection : Allan Greer and Carolyn Podruchny

This series features studies of the history of the northern half of North America – a vast expanse that would eventually be known as Canada – in the era before extensive European settlement and extending into the nineteenth century. Long neglected, Canada-before-Canada is a fascinating area of study experiencing an intellectual renaissance as researchers in a range of disciplines, including history, geography, archeology, anthropology, literary studies, and law, contribute to a new and enriched understanding of the distant past. The editors welcome manuscripts in English or French on all aspects of the period, including work on Indigenous history, the Atlantic fisheries, the fur trade, exploration, French or British imperial expansion, colonial life, culture, language, law, science, religion, and the environment.

Cette série de monographies est consacrée à l'histoire de la partie septentrionale du continent de l'Amérique du nord, autrement dit le grand espace qui deviendra le Canada, dans les siècles qui s'étendent jusqu'au début du 19e. Longtemps négligé par les chercheurs, ce Canada-avant-le-Canada suscite beaucoup d'intérêt de la part de spécialistes dans plusieurs disciplines, entre autres, l'histoire, la géographie, l'archéologie, l'anthropologie, les études littéraires et le droit. Nous assistons à une renaissance intellectuelle dans ce champ d'étude axé sur l'interaction de premières nations, d'empires européens et de colonies. Les directeurs de cette série sollicitent des manuscrits, en français ou en anglais, qui portent sur tout aspect de cette période, y compris l'histoire des autochtones, celle des pêcheries de l'atlantique, de la traite des fourrures, de l'exploration, de l'expansion de l'empire français ou britannique, de la vie coloniale (Nouvelle-France, l'Acadie, Terre-Neuve, les provinces maritimes, etc.), de la culture, la langue, le droit, les sciences, la religion ou l'environnement.

1 A Touch of Fire
Marie-André Duplessis, the Hôtel-Dieu of Quebec, and the Writing of New France
Thomas M. Carr, Jr

2 Entangling the Quebec Act
Transnational Contexts, Meanings, and Legacies in North America and the British Empire
Edited by Ollivier Hubert and François Furstenberg

Entangling the Quebec Act

Transnational Contexts, Meanings, and Legacies in North America and the British Empire

Edited by
OLLIVIER HUBERT
and
FRANÇOIS FURSTENBERG

McGill-Queen's University Press
Montreal & Kingston • London • Chicago

ISBN 978-0-2280-0389-2 (cloth)
ISBN 978-0-2280-0390-8 (paper)
ISBN 978-0-2280-0463-9 (ePDF)
ISBN 978-0-2280-0464-6 (ePUB)

Legal deposit fourth quarter 2020
Bibliothèque nationale du Québec

Printed in Canada on acid-free paper that is 100% ancient forest free (100% post-consumer recycled), processed chlorine free.

This book has been published with the help of a grant from the Canadian Federation for the Humanities and Social Sciences, through the Awards to Scholarly Publications Program, using funds provided by the Social Sciences and Humanities Research Council of Canada.

Funded by the Government of Canada | Financé par le gouvernement du Canada | Canada

Canada Council for the Arts | Conseil des arts du Canada

We acknowledge the support of the Canada Council for the Arts.

Nous remercions le Conseil des arts du Canada de son soutien.

Library and Archives Canada Cataloguing in Publication

Title: Entangling the Quebec Act : transnational contexts, meanings, and legacies in North America and the British empire / edited by Ollivier Hubert and François Furstenberg.
Names: Hubert, Ollivier, 1968– editor. | Furstenberg, François, editor.
Description: Series statement: McGill-Queen's studies in early Canada ; 2 | Includes bibliographical references and index.
Identifiers: Canadiana (print) 20200329316 | Canadiana (ebook) 20200329367 | ISBN 9780228003908 (paper) | ISBN 9780228003892 (cloth) | ISBN 9780228004639 (ePDF) | ISBN 9780228004646 (ePUB)
Subjects: LCSH: Québec (Province). Quebec Act.
Classification: LCC FC414 .E48 2020 | DDC 971.4/02—dc23

This book was typeset by True to Type in 10.5/13 Sabon

Contents

Table and Figures

TABLE

FIGURES

Acknowledgments

For their support for the initial conference that made this volume possible, our thanks go to the Omohundro Institute of Early American History and Culture, the Social Sciences and Humanities Research Council of Canada, the Bibliothèque et Archives nationales du Québec, and the Faculté des arts et des sciences de l'Université de Montréal. Thanks in particular to Karin Wulf, Isabelle Crevier, and Sophie Montreuil, as well as to Alain Beaulieu, Christopher Leslie Brown, and Jean-François Palomino, who helped us organize the international colloquium on the Quebec Act held in Montreal in October 2013. Special thanks to Jack P. Greene and Denys Delâge for their valuable comments on this occasion: they inspired us in the conceptualization of this book. We're also grateful to Pierre Tousignant for his valuable advice and encouragement. Alexandre Trépanier and Adina Ruiu provided invaluable assistance in moments of stress. We should take a moment here to remember the late Ronald Hoffman, who initially supported the idea for a conference on the Quebec Act.

Thanks, also, to our friends from the French Atlantic History Group: Catherine Desbarats, Nicholas Dew, Helen Dewar, Carolyn Fick, Allan Greer, Jean-Pierre Le Glaunec, and Thomas Wien. They have been our intellectual comrades in arms in this, as in so many other projects.

We would like to express our gratitude to the anonymous reviewers for their outstanding comments, to the entire team at McGill-Queen's University Press, to Patricia Kennedy for her superb copy-editing, to Lisa Aitken for seeing the manuscript through production with such competence, to Judy Dunlop for her expert help on the index, and especially to Jonathan Crago for his always sage advice and unfailing support throughout the editorial process.

ENTANGLING THE QUEBEC ACT

INTRODUCTION

Entangling the Quebec Act

Ollivier Hubert and François Furstenberg

Although it features in many historical accounts, the Quebec Act too often remains on the sidelines. National narratives – which most often structure historical writing – highlight other foundational events instead. Quebec and Canadian history both make *La Conquête* a central turning point: the conquest of 1759–60, when New France fell, and landed (providentially or tragically, depending on one's perspective) in the British Empire. In Native American history, the Royal Proclamation of 1763 stands as a milestone: indigenous resistance to British power resulting in the creation of a Native American territory off limits to European settlement, establishing land and treaty rights that would persist into the present. The United States, meanwhile, dates its foundation from 1776, the year when settler resistance to British power culminated in a Declaration of Independence and a war for nationhood. As for the British Empire, 1783 marks the date at which the first empire ended and the second began. Even the events of 1812 have recently joined the mix, now reframed as "the fight for Canada" waged by the nation's three founding peoples, French, English, and Native American. In these and other narratives, the Quebec Act of 1774 plays a bit part – if it plays any at all.[1]

Thus does the Quebec Act fall through the scholarly cracks. (The last sustained analysis of the Act is now thirty years old.[2]) And yet today, more than ever, there are good reasons to question its marginality. Recent attempts to approach history from transnational perspectives offer an opportunity to reinterpret the Quebec Act across these and other historiographical boundaries. The growing practice of entangling histories – *histoire croisée*, as the French term puts it –

enables a reconsideration of the Quebec Act from Canadian, North American, Native American, and British imperial perspectives.[3]

This volume has two principal objectives. First, it brings cutting-edge methodological, geographical, and thematic perspectives to bear on the Quebec Act. Moving beyond a national frame, this book highlights the multi-faceted importance of an event whose significance, we hope to demonstrate, is greater than the sum of its many fractured historiographical parts. By resituating the Act in light of the last generation of scholarship, we also point to new directions for future research. Second, by focusing on one event – a social, legal, revolutionary, and imperial phenomenon that crosses multiple national and historiographical borders – this volume makes a methodological contribution. Operating at multiple scales of spatial analysis and juxtaposing multiple historical perspectives, this book hopes to serve as a case study in the practice of "entangling" conceptually distinct historical fields. In this regard, our volume joins recent scholarship that has been showing the interconnectedness of national histories and, indeed, methodological approaches, from legal to cultural, political to religious, and beyond.

This introduction first traces the historiography on the Quebec Act from multiple national perspectives that have framed the scholarship. From there, it offers a brief overview of the essential historical contexts – Canadian, Native American, and imperial – that situate our renewed understanding of the Act, before introducing the individual essays.

A FRACTURED HISTORIOGRAPHY

Varied interpretations of the Quebec Act reflect divergent opinions of colonial society and British imperialism in North America. Not surprisingly, some of the richest analyses originate in Canada. Nationalist Quebec historians, critical of British power, portray the Act as a purely tactical concession made to *Canadiens* to secure their loyalty during a troubled period. A second view, by contrast, describes it as a charter to safeguard French-Canadian distinctiveness within the empire, and laying the foundation for a multi-ethnic political space. According to a third line of argument, the Act was an unfortunate attack on, and ultimately a barrier to, the development of political and economic liberalism in Canada. In contrast to the extended debate Canadian scholarship accords the Quebec Act, US historiography – still disentangling itself from a reading of colonial America that leads inevitably to revolution – has marginalized it. Most often the Act is relegated to one of the "Coercive" or "Intolerable" acts that led to the American Revolution. The historiography on the British Empire, meanwhile, reads the Quebec Act as the product of a complicated set of local and imperial interactions. In that tradition's most ambitious interpretations, the Quebec Act emerges as a first step in the reformulation of the Second British Empire. A brief survey of these varied scholarly traditions will help lay the groundwork for this volume's methodological and interpretive intervention.

Quebec resident William Smith published the first study of the period in 1815. Disturbed by even the limited persistence of a French civilization he considered inferior, Smith portrayed the Quebec Act as the unfortunate result of lobbying by Franco-Catholic elites. By exploiting a favourable political context – the imperial crisis of the 1770s – they secured the Canadien population's loyalty to the British Crown. Their success, however, came at a high cost: preserving feudalism in the St Lawrence Valley.[4]

The first French-Canadian historians interpreted the political culture of the St Lawrence Valley very differently. The regime established by the Constitutional Act of 1791 gave little autonomy to the colonial assembly. The resulting political dynamic pitted the elected representatives of an essentially Franco-Catholic population against a government dominated by Anglo-Protestants, leading to a growing cleavage of politics along ethnic lines.[5] These tensions erupted in crisis in 1837 and 1838, culminating in armed insurrections justified by republican ideals, which elicited a ruthless repression and a temporary return to the constitutional authoritarianism of 1774. In 1840, a new constitution further diluted the influence of the French-speaking population within a new assembly made subordinate to heavy-handed imperial authorities. In this context of imperial domination, French-Canadian interpretations of the Quebec Act began to take shape. François-Xavier Garneau, who published his ambitious *History of Canada* in three volumes starting in 1845, saw the Act as an early moment in a continuous struggle for Canadien liberty that stretched back to the fall of the French Empire. Abandoned by France and humiliated by the English, Canadiens found themselves treated "like a barbarian nation without government and without laws," while authorities in London sought to "denationalize the country" and "repeat in Canada what had been done in Ireland." From this perspective, the Quebec Act foreshadowed a long battle of future generations to free themselves of foreign domination and forge their own nation.[6]

Building on this interpretation in the 1920s, Lionel Groulx cast the Conquest as a catastrophic event that opened the way to a "policy of assimilation." For this dominant figure among Quebec historians, the Quebec Act was an insignificant concession that bought the support of a small aristocratic and clerical elite in anticipation of conflict with the Thirteen Colonies. The 1774 constitution gave a risibly small amount of power to "a minority kept on a short leash."[7] Neo-nationalist historians at the Université de Montréal further developed this line of argument after the Second World War, interpreting the Conquest as the beginning of the political and economic subjugation of French Canadians. Excluded from the military service that underpinned its dignity, the Canadien gentry humiliated itself by slavishly supporting the conquerors in exchange for a few sparingly distributed honours. In this analysis, the Quebec Act did nothing to improve the Canadiens' situation. To the contrary, a "social decapitation" ensured that they remained a subjugated people, without any control over their destiny.[8]

Michel Bibaud (1792–1857) and like-minded historians came to a very different view of the Quebec Act.[9] Bibaud, a French-Canadian monarchist, did not link the Act to agitation in the Thirteen Colonies. Rather, he presented it as the product of careful reflection by imperial authorities concerned with the effective administration of Canada, and more sensitive to the interests of the Canadiens than to the English merchant lobby. Likewise, Tomas Chapais dismissed the role of the impending American Revolution in the Act's origins. In his 1919 study, this loyalist Catholic historian, worried about the dissolution of the British Empire in the wake of the First World War, described it as "liberating and reconstructive legislation" that advanced "our religious emancipation and our national emancipation."[10]

Anglo-Canadian historiography of the twentieth century removed the Quebec Act from the imperial context, casting it as an initial step in the creation of a binational Canada founded on mutual respect between two separate peoples. Alfred Leroy Burt's 1933 study argued that the Quebec Act advanced the equal rights of two distinct peoples, making it possible for them to coexist within a supranational political framework. While this liberal approach did not extend to other parts of Britain's multi-ethnic empire, Burt believed it was appropriate for Canada, because "the French possessed a civilization as ancient and as fixed as that of the English."[11] In his *Colony to Nation: A History of Canada* (1946), Arthur Lower agreed. The Act, he argued, was "a great constitutional land-mark in Canadian history and the history of the British Empire." It lay the foundation for a Canada defined by the improbable marriage of two opposed world views, ensuring the survival of an older, premodern French-Canadian mentality, which would henceforth temper the excessively individualistic and industrious mentality of English Canadians.[12] A fairly narrow interpretative framework, which reflected debates among national elites, thus constrained interpretations of the Quebec Act.

In the 1960s, Fernand Ouellet broke new ground. A practitioner of socio-economic history and a follower of the French Annales school, Ouellet focused on the emergence of a dynamic merchant bourgeoisie between 1760 and 1774. That bourgeoisie, he argued, remained too small to serve as a reliable ally to London. To consolidate their authority, imperial officials thus turned to the only viable alternative: the landed gentry. Determined to deconstruct ethnic understandings of the Quebec Act, Ouellet abandoned "the famous themes of the 'struggle for survival,'" blaming a "reactionary nobility, as much enamored of political absolutism and social inequality as in the past," for the future struggles of Quebec society.[13] Hilda Neatby similarly avoided analyzing the 1774 constitution in terms of anachronistic Canadian nationalisms. Unlike Ouellet, however, she located the Quebec Act firmly within a British imperial framework. Imperial authorities were not trying to guarantee the fundamental rights of a Franco-Catholic population, she argued, nor were they looking south to the thirteen rebellious colonies. Rather, they hoped to solve the problem of instability in the Ohio Valley and provide for the efficient administration of the Province of Quebec.[14]

In the 1970s, Pierre Tousignant made an incisive contribution to the study of the Quebec Act by exploring a vast corpus of official documents, both colonial and imperial. Fusing social, political, strategic, diplomatic, economic, and cultural perspectives, he placed the Quebec Act in a far broader context than any previous historian, casting it as both the product and the manifestation of a shift in imperial policy that followed the failure of Lord Halifax's continental strategy.[15] Granted, the centralizing and authoritarian turn in imperial policy had been under way for several decades, as testified to by events in the Thirteen Colonies.[16] He insisted that the adoption of the Act on 22 June 1774 had to be understood in the context of the Massachusetts

Government Act, passed one month earlier. Rather than seeing the Act as an ad-hoc response to local circumstances, however, he argued that it resulted from a long set of deliberations by officials in London.

No historiography of equivalent richness on the Quebec Act exists in the US-based scholarship, where the American Revolution exerts an almost irresistible gravitational pull on the events of the 1770s. Framed in the context of US national history, the Quebec Act nearly always gets subsumed within the so-called "Intolerable" or "Coercive" acts that pushed British settlers towards independence. This perspective has made it impossible to understand the Quebec Act on its own terms: as legislation of national or transnational significance. Coming right after the Boston Tea Party and two years before the American Declaration of Independence, the Quebec Act becomes but one more step in the teleological coming of the Revolution.

Nineteenth-century US historians framed the Quebec Act in reference to the tensions between the Thirteen Colonies and the empire. "In the belief that the loyalty of its possessions had been promoted by a dread of French settlements on their northern and western frontier," wrote George Bancroft, the foremost national historian of the nineteenth-century United States, "Britain sought to create under its own auspices a distinct empire, suited to coerce her original colonies, and restrain them from aspiring to independence. For this end it united into one province the territory of Canada, together with all the country northwest of the Ohio to the head of Lake Superior and the Mississippi, and consolidated all authority over this boundless region in the hands of the executive power."[17] Francis Parkman, unremittingly fascinated with French colonial history in North America, did manage to escape the national framework. His brief mention of the Act suggested, however, that he less successfully escaped the prejudices of his Protestant background. "Civil liberty was given them by the British sword," Parkman wrote at the conclusion of his great *Montcalm and Wolfe*, in an analysis that echoed that of William Smith's 1815 study, "but the conqueror left their religious system untouched, and through it they have imposed upon themselves a weight of ecclesiastical tutelage that finds few equals in the most Catholic countries of Europe."[18] That the Quebec Act bore intrinsically on the American Revolutionary fervour by its annihilation of the Thirteen Colonies' all-important western land claims seems to have eluded most historians interested in the subject. Even Thomas Perkins Abernethy's still-useful account of the importance of western lands to the American Revolution barely mentioned the Act.[19]

Bancroft's perspective – understanding the Quebec Act in relation to the American Revolution – has continued in the modern scholarship on colonial politics of the 1770s, which inevitably looks forward to the American Revolution. "Because of its timing and provisions, the Quebec Act was also considered by the colonists to be a part of this punitive legislation," notes one essay on the Coercive Acts in the Blackwell *Companion to the American Revolution*, edited by Jack P. Greene and John R. Pole. "In fact the Act was an enlightened effort on the part of the British Government to organize the recently acquired colony of Quebec."[20] Most modern accounts don't even bother to make the distinction, simply lumping the Quebec Act in as part of the Coercive Acts.[21] In his study of political culture that explicitly shies away from a teleological reading of the thirteen mainland colonies, Brendan McConville points to the Quebec Act as "a particularly lurid example of what awaited the American colonists under the new, militarized tyranny." McConville thus explores the Act as the final nail in the coffin of a Protestant political culture that had built itself around the cult of a benevolent monarch and dominated the colonies for more than a century. "To provincials, it looked like the establishment of popish government in full bloom right on their doorsteps."[22] One recent study gives greater attention to the Quebec Act, providing an insightful analysis grounded in the politics of the St Lawrence Valley and emphasizing the Act's effects on religious and territorial issues, thus offering an essential context for the Act's reception in the lower Thirteen Colonies. Nonetheless, the analysis ultimately remains in the service of explaining the American Revolution, as suggested by the title of the work, *The Battle for the Fourteenth Colony*.[23]

The major exception to the Revolution-centric analysis of the Quebec Act in US scholarship lies in Native American history, which occasionally examines the Quebec Act in the light of contested sovereignties in the Ohio Valley. Even then, however, the transfer of the Ohio Valley to the Province of Quebec has seemed like the most transient of events in the long-contested extension of US settlement into the continental interior. The Ohio Valley became part of Quebec only six months before fighting broke out in Lexington, Massachusetts. Almost immediately, the region became a war zone, as it had been for decades. Indeed, fighting continued in the Ohio Valley after Yorktown, after it had ceased in other parts of the continent, growing in 1782, 1783, and even into 1784, as Shawnee and Iroquois warriors battled forces led by George Rogers Clark. The sudden and dramatic cession of what would soon be called the Northwest Territory in the "Infamous treaty" of 1783 means that Quebec's extension into the Ohio Valley was fleeting in theory and never realized in practice; for that reason, it is largely seen as the briefest of moments in a long war for control of the trans-Appalachian West. Not surprisingly, in a historiography that emphasizes Native agency and resistance against settler pressures, attention to imperial laws tends to get overlooked in favour of social dynamics on the imperial periphery. The attention of historians thus shifts to the next stage of that war, in the 1780s and 1790s, when the newly formed Ohio Confederacy resisted US encroachment north of the Ohio River.[24]

It is from the perspective of British imperial history that the Quebec Act has been most fruitfully explored in English-language scholarship. The notable figure here is Clarence Walworth Alvord (1868–1928), who studied at Amherst College and the Friedrich Wilhelm University in Berlin, eventually earning his PhD from the University of Illinois. Building on the scholarship of his contemporaries in the "Imperial School" of historians, such as Charles McClean Andrews (1863–1943) and Herbert Levi Osgood (1855–1918) – and, like his contemporaries, firmly grounded in the British archives – Alvord pushed the politics of the British Empire deep into the North American continent. "Whenever the British ministers soberly and seriously discussed the American problem," his influential *The Mississippi Valley in British Politics* began, "the vital phase to them was not the disturbances of the 'madding crowd' of Boston and New York but the development of that vast transmontane region that was acquired in 1763 by the Treaty of Paris."[25] Jack Sosin's *Whitehall in the Wilderness*, published in 1961, built on Alvord's insights to show how the Quebec Act resulted from a series of repeated failures of British policy in the continental interior. Sosin particularly emphasized the importance of maintaining peace with Native peoples west of the Appalachians.[26]

British imperial scholarship on the Quebec Act fell into rapid decline after Canada and the other dominions of the Empire gained autonomy in the 1930s; Reginald Coupland, a historian of imperialism, published the last major work in 1932.[27] Coupland believed in the superiority of British imperial governance, which sheltered inferior cultures under its benevolent protection. From this premise, the skilful and liberal management of French Canada's cultural distinctiveness in 1774 exemplified British generosity and toleration; it could serve as a model for latter-day British authorities managing the transition to a commonwealth of nations. Coupland's confidence in the Empire's benevolent capacities could not outlast the Second World War and the violent upheavals of decolonization.[28] However, attempts to interpret the Quebec Act in the context of British imperial politics continued. In 1961, Peter D. Marshall emphasized "the significance of the Quebec example in establishing the constitutional form of the Second British Empire," raising the question not just of the consequences for Quebec of its incorporation into the British Empire, but of "the effect upon the British Empire of its incorporation of Quebec."[29]

Philip Lawson, a historian trained in the United Kingdom and living in Alberta, launched a renewed imperial perspective in 1989. In his masterful work, based on an intensive study of the official archives, as well as of British public opinion, Lawson interpreted the debates surrounding Quebec as a defining moment in British history, locating them in the context of late-eighteenth-century ideologies on identity and the nature of citizenship.[30] On the one hand, Lawson highlighted the problem posed by the Canadiens' Catholicism. On the other hand, he explored how the cultural diversification of Britain's colonial possessions after the Seven Years' War affected ideas of citizenship – not necessarily in the Empire at large, but in the British Isles in particular.[31] By asking "what effect the conquest of Quebec had on Britain" – a question that seems obvious in the current post-colonial historiographical context but which, in the 1980s, was truly pioneering – Lawson opened a path that several essays in this book have followed.[32] David Milobar continued that tradition in a series of articles published in the 1990s, reading the political debates surrounding the Quebec Act through the rich scholarship on "Country" ideology burgeoning at the time, and setting them in "the context of broader intellectual traditions that underpinned the eighteenth-century British Atlantic."[33] He concluded that the Quebec reforms "constitute a historical barometer of the most sensitive issues within the British Atlantic empire."[34]

In recent decades, post-colonial studies have reinvigorated the field of imperial history, resulting in important work that pushes beyond stodgy accounts of benevolent administrators in the metropole to emphasize the mutual interrelation of centres and peripheries, the interaction among a variety of state and non-state actors, and the centrality of cultural practices and imperial subjectivities to the construction of empire. Several of the essays in the volume follow on the magisterial work of P.J. Marshall, who emphasizes the interrelated nature of the Empire in the Americas and South Asia, and whose research on Quebec takes a more global approach than any other.[35]

Taken together, the scholarship on the Quebec Act emerges as one divided not just by nation but also by scale of analysis. Whether set at provincial, continental, Atlantic, or global levels, the insights from these rich and varied approaches have too often remained siloed. Recent historiographical developments now make it possible to consider the Quebec Act from a fresh set of perspectives.

THE CONQUEST OF NEW FRANCE: IMPERIAL GOVERNANCE AND THE ST LAWRENCE VALLEY

It was from the mundane process of governance in the St Lawrence Valley that a new vision for British imperial governance would eventually emerge. When negotiations between France and Britain opened in 1761 after the collapse of France's North American Empire, a hawkish William Pitt envisaged a "punitive peace" that would strip France of its colonies.[36] French negotiators, meanwhile, intended to recover Canada, which they considered the key to their American possessions.[37] If British diplomats soon pared back their demands – the country's shrewder negotiators recognizing that humiliating a defeated power only plants the seeds of future wars – they remained unbending on the issue of Canada. The war, after all, had stemmed from the French military presence in North America, and the British were determined to remove that cause for good. They therefore decided to return French possessions in the Caribbean in exchange for the withdrawal of French troops in Europe.

As François-Joseph Ruggiu has shown, France and Britain each reversed its colonial policy in the Treaty of Paris negotiations.[38] Where the French had long pursued imperial, territorial, and military dominance, they would henceforth focus on commercial and economic profitability. Britain, by contrast, expanded territorially and bureaucratically; it found itself burdened with a collection of new colonies that had cost dearly to acquire, whose administration promised to be expensive, and whose profitability remained uncertain. The exhilaration of military victory soon gave way to a drearier process of imperial governance.

British authorities seem to have assumed that, after the Conquest of New France, Britain would simply impose its laws on the occupied territories. General Jeffrey Amherst flatly rejected any protections of "the Laws and usages" of New France in the 1760 Articles of Capitulation of Montreal. French-Canadians were to "become Subjects of the King," by which Amherst meant that they would become subject to English law.[39] The same assimilationist vision prevailed in London, where authorities hoped to establish more rational and uniform policies across their vast new empire. The Royal Proclamation of 1763 created four new colonies – Quebec, West Florida, East Florida, and Grenada – to be peopled, it was assumed, by Protestants accustomed to living under English law. At the same time, it forbade settlement west of the Appalachian Mountains, reserving the territory for Native Americans, and centralized authority for treaty-making with the imperial government.

But what to do about the existing population in the meantime? Although the Treaty of Paris gave residents of the St Lawrence Valley the option of leaving for metropolitan France, very few did so. Members of the military nobility faced doubtful prospects in France: their titles were often uncertain, their futures in the French military cloudy, and no one knew if or how the wealth built in Canada could be transferred to France. In Canada, they were firmly rooted by entrenched trade networks, and especially by the socio-economic power they wielded as landowners. Unsurprisingly, most chose to stay in Canada. The prosperous communities of Canadien merchants in Quebec and Montreal made the same calculation and arrived at the same decision. Among the elite, only the members of the civil administration emigrated in significant numbers. As for the artisans and peasants, they remained firmly attached to the society into which they had been born.[40]

The colonists of French ancestry in the St Lawrence Valley, with their growing sense of collective identity,[41] posed an obvious threat to British sovereignty.[42] The Acadian experience seemed to confirm the worst British fears. After its territory was ceded to Britain in 1713, the French-speaking Catholic population had resisted submission to British authority, refusing to take up arms against the French during the Seven Years' War. To British officials, the Acadians exemplified a conquered people's tendency to treason.[43] Although deportation was ultimately used against the Acadians, such a measure does not appear to have been considered in the Canadien case.[44] Instead, officials in London set out to assimilate the inhabitants of the St Lawrence Valley. Some believed that the Canadiens, finally liberated from the oppression of Bourbon absolutism and irresistibly attracted to enlightened English governance, would gratefully transform themselves into Anglo-Protestants.[45] More sober analysts, however, counted on the large-scale immigration of Anglo-Protestant settlers to neutralize the Canadien influence.

In pursuit of this goal, the Board of Trade, led by the Anglo-Irish proprietor, Wills Hill, 1st Earl of Hillsborough, implemented policies to attract Protestant migrants to the new territories by keeping them out of the trans-Appalachian West. "The aim," writes Bernard Bailyn, "was a slow and controlled expansion of western settlement and the gradual introduction of civil government in the west." A 1763 Board of Trade memorandum outlined the steps needed to implement the policy in Quebec: Establish a capital named "British Town," to be settled by new migrants, who would bring with them "the English language, the English manners, & a Spirit of Industry, among the French Canadians." This assimilationist vision prevailed in the early stages of drafting the Quebec Act, with authorities assuming that French law would eventually give way to British law.[46]

It was not long, however, before British imperial control ran up against realities on the ground. Within several years, the demographic and political situation in the St Lawrence Valley (and elsewhere in the empire) had made itself manifest. Aside from a small but notable cohort of Scottish merchants, waves of Anglo-Protestant migration were not flooding into Quebec. Meanwhile, the Canadiens retained a firm hold on the lands bordering the St Lawrence River. Officials in London had no choice but to deal with them.[47] "Whatever might have been intended in 1763," P.J. Marshall aptly remarks, "accommodations with the huge French majority could not be avoided."[48] These necessary accommodations would eventually give rise to a form of imperial governance more open to cultural and religious diversity and more firm in curbing colonial autonomy.

Although no one would have recognized it at the time, the roots of a form of imperial governance stretched back to the 1760 Articles of Capitulation of Montreal. Articles 27, 39, and 40 provided for the free exercise of Catholicism, and promised residents, both Indigenous and European, that they would not be relocated by force, while article 37 guaranteed property rights to existing residents.[49] Although these agreements were meant only as temporary measures, by guaranteeing property rights, in particular, the terms of surrender maintained the seigneurial regime, a social order dominated by the military aristocracy, the landed gentry, and the Catholic Church.[50] From the first conquest, then, reassuring the Canadien elites was the highest priority of the "military regime" (1760–1763).[51] The civil government established by the Royal Proclamation of 1763 maintained these priorities and policies. Although some of the document's provisions restricted the rights of Catholics on paper, colonial administrators' need for local expertise meant that most of the discriminatory measures banning Catholics from public office were not put into practice.[52]

From these early accommodations grew a vision of the St Lawrence Valley's integration into the British Empire that would not depend on Canadiens' embrace of English liberty, but would rely, instead, on their attachment to the land itself, and to the seigneurial system that supported their social structure. As Heather Welland has pointed out, for many British officials the peculiarities of Canadian society (its Catholicism and its feudal regime) created an opportunity for more effective governance rather than an aberration that needed to be eliminated.[53] This view was especially prevalent among those neo-Tories who favoured a more centralized empire, with each colony dependent on the mother country, rather than a wider and more decentralized imperial commercial network. In the eyes of such observers, Canada's hierarchical institutions gave it the characteristics of an ancien régime French province they construed as an archetypal feudal society.[54] Because this view of the social order served their authoritarian political vision, the first two governors of the province placed particular emphasis on the Catholic, rural, and aristocratic character of Canada. A large part of subsequent Canadian historiography would retrospectively paint a portrait of Quebec that conformed to this initial (and tactical) portrayal: of an exotic peasant society, endowed with all the qualities of simplicity, subject to the cycles of nature and the rites of a medieval Church, frozen in time and consequently incapable of governing itself.[55]

The problem with this view of Canada is that it did not conform to the existing social order. In Quebec and Montreal, prosperous families of merchants and artisans formed an educated petite bourgeoisie that offered its services to the state.[56] These literate Canadiens largely ensured the operation of the colonial administration after the departure of the French civil administrators. They also embodied a French-speaking public opinion, as revealed in debates surrounding the drafting of the Quebec Act. Far from it being the sole prerogative of a minority of radical British colonists, French-speaking Canadians also demanded political autonomy, mobilizing a discourse of liberty very early on, and shaping it in dialogue with their English-speaking counterparts.[57] But these elements of the political culture along the St Lawrence Valley served no useful political end in the debates in London leading up to the Quebec Act. Thus, the discursive construction of "Canadiens" as a homogenous and feudal people clinging to an aristocratic form of government reduced the province's population to two groups whose characteristics and interests were diametrically opposed: the good Canadiens, frozen in time and submissively waiting for an opportunity to be constitutionally protected by the Empire, and a nasty group of radical English merchants attempting to seize power for their own benefit.

Ensuring the participation of Canadiens in the political and administrative structures of the colony required more than mere accommodation of the principles of cultural and religious toleration. It required an institutional recognition of the Catholic Church itself – no easy feat in the immediate wake of a bitter global struggle waged under the banner of an apocalyptic struggle between Protestant freedom and Popish slavery. Local authorities proceeded cautiously. Although abolished in principle, the collection of the tithe (which provided for the subsistence of the clergy in New France) was maintained in practice.[58] Similarly, the network of Catholic parishes inherited from New France remained. The Privy Council received numerous opinions on the religious question, and was particularly attentive to the views of the Canadien gentry. In February 1763, Joseph-Marie de la Corne, a Canadien aristocrat, experienced diplomat, and representative of the high clergy, contacted Lord Shelburne with a plan for establishing a Canadian Catholic Church that would be loyal to the king.[59] The British military commander in Quebec had similar ideas, hoping to encourage the development of a Catholic and French-speaking society in Quebec. In June 1765, jurists submitted a report to the Board of Trade urging that Canadiens "not [be] subject to the incapacities, disabilities, and penalties to which Roman Catholics in this kingdom are subject by the Laws thereof."[60] According to Philip Lawson, this was the moment when officials in London definitively abandoned the vision of a Protestant Quebec.[61] It represented a turning point in the history of British imperial governance and of the principle of religious tolerance. On 29 June 1766, Mgr Jean-Olivier Briand triumphally disembarked at Quebec as the new Catholic bishop.[62] The Church had become the authorities' preferred representative of the Canadien people. And thanks to a particularly efficient system of cultural and moral regulation, the clergy had become the main guarantor of Canadiens' loyalty, a fact that had a lasting impact on the collective consciousness of Quebec.[63]

In a remarkably short time, imperial administrators had concluded that Canada's bedrock institutions were not to be disrupted and could even be reinforced to better ensure the province's loyalty. Still, they needed to persuade the British parliament. That task was given to the experts who, between 1766 and 1774, developed and drafted what would become the Quebec Act. The Earl of Shelburne, in charge of American affairs, placed particular emphasis on Great Britain's responsibility to recognize certain rights of the peoples it conquered. When Guy Carleton replaced James Murray as governor of Canada in 1766, adherents to ideologies of Anglo-Protestant supremacy expected a return to policies of forced assimilation. Those hopes were soon dashed, however: the new governor continued his predecessor's policies, ignoring the demands of British merchants and establishing closer ties to the "traditional" Franco-Catholic elites. He also extended the authority of the Court of Common Pleas, a tribunal that operated largely in French and according to principles of French law.

During the months of May and June 1774, the British parliament debated a bill confirming the perpetuation of the social, legal, economic, administrative, cultural, and territorial frameworks that Canada had inherited from the French regime. It was the subject of particularly stormy arguments in the House of Commons. Combining anti-Catholic prejudice with an alarmist defence of the Bill of Rights (1688), the popular English press sought to turn public opinion against the proposal. In response, the government delegated Carleton, a key architect of the plan, to defend the bill in parliament. He did so brilliantly. *An Act for Making More Effectual Provision for the Government of the Province of Quebec in North America* (14 Geo. III, c. 83) was approved by a large majority (fifty-six for and twenty against) in the Commons on 18 June 1774, and received royal assent four days later. The Quebec Act came into force on 1 May 1775. In the absence of an elected colonial assembly, the governor would be assisted by a nominated legislative council. As it happened, all the Catholic councillors were members of the landed gentry.

THE OHIO VALLEY AND NATIVE AMERICAN ALLIES

To understand the Quebec Act as a result of ten years of struggle between French Catholics, Protestant settlers, and imperial administrators, however, leaves out some of the most essential features – and actors – in its construction. Perhaps because scholars tend to project the modern-day borders of Quebec back in time, too little research on the Act has looked south to the Ohio Valley and west to the Great Lakes. The Quebec Act was not passed just to appease settlers along the St Lawrence Valley, after all; its reach stretched deep into the Ohio Valley and across the *pays d'en haut*, where it reinforced a set of concessions to Native Americans that dated back to the Royal Proclamation of 1763.

Whatever the lines and colours on European maps proclaimed, Great Britain had not extended its sovereignty into Indian Country after the Seven Years' War. Just as early plans to assimilate or overwhelm the French-Canadian population in Quebec collapsed in the early 1760s, so British policies in the trans-Appalachian West dissolved amidst the fierce resistance of the inhabitants. Native peoples long allied with French power and linked to New France through kinship, trade, and diplomatic networks had not, after all, capitulated in Montreal or surrendered alongside Montcalm. "Although you have conquered the French," warned an Ojibwa chief to a British trader, "you have not yet conquered us!" In 1763, Native peoples allied under the Ottawa chief Pontiac launched a series of devastating assaults on British forts and settlements. The vast uprising across the Great Lakes and the Ohio Valley panicked British imperial officials with the prospect of a costly new war coming hard on the heels of their recent victory. The resulting concessions to Native nations, enshrined in the Royal Proclamation of 1763, created the Province of Quebec, and laid down a set of principles intended to protect Native landholdings, centralize trade and diplomacy with imperial officials rather than fractious provincial governments, ban colonial settlement west of the Appalachian Mountains, and ensure that future Native cessions only occurred by treaty with the central government.

This policy focused particularly on the Ohio Valley, where the settler-Native-imperial tensions were at their most intense. By the late-eighteenth century, wars for control of the region had been waging for centuries. Britain was a relative newcomer. If the St Lawrence Valley was a world of European settlements, with *habitants* living on fixed seigneuries, the Ohio Valley looked entirely different: a fluid, highly mobile, and decentralized Native world, where British sovereignty remained exceedingly tenuous. A robust trade continued in the Illinois Country, on the western edge of the Ohio Valley. Meanwhile, to the south, the French governor of Louisiana was reaching out to Cherokees, Choctaws, Abekas, Alibamos, and others to consolidate French alliances as late as 1762. "If the British wished to occupy the French posts and establish a trade with the western nations," as Michael A. McDonnell has remarked, "they would have to do so on Indian terms."[64] Only by strengthening their own networks of Native alliances could British officials effectively assert their sovereignty in the region. The oldest and most important of British allies were the Haudenosaunee, centred along the Mohawk Valley, and the Cherokee, centred along the Tennessee River. Since these two groups of Iroquoian-speaking people controlled two major waterways into the Ohio Valley, alliances with them in north and south became the key to British control of the region. Confronted with common enemies in the Illinois Country and around the Great Lakes, the Haudenosaunee and Cherokees finally established an uneasy peace.[65]

It wasn't just Native American politics in the Ohio Valley that were exceedingly decentralized. So too were the settler politics of the British Empire. Both proved baffling to British imperial administrators seeking to establish sovereignty in the continental interior. In response to Iroquois and Cherokee demands, authorities continually promised, in vain, to keep white settlement out of Indian Country. Meanwhile, colonial governments undermined imperial authority by negotiating separate land cessions with Indians and granting vast tracts of land to well-connected speculators, while hundreds of settlers heedlessly flouted treaty obligations to settle on Indian lands. "You often tell us we don't restrain our people, and that you do so with yours," an Iroquois delegate chastised Superintendent of Indian Affairs William Johnson. And yet, he pointed out, "your Words differ more from your Actions than ours do." By the early 1770s, the upper Ohio Valley was a war zone among various Native people and between settlers invading the country and Indians fighting to retain their sovereignty. In response to the chaos, one solution beckoned: the imperial government would consolidate its authority in more reliable hands than those of colonial governments and uncontrollable settlers. New borders would be drawn, not along the crest of the Appalachians, as in the 1763 Royal Proclamation, but rather following the massive cession of Iroquois (formerly Alongonquian) lands in the 1768 Treaty of Fort Stanwix and of Cherokee rights in the 1768 Treaty of Hard Labour, both of which pushed the eastern border of Indian Country to the Ohio River.

The Quebec Act was thus the result of more than a decade of attempts to consolidate British authority in the Ohio Valley by strengthening Indian control and discouraging settler incursions. At stake was the fate of British authority in the West – and, in a sense, the fruits of the great victory achieved in the Seven Years' War. The new province built on previous French travel routes connecting the Ohio and the St Lawrence valleys, reorienting trade and governance away from the seaboard colonies to the east, and signalling the centrality of Native-French-Métis trade networks over those of British settlers. Both the geographical and legal features were written, as Undersecretary of State for the Colonies William Knox put it, "for the avowed purpose of excluding all further settlement" in the Ohio Valley.[66] Colonial officials believed that preventing the extension of British law into Indian Country would further discourage Anglo-Protestant settlement. As Edmund Burke, a fierce critic of the law, complained, it would "draw a line which is to separate a man from the right of an Englishman." For its proponents, this was a feature, not a bug, of the new policy. Just as earlier officials had believed British law in Quebec would attract Protestant settlers, so, by the same logic, they now believed that maintaining French law in the trans-Appalachian West would keep settlers out. Proponents of the Quebec Act were clear about their intentions. "If it is not wished that British subjects should settle that country," wrote Lord Dartmouth, Secretary of State for the Colonies, "nothing can more effectually tend to discourage" British settlement than maintaining French law in the Ohio Valley. It was a point on which both proponents and opponents of the policy could agree. For opposition Whig Charles Pratt, 1st Earl of Camden, a fierce critic of the act, the Quebec Act would serve as "an eternal barrier ... [a] Chinese wall, against the further extension of civil liberty and the Protestant religion."[67]

Eternal it was not to be, however. Only a year after the Quebec Act was passed, British settlers in New England were in armed insurrection against the British Empire. By 1783, Lord Shelburne – a strong supporter of the Quebec Act – would agree to cede the Ohio Valley back to the seaboard colonists. Its history as part of Quebec was vanishingly short, and it is thus tempting to view it as an anomaly. Nonetheless, some of the elements embedded in the Act persisted. Most notably, the principle that treaty-making power be centralized and not ceded to the individual states was enshrined in the 1787 United States Constitution. On the other hand, the United States would endorse some of the principles articulated by the Quebec Act's opponents. When the US Congress began to organize the Northwest Territory in the 1780s, it did so in the expectation that regular government in the region would foster settlement. Indeed, as Christian Burset notes in this volume, the Northwest Ordinance of 1787 "essentially codified the compromise the Act's opponents had offered." If British common law had failed to extend to Quebec in the 1770s, it ultimately succeeded in doing so in the United States in the 1780s. The ironies remain striking, even today: it was Great Britain that extended French law into the Ohio Valley and Great Lakes in the 1770s, and the United States that would extend British law into the same region in the 1780s.

EXPANSION OF EMPIRE

The significance of the Quebec Act was not limited to the history of the St Lawrence or Ohio valleys, however. In its broadest frame, the Act was more than a Canadian, or even a North American, event: it was a British imperial event, which resulted from a radically expanded empire confronting a demographic, legal, religious, and cultural diversity unprecedented in its history.

The territories conquered by Britain in the Seven Years' War extended far beyond the borders of current-day Quebec. They spanned the St Lawrence River, into the Great Lakes, and north to Hudson Bay to encompass most of today's Canada. From there, they stretched south across the trans-Appalachian West to the Gulf of Mexico, including Florida (East and West), and across the Gulf to the Caribbean Sea, including the stretch of the Windward Islands in the Caribbean from Martinique to St Lucia, St Vincent, and Grenada. The scale of these new American possessions would have been daunting enough, but still they were only a fraction of the new territories won in the war. From the Caribbean, Britain's vastly expanded empire stretched across the Atlantic to the slave-trading colony of Saint-Louis and along the

Senegal River, through the Mediterranean to Gibraltar and Minorca, and then, most consequentially of all, encompassed extensive sections of the Indian subcontinent, including the state of Bengal, with a population far exceeding any other European colonial possession.[68]

An island nation, controlling a maritime space, had suddenly become a territorial empire. Britain's American territories alone stretched across half a billion acres of land, making up only one part of a global empire that now encompassed millions of peoples of vastly differing languages, religions, manners, and legal codes. Each new region was deeply faction-ridden, with quarrelling populations – European and indigenous; slave and free; French, Spanish, and English; Hindu, Muslim, and Christian – including most notably Britain's "old subjects," all of them with conflicting political objectives. Each new territory, moreover, had a varied set of hopelessly muddled legal traditions to sort through. An innumerable number of assertions of local authority now confronted attempts at a more centralized, imperial authority. There simply was no precedent for managing a polyglot British Empire on this scale.[69]

In North America, General Jeffery Amherst had taken the first stab in the wake of the French defeat, but his assertive policies had failed in Quebec and across the trans-Appalachian West. The following decade, similarly assertive policies inspired rebellion among Caribs in St Vincent. Meanwhile, governments in the imperial centre were rising and falling, Bengal was starving, and British colonists in the thirteen seaboard colonies were proving themselves immune to even the mildest imperial regulations. Indeed, from that last perspective it was hardly obvious that imposing Protestant religion and English manners would unify or pacify distant populations. After all, the very opposite was just then taking place among the largely English and Protestant colonies to the south of the St Lawrence Valley. Given the chaotic political context, offering concessions to a population of French Catholics beckoned as the most obvious way to negotiate the conflicting claims of local versus imperial control.

What began as a response to forces on the ground and contingent factors elsewhere, however, soon became enmeshed in broader debates about imperial governance and about the nature of empire itself. As British officials searched for precedents in crafting a new imperial policy, they found few places to turn. The tiny Mediterranean island of Minorca appeared recurrently in the discussions surrounding the Quebec Act (as it does in this volume). There, Britain had taken possession of the island earlier in the eighteenth century and preserved Spanish language and law. The Caribbean island of Grenada, also acquired in the Seven Years' War, served as another example. There, the British were finding ways to accommodate the French-Catholic settler population. And, of course, the Irish case was of central importance, looming over much of the debate.[70]

But the Quebec Act pointed to something fundamentally new, reflecting the new scope of the British Empire. "The scale of the problem," as P.J. Marshall observes, had "suddenly become vastly greater." Old, homogenizing approaches grounded in a common religion and manners were not just impractical; they began to seem downright tyrannical. When one Member of Parliament claimed, in the debates surrounding the Quebec Act, that imposing English laws on a conquered nation was an "act of the grossest and absurdest and cruelest tyranny," it signalled how far opinion had moved in just one generation. Even the "Mussulman, the Ottoman, the Turks, the worst of all conquerors, in the countries they subdued," declared Solicitor General Alexander Wedderburn, "left the people in possession of their municipal laws." This new line of thought revealed an openness to a legally and religiously diverse empire that stood in stark contrast to the traditional definition of a militantly Protestant British imperial nationalism. It suggested that Britons and their conquered peoples had suddenly entered a moment of rich, profound, and fundamentally original reflection on the nature of the British Empire specifically and of empire more generally.

From this reflection, as Hannah Muller puts it in this volume, "a new vision of governance" would arise, and it is in this broader imperial context that the Quebec Act of 1774 emerges as an important turning point: the moment "when a truly imperial subjecthood was imagined and realized." With its acceptance of legal, cultural, and religious pluralism within the empire, the Quebec Act inaugurated new debates about imperial authority and administration, the thematic contours of which would persist through much of the next century. Although it was hardly uncontested, the Quebec Act of 1774 marked a decisive turn away from a conception of the British Empire as, in David Armitage's pithy formulation, "Protestant, commercial, maritime and free." From a longer-term perspective, historians may want to consider the possibility that the second British Empire began not so much with the loss of the American colonies in 1783, but rather in 1774, with the foundation of the conceptual bases for a new empire.[71]

As this volume emphasizes, this new vision of imperial governance resulted from a host of factors operating at different political and geographical scales, and from the complex negotiations between local struggles on the imperial periphery and officials in the metropolitan centre. The debate pushed beyond the practicalities of imperial governance to address the meaning of British subjecthood itself, both in the colonies and in the metropole – debates that paralleled the more famous ones taking place just to Quebec's south. Imperial innovations on this scale were bound to foster dissent. After all, not everyone agreed that British subjecthood should be so fluid, and legal systems so flexible. Protestant English-speaking settlers across North America saw their empire being pulled out from under their feet. Indeed, from a broader imperial perspective, the American Revolution and the collapse of the first British Empire emerges more as a consequence than a cause of these debates over imperial governance.

Whatever the context in which the Quebec Act is located – be it US, Canadian, Indigenous, or imperial – the event, as we hope this volume shows, was of greater importance than any single body of scholarship recognizes. In this regard, a study of the Quebec Act offers a fruitful example of the methodological payoff of an "entangled" approach to history, highlighting the interconnected nature of early modern history more generally. Like the proverbial butterfly flapping its wings, a small Act could have a variety of unanticipated and unintended consequences bearing on a variety of interconnected peoples of North America and the British Empire, each of them redounding on the other to determine the course of so many interconnected histories.

THE VOLUME

Part I of the volume, "Quebec, Law, and Empire," lays out the broadest geographical context for the Quebec Act, setting it principally in the scholarship on law and empire. Hannah Muller begins by presenting the stakes of the debate from an imperial perspective. The Quebec Act, she argues, did not simply lay out a new vision for governing the empire; it was also a fundamental redefinition of British subjecthood. Before the Seven Years' War, little consensus existed on the precise rights of British subjects. Most writers simply referred back to a vaguely defined ancient constitution. Old and New Subjects agreed that British subjects were protected by law. But which law? Canadiens paved new ground by arguing that British subjecthood required the preservation of French civil law, which would "render them more able to serve their monarch as loyal subjects." The argument was taken up in London by figures like Solicitor General Alexander Wedderburn, who insisted that the Quebec Act would "bring the Canadians much more to the resemblance of British subjects than they are at present." Old Subjects, by contrast, argued that British subjecthood required the preservation of English law. For them, the Act was, as William Pitt put it, "the most cruel, oppressive and odious measure" that would alienate many subjects. Crucially, these new meanings of subjecthood resulted directly from the debates playing themselves out on the ground in Quebec. From periphery to centre and out again, debates in Quebec launched "a profound redefinition of the rights of British subjects" – not just in Canada but throughout the British Empire – resulting, for the first time, in "a truly imperial subjecthood."

Donald Fyson's essay serves as an essential counterpoint to the imperial and transnational approach that animates the other contributions in this volume. It brings attention to the local practice of administrative power rather than to imperial discourse, and to the concrete consequences of the Quebec Act on Franco-Catholic settlers. Fyson argues robustly against portrayals of the Quebec Act as a Magna Carta of a nation in the making. For him, it was essentially the constitutional ratification of a series of pragmatic policies undertaken by governors – the same pragmatic response that had already inspired many of the articles of the Capitulation of Montreal (1760) and the Treaty of Paris (1763). More fundamentally, Fyson demonstrates that religious, legal, and judicial policies had been imposed on the ground by the Canadiens themselves, and were implicitly recognized by colonial rulers as an effective form of social regulation. The Quebec Act therefore cannot be considered as the founding moment of Canadiens' political identity within the Empire; it was merely the official recognition of a state of affairs based on mutual accommodation that had gradually emerged in previous years. This reading the Quebec Act's marginal consequences on the daily lives of old settlers nonetheless highlights its historical importance. By its constitutional ratification, it emerges as a manifestation of considerable evolution in theorizations of empire during the period, and as proof of the integration of a predominantly French and Catholic colony in this evolution.

If the Quebec Act was thus the response to forces on the ground, and in this sense the product of highly contingent factors, there was nothing impulsive about the new policy. Michel Morin shows that the

Quebec Act was not ad hoc, but resulted from the detailed study of French legal codes, extensive consultation with jurists, and careful deliberation among policy officials. Reconstructing the debates and controversies in Quebec and in London, Morin follows legal officials as they drafted reports on the implementation of British law in conquered territories. No longer were they proposing legal accommodations as temporary measures. By the late 1760s, influential voices began to push back, not just against the practicality, but against the very principle of a legally uniform British Empire. The "British Form of government, never will produce the same Fruits as at Home," Governor Carleton wrote Lord Shelburne in 1768. "It is impossible for the Dignity of the Throne to be represented in the American Forests." The implementation of legal uniformity in an empire now spanning an unprecedented variety of climates, peoples, and manners made little sense, according to these theorists. It was, Attorney General Edward Thurlow argued in a 1773 report, both "unattainable" and "useless."[72]

Christain Burset brings a broad coherence to the various pro– and anti–Quebec Act voices, reading the debate through the lens of the scholarship on legal pluralism, and arguing that the dispute over the Quebec Act was part of a "broader debate over the place of English law in the British Empire," notably including Bengal. Until the second half of the eighteenth century, Burset argues here, British imperial policy followed Edward Coke's dictum that a "union of lawes is the best meanes for the unity of countries." Imperial administrators followed this principle in imposing English law on Ireland, Wales, as well as conquests abroad like New York. Some diversity existed within the law, to be sure, but advocates of legal pluralism remained marginal through the middle of the eighteenth century. It was only after the Seven Years' War that a loosely organized movement that Burset identifies as "authoritarian Whigs" began to cohere. These figures – who included Wedderburn, Carleton, and Chief Justice William Murray, 1st Earl of Mansfield – abandoned the traditional pursuit of legal uniformity in favour of a new commitment to legal pluralism, which they believed would allow Britain to more efficiently govern its colonies, while maintaining them in a state of economic subordination. The authoritarian Whigs were opposed by a coalition of radical Whigs, who saw the lurking threat of governmental tyranny in the efforts to limit the universality of English common law, and establishment Whigs, who were willing to compromise on some elements of legal pluralism but insisted that English commercial and procedural law should govern the colonies. The vision of the authoritarian Whig ultimately won out. Their conception of legal pluralism imposed across the Empire amounted to a major break with past practice and would affect all realms of the British Empire going forward. "From 1774," Burset concludes, "the question would no longer be whether to embrace mandatory legal pluralism, but how."[73]

Part II, "Religious and Ethnic Conflict," moves beyond the legal and administrative frameworks of the first four essays to explore the controversial religious aspects of the law. After all, the Quebec Act was "not solely an example of legal pluralism or negotiated authority," as Aaron Willis notes in his essay. It also served "as a critical example of religious and cultural pluralism within British imperial civil society."

Willis reconstructs the debates that led to the Quebec Act's formulation, showing the powerful influence of what many officials by then considered the failed Irish experience on the discussions. "The reappraisal of the Catholic question in Ireland," Willis argues, prompted "a rethinking of policy in the ceded territories in North America." As they debated how to manage a new Catholic population, polemicists and policy-makers looked back to past experience and found it wanting. What, they asked, had gone wrong in Ireland? "*In a country so highly favoured by nature*," read a 1770 pamphlet published in London, "the inhabitants could not be miserable, *without some defect in our laws*." The parliamentary debates over the Quebec Act repeatedly referred to the Irish experience, where, as supporters of the Act pointed out, the penal laws had proven counterproductive, leading to the impoverishment of the Catholic population, pushing them toward rebellion, requiring the continual presence of (expensive) British garrisons, and driving them to cling with ever greater tenacity to the Catholic Church. Irish laws, wrote William Knox, the Irish-born undersecretary for the American department, who served under Hillsborough at the Board of Trade, had not "served in any degree to recommend them for our imitation in Quebec." Indeed, several of the officials promoting a more pluralist model for Quebec – including Carleton and Knox – were themselves Irish born. Their experiences in Ireland gave them good reason to doubt the efficacy of an assimilationist approach to imperial governance. Central to their redesigned model of imperial governance was an emphasis on the seigneurs, whose loyalty and collaboration was seen as essential in maintaining imperial control over the larger population of Canadiens. This new emphasis on pluralism through concessions to local elites amounted to a paradigm shift. "The Quebec

Act was not simply a localized, pragmatic policy," Willis concludes. "Experiments in Quebec would lay the foundation of collaborative strategies deployed across the British Empire in the nineteenth and twentieth centuries."

By breaking radically with the Empire's past treatment of Catholics, the Quebec Act pointed toward a new policy of religious pluralism abroad – and at home. Luca Codignola paints a striking portrait of ecclesiastical networks stretching across the new and old territories of the British Empire, connecting authorities in Rome to Quebec, London, Grenada, Minorca, Florida, and Newfoundland; officials in older parts of the Empire, such as Ireland; as well as a related-but-distinct Jesuit network linking London and the North American British colonies (later the United States). Initially, Church authorities in London, led by an aging vicar apostolic, showed little interest in the formulation of the Act. That indifference is ironic, because, in the end, Codignola argues, the Act would play a significant role in English Catholic history – and, perhaps more importantly, in situating London at the heart of Catholicism in the British Empire. By the 1820s, London's vicar apostolic had become the centre of a Catholic network spanning the globe from America to the East Indies, and the Pacific. From this longer temporal perspective, the Quebec Act emerges as an important step in the creation of the modern British Catholic Church. It shaped precedent not just for the governance of empire, but of the metropole too, foreshadowing Catholic emancipation and the transformation of the Church's place in British life. The Quebec Act also played a decisive role in the construction of the Canadian Catholic Church. Traditionally Gallican, it gradually redefined the nature of its relations with the colonial authorities and established closer relations with the Holy See, thus gaining an unprecedented level of autonomy from the state. The negotiations surrounding the status of Catholicism in Quebec also mark an important step in the Vatican's consideration of North American churches. Codignola's text, which is based on a thorough and rare knowledge of religious archives, offers fascinating insight into an aspect of Quebec and Church history neglected by the scholarship on the period.

It is impossible to understand the caution with which the British Catholic Church and the imperial government inched towards religious tolerance without assessing the centrality of a militant Protestant patriotism in the British imperial identity. Brad A. Jones provides a striking illustration in his analysis of the Quebec Act's reception in the

New York and Halifax press. He shows how the Act catalyzed latent but powerful anti-Catholic strains in British political culture, fuelling an extreme paranoia about a Catholic plot and even a Catholic invasion. Recall that, by 1774, not even a century had passed since King James II had been overthrown in the Glorious Revolution of 1688. The event was about as far from peoples' living memory then as the Great Depression of the 1930s is to us today. A plot to secretly restore Catholicism might not have seemed so far-fetched as many historians now view it.[74] Little wonder Protestants in New York and New England – where a language of Popery had long featured in the political discourse and where bitter memories of the French and Native attacks on British settlements remained vivid – were so quick to react violently. The timing of the Quebec Act – promulgated just as imperial tensions reached a boiling point – could hardly have been worse. "What," asked one New Yorker, could have led officials to pass a bill meant "to rob, enslave and murder their fellow subjects at the expense of the *protestant cause*?" So powerful were anti-Catholic sentiments, they could even shake settlers' faith in "Popish King George" himself, who "had broken his coronation oath, and established the popish religion in Canada." Well before Thomas Paine published *Common Sense*, pushing reluctant colonists to break with their monarchical political culture, Jones argues that the Quebec Act's concessions to French Catholics had "brought the King to the centre of the conflict," forcing colonists "to think more seriously about the place of the monarch in popular articulations of Protestant British patriotism."

Part III, "Indigenous Peoples and European Borders," looks away from the Atlantic littoral to focus on the Ohio Valley, and on the essential role of Native peoples in the Quebec Act. As Jeffers Lennox emphasizes, anti-Catholic sentiments were not the only factors shaping the Quebec Act's reception. "The Act's 'intolerable' element was not the accommodations it offered French subjects," he argues, "but rather the borders it provided for the province." Perhaps because so few contemporary maps represented Quebec's contours as laid out by the 1774 Act – the mostly patriotic printers in Great Britain found it difficult to represent an empire divided against itself – the implications of its extension into the Ohio Valley have gone largely unrecognized by historians since. For Lennox, the Act's most salient feature was the size of the province it created, stretching from the St Lawrence Valley down the Ohio River and up around the Great Lakes. In so doing, it nullified the territorial claims that British settlers had only recently secured. Even worse, perhaps, by centralizing authority over land cessions in the Ohio Valley in Quebec, it reinforced the principle that British settlers would not push into Native territory without the permission of imperial authorities. "The people here," as Frederick Haldimand wrote from New York, "do not want to see a chain pulled along the backs of their settlements." Settlers may have protested, but Lennox shows that those borders were very intentional – the product of extensive reflection and debate among colonial administrators. Although they possessed little geographic knowledge of the North American interior, authorities in London were well aware of the settler-Native dynamics that prevailed. William Johnson, among others, had relayed the unhappiness of Indigenous nations demanding, in the words of one Huron diplomat, that "we may be supported in the right and privileges granted us by our present Royal Sovereign and father by his proclamation of 7th October 1763." Governments along the coast had proven unwilling to enforce the borders of 1763. A new government in Quebec might prove more successful.

British officials in London spent extensive time debating Quebec's new borders, but they would have to be imposed on the ground. And as Kristofer Ray argues, those cartographical boundaries "meant little in a fluid world, where Northern, Western, and Southern Indians interacted and competed with one another." The Ohio Valley was "an Indigenous world," Ray emphasizes, that "Britons simply could not control" – a world of "geopolitical fluidity" marked by extensive Native mobility, the creation and collapse of alliances, and almost continuous warfare. British power barely extended to the region; insofar as it did, it worked through alliances with Native American nations. Ray dwells partly on the various Cherokee tribes in the south, along the Tennessee River, and the Haudenosaunee to the north, both of whom had long-standing claims to parts of the Ohio Valley. Although these two Iroquoian-speaking peoples had fought bitterly for decades, both were simultaneously at war with Western nations in the Illinois Valley and around the Great Lakes. By the mid 1760s, the Ohio Valley had become the tense meeting point between all these warring people. Thanks to their common wars with Western nations (Aninshnaabeg, Illinois, Mascoutens, Miamis, and others), the British had succeeded in brokering a peace between the Cherokee and Haudenosaunee in the late 1760s. Alas, these long-standing and expensive efforts to stabilize the West were continually undermined by rapacious British settlers and venal provincial governments. Imperial authorities were well aware of the "fraudulent and bad Practices" that prevailed. "I have heard of those Complaints as long as I have heared [*sic*] of America," General Gage reported. Through these and other channels, officials in London were well aware that the "Thirteen seaboard colonies were utterly ill- equipped to deal with the palpable instability of Native affairs." It had become clear that "only centralized power could stabilize the west and bring order to the North American Empire" by managing trade and diplomacy with Native Americans. The Quebec Act thus emerges, in Ray's telling, as a belated attempt to stabilize a chaotic region, and fulfill the promises made in 1763. Had it come earlier, perhaps it would have succeeded.

It might seem odd to view the Quebec Act as an extension of the Royal Proclamation. On its face, the Act reorganized much of the territory encompassed by the Royal Proclamation, and was entirely silent on Native American issues. Did it overturn the rights established in 1763? The question is not just, so to speak, academic; it carries major implications for current legal debates about Indigenous land rights in Canada. Although the 1774 Act figures in the lineage of laws that compose Canada's unwritten Constitution, when it comes to the history of Canada's Indigenous peoples, as Alain Beaulieu explains, it is the 1763 Royal Proclamation that takes on a canonical status. Alongside it, the Quebec Act plays a minimal – and indeed embarrassing – role. While the 1763 Proclamation asserted Indigenous land rights and established the precedent that Native lands could only be ceded by treaty, the Quebec Act failed to mention Native peoples, overturning the more generous Royal Proclamation. Nevertheless, as Beaulieu argues, there are good reasons to see the 1774 Quebec Act as an extension of the 1763 Royal Proclamation. Indeed, it was an extension of earlier French imperial policy in North America. By the 1770s, British officials had become convinced of the "superiority of French Indian policy" enacted through a complex set of Native alliances. So effective were they, according to William Johnson, that even after the collapse of the French Empire, French people in the West "maintain their Influence, enjoy the major part of the Trade, whilst our Traders are considered as Interlopers."[75] By centralizing Native American relations under a single governor in Quebec, the imperial government hoped to better manage their new system of alliances stretching into the Ohio Valley and the Great Lakes and the treaties that undergirded them. Enforcing treaty requirements would appease Indian nations, while also asserting a firmer control over unruly British settlers.

From these discussions, the role of Native American relations with European empires emerges as one of the key factors shaping the Quebec Act. And here one final irony becomes clear: the centralized authority over Indian affairs the Act meant to implement – and which was so vociferously rejected by rebellious settlers along the Atlantic coast – would remain in the Constitution those same settlers enacted in 1787. By then, those colonists rebelling against an empire had become an imperial power of their own.

NOTES

1 On national narratives and history, important theoretical works include: Benedict Anderson, *Imagined Communities: Reflections on the Origin and Spread of Nationalism* (London: Verso, 1983; rev. ed., 1991); Eric Hobsbawm and Terrence Ranger, eds, *The Invention of Tradition* (Cambridge: Cambridge University Press, 1983); Partha Chatterjee, *Nationalist Thought and the Colonial World: A Derivative Discourse?* (London: Zed Books, 1986); John R. Gillis, ed., *Commemorations: The Politics of National Identity* (Princeton: Princeton University Press, 1994). On these subjects as they pertain to the area concerned by the Quebec Act, see: Jeremy Adelman and Stephen Aron, "From Borderlands to Borders: Empires, Nation-States, and the Peoples in Between in North American History," *American Historical Review* 104, no. 3 (June 1999): 814–41, along with the responses in "Forum Essay: Responses," *American Historical Review* 104, no. 4 (October 1999): 1221–39, and the works cited therein; Joyce E. Chaplin, "Expansion and Exceptionalism in Early American History," *Journal of American History* 89, no. 4 (2003): 1431–55; Thomas Bender, *A Nation Among Nations: America's Place in World History* (New York: Hill and Wang, 2006); Jack P. Greene, "Colonial History and National History: Reflections on a Continuing Problem," *William and Mary Quarterly*, Third Series 64, no. 2 (2007): 235–50; Christopher Grasso and Karin Wulf, "Nothing Says 'Democracy' Like a Visit from the Queen: Reflections on Empire and Nation in Early American Histories," *Journal of American History* 95, no. 3 (2008): 764–81; Rosemarie Zagarri, "The Significance of the 'Global Turn' for the Early American Republic: Globalization in the Age of Nation-Building," *Journal of the Early Republic* 31, no. 1 (2011): 1–37; Catherine Desbarats and Thomas Wien, "Introduction: La Nouvelle-France et l'Atlantique, *Revue d'histoire de l'Amérique française* 64, no. 3–4 (2011): 5–29; Cécile Vidal, ed., *Louisiana: Crossroads*

of the Atlantic World (Philadelphia: University of Pennsylvania Press, 2013); Daniel H. Usner, "Rescuing Early America from Nationalist Narratives: An Intra-Imperial Approach to Colonial Canada and Louisiana," *Historical Reflections* 40, no. 3 (2014): 1–19. On the fight for Canada, see www.1812.gc.ca; Karim M. Tiro, "Now You See It, Now You Don't: The War of 1812 in Canada and the United States in 2012," *The Public Historian* 35, no. 1 (2013): 87–97; Claire Turenne Sjolander, "Through the Looking Glass: Canadian Identity and the War of 1812," *International Journal: Canada's Journal of Global Policy Analysis* 69, no. 2 (2014): 152–67; Yves Frenette, "Conscripting Canada's Past: The Harper Government and the Politics of Memory," *Canadian Journal of History* 49, no. 1 (2014): 49.

2 Philip Lawson, *The Imperial Challenge: Quebec and Britain in the Age of the American Revolution* (Montreal: McGill-Queen's University Press, 1989).

3 On entangled history or *histoire croisée*, see esp. Michael Werner and Bénédicte Zimmermann, "Penser l'histoire croisée: entre empirie et réflexivité," *Annales. Histoire, sciences sociales* 58, no. 1 (2003): 7–36, translated as Michael Werner and Bénédicte Zimmermann, "Beyond Comparison: Histoire Croisée and the Challenge of Reflexivity," *History and Theory* 45, no. 1 (2006): 30–50; Sanjay Subrahmanyam, "Connected Histories: Notes towards a Reconfiguration of Early Modern Eurasia," *Modern Asian Studies* 31, no. 3 (1997): 735–62; Subrahmanyam, *From the Tagus to the Ganges* (New Delhi, 2005); Subrahmanyam, "Holding the World in Balance: The Connected Histories of the Iberian Overseas Empires, 1500–1640," *American Historical Review* 112, no. 5 (December 2007): 1359–85; Eliga H. Gould, "Entangled Histories, Entangled Worlds: The English-Speaking Atlantic as a Spanish Periphery," *American Historical Review* 112, no. 3 (June 2007): 764–86; Gould, "Entangled Atlantic Histories: A Response from the Anglo-American Periphery," *American Historical Review* 112, no. 5 (December 2007): 1415–22. The British Conquest of Quebec has recently been the subject of important publications that place the event in a broader imperial context: Phillip A. Buckner and John G. Reid, eds, *Remembering 1759: The Conquest of Canada in Historical Memory* (Toronto: University of Toronto Press, 2012); Phillip A. Buckner and John G. Reid, eds, *Revisiting 1759: The Conquest of Canada in Historical Perspective* (Toronto: University of Toronto Press, 2012); Laurent Veyssière and Bertrand Fonck, eds, *La Guerre de Sept Ans en Nouvelle-France* (Quebec: Septentrion, 2012); Sophie Imbeault, Denis Vaugeois, and Laurent Veyssière, eds, *1763: Le traité de Paris bouleverse l'Amérique* (Quebec: Septentrion, 2012); Laurent

Veyssière and Bertrand Fonck, eds, *La fin de la Nouvelle-France* (Paris: A. Colin, 2013); Laurent Veyssière, ed., *La Nouvelle-France en héritage* (Paris: A. Colin / Ministère de la Défense, 2013); Laurent Veyssière and Bertrand Fonck, eds, *La chute de la Nouvelle-France: De l'affaire Jumonville au traité de Paris* (Quebec: Septentrion, 2015).

4 William Smith, *History of Canada: From Its First Discovery, to the Year 1791* (Quebec: J. Neilson, 1815), 2: 64–74.

5 For a recent analysis of the Quebec Act as the source of future difficulties, see Louis-Georges Harvey, "L'intégration de l'ancienne Nouvelle-France à l'Empire britannique, 1760–1774," in *La Nouvelle-France en héritage*, ed. Laurent Veyssière, 29–44 (Paris: Armand Colin, 2013).

6 The relevant section is in the first chapter of the eleventh book of the third volume of the original edition: François-Xavier Garneau, *Histoire du Canada depuis sa découverte jusqu'à nos jours* (Quebec: N. Aubin, 1848).

7 Lionel Groulx, *Vers l'émancipation: Cours d'histoire du Canada à l'Université de Montréal, 1920–1921* (Montreal: Bibliothèque de l'Action française, 1921), 227. See also *Lendemain de Conquête: Cours d'histoire du Canada à l'Université de Montréal, 1919–1920* (Montreal: Bibliothèque de l'Action française, 1920).

8 Michel Brunet, "La Conquête anglaise et la déchéance de la bourgeoisie canadienne (1760–1793)," *Amérique française* 13, no. 2 (June 1955): 19–84. On the subject of this interpretation, see Cameron Nish, *The French Canadians, 1759–1766: Conquered? Half-Conquered? Liberated?* (Vancouver and Toronto: Copp Clark, 1966); Dale Miquelon, ed., *Society and Conquest: The Debate on the Bourgeoisie and Social Change in French Canada, 1700–1850* (Vancouver: Copp Clark, 1977); Serge Gagnon, *Quebec and Its Historians: The 20th Century* (Montreal: McGill-Queen's University Press, 1985); S. Dale Standen, "The Debate on the Social and Economic Consequences of the Conquest: A Summary," in *Readings in Canadian History: Pre-Confederation*, ed. Robert Douglas Francis and Donald Boyd Smith, 246–55 (Toronto: Holt, Rinehart and Winston, 1990); Jean Lamarre, *Le devenir de la nation québécoise selon Maurice Séguin, Guy Frégault, et Michel Brunet (1944–1969)* (Sillery: Septentrion, 1993); Ronald Rudin, *Making History in Twentieth-Century Quebec* (Toronto: University of Toronto Press, 1997). On Anglo-Canadian historiography, see Carl Berger, *The Writing of Canadian History: Aspects of English-Canadian Historical Writing, 1900–1970* (Toronto: Oxford University Press, 1976).

9 Michel Bibaud, *Histoire du Canada et des Canadiens sous la domination anglaise* (Montreal: Lovell and Gibson, 1844).

10 Thomas Chapais, *Cours d'histoire du Canada* (Quebec: J.P. Garneau, 1919), vol. 1. See the very good article by Damien-Claude Bélanger, "Thomas Chapais, loyaliste," *Revue d'histoire de l'Amérique française* 65, no. 4 (2012): 439–72.

11 Alfred L. Burt, *The Old Province of Quebec* (Minneapolis: University of Minnesota Press, 1933), 200.

12 Traces of this paradigm can still be found in Donald G. Creighton, *The Empire of the St Lawrence* (Toronto: Macmillan, 1956) and Fernand Ouellet, *Lower Canada, 1791–1840: Social Change and Nationalism* (Toronto: McClelland and Stewart, 1980).

13 Fernand Ouellet, *Economic and Social History of Quebec, 1760–1850: Structures and Conjonctures* (Toronto: Gage Publishing, in association with the Institute of Canadian Studies, Carleton University, 1980).

14 Hilda Neatby, *Quebec: The Revolution Age, 1760–1791* (Toronto: McClelland and Stewart, 1966).

15 Pierre Tousignant began by publishing a PhD thesis on the period: "La genèse et l'avènement de la constitution de 1791" (Université de Montréal, 1971). It was followed by a long article: "The Integration of the Province of Quebec into the British Empire, 1763–791. Part I: From the Royal Proclamation to the Quebec Act," in *Dictionary of Canadian Biography* 4: xxxii–xlix (Toronto and Quebec: University of Toronto Press and Presses de l'Université Laval, 1979).

16 On this subject, see Elizabeth Mancke, "Another British America: A Canadian Model for the Early Modern British Empire," *The Journal of Imperial and Commonwealth History* 25, no. 1 (1997): 1–36.

17 George Bancroft, *History of the United States of America, from the Discovery of the Continent* (Boston: Little, Brown and Company, 1876), 4: 156.

18 Francis Parkman, *Montcalm and Wolfe: The French and Indian War* (Boston, MA: Da Capo Press, 1995), 546.

19 Thomas Perkins Abernethy, *Western Lands and the American Revolution* (New York: D. Appleton–Century Company, for the Institute for Research in the Social Sciences, University of Virginia, 1937).

20 David Ammerman, "The Tea Crisis and Its Consequences, through 1775," in *A Companion to the American Revolution*, ed. Jack P. Greene and J.R. Pole, 198 (Oxford: Blackwell, 2000).

21 Ibid., 227.

22 Brendan McConville, *The King's Three Faces: The Rise and Fall of Royal America* (Chapel Hill: Published for the Omohundro Institute of Early

American History and Culture, Williamsburg, Virginia, by the University of North Carolina Press), 288.

23 Mark R. Anderson, *The Battle for the Fourteenth Colony: America's War of Liberation in Canada, 1774–1776* (Lebanon, NH: University Press of New England, 2013), 31–44. See also Alan Taylor, *American Revolutions: A Continental History, 1750–1804* (New York: W.W. Norton, 2016), 83–6.

24 Daniel Richter, *Facing East from Indian Country: A Native History of Early America* (Boston, MA: Harvard University Press, 2001), 206–16; Colin G. Calloway, *The Scratch of a Pen: 1763 and the Transformation of North America* (Oxford: Oxford University Press, 2006), 112–32. See also Eric Hinderaker, *Elusive Empires: Constructing Colonialism in the Ohio Valley, 1673 –1800* (New York: Cambridge University Press, 1997); and François Furstenberg, "The Significance of the Trans-Appalachian Frontier in Atlantic History," *American Historical Review* 113, no. 3 (2008), 647–77.

25 Clarence Walworth Alvord, *The Mississippi Valley in British Politics: A Study of the Trade, Land Speculation, and Experiments in Imperialism Culminating in the American Revolution*. 2 vols. (Cleveland: The Arthur H. Clark Company, 1917), 1: 13. His discussion of the Quebec Act appears on 2: 209–51.

26 Jack M. Sosin, *Whitehall and the Wilderness: The Middle West in British Colonial Policy, 1760–1775* (Lincoln: University of Nebraska Press, 1961), 239–55).

27 Reginald Coupland, *The Quebec Act: A Study in Statesmanship* (Oxford: Clarendon Press, 1925).

28 Philip Lawson, "A Perspective on British History and the Treatment of Quebec," *Journal of Historical Sociology* 3 (1990): 253–71.

29 Peter Marshall, "The Incorporation of Quebec in the British Empire," in *Of Mother Country and Plantations: Proceedings of the Twenty-seventh Conference in Early American History*, ed. Virginia Bever Platt and David Curtis Skaggs, 61, 62 (Bowling Green, OH: Bowling Green State University Press, 1971).

30 Lawson, *The Imperial Challenge*.

31 In this same vein, see Karen Stanbridge, "Quebec and the Irish Catholic Relief Act of 1778: An Institutional Approach," *Journal of Historical Sociology* 16, no. 3 (2003): 375–404.

32 Lawson, *The Imperial Challenge*, x.

33 David Milobar, "Conservative Ideology, Metropolitan Government, and the Reform of Quebec, 1782–1791," *International History Review* 12 (Feb. 1990): 45–64; David Milobar, "The Origins of British-Quebec Merchant Ideology: New France, the British Atlantic, and the Constitutional

Periphery, 1720–1770," *Journal of Imperial and Commonwealth History* 24 (Sept. 1996): 364–90; quotation at 165.

34 David Milobar, "Quebec Reform, the British Constitution and the Atlantic Empire, 1774–1775," *Parliamentary History* 14 (Jan. 1995), 65.

35 P.J. Marshall, ed., *The Oxford History of the British Empire*, vol. 2, *The Eighteenth Century* (Oxford: Oxford University Press, 1998); P.J. Marshall, *The Making and Unmaking of Empires: Britain, India, and America c.1750–1783* (Oxford: Oxford University Press, 2005). Another important point of reference is Lauren Benton's focus on "legal pluralisms," in which various legal regimes at the local, national, and supra-national level clash up against each other and also against non-state entities. See Lauren A. Benton, *Law and Colonial Cultures: Legal Regimes in World History, 1400–1900* (Cambridge: Cambridge University Press, 2002); Richard J. Ross and Lauren Benton, *Legal Pluralism and Empires, 1500–1850*. (New York: NYU Press, 2013). See also the foundational work by Jack P. Greene. Greene, *Peripheries and Center: Constitutional Development in the Extended Polities of the British Empire and the United States, 1607–1788* (Athens: University of Georgia Press, 1986).

36 Edmond Dziembowski, *Les Pitt: L'Angleterre face à la France, 1708–1806* (Paris: Perrin, 2006), 122. George III was in favour of settling the conflict as quickly as possible, while France exploited a newfound ability to draw out negotiations, thanks to the alliance it negotiated with Spain in August 1761.

37 Jean-Pierre Poussou, "Les conséquences économiques de la guerre de Sept Ans," in *La fin de la Nouvelle-France*, ed. Bertrand Fonck and Laurent Veyssière, 433–48 (Paris: Armand Colin and Ministère de la Défense, 2013). Laurent Veyssière, "Le traité de Paris de 1763, une paix 'ni bonne ny glorieuse,'" in *1763: Le traité de Paris bouleverse l'Amérique*, ed. Sophie Imbeault, Denis Vaugeois, and Laurent Veyssière, 18 (Quebec: Septentrion, 2013).

38 François-Joseph Ruggiu, "Falling into Oblivion? Canada and the French Monarchy, 1759–1783," in Buckner and Reid, *Revisiting 1759*, 69–94.

39 "Articles de la capitulation de Montréal" (1760), http://www.axl.cefan.ulaval.ca/francophonie/Montreal – capitulation – 1760.htm, accessed Aug. 30, 2017.

40 Article 4 of the Treaty of Paris states that, "His Britannick Majesty further agrees, that the French inhabitants, or others who had been subjects of the Most Christian King in Canada, may retire with all safety and freedom wherever they shall think proper, and may sell their estates, provided it be to the subjects of his Britannick Majesty, and bring away their

effects as well as their persons, without being restrained in their emigration, under any pretence whatsoever, except that of debts or of criminal prosecutions: The term limited for this emigration shall be fixed to the space of eighteen months, to be computed from the day of the exchange of the ratification of the present treaty." Adam Shortt and Arthur G. Doughty, *Documents Relating to the Constitutional History of Canada, 1759–1791* (Ottawa, S.E. Dawson, 1921), 86. On the general question of emigration, see Robert Larin, *Canadiens en Guyane, 1754–1805* (Paris: Presses de l'Université Paris–Sorbonne, 2006); Marcel Trudel, *Le régime militaire et la disparition de la Nouvelle-France, 1759–1764* (Montréal: Fides, 1999), 491–511. On the difficult experiences of Canadians who chose to settle in France, see Robert Larin, *L'exode de Canadiens à la Conquête, le Petit-Canada de la Touraine, 1760–1840* (Montreal: Société généalogique canadienne–française, 2008). On the Canadian gentry and its equivocation, see Roch Legault, *Une élite en déroute: Les officiers canadiens après la Conquête* (Outremont: Athéna éditions, 2002); Sophie Imbeault, *Les Tarieu de Lanaudière: une famille noble après la conquête, 1760–1791* (Québec: Septentrion, 2004); François-Joseph Ruggiu, "Le destin de la noblesse du Canada, de l'Empire français à l'Empire britannique," *Revue d'histoire de l'Amérique française* 66, no. 1 (2012): 37–63; Lorraine Gadoury, "L'impact de la Conquête sur la noblesse canadienne," in *La Nouvelle-France en héritage*, ed. Laurent Veyssière, 119–36 (Paris: Armand Colin and Ministère de la défense, 2013). On the Catholic Church after the Conquest, see Marcel Trudel, *L'Église canadienne sous le régime militaire, 1759–1764* (Montreal and Quebec: Institut d'histoire de l'Amérique française and Presses de l'Université Laval, 1956–57); Lucien Lemieux, *Histoire de catholicisme québécois: Les années difficiles (1760–1839)* (Montreal: Boréal, 1989). On the merchants, see José Igartua, "The Merchants and Négociants of Montreal, 1750–1775: A Study in Socio-economic History" (PhD thesis, Michigan State University, 1974). On the question in general, see Jacques Mathieu and Sophie Imbeault, *La guerre des Canadiens* (Quebec: Septentrion, 2013).

41 Using reports and petitions to help shape imperial knowledge, along with colonial and British public opinion, Canadian elites established themselves as representatives of a new "people," a people they helped to create through their very discourse. See Anne Trépanier, "La parade d'une seconde Conquête: l'Acte de Québec comme moment refondateur," in *La Rénovation de l'héritage démocratique: Entre fondation et refondation*, ed. A. Trépanier (Ottawa: Les Presses de l'Université d'Ottawa/University of Ottawa Press, 2009), 178–219.

42 The Treaty of Paris merely signalled a temporary pause in hostilities between the two rival European powers. The French, convinced that the British were seeking to impose their supremacy on overseas trade, pursued hostile policies towards their rival. During the 1760s and 1770s, this approach fed an unfounded yet frequently surfacing rumour, according to which France was infiltrating Canada with spies and was developing plans for a reconquest. During the American War of Independence, France was falsely accused of trying to capitalize on the situation to take back Canada. See Marcel Trudel, *La Révolution américaine: Pourquoi la France refuse le Canada (1775–1783)* (Sillery: Boréal Express, 1976), 130, 186–90.

43 On the common history shared by the Acadians and the Mi'kmaq, see Geoffrey G. Plank, *An Unsettled Conquest: The British Campaign against the Peoples of Acadia* (Philadelphia: University of Pennsylvania Press, 2001). Another cause for concern among the British was Pontiac's Rebellion (1763–65) in the Great Lakes region, during which Indigenous forces sought to rally French-speaking colonists to their cause.

44 Stephen Conway, "The Consequences of the Conquest: Quebec and British Politics, 1760–1774," in Buckner and Reid, *Revisiting 1759*, 143.

45 Douglas Hay, "The Meanings of the Criminal Law in Quebec, 1764 to 1774," in *Crime and Justice in Europe and Canada*, ed. Louis Knafla, 83 (Waterloo, ON: Wilfrid Laurier University Press, 1981).

46 Bernard Bailyn, *Voyagers to the West: A Passage in the Peopling of America on the Eve of Revolution* (New York: Knopf, 1986), 29; Memorandum to the Board of Trade, quoted in Burset, Chapter 4 in this volume, 141.

47 At the time, colonial administrators estimated the French-speaking population of the Province of Quebec at fifty thousand individuals. Research conducted by historical demographers have since produced higher estimates, placing the number of French-speaking Catholics settled in the St Lawrence Valley in 1760 at between seventy and eighty thousand. See Trudel, *Le régime militaire et la disparition de la Nouvelle-France*, 83. By 1774, there would have been almost a hundred thousand Franco-Catholics in the colony, and possibly a few thousand Anglo-Protestants. See Hubert Charbonneau, ed., *La Population du Québec: Études rétrospectives* (Trois-Rivières: Les Éditions du Boréal Express, 1973), 43; Robert Larin, *Brève histoire du peuplement européen en Nouvelle-France* (Sillery: Septentrion, 2000), 164; Fernand Ouellet, *Histoire économique et sociale du Québec, 1760–1850* (Montreal: Fides, 1966), 599. Donald Fyson suggests a figure of 750 adult male Protestants

in 1775 in "The Conquered and the Conqueror: The Mutual Adaptation of the Canadiens and the British in Quebec, 1759–1775," in Buckner and Reid, *Revisiting 1759*, 212–13.

48 Marshall, *Making and Unmaking*, 189.

49 A separate accord, the Treaty of Oswegatchie of 30 August 1760, laid the groundwork for a new system of alliances with the British. Another treaty, signed on 16 September 1760, formalized the new system by placing seven allied peoples under the leadership of Kahnawake. Alain Beaulieu, "Les garanties d'un traité disparu: Le traité d'Oswegatchie, 30 août 1760," *Revue juridique Themis* 34, no. 2 (2000): 369–408; Denys Delâge and Jean-Pierre Sawaya, *Les traités des Sept-Feux avec les Britanniques: Droits et pièges d'un héritage colonial au Québec* (Montreal: Septentrion, 2001); Jean-Pierre Sawaya, *Alliance et dépendance: Comment la Couronne britannique a obtenu la collaboration des Indiens de la vallée du Saint–Laurent entre 1760 et 1774* (Sillery: Septentrion, 2014).

50 John A. Dickinson and Brian J. Young, *A Short History of Quebec* (Montreal: McGill-Queen's University Press, 2008), 41; Benoît Grenier, *Seigneurs campagnards de la Nouvelle France: Présence seigneuriale et sociabilité rurale dans la Vallée du Saint-Laurent à l'époque préindustrielle* (Rennes: Presses universitaires de Rennes, 2007). Bruce Curtis, "Pastoral Power, Sovereignty and Class: Church, Tithe, and Simony in Quebec," *Critical Research on Religion* 5, no. 2 (2017): 151–69; Article 47 specifies that "Negroes and panis" were included in the protected property.

51 Marcel Trudel, *Le régime militaire dans le gouvernement des Trois-Rivières, 1760–1764* (Trois-Rivières: Éditions du bien public, 1952); Trudel, *L'Église canadienne sous le Régime militaire* (vol. 1, *Les problèmes*; vol. 2, *Les institutions*) (Montréal: Institut d'histoire de l'Amérique française, 1956 and 1957); Trudel, *Histoire de la Nouvelle-France*, vol. 10, *Le régime militaire et la disparition de la Nouvelle-France, 1759–1764* (Montréal: Fides, 1999).

52 Donald Fyson, "The Conquered and the Conqueror," 190–217.

53 Heather Welland, "Commercial Interest and Political Allegiance: The Origins of Quebec Act," in Buckner and Reid, *Revisiting 1759*, 166–89.

54 See, in particular, Louise Dechêne, *Habitants et marchands de Montréal au XVIIe siècle* (Paris: Plon, 1974); Allan Greer, *Peasant, Lord, and Merchant: Rural Society in Three Quebec Parishes, 1740–1840* (Toronto: University of Toronto Press, 1985), 6–15; Louise Dechêne, *Le Peuple, l'État et la guerre au Canada sous le régime français* (Montreal: Boréal, 2008), 137–48; Benoît Grenier, *Brève histoire du régime seigneurial* (Montreal: Boréal, 2012).

55 On the long history and staying power of these clichés, see José E. Igartua, "The Genealogy of Stereotypes: French Canadians in Two English-language Canadian History Textbooks," *Journal of Canadian Studies / Revue d'études canadiennes* 42, no. 3 (2008): 106–32. On the academic work of deconstruction that this situation has inspired, see Catherine Desbarats and Thomas Wien, "Introduction: La Nouvelle-France et l'Atlantique," *Revue d'histoire de l'Amérique française* 64, nos. 3–4 (Winter/Spring 2011): 5–29.

56 Bernard Andrès, ed., La *conquête des lettres au Québec (1759–1799)* (Quebec: Presses de l'Université Laval, 2007); Andrès, *Histoires littéraires des Canadiens au XVIIIe siècle* (Quebec: Presses de l'Université Laval, 2013); Yvan Lamonde, *Histoire sociale des idées au Québec (1760–1896)* (Montreal: Fides, 2000); Louise Bienvenue, Ollivier Hubert, and Christine Hudon, *Le collège classique pour garçons: Études historiques sur une institution québécoise disparue* (Montreal: Fides, 2014).

57 Jean-Pierre Wallot, "L'Acte de Québec, ses causes, sa nature et 'l'Ancien Régime,'" *Cahier de programme d'études sur le Québec, Université McGill* 21 (2001): 2–8. More generally, see Jean-Pierre Wallot, *Un Québec qui bougeait* (Montreal: Boréal Express, 1973); Tousignant, "La genèse et l'avènement de la Constitution de 1791."

58 Georges-Étienne Proulx, "Les Canadiens ont-ils payé la dîme entre 1760 et 1775," *Revue d'histoire de l'Amérique française* 11, no. 4 (1958): 533–62.

59 Lemieux, *Histoire de catholicisme québécois*, 18–26. There were numerous and early allusions to the need for a truly Canada clergy, that is to say, free from the influence of Rome and Paris, in the official documents published in Hilda Neatby, *The Quebec Act*.

60 Report by Fletcher Norton and William de Grey, 10 June 1765, as cited in Lawson, *The Imperial Challenge*, 45.

61 See also Peter Marshall, "The Incorporation of Quebec in the British Empire, 1763–1774," in *Of Mother Country and Plantations: Proceeding of the Twenty-seventh Conference in Early American History*, ed. V.B. Platt and D.C. Skaggs (Bowling Green: Bowling Green State University Press, 1971), 52–7.

62 Nationalist Quebec historiography has gone so far as to brand Briand as a collaborator, complicit in British colonialism. See Michel Brunet, "L'Église catholique dans la période d'après la Conquête," in *Les Canadiens après la Conquête, 1759–1775* (Montreal: Fides, 1969), 127–33; Luca Codignola, "Quoi de neuf sur la prétendue servitude de Monseigneur Briand (1760 à 1766)? Une nouvelle lecture historiographique de l'après-Trudel à partir des archives romaines," in *Le Saint-Siège, le*

Québec et l'Amérique française: Les archives vaticanes, pistes et défis, ed. Martin Pâquet, Matteo Sanfilippo, and Jean-Philippe Warren (Quebec: Presses de l'Université Laval, 2013), 109–31.

63 Raymond Lemieux, "Penser la religion au Québec," *Globe: Revue internationale d'études québécoises* 11, no. 1 (2008): 225–36.

64 Michael McDonnell, *Masters of Empire: Great Lakes Indians and the Making of America* (New York: Hill and Wang, 2015), 199.

65 The literature on Native Americans and European empires in the Ohio Valley is vast and continually growing. Important accounts include: Richard White, *The Middle Ground: Indians, Empires, and Republics in the Great Lakes Region, 1650 –1815* (Cambridge: Cambridge University Press, 1991); Eric Hinderaker, *Elusive Empires: Constructing Colonialism in the Ohio Valley, 1673–1800* (Cambridge: Cambridge University Press, 1999); Alan Taylor, *The Divided Ground: Indians, Settlers, and the Northern Borderland of the American Revolution* (New York: Knopf, 2006); Rob Harper, *Unsettling the West: Violence and State Building in the Ohio Valley* (Philadelphia: University of Pennsylvania Press, 2018); Patrick Spero, *Frontier Rebels: The Fight for Independence in the American West, 1765–1776* (New York: W.W. Norton & Company, 2018); Susan Sleeper-Smith, *Indigenous Prosperity and American Conquest: Indian Women of the Ohio River Valley, 1690–1792* (Chapel Hill: Omohundro Institute of Early American History & Culture / University of North Carolina Press, 2018). Quotes from Ray, chapter 9 in this volume.

66 Knox quoted in Lennox, chapter 8 in this volume.

67 Morin, chapter 3 in this volume; Burke and Dartmouth, quoted in Lennox, 276.

68 The best study of these events is Fred Anderson, *Crucible of War: The Seven Years' War and the Fate of Empire in British North America, 1754–1766* (New York: Vintage Books, 2001). For the aftermath, see esp. Marshall, *Making and Unmaking of Empires*; Max S. Edelson, *The New Map of Empire: How Britain Imagined America before Independence* (Cambridge, MA: Harvard University Press, 2017).

69 John Brewer, *The Sinews of Power: War, Money, and the English State, 1688–1783* (Cambridge, MA: Harvard University Press, 1990); Richard White, *The Middle Ground: Indians, Empires, and Republics in the Great Lakes Region, 1650–1815* (Cambridge: Cambridge University Press, 1991); Eric Hinderaker, *Elusive Empires: Constructing Colonialism in the Ohio Valley, 1673–1800* (Cambridge: Cambridge University Press, 1999); Eric Hinderaker and Peter C. Mancall, *At the Edge of Empire: The Backcountry in British North America* (Baltimore: Johns Hopkins University

Press, 2003); Fred Anderson and Andrew Cayton, *The Dominion of War: Empire and Liberty in North America, 1500–2000* (New York: Penguin, 2005), 135–59; Marshall, *Making and Unmaking*; Emma Rothschild, *The Inner Life of Empires: An Eighteenth-century History* (Princeton: Princeton University Press, 2011).

70 Willis, essay, chapter 5 in this volume.

71 David Armitage, *The Ideological Origins of the British Empire* (Cambridge: Cambridge University Press, 2000), 8.

72 Carleton and Thurlow quoted in Morin, chapter 3 in this volume, 110.

73 Coke quoted in Burset, chapter 4 in this volume, 145. On the application of legal pluralism in the Province of Quebec in the years surrounding the Quebec Act, see: Arnaud Decroix, "La controverse sur la nature du droit applicable après la conquête," *McGill Law Journal / Revue de droit de McGill* 56, no. 3 (2011): 489–542; David Gilles, *Essais d'histoire du droit: De la Nouvelle-France à la Province de Québec* (Sherbrooke: Les Éditions de la Revue de Droit, 2014) and Michel Morin, "Les revendications des nouveaux sujets, francophones et catholiques, de la Province de Québec, 1764–1774," in *Essays in the History of Canadian* Law, vol. 11, *Quebec and the Canadas*, ed. G. Blaine Baker and Donald Fyson (Toronto: University of Toronto Press, 2013), 131–86; Michel Morin, "Les débats concernant le droit français et le droit anglais antérieurement à l'adoption de l'Acte de Québec de 1774," *Revue de droit de l'Université de Sherbrooke* 44 (2014): 259–306; Michel Morin, "The Discovery and Assimilation of British Constitutional Law Principles in Quebec, 1764–1774," *Dalhousie Law Journal* 66, no. 2 (2013): 581–616; Michel Morin, "Blackstone and the Birth of Quebec's Distinct Legal Culture, 1765–1867," in *Re-Interpreting Blackstone's Commentaries: A Seminal Text in National and International Contexts*, ed. Wilfrid Prest (Oxford: Hart Publishing, 2014), 105–24.

74 Richard Hofstadter, *The Paranoid Style in American Politics, and Other Essays* (New York: Knopf, 1965); Gordon S. Wood, "Conspiracy and the Paranoid Style: Causality and Deceit in the Eighteenth Century," *The William and Mary Quarterly* 39, no. 3 (1982): 402–41.

75 Quoted in Calloway, *Scratch of a Pen: 1763 and the Transformation of North America* (New York: Oxford University Press, 2006), 130–1.

PART ONE

Quebec, Law, and Empire

I

"As may consist with their Allegiance to His Majesty": Redefining Loyal Subjects in 1774

Hannah Weiss Muller

When it was passed in 1774, the Quebec Act became the first parliamentary legislation to address the government of a specific British colony, as well as the first statute to tackle the question of privileges owed to the province's predominantly French Catholic subjects.[1] Among other things, the Quebec Act granted Catholics the free exercise of their religion, subject to the king's supremacy, and the right to assume offices of trust by taking an oath designed for those purposes rather than subscribing to the Test.[2] Perhaps most significantly, the act determined that "His Majesty's Canadian Subjects ... may also hold and enjoy their Property and Possessions, together with all Customs and Usages relative thereto, and all other their Civil Rights ... as may consist with their Allegiance to His Majesty."[3] By finally resolving the question of which laws would apply to the province and by formally allowing the coexistence of English criminal law and French civil law, the Quebec Act redefined the inheritance of loyal subjects, upholding their right to live under time-honoured customs, even if those customs were French.

Both eighteenth-century observers and historians in subsequent centuries have seen in the Quebec Act a range of possibilities, limitations, and motives, both conciliatory and oppressive. In the years surrounding the statute's passing, contemporaries either applauded the efforts of government or excoriated ministers for having betrayed them. Frederick Haldimand, Governor of Quebec, praised the Quebec Act as having ensured the relative tranquility of the province during the American Revolutionary War, and insisted that allowing French Catholics to continue under their ancient laws was "the most likely means to attach the people to the mother country."[4] But other observers were persuaded that the Act would turn subjects against the British Empire – that it would "shake the affections and confidence of his Majesty's subjects in England and Ireland, and finally lose him the hearts of all the Americans."[5] Given the fierce reactions this Act precipitated, perhaps it is not surprising that scholars began to grapple with the legacy of 1774 almost immediately. One enduring line of argument has seen in the Quebec Act the birth of the "nation within a nation," viewing the protection accorded to the Catholic Church and to French civil law as the means of ensuring the survival of a distinct national group.[6] The North American backdrop to this legislation passed in 1774 has also consistently attracted historians. Given the many eighteenth-century critics who proclaimed the Quebec Act to be one of the "intolerable acts," some scholars have related its passage to troubles that were brewing in the thirteen colonies to the south, while others have sought to prove that it bound Canada to the British Empire when its other rebellious colonies declared their independence.[7]

Finally, another more recent historiography, which is significantly enhanced by numerous essays in this volume, situates the Quebec Act within broader policy shifts in the British Empire. Scholars ranging from A.L. Burt, to Vincent Harlow, to Peter Marshall have argued that the Quebec Act represented a new form of governing and managing the empire.[8] For many imperial historians, the Quebec Act signalled a move away from the assimilative policies embodied in the Proclamation of 1763 to "policies of toleration and acceptance of the customs of peoples alien in language and religion."[9] For Stephen Conway, the shift in the models applied in 1763 and 1774 – a shift from the Irish-style model of governance, in which English constitutional forms and laws were imposed on a conquered population, to a more Minorcan-style model of governance, in which local populations were allowed to maintain their own systems of local governance and laws – reflected a reorientation of official policy.[10] Philip Lawson observes that, whereas traditional antipathy to Catholics had shaped the Proclamation of 1763 and little attention had been paid to the needs of the conquered population after the Seven Years' War (1756–1763), this more narrow-minded approach did not survive the decade but underwent a major revision by 1774.[11] For David Milobar, the metropolitan government, which initially viewed French colonial institutions with suspicion and was committed to upholding traditional understandings of the British constitution immediately before and after the Seven Years' War, began to view non-British institutions with greater acceptance and to understand their utility to the imperial government.[12] As Pierre Tousignant puts it so succinctly, the British government's "means of achieving its objectives was changing."[13] Thus, although there are differences among these historians, most agree that a new vision of governance materialized between the Royal Proclamation of 1763 and the Quebec Act of 1774. Metropolitan officials became less convinced that new subjects needed to be assimilated and more committed to policies that protected the rights of varied groups within the larger whole.

The willingness of colonial governors and metropolitan officials to move away from strict interpretations of the Protestant constitution, however, created new uncertainties about the meanings and boundaries of British subjecthood. The British Empire that emerged after the Seven Years' War included many who were non-Protestant, non-British, and non-white, and debates about the rights of British subjects occurred in almost all of its new territories.[14] Moreover, questions about whether a house of assembly should be called for Quebec or about whether English or French law applied in the province reflected not only differing interpretations of the British constitution; they also revealed profoundly conflicting understandings of how the rights of the "British subject" were to be defined. Almost a century ago, Reginald Coupland noted that the Quebec Act represented a "square fight between the claims of the new subjects ... and those of the old."[15] This was undoubtedly the case. But the end result of this "square fight" was a radical redefinition of the inheritance of British subjects. While English law had typically been held up as the ancient right of British subjects, the passing of the Quebec Act signalled that, within the highest echelons of government, a majority had deemed it "consistent with their allegiance" for British subjects to live under "foreign" law.

Much recent imperial historiography has also detailed the Quebec Act's long genesis. The origins of this landmark legislation can be found in a variety of Board of Trade and legal reports produced in the 1760s and early 1770s, which attempted to resolve whether English law, French law, or some combination of the two, was applicable to this new British province.[16] Less scholarship, however, connects policy debates in London to arguments made by subjects themselves. As we will see, petitions generated by inhabitants of Quebec during this period are essential to understanding the statutory redefinitions that occurred in 1774. Revisiting these memorials reveals that the questions of law addressed by parliament were intimately linked to a range of pre-existing understandings about what it meant to be a British subject. These understandings of subjecthood, many of which were conflicting, were put forward both by "new subjects," the predominantly French-Catholic population that had been adopted into the British Empire upon the cessions of 1763, and also by "old subjects," the predominantly British Protestant population of merchants and traders who were typically identified as natural-born subjects. These petitions offer new insight into the parliamentary discussions of 1774, demonstrating that politicians not only weighed what might be an appropriate constitutional settlement for Quebec – they also redefined the loyal subject's inheritance, drawing on ideas and arguments that were being made in the colony itself. This approach reveals that a range of inhabitants were instrumental in redefining the privileges of subjecthood and in articulating arguments about subject status, a dialogic process that culminated in parliamentary discussion and passage of the Quebec Act.

ADDRESSING THE RIGHTS OF SUBJECTS

When Canada was ceded to the British Empire under the Treaty of Paris (1763), colonial administrators initially hoped that they would draw numerous Protestant settlers to the newly constituted Province of Quebec.[17] Treaties and proclamations proposed simultaneous settlements for all of the ceded colonies and sought to integrate them under a broader constitutional model familiar to the Atlantic world – a model that embraced government by representative assembly and judgment according to English law. As many scholars have noted, promises of a representative assembly, "as soon as the circumstances shall permit," and of English law were intended to attract British Protestant settlers. The Proclamation of 1763, however, paid little attention to the existing demography of Quebec. It soon became apparent that the constitution of government envisioned in the early 1760s was not appropriate to governing a territory where the French-Catholic majority would remain predominant and seemed particularly concerned with preserving the security of property provided under their own traditional laws.

In the 1760s, the French Catholic population of Quebec numbered somewhere between sixty and seventy thousand, while the population of British merchants and traders hovered between two and three hundred. [18] Although British administrators intended to attract more British-born inhabitants to offset this imbalance, the predominance of the Canadiens only became more pronounced by the 1770s, given that merely one in two hundred of them had chosen to leave the colony after the peace and that few Protestant settlers had arrived.[19] Indeed, when parliament considered questions relating to the province of Quebec in the 1770s, observers noted that there were anywhere from eighty thousand to a hundred and fifty thousand French Catholics as compared to a few thousand British Protestants.[20] Only with the influx of around six thousand Loyalists in the 1780s did this demographic imbalance begin to be redressed.[21] The numerical predominance of non-Protestants therefore persisted in Quebec and would profoundly affect the outcome of debates over subjects' rights.

It is important to note that the Canadiens were widely recognized as "British subjects" after the conquest of Canada – in fact, virtually no one suggested anything to the contrary, generally accepting the renaming of these formerly French enemies as "adopted" or "new" subjects. In the Articles of Capitulation of September 1760, for example, the "French, Canadians, and Acadians of what state and condition soever, who shall remain in the colony," were deemed "Subjects of the King."[22] They were welcomed as "His Majesty's New Roman Catholic Subjects" under the Treaty of Paris.[23] As General Gage wrote in 1762, "no distinction has been made betwixt the Briton and the Canadian, but [they have been] equally regarded as subjects of the same Prince."[24] In the petitions and official correspondence of the 1760s and 1770s, both Catholic and Protestant inhabitants, as well as colonial officials, widely referred to the Canadiens as subjects. Even the Continental Congress, which addressed the diverse inhabitants of Quebec in 1774 and 1775, referred to them as "fellow-subjects," noting that the fortunes of war "had incorporated you with the body of English subjects."[25] However, if most agreed that the French Catholics were "British subjects," there was little agreement as to their exact rights as such. Instead, debates over the rights due British subjects were to become a feature of the era.

It also bears noting that governors of Quebec believed their "new subjects" were essential to ensuring the stability and productivity of the colony, and that a climate of relative conciliation towards subjects who were neither "British" nor "Protestant" was the wisest approach in the 1760s and 1770s. Beginning in 1764, James Murray, the first civil governor of Quebec, wrote to the Lords Commissioners indicating how important it was to win over the new subjects upon whom the empire depended:

> Little, very little will content the New Subjects ... a Race who could they be indulged with a few Privileges which the Laws deny to Roman Catholicks at home ... might become the most faithfull, and most useful, set of men in this American Empire ... and certain I am, unless the Canadians are admitted on Juries, and are allowed Judges and Lawyers who understand their Language that His Majesty will lose the greatest part of this valuable People.[26]

His successor, Guy Carleton, went even further in urging concessions. He recommended trade indulgences so that the Canadiens might contribute to British rather than French commercial growth; admission to places of trust, which would encourage Catholics to forget their former sovereign; and acceptance of some of the Canadian *noblesse* into the Council, because the "only way to make them faithful subjects is to place a prudent confidence in and employ them."[27] Similarly, Lieutenant-Governor Hector Theophilus Cramahé, of Swiss-Huguenot origin, argued that indulgence of the Catholic religion and confirmation of French laws of property were the only "sure and effectual method of gaining the affections of His Majesty's Canadian Subjects."[28] Governors might readily draw on memorials from inhabitants themselves when they urged the metropolitan government to be generous to its new subjects: an address from the Abbé de la Corne had promised that if some assurances were provided for the Catholic religion, George III "would not have in all his possessions subjects more submissive, more tenderly attached than they."[29] Hopeful that liberal concessions might make the Canadiens the most faithful among British subjects, colonial governors consistently recommended granting them privileges that did not contravene stipulations in the Treaty of Paris.

Recognizing that many administrators looked upon them with favour and were inclined to allow them a range of rights to which fellow Catholics living under the penal laws of Ireland and England were not entitled, a number of the French Catholics began to make their wishes known. Although a few would petition for access to offices of trust, and others would engage in debating whether a house of assembly was appropriate for the colony, their more consistent concern related to the laws under which adopted British subjects might live. It was therefore on the terrain of law that the rights of British subjects were first successfully renegotiated in Quebec.

Indeed, shortly after Canada's cession, the Canadiens began addressing George III and expressing concern about the precarious legal system, using a series of memorials not only to entreat the king's intervention, but also to proclaim their new status as his subjects. Presenting themselves as loyal subjects, they underlined their utility to the imperial enterprise, as well as their membership in the broader community of British subjects. As they petitioned their new monarch, however, they also proposed interpretations of subject status that would directly conflict with those put forth by their British and Protestant fellow subjects, articulating the idea that subjects were entitled to live under their own ancient laws. Initially, many Canadiens sought to appeal to George III's humanity toward all his subjects, imploring him to confirm the legal system that had been in place under their former sovereign. As inhabitants testified in an early petition from 1764, they worried that, unless their customs were upheld, they would become "veritable Slaves" instead of "favoured Subjects of Your Majesty."[30] Petitioners thus very clearly linked their status as free subjects with their time-honoured customs, drawing on enduring ideas that English subjects were distinguished from enslaved persons because of their protected rights to law.

Within a few years, however, this argument about "ancient laws" and subject status had been extended further. Petitioners in 1770, for example, argued that restoration of their ancient usages would actually enable them to understand their rights more fully and render them more able to serve their monarch as loyal subjects.[31] According to this argument, it was access to one's ancient laws that allowed individuals to realize their subjecthood. That these customs were influenced by French precedent was immaterial. As they pleaded that their privileges and customs be established as the law of the province in 1773, the new subjects once again entreated the king "to grant us, in common with your other subjects, the rights and privileges of citizens of England." Throughout this important petition, they repeatedly asked the monarch to eliminate the remaining differences between his subjects: "Vouchsafe to bestow your favours equally upon all your subjects in the province, without any distinction."[32] By doing so, the Canadiens were evoking membership in a broader community of English citizens and subjects, and they were arguing that all of these members were equally entitled to live under their particular and time-honoured customs. Throughout the 1760s and 1770s, the French Catholics increasingly and deftly used the language of subjecthood and citizenship to articulate a connection between law and the status of freeborn subjects.

In response, numerous other inhabitants, mostly British Protestants, proposed a conflicting vision of subjecthood, insisting that English law was an integral part of the rights of the subject. Not only did they attack the inferior courts responsible for administering French law as "tiresome litigious and expensive in this poor Colony," but, more significantly, they insisted that a government that allowed foreign civil law violated the constitution and laws of England, denying the British subject his birthright.[33] When, in November 1774, many of these same subjects sought to have the Quebec Act repealed before it actually went into effect, they asked for the "benefit and protection of English laws" and pleaded that "their liberty may be ascertained according to their ancient constitutional rights and privileges heretofore granted to all his Majesty's dutiful subjects throughout the British Empire."[34] These arguments about the subject's birthright were ones the Loyalists would bring back well into the 1780s. Shortly after their arrival in the province, many of these refugees tried to persuade administrators that "they were born British Subjects & have ever been accustomed to the Government & Laws of England." They demanded the blessings of the British constitution and detailed the hardships they feared if forced to live under French laws and land tenures.[35] All of these British Protestant petitioners, however, linked the status of subjects to the question of law.

As each of these various memorials made clear, there was little agreement as to how the rights of subjects were to be defined. While the French Canadians contended that true subjects were those entitled to their ancient laws, many British-born subjects claimed just as passionately that bona-fide subjects were those who lived under English law. Both positions drew on familiar arguments that British liberties were protected by law and that the British subject was entitled to enjoy time-honoured customs, but each offered a radically different interpretation of how that "inheritance" and those "ancient usages" were to be defined. These were issues that members of parliament would need to resolve as they considered the "Act for making more effectual provision for the Government of the Province of Quebec" in 1774.

EXPLAINING THE MANY AND CONFLICTING RIGHTS OF SUBJECTS

There were a number of reasons that French Catholics and British Protestants were repeatedly and forcefully able to articulate these diametrically opposing ideas about subjecthood – and that both were given serious consideration by administrators in Quebec and in London over the years. Some related to particular circumstances in the Province of Quebec, whereas others stemmed from ambiguities relating to the rights of British subjects across the British Empire. The demographic realities of Quebec, as well as the climate of relative conciliation discussed earlier, were certainly important. So, too, was the murky legal situation that prevailed in Quebec in the aftermath of the Seven Years' War.

As Governor Guy Carleton noted in one of his many letters to the secretary of state, confusion about which law was applicable to Quebec had begun as early as 1763, and disagreements over which law might be used to regulate the affairs of its diverse inhabitants merely intensified in the years after Canada's cession to Britain.[36] On the one hand, both the Royal Proclamation of 1763 and the commission sent to Quebec's first civil governor had established English law to the satisfaction of British-born Protestants. On the other hand, many believed that French civil law had actually been accorded to the Canadiens, since, during the period of military rule that lasted from the conquest of Quebec in September 1759 until August 1764, many of the courts of first instance, constituted by officers of the Canadian militia, actually continued to judge disputes according to the customary Coutume de Paris.[37] Even where many accepted that the proclamation appeared to have introduced English civil and criminal law, several local ordinances continued to allow French laws and customs even after the period of military rule, generating further uncertainty as to which laws were actually in effect.[38] If the Canadiens were understandably concerned about preserving access to their time-honoured customs, based largely on the Coutume de Paris, British-born inhabitants were equally worried about maintaining familiar English laws that they understood and could navigate. It was not surprising, therefore, that the rights of British subjects were negotiated on the terrain of law in the Province of Quebec.

Although these local realities certainly affected debates in the 1760s and 1770s, a number of other ambiguities relating to a subject's rights across the empire shaped the willingness of contemporaries to entertain arguments about British subjects' rights. The first was that the rights of subjects were not well defined by case law or by statute at the time. A series of cases had established that subjects held the rights to own freeholds in England, to sue before the courts in England, and to petition the king.[39] The 1689 Declaration of Rights had referred to many of a subject's liberties within the realm, but the only clause relating explicitly to a "right of subjects" was the one linked to petitioning the king, a liberty that had come under attack in the seventeenth century.[40] Put together, however, these were hardly more than very limited rights.

Furthermore, although judges had ruled that subjecthood extended to those individuals born within the king's dominions and allegiance, a series of opinions offered conflicting ideas about the laws under which those numerous subjects might live. In 1608, for example, *Calvin v. Smith* suggested that subjects did not have to be born within the ambit of the common law to be subjects, and that individuals who lived under a wide variety of laws were still subjects to the same monarch.[41] Other cases, such as *Dutton v. Howell* (1693), established that in an uninhabited country settled by British subjects, the common law "must and doth oblige," suggesting that the common law was deemed the "birthright" of subjects who "no more abandoned the English laws than they did their Natural Allegiance, which they did not."[42] Though Quebec was clearly not an "uninhabited country," a familiar legal discourse nonetheless existed positing common law as the inherent right of subjects. This understanding stood in apparent contradiction to the well-established idea that subjects might theoretically live under diverse laws, though each of these two discourses would work to legitimize the different arguments about law and rights presented by inhabitants in Quebec.

Finally, many administrators in the 1760s and 1770s countenanced conflicting ideas about the rights of subjects because of a long-standing tradition of declaring rights both within Great Britain and throughout its empire. From the 1689 Declaration of Rights to a range of colonial charters of liberties, to pamphlets such as the 1766 *British Liberties, or the Free-Born Subject's Inheritance*, peoples throughout Great Britain and its empire had traditionally proposed and associated a seemingly limitless number of "rights and privileges" with subjecthood. In addition, a rich tradition of petitioning had encouraged many both to express their grievances as loyal subjects and to plead for rights they believed to be their due. Ironically, despite the proliferation of such declarations and petitions, particularly in the seventeenth and eighteenth centuries, there was little official agreement as to what the rights of subjects actually were. Subjects themselves had remarkably varied ideas about their rights and, far from discouraging individuals from making claims, the lack of consensus about the meanings of subjecthood merely seems to have precipitated further demands for rights.[43]

For several reasons, then, the conflicting claims about the rights of subjects put forward by French-Catholic and British-Protestant inhabitants in Quebec were accorded significant attention. It also bears noting that, by the mid 1770s, leading voices of the legal world had begun to articulate that law, even if this meant French law, was part of a subject's inheritance. When Chief Justice Lord Mansfield wrote to the prime minister with his ideas about a legal settlement for Quebec in the early 1760s, he had noted that there was no instance "so rash and unjust" as of a conqueror abolishing the laws and customs of a conquered people.[44] In Quebec, where so many new subjects were accustomed to French law, Mansfield believed that it was a manifest failure of justice to deny them access to the laws with which they were familiar. By 1772, his contemporary Alexander Wedderburn, then solicitor general, observed that "no other right can be founded on conquest but that of regulating the political and civil government of the country, leaving to the individuals the enjoyment of their property, and all privileges not inconsistent with the security of conquest."[45] Perhaps even more tellingly, Mansfield had begun to outline the rights of conquered peoples in a 1774 King's Bench case originating in the ceded colony of Grenada. He ruled, among other things, that "conquered inhabitants once received into the conqueror's protection become subjects," and that the laws of the conquered country continued in force until they were altered by the conqueror.[46] According to these interpretations, inhabitants of conquered territories might continue to live under their traditional laws until those laws were altered, all the while being considered subjects of the king. For many legal luminaries of the 1760s and 1770s, colonial administrators were responsible for protecting the rights of subjects, and these included access to a law that was not necessarily English.

THE QUEBEC ACT AND THE RIGHTS OF SUBJECTS

By 1774, therefore, subjects in Quebec had proposed conflicting definitions of the British subject's inheritance, each of which had its supporters among colonial administrators in Quebec and London. Neither had yet received the official sanction of parliament. Although the Board of Trade had considered innumerable reports and proposals for necessary reform of the constitutional and legal system in Quebec, it remained unsuccessful in deciding upon or implementing any of them. Indeed, administrative opinion remained polarized about whether granting French Catholics access to their ancient usages in Quebec was "cruel and oppressive" or "just and humane."[47]

Furthermore, as "anarchy" and "confusion" continued to characterize the legal system of Quebec, most inhabitants and administrators recognized that some official resolution was absolutely essential for the sake of all subjects.[48] The Lord Chancellor expressed his deepest concern about the delay in agreeing to a plan for the province, noting that it was "a disgrace to Government, I had almost said to Humanity, to leave them [the inhabitants of Quebec] in their present deplorable situation."[49] With growing disaffection with British rule in New England, discontent in Quebec became an issue of growing concern to the central government, and the loyalty of an ever-increasing Canadien population began to seem even more essential. And as debates between old and new subjects proved inconclusive, and local settlements continued to be inadequate, many began to accept the argument that only an act of parliament could overturn the legal system in place and the rights that had been established by the Royal Proclamation of 1763 and by the series of governors' commissions.[50]

Pushed through both houses at the end of the parliamentary session, the Quebec Act attracted both euphoric endorsement and virulent criticism. Although the ideas embedded in the Quebec Act had been aired in petitions and legal reports for nearly a decade, many saw the 1774 legislation as dramatically innovative, whether that was because it ushered in an era of toleration or because it upheld some of the dangerous new principles prevalent in the other intolerable acts. When George III assented to the bill in a short speech, he praised it as "founded on the clearest principles of justice and humanity" and believed it would "have the best effect, in quieting the minds and promoting the happiness of his Canadian subjects." By contrast, William Pitt, Earl of Chatham, not only called it "the most cruel, oppressive and odious measure, tearing up justice and every good principle by the roots," but also argued that it would turn many subjects against the empire.[51] It was apparent, however, that members of parliament from all ends of the political spectrum believed that the outcome of these debates would determine whether subjects remained consistent in their allegiance to George III.

Because the plan for administering Quebec reached the halls of parliament, the ensuing discussions were reasonably well-documented and reveal that observers actively engaged arguments that had been made throughout the 1760s and 1770s about subjects' rights, particularly those made by "new" and "old" subjects. Although these discussions have been analyzed on many occasions, revisiting them in relation to earlier ideas presented by subjects in the Province of Quebec reveals that politicians were not only weighing what might be an appropriate constitutional settlement for the colony. They were also grappling with which concessions were most likely to secure loyal British subjects for the empire and were redefining the rights associated with that subjecthood.

In general, proponents of the act enthusiastically argued that the bill reinforced the constitution; because it upheld English criminal law but still permitted the Canadiens to live under the laws they had known for over one hundred years, the act secured rights for subjects. Indeed, for defenders of the Quebec Act, imposing English laws upon a conquered nation was an "act of the grossest and absurdist and cruelest tyranny," and the bill was intended to remove such a stain of tyranny from the province.[52] Opponents of the bill lamented that it, in fact, overturned the constitution given to the province in 1763 and violated promises made to British settlers who had relocated there under the assumption that they would live under English law and the "British constitution."[53] As they discussed the Quebec Act, ministers were attempting to resolve which laws should apply to the province, but they were also debating the meanings of the "ancient constitution" and the "inheritance" of subjects more generally.

Perhaps most significantly, in the words of pamphleteer William Knox, the Quebec Act was intended to resolve to what extent the

French Catholics were "entitled to the common rights of British subjects in that country" and how they might best be "attached to the English government."[54] Those supporting the Quebec Act argued that embracing the French Catholics and allowing them to live under their own laws was the only way to ensure that they became British subjects. Alexander Wedderburn believed that, unless the French Catholics themselves wanted to accept English laws, imposing them would have little effect. Rather, leaving the Canadiens to their ancient customs and encouraging gradual change "will bring the Canadians much more to the resemblance of British subjects than they are at present."[55] During his examination in the House of Commons, William Hey, former chief justice for Quebec, noted that only "proper indulgence" of the Canadiens could turn them away from the French government, bring them to a "perfect submission to the Crown," and make them "good British subjects."[56] Supporters of the bill believed that a guarantee of access to ancient laws was essential to subjecthood. Like many colonial governors, they proposed that subjecthood could accommodate not only those who spoke French or attended Catholic mass, but also those who lived under French laws.

By contrast, most opponents of the bill accused the government of reneging on its sacred duty to promulgate liberty by not insisting that the Canadiens live under English laws. As Edmund Burke would assert during the debates of 1774, "it is a violation of the faith of Great Britain held out to the Canadians ... a violation of a promise to give them the benefit of the laws of England ... I would have English liberty carried into the French colonies, but I would not have French slavery brought into the English colonies ... to deprive the English subject of the benefit of the laws of England."[57] Serjeant Glynn echoed these concerns, noting that it was the government's "duty, by all gentle means, to root those prejudices from the minds of the Canadians." He believed that parliament, misguided by toleration, was betraying its newest inhabitants: "is it then, wise, I ask, out of compassion to the prejudices of those who have been born under the arbitrary law of another country, to perpetuate a system of government, which will deprive all those who may hereafter be born, from the enjoyment of the privileges of other British subjects."[58] For these critics, instead of transforming Canadiens into "British subjects" by introducing English law and fully assimilating them into English liberties, members of parliament were eschewing their duties and depriving their newest subjects of their rights to English law.

According to these arguments, allowing French Catholics to continue living under French law and French tyranny would result in a failure to create British subjects. Members of the opposition refused to accept that granting French Catholics their "ancient usages" was the best way to turn them into useful subjects. Lord John Cavendish noted that he "would assimilate them as much as possible, that they might become fitter subjects of Great Britain. For that reason, I should think it material not to give them directly their own law again."[59] Burke would again proclaim: "give them English liberty – give them an English constitution – and then, whether they speak French or English, whether they go to mass or attend our own communion, you will render them valuable and useful subjects of Great Britain."[60] For many of these critics, British subjects might speak different languages and belong to various Christian denominations, but they must be protected by English law in order to become "useful subjects." Not only was the British government sworn to uphold the English law and constitution introduced in 1763, but it was "English liberty" that would secure the allegiance of its newest additions and make "fit subjects" of the Canadiens.

The Quebec Act, which received the royal assent on 22 June 1774, had undergone several revisions as a result of ministerial and parliamentary debate. A crucial phrasing, however, remained consistent in the second draft, the third draft, the draft amended and returned by the House of Commons, and the final version passed by the House of Lords. The second draft proposed "that *His Majesty's Subjects* of and in the said Province of Quebec ... may have hold and enjoy their Property, Laws, Customs, and Usages ... *as may consist with their allegiance to His Majesty and subjection to the Crown and Parliament of Great Britain* [italics added]." In the third draft, this phrasing was amended slightly, specifying that "His Majesty's *Canadian* Subjects within the Province of Quebec ... may also hold, and enjoy their Property & Possessions together with all Customs & Usages relative thereto, and all other their Civil Rights ... *as may consist with their Allegiance to his Majesty & Subjection to the Crown and Parliament of Great Britain* [italics added]." Subsequent passages then explained that, in matters of property and civil rights, both Canadian and English subjects were to have recourse to the "Laws of Canada and not the Laws of England," whereas the criminal law would remain that of England. The draft returned from the House of Commons retained the phrasing of the third draft, explaining that "His Majesty's Canadian Subjects" were to live under their customs and laws "as may consist with their Allegiance to His Majesty, etc.," but then detailing that these laws applied to issues of property and civil rights, and that the criminal law of England was maintained. The final version accepted the phrasing of the third and Commons drafts, enshrining a definition of the subject's rights that had hitherto been hotly contested.[61] Indeed, despite popular backlash and an attempted repeal in 1775, the Quebec Act's successful passage upheld a controversial new notion: subjects were entitled to live under their ancient "customs and usages," even if those were French, and this was deemed consistent with their allegiance to king and parliament.

Nor was it just the book of statutes that reflected this expanded understanding of British subjecthood. The range of grateful and angry memorials, which reached the king in 1774 and 1775, clearly regarded the act as having either granted or dismissed the rights of subjects. Those from French Catholics in Montreal noted their gratitude at having been "adopted as sons of the Nation and as English citizens." The address from their compatriots in Trois-Rivières referred to their joy at being favoured with the "rights, advantages, and prerogatives of British subjects."[62] Looking back from the vantage point of 1783, many of these same subjects praised the passing of the Quebec Act as the moment when they were "recognized as authentically British subjects," the moment at which their ancient system of laws, among other things, had been upheld.[63] In answer to a range of petitions generated in 1783, the council proposed to enter on the books an address to George III, "begging him to maintain in its integrity that 'precious charter' by favour of which Canadians 'will in a short time be indissolubly incorporated into the British nation.'"[64] It was the Quebec Act and the protections that it accorded to religion and to ancient laws that had truly incorporated the Canadiens into the British nation and community of subjects.

The representations from British Protestants, however, protested that, by the act of parliament, individuals had lost the "protection of the English Laws ... disgraceful for us as Britons."[65] Yet another petition to the House of Commons noted that the Quebec Act "deprives His Majesty's ancient subjects of all their rights and franchises" and pleaded that their liberties be ascertained not by French law but "according to their ancient constitutional rights and privileges heretofore granted to all His Majesty's dutiful subjects throughout the British Empire."[66] In each of these very different petitions, subjects evoked their membership in a broader community of British subjects and asserted that the Quebec Act had either upheld or betrayed their rights as subjects to time-honoured customs. If members of parliament had engaged arguments articulated by petitioners in the 1760s and early 1770s, subjects would in turn respond to the legislation passed in 1774 for decades to come.

CONCLUSION

While the Quebec Act would continue to have its vocal detractors, it was ultimately endorsed by a central government which recognized that an inclusive definition of subjecthood was more appropriate for a territory where the French-Catholic population, whose continued loyalty was paramount given discontent brewing in the thirteen colonies to the south, continued to grow.[67] As recent historiography has shown, the priorities of the central government had also changed between 1763 and 1774. The more assimilative policies of 1763 had lost momentum, and many administrators had become more inclined to recognize the diversity of religions and laws across the British Empire as policies of toleration were countenanced. The settlements after the Seven Years' War had attempted to integrate Quebec into the constitutional framework of the Atlantic World, embracing the idea that each would be governed by a representative assembly and by English law. The drawbacks of this approach for Quebec, however, had become clear by the 1770s, as the persistent French-Catholic majority in Quebec seemed to express uncertainty about representative assemblies and appeared to favour the continuance of French civil law. Policies like the Quebec Act thus increasingly needed to consider particular exigencies within the Province of Quebec and, perhaps more significantly, to imagine alternative means of incorporating diverse groups of subjects.

Indeed, although the British government had permitted Minorcans to continue living under Spanish law beginning in the early eighteenth century, the 1770s and 1780s saw a marked increase in such occurrences. Legal pluralism along the Minorcan and Québécois models became a more recognized practice. Analogous practices and regulations appeared in the 1770s and 1780s that enabled Hindus and Muslims to be judged according to "Hindu" and "Muslim" law, respectively, in East India Company territories. Perhaps just as importantly, the move towards legal pluralism addressed by Christian Burset in this volume, was paralleled by new and flexible understandings of subject status. Historians have recognized that a decision about law was foundational to the revised imperial policies of the 1770s and 1780s, but few have understood that resolving the question of which law applied in the case of the Province of Quebec also entailed a profound redefinition of the rights of British subjects. The parliamentary decision about which law applied to inhabitants of Quebec confirmed not only that the "rights of subjects" might include the right to time-honoured customs, but it also suggested that increasing numbers of inhabitants and administrators were willing to accept that subjects might be loyal even if they lived under diverse laws and were scattered throughout an empire.

When French Canada was ceded to Britain in 1763, it joined an empire in need of reinvention. The massive transfers of territory occasioned by the Treaty of Paris and the accelerating expansion of the East India Company into Bengal brought new peoples into the empire whose rights and status were far from clear. Conceived as an empire that was Protestant, commercial, maritime, and free,[68] it was now an empire that included "subject populations of Native Americans, French Canadians, and Indians, none of whom were Protestant, British, or free, according to 'British notions of freedom.'"[69] The debates about subjects' rights in the Province of Quebec and the ideas about subjecthood embedded in the Quebec Act were therefore intimately linked to a broader shift that was recognizable across the British Empire. The legislation of 1774 marked a moment when a truly imperial subjecthood was imagined and realized – a subjecthood that could accommodate the many peoples and the many laws of the British Empire.

NOTES

1 Peter Marshall, "The Incorporation of Quebec in the British Empire, 1763–1774," in *Of Mother Country and Plantations: Proceedings of the Twenty-seventh Conference in Early American History*, ed. V.B. Platt and D.C. Skaggs, 63 (Bowling Green, OH: Bowling Green State University Press, 1970). It should be noted that the Regulating Act (1773) made comparable provisions and established an administration of justice for Bengal. However, Bengal was technically a territory governed by the East India Company rather than by colonial administrators such as the

Lords Commissioners, the secretaries of state, and the governors who were responsible for Quebec. Some of this chapter has been adapted from material originally published in *Subjects and Sovereign: Bonds of Belonging in the Eighteenth-century British Empire* by Hannah Weiss Muller, and has been reproduced by permission of Oxford University Press (https://global.oup.com/academic/product/subjects-and-sovereign-9780190465810). For permission to reuse this material, please visit http://global.oup.com/academic/rights.

2 The Test Acts of 1672 and 1678 were a series of penal laws requiring that occupants of public offices and members of the Houses of Lords and Commons take not only the oaths of supremacy and allegiance, but that they also subscribe to a declaration against transubstantiation. This theoretically rendered all practising Catholics ineligible for offices of trust. Many assumed that the penal laws, including the Test Acts, automatically extended to new colonies with Catholic populations. However, reports submitted in 1765 by the attorney general and solicitor general, and in 1768 by the king's advocate, attorney general, and solicitor general, both insisted that the penal laws did not apply to the colonies ceded to Britain in 1763. For printed copies of these reports, see Adam Shortt and Arthur G. Doughty, eds, *Documents Relating to the Constitutional History of Canada, 1759–1791* (Ottawa: J. de L. Taché, 1918).

3 "The Quebec Act" (1774), in Shortt and Doughty, *Documents Relating to the Constitutional History of Canada*, 373.

4 Colonial Office [hereafter CO] 42/46 – Letter from Haldimand to the Lords of the Privy Council dated 6 May 1784.

5 J. Wright, ed., *Debates of the House of Commons in the year 1774, on the Bill for Making More Effectual Provision for the Government of the Province of Quebec* (London: 1839), iv.

6 In *The Quebec Act, 1774* (Montreal: Gazette Printing Company, 1891), Gerald Hart argued that the Quebec Act assured the growth of "a nation within a nation" (20). This was, as Hilda Neatby notes in *The Quebec Act: Protest and Policy* (Scarborough: Prentice-Hall of Canada, 1972), an argument that Lord Durham first signalled in the 1830s, when he spoke indirectly of the Quebec Act, suggesting that the "Government deliberately constituted the French into a majority, and recognized and strengthened their distinct national character" (71). It should be noted that, although Hart and Durham both viewed the growth of a distinct national group as problematic, even detrimental, to the development of Canada, other historians have argued that the survival of this national

group was foundational in Canadian – and, more particularly, French-Canadian – history.

7 See, for example, the work of Victor Coffin, Reginald Coupland, Philip Lawson, and Hilda Neatby. It is Coupland who argues in *The Quebec Act: A Study in Statesmanship* (Oxford: Clarendon Press, 1925) that "without the Quebec Act [Britain] would still have lost the thirteen colonies. With it Canada was at least saved" (122).

8 Alfred LeRoy Burt, *The Old Province of Quebec* (Minneapolis: University of Minnesota Press, 1933); Vincent Harlow, *The Founding of the Second British Empire, 1763–1793*, 2 vols. (London: Longman's, 1952–64); Marshall, "The Incorporation of the Province of Quebec."

9 This is an interpretation of Coupland presented by Neatby in *The Quebec Act*, 104.

10 Stephen Conway, "The Consequences of the Conquest: Quebec and British Politics, 1760–1774," in *Revisiting 1759: The Conquest of Canada in Historical Perspective*, ed. Philip Buckner and John G. Reid, 141–65 (Toronto: University of Toronto Press, 2012).

11 Philip Lawson, *The Imperial Challenge: Quebec and Britain in the Age of the American Revolution* (Montreal: McGill-Queen's University Press, 1989), 44.

12 See Karl David Milobar, "The Constitutional Development of Quebec from the Time of the French Regime to the Canada Act of 1791" (PhD diss., University of London, 1990); "Quebec Reform, the British Constitution and the Atlantic Empire: 1774–1775," *Parliamentary History* 14, no. 1 (1995): 65–88; "The Origins of British-Quebec Merchant Ideology: New France, the British Atlantic, and the Constitutional Periphery, 1720–70," *Journal of Imperial and Commonwealth History* 24, no. 3 (1996): 364–90.

13 Pierre Tousignant, "The Integration of the Province of Quebec into the British Empire, 1763–1791," in *Dictionary of Canadian Biography*, vol. 4 (Toronto: University of Toronto Press, 1979), xl.

14 For more on this argument, see Hannah Weiss Muller, *Subjects and Sovereigns*, and "Bonds of Belonging: Subjecthood and the British Empire," *Journal of British Studies* 53, no. 1 (January 2014): 29–58.

15 Coupland, *The Quebec Act*, 70.

16 See, in particular, Lawson, *The Imperial Challenge*; Peter Marshall, "The Incorporation of Quebec in the British Empire"; Carolee Ruth Pollock, "His Majesty's Subjects: Political Legitimacy in Quebec, 1764–91" (PhD diss., University of Alberta, 1996). The December 1772 report of Alexander Wedderburn was particularly influential in shaping the Quebec Act.

17 I will use the term "the Province of Quebec" or "Quebec" to refer to the Province of Quebec as it was defined after the cession of "Canada" to the British in 1763. The three districts of Québec, Trois Rivières, and Montréal remained united in the British "Province of Quebec." When appropriate, I will also use the term "Canada" to refer to this same region during the period of French rule. "Canada" was one of the French territories in North America known as "New France," which also included Acadia, Hudson Bay, Newfoundland, and Louisiana at various points in the seventeenth and eighteenth centuries.

18 Population figures for Quebec are estimated based on several sources: Philip Lawson, *The Imperial Challenge*; Pierre George, *Le Québec* (Paris: PUF, 1979); Pierre Tousignant, "The Integration of the Province of Quebec." Tousignant puts the number of French Catholics at sixty thousand in the early 1760s; George at sixty-five thousand in 1763; Lawson at seventy thousand for the 1760s.

19 Tousignant, "The Integration of the Province of Quebec," xxxiv. In *The Scratch of a Pen: 1763 and the Transformation of North America* (New York: Oxford University Press, 2006), Colin Calloway notes that only 270 Canadiens left the colony after the peace (114). Article IV of the Treaty of Paris gave inhabitants eighteen months to emigrate from the colony "with all safety and freedom."

20 Studies of the Quebec Act tend to concur that there were approximately ninety thousand inhabitants in "Canada," of whom the vast majority were of French origin in 1774. However, contemporaries offered a range of other estimates. Tousignant notes that the reports of law officers suggested that there were more like eighty thousand "new subjects" (see, "The Integration of the Province of Quebec," xlvii). Examined by the House of Commons in 1774, both Francis Maseres and Guy Carleton stated that there were 150,000 Canadiens then in the province. Carleton also referred to a 1770 return that listed 360 Protestants in the province of Quebec. For more information about these hearings and an analysis of the population of Quebec in the 1770s, see Wright, *Debates of the House of Commons in the Year 1774*, 103–31.

21 See Maya Jasanoff, *Liberty's Exiles: American Loyalists in the Revolutionary World* (New York: Knopf, 2011), 354. Jasanoff notes that "between the 5,628 individuals listed on the 1784 muster, the further contingent of Mohawks, and those who emigrated without getting land grants, one can easily justify a minimum population figure of 6,000 refugees in

Quebec – and again plausibly imagine the total number to have been up to 10 percent higher."

22 For a copy of these capitulations in English, see Shortt and Doughty, *Documents Relating to the Constitutional History of Canada*, 21–9.

23 For an easily accessible copy of the Treaty of Paris, see Shortt and Doughty, *Documents Relating to the Constitutional History of Canada, 1759–1791*, 113–22.

24 As quoted in Coupland, *The Quebec Act*, 19.

25 "Address to the Inhabitants of the Province of Quebeck" (1774) in *Documents of the Canadian Constitution, 1759–1915* (Toronto: Oxford University Press, 1918), 139–43. The "Letter to the Inhabitants of Canada" (1775) can be found at http://www.avalon.yale.edu/18th_century/contcong_05-29-75 (accessed 6 September 2020).

26 CO 42/2 – Letter from Murray to the Lords Commissioners, dated 29 October 1764.

27 CO 42/27 – Letter from Carleton to Lords Commissioners of Trade, dated 28 March 1767; CO 42/7 – Letter from Carleton to Shelburne, dated 20 January 1768; CO 42/27 – Letter from Carleton to Hillsborough, dated 15 March 1769.

28 CO 42/8 – Letter from Cramahé to Dartmouth, dated 22 June 1773; and CO 42/33 – Letter from Cramahé to Dartmouth, dated 12 December 1773.

29 As quoted in Lawrence Henry Gipson, *The Triumphant Empire: New Responsibilities within the Enlarged Empire, 1763–1766* (New York: Knopf, 1956), 160.

30 "Address of French Citizens to the King regarding the legal system," in Shortt and Doughty, *Documents Relating to the Constitutional History of Canada*, 228. The petition was read on 7 January 1765, suggesting that it had been composed in late 1764.

31 "Petition for the Restoration of French Law and Custom" (dated sometime in 1770), in Shortt and Doughty, *Documents Relating to the Constitutional History of Canada*, 419–22.

32 "A Petition of diverse of the Roman-Catholick Inhabitants of the Province of Quebeck to the King's Majesty (signed December 1773 and presented February 1774)," in Shortt and Doughty, *Documents Relating to the Constitutional History of Canada*, 504–8.

33 "Presentments of the Grand Jury of Quebec," in Shortt and Doughty, *Documents Relating to the Constitutional History of Canada*, 212–15.

34 "Petition to the House of Commons (12 November 1774)," in ibid., 417–18.

35 CO 42/47 – The Petition of Sir John Baronet and others ... Loyalists, their Associates, who have taken Refuge in Canada, dated 11 April 1785.

36 CO 42/7 – Letter from Carleton to Shelburne, dated 24 December 1767.

37 Tousignant, "The Integration of the Province of Quebec." See also, Michel Morin, "The Reactions of the 'New' Subjects of Quebec to British Justice, 1760–1774" (unpublished paper, University of Illinois, presented October 2012), and "The Discovery and Assimilation of British Constitutional Law Principles in Quebec, 1764–1774," *Dalhousie Law Journal* 36, no. 2 (Fall 2013): 581–616.

38 In September 1764, for example, a three-tiered legal system was established in which a second, inferior, Court of Common Pleas allowed French law and customs at the same time that a superior court continued to hear and determine all civil and criminal cases according to the laws of England. Over the years, local ordinances were passed that allowed Catholics to sit on juries (1764 and 1766), enabled the laws and customs of the previous era to prevail concerning tenure, inheritance, and alienation of lands (1767), and moved the effectual administration of justice out of the hands of justices of the peace and into the hands of the Court of Common Pleas, where French law was allowed (1770). The scholarship about the legal system in the province of Quebec during the 1760s and early 1770s is extensive. For recent and innovative treatments of this topic, see Donald Fyson, "The Conquered and the Conqueror: The Mutual Adaptation of the Canadiens and the British in Quebec, 1759–1775," in *Revisiting 1759*. See also the work of Michel Morin, particularly Morin, "The Reactions of the 'New' Subjects of Quebec to British Justice."

39 The rights to own freeholds in England and to sue before the courts in England were affirmed in *Calvin v. Smith* (1608) and in subsequent cases tried before the common-law courts. *Christian v. Corren* (1716) was one of the few cases to address the issue of additional rights for subjects. In this case, the court confirmed that it was the "right of subjects to appeal to the sovereign to redress a wrong done to them in any court of justice," a right of subjects that had actually already been confirmed by statute on several occasions.

40 The text of "The Declaration of Rights" can be found in Lois Schwoerer, *The Declaration of Rights, 1689* (Baltimore: John Hopkins University Press, 1981). For further discussion of parliamentary definition of subjects' rights, see Muller, *Subjects and Sovereign*, 16–44.

41 Because allegiance was due to the sovereign by "law of nature," subjects might be part of a "union of ligeance" without living under a correspond-

ing "union of laws." See "Calvin's Case," in *The Seventh Part of the Reports of Sir Edward Coke* (London: 1738), 13–15. The case can also be found under *Calvin v. Smith* 7 Co. Rep. 1b, 77 *English Reports* 377.

42 *Dutton v. Howell* (1693) Shower 24, 1 *English Reports* 17.

43 For more about this argument, see Muller, *Subjects and Sovereign*, 45–79.

44 Lord Mansfield to George Grenville, dated 24 December 1764, *Grenville Papers* 2: 476–7, as quoted in Lawson, *The Imperial Challenge*, 58.

45 As quoted in Lawson, *The Imperial Challenge*, 121.

46 For an accessible version of Mansfield's decision in *Campbell v. Hall* (1774) and his propositions at large, see Shortt and Doughty, *Documents Relating to the Constitutional History of Canada*, 525–6.

47 In June 1767, the secretary of state wrote to Governor Carleton asking him for advice about how "practicable and expedient" it would be to blend the English and French laws. This was followed by a series of requests for reports. In August 1767, the Privy Council requested a report from Quebec on its constitutional settlement. By July 1769, the Board of Trade had responded to the Privy Council's request with a report that duly criticized the lack of a constitutional settlement for Quebec. A few local ordinances, including the 1770 ordinance "for the more effectual administration of justice," temporarily ameliorated the access of Canadiens to their own laws, but also succeeded in alienating many of the British-born Protestants. By June 1771, the solicitor general of Britain, Alexander Wedderburn, was directed to take into consideration the many years of reports and papers relating to laws and courts in Quebec and to prepare a plan that detailed a revised civil and criminal legal administration for the colony. Wedderburn submitted his report at the end of 1772, but both the advocate general and attorney general also submitted reports in 1773, neither of which was in full agreement with Wedderburn's very thoughtful consideration of affairs in Quebec. For details of these many reports and discussions, see Pollock, "His Majesty's Subjects" and Lawson, *The Imperial Challenge*.

48 These were the words of Thomas Townshend in 1774. See Wright, *Debates of the House of Commons in the year 1774*, 3.

49 As quoted in Neatby, *The Quebec Act*, 33.

50 Philip Lawson argues that, as early as the summer of 1766, administrators were committed to resolving the problems in Quebec through parliamentary legislation rather than through an act of council. See Lawson, *The Imperial Challenge*, 87. However, many others have suggested that administrators were not committed to an act of parliament for several more years.

51 Wright, *Debates of the House of Commons in the year 1774*, iv. In *The Quebec Act*, Coupland notes that George III gave this short speech of assent after having traversed an angry mob hurling cries of "No Popery" (104).

52 Wright, *Debates of the House of Commons in the year 1774*, 29. Attorney General Edward Thurlow repeatedly noted that it was an act of humanity to leave a country in the possession of its laws. Solicitor General Alexander Wedderburn also noted that even the "Mussulman, the Ottoman, the Turks, the worst of all conquerors, in the countries they subdued, left the people in possession of their municipal laws" (Wright, 51). More generally, proponents of the bill insisted that government by governor and council was best suited to introduce slow change in accordance with the habits of the Canadiens. They confirmed that an assembly made up exclusively of a small minority of Protestant settlers could not be granted, because it would be oppressive to the Catholic majority. Finally, they argued that the Catholic Church had not been established, given that it was still subject to the king's supremacy. Instead, the government was committed to supervising a church that accepted Canadian born-and-bred priests rather than alienating clergymen and thereby encouraging them to look to France for succour.

53 More generally, opponents worried that, by allowing the collection of tithes, the Quebec Act was perceived to have established the Catholic Church in Canada. Overall, critics believed that the act introduced a language of despotism and that, by failing to institute an assembly, it had introduced tyrannical government, a fear that was echoed in representations from the Continental Congress and the Assembly of New York. See "Address to the Inhabitants of the Province of Quebeck" (1774) and "Letter to the Inhabitants of Canada" (1775). Representatives of the Continental Congress sympathized with the Canadians who had been deprived of representative assemblies and trial by jury, among other things. See also "The Representation and Remonstrance of the General Assembly of the Colony of New-York," in *Parliamentary History of England from the Earliest Period to the Year 1803*, vol. 18, ed. T.C. Hansard (London: 1812–20). Representatives from New York raised concerns about the "jealousies which have been excited in the Colonies by the extension of the limits of the Province of Quebec, in which the Roman Catholick religion has received such ample support."

54 William Knox, *The justice and policy of the late act of Parliament for making more effectual provision for the government of the province of Quebec, asserted and proved* (London: 1774), 30, 18.

55 Wright, *Debates of the House of Commons in the year 1774*, 57.

56 Ibid., 160.
57 Ibid., 213.
58 Ibid., 264.
59 Ibid., 44.
60 Ibid., 289.
61 For copies of these various drafts, with appended notes, see Shortt and Doughty, *Documents Relating to the Constitutional History of Canada*, 532–75.
62 CO 42/34 – Petitions of 1774 from "His Majesty's Canadian Subjects at Montreal" and "His Canadian Subjects at Trois Riveres." Original French texts read: "nous sommes adoptés comme fils de la Patrie et Citoiens anglois" and "la jouissance de tous les droits avantages & prerogatives des sujets Britanniques."
63 CO 42/45 – La tres humble Adresse des Citoyens de tous Etats et autres Habitans Catholiques dans la Province de Quebec en Canada (enclosed in Governor Haldimand's letter of 14 October 1783). The original French reads: "dans la quatorzieme annee de Regne de Votre Majeste, il vous plut tres gracieusement par un Acte emane de Votre Parlement nous reconnoiter authentiquement Sujets de Votre Majeste et autoriser en cette Province le Culte [?] de Notre Religion et le Systeme de nos Loix municipals."
64 As quoted in Hilda Neatby, *Quebec: The Revolutionary Age, 1760–1791* (Toronto: McClelland and Stewart, 1966), 191.
65 CO 42/34 – Petitions of 1774.
66 Copy of Petition to the House of Commons dated 12 November 1774 in Francis Maseres, *An Account of the Proceedings of the British and other Protestant Inhabitants ... in order to obtain an House of Assembly* (London: 1775), 258.
67 If the governor of the province was repeatedly frustrated by these new subjects' failure to mobilize for the war effort against the thirteen mainland colonies, the French Catholics did not rally to the American or French causes en masse. See CO 42/38 – Sketch of the Military State of the Province of Quebec dated 25 July 1778. In 1778, Haldimand worried that "the Clergy, the Noblesse, and some Part of the Beourgeoisie in the Towns, excepted, the Canadians are not to be depended upon, especially if a French War breaks out." A little over a year later, Haldimand observed that "some of the Canadian Habitans might have been brought in time to act with vigour too, against the American Rebels, but should a French ship or two make their appearance, Bourgainville or any other French Officer known to them, come with 400 or 500

French or other men cloathed in white, they most probably would take their part, & appear in Arms against us." See CO 43/14 – Secret and Confidential Letter from Haldimand dated 14 September 1779. And, in 1781, Haldimand noted that the French alliance with the American rebels had had a dangerous effect upon the minds of the Canadiens. He mentioned, however, that British successes in battle, when combined with his vigilant attention to the Canadiens' conduct, "have hitherto kept them if not within the limits of their Duty, at least within those of decency." See CO 42/42 – Most Secret Letter from Haldimand dated 23 November 1781.

68 David Armitage, *The Ideological Origins of the British Empire* (New York: Cambridge University Press, 2000), among others.

69 P.J. Marshall, *The Making and Unmaking of Empires: Britain, India, and America, 1750–1783* (New York: Oxford University Press, 2005), 6–7.

2

The Quebec Act and the Canadiens: The Myth of the Seminal Moment

Donald Fyson

The Quebec Act is often presented as a seminal moment in the history of Quebec, of British North America, and of the British Empire. This is especially true of popular views of the Act. As the current iteration of the relevant English-language Wikipedia article asserts: "The Act had wide-ranging effects, in Quebec itself as well as in the Thirteen Colonies."[1] The idea of a fundamental turning point has traditionally been particularly strong with regard to the British colonial state's relationship with the main group that the Act sought to address: the Canadiens, the francophone and Catholic inhabitants of Quebec, mostly descended from the pre-Conquest French settlers and the ancestors of most francophone Quebecers today. To cite Quebec intellectual François-Albert Angers, writing in the neo-nationalist *L'Action nationale* in 1974, "This year we celebrate a major anniversary. The most important anniversary in our history after the very foundation of Quebec. 1974 is the 200th anniversary of the Quebec Act. And 1774 was the year of the second foundation of French Quebec." The Act is indeed still sometimes today presented as "French Canada's Magna Carta" or as "the first constitutional recognition of the distinct character of [Canadien] society."[2]

This interpretation of the Quebec Act forms a crucial part of broader debates regarding the effects of the British conquest of Quebec.[3] For some, the Act was the result of a benevolent humanistic impulse emanating from a wise imperial government repairing the ills it had caused in the colony's governance by its hastily drafted Royal Proclamation of 1763.[4] For others, the Act was a Machiavellian attempt on the part of a desperate imperial power to ensure the loyalty of the Canadiens (or at least, of their supposed natural leaders, the seigneurs and the clergy) in the face of the rising threat of American unrest, all the while reinforcing traditional power structures, such as the seigneurial system, the Church, and authoritarian unelected government.[5] In this last view, the apparent generosity and openness of the Act was undermined by the governors' instructions (which were not made public), directives whose basic intent was the long-term assimilation of the *Canadiens*. But regardless of whether the Act is seen in a positive or a negative light, the Act is taken as a pivotal moment for the Canadiens in their rapport with the colonial state.

In recent years, historiographical debates concerning the Quebec Act's place within the history of Quebec itself and its effects on the Canadien population have largely died down. We can no longer affirm, as did Séraphin Marion in 1963, that "The history of Canada probably affords no question that, even today, raises more controversy than the Quebec Act."[6] As is shown by recent work on the Act, including many of the essays in this collection, the attention of scholars has shifted elsewhere: to the Act in its imperial and comparative context; to its role in the American Revolution; to its impact on Indigenous peoples; in short, towards questions where, if the Canadiens are evoked at all, it is either in passing or as objects of an external gaze.[7] Another feature of more recent work on the Quebec Act, again including several of the pieces in this book, is its emphasis on discourse. While exchanges continue over the origins of the Act and the intent of the imperial government, far-less-recent work has focused on whether these intentions were actually fulfilled in the years following the Act. Given the rich debates around the Act in Quebec, in Britain, and in the American colonies, the turn to discourse is understandable and indeed necessary. For example, much recent work on the Act has sought to restore historiographical appreciation of the complexity of British and American discourse on issues such as anti-Catholicism, liberty, and subjecthood.

This shift in focus toward a less internalist, more comparative, analysis of the Quebec Act, and a broader understanding the discursive basis and impact of the Act, has been salutary. And yet, there is still room for approaches focused on how the Act worked "on the ground" in Quebec itself. Fundamentally, what most influenced how the Canadien population (or rather, the very different groups that made it up) experienced colonial rule was the concrete practices of governance implemented in the colony. What governors James Murray or Guy Carleton or Frederick Haldimand wrote in private letters or confidential dispatches, or what was written by British and American pamphleteers, is certainly worthy of study, but it had less direct impact on ordinary Canadiens. Even the debates in Quebec's few newspapers, especially in English, could matter only peripherally to most of the Canadien population, given the relatively low rates of literacy, their virtually non-existent command of English, and the limited circulation of these newspapers. What mattered far more to the Canadien population were the very specific practices and experiences of colonial rule put in place by governors and other colonial administrators.

A case in point is the importance of the Quebec Act itself in establishing the relationship between Canadien society and British colonial rule. But what if, despite its pre-eminent position in the post-Conquest historiographical canon, we have been mistaken in attributing such great import to the Act, at least insofar as its actual impact on the Canadiens is concerned? This is not an entirely new question, having been raised from time to time by previous historians. Already in 1951, Elizabeth Arthur asserted that "the Quebec Act has so often been called the Magna Carta of French-Canadian liberties that it is easy to attribute to it a cataclysmic quality that it did not possess." And Hilda Neatby went further: in the brief Editor's Note at the very end of the sourcebook she edited on the Quebec Act in 1972, she suggested that "If the Quebec Act was a charter for Canadians, like some other charters it may be said only to have confirmed ... what had already been conceded in practice."[8]

That is the focused question this paper addresses: the impact of the Quebec Act on the practices of colonial governance in Quebec, as they concerned the Canadien population. A close review of the various provisions of the Act in this regard raises questions about the notion of a seminal moment. Most importantly, as Neatby noted, many of the Act's most striking provisions concerning the relationship between the Canadiens and the colonial state were declaratory – not in the classic legal sense of declaring existing law, but rather, declaratory of existing fact. Many of the radical changes the Act appeared to bring about de jure – which raised so much opposition in England and in the American colonies – had already progressively been put in place de facto, or even de jure, under the colonial administration since the Conquest. For the Canadiens, the Quebec Act's importance was less in making these changes, than in constitutionally confirming and entrenching changes already made over the previous fifteen years.[9]

THE QUEBEC ACT: CONTINUITY AND CHANGE

To begin, take the main provisions of the Quebec Act that most concerned the relationship of the Canadiens to the colonial state. The first section of table 2.1 summarizes these provisions, in the order they appear in the Act. The right-hand column indicates whether this was truly a new measure; a provision that simply repealed existing provisions; a measure already in force de jure by other formal means; and provisions which, while not yet formally established, were already fully or largely in force de facto. However, limiting the analysis to provisions explicitly detailed in the Act provides only a partial view of the Quebec Act's potential impact on the Canadiens. Measures that were at the heart of contention over the Act, such as the abolition of juries in civil cases or the apparent refusal of the right to habeas corpus, were not mentioned explicitly in the text, nor were other fundamental administrative changes that have provoked less debate. Instead, these were implicit in the Act's provisions. Some of the most important of these are summarized in the second section of table 2.1.

What is immediately evident is the number of provisions that did not represent change, but rather confirmed existing law and existing practices. A more detailed analysis is thus in order, looking both at the continuities that the Act embodied, and the changes it actually wrought.

CONTINUITIES

Let us begin with the continuities in governance: measures that the Quebec Act confirmed. Some were simply re-enactments of what had already been established de jure under various previous legal or quasi-legal enactments. Others represented the formal legislative confirmation of de-facto practices already adopted since the Conquest, under the military regime and the civil government that followed it in 1764. Finally, in some instances, the British administration had never really changed pre-Conquest French regime structures at all, and also changed nothing with the Act.

Table 2.1
Key provisions of the Quebec Act of Relevance to the Canadiens

Section	*Provision*	*Status*
1. EXPLICIT PROVISIONS		
1	Annexation of Labrador, the Great Lakes basin, etc. to Quebec	new
4	Revocation of Royal Proclamation as it pertained to Quebec	repeal of existing provisions
4	Revocation of existing Quebec commissions	repeal of existing provisions
4	Revocation of existing Quebec ordinances	repeal of existing provisions
	Freedom to exercise Roman Catholicism	already in force de jure (Treaty of Paris)
5	Clergy to receive its accustomed dues (tithe)	already in force de facto
7	Catholics exempted from Test Oaths	partly new, partly already in force de facto
8	Guarantee of property rights of Canadiens	already in force de jure (Capitulation of Montreal)
8	Non-recognition of property rights of religious orders and communities	new
8	Confirmation of full civil rights of Canadiens	already essentially in force de facto
8	Re-establishment of the "Laws of Canada" for property and civil rights	already in force de facto
10	Freedom of willing	already in force de jure
11	Continuation of English criminal law	already in force de jure (reception as of 1763)
12–16	Establishment and powers of Legislative Council	already in force de jure (governors' commissions, instructions, etc.)
2. IMPLICIT PROVISIONS		
(8)	Maintenance of seigneurial system	already in force de facto
(8)	Maintenance of notarial system	already in force de facto
(8)	Use of French before the courts	already in force de facto
(8)	Suspension of habeas corpus	new (possibly)
(4, 8)	Abolition of juries in civil cases	new
(4)	Abolition of parish bailiffs	new
(4, 8)	Abolition of registration of deeds	new

First and most clearly, the Quebec Act re-enacted several provisions that had already been established de jure before 1775 in formal instruments such as the 1760 Articles of Capitulation of Montreal (which were in effect the articles of capitulation of the whole of Canada), or the 1763 Treaty of Paris. For example, when the Quebec Act stated that Catholics might "have, hold, and enjoy, the free exercise of the Religion of the Church of Rome," subject to the king's supremacy, it did nothing more than repeat what had already been agreed on in the Treaty of Paris.[10] This also confirmed a de-facto situation, since the penal provisions of the English anti-Catholic laws had never been implemented in the colony, despite agitation from some of the colony's more rabidly Protestant, anti-papist British settlers.[11] Or again, the stipulation that all Canadien subjects, apart from the religious orders and communities, could "hold and enjoy their Property and Possessions" simply reaffirmed what had already been promised in the 1760 Articles of Capitulation of Montreal, and which had never been seriously questioned since.[12] Similarly, when the Quebec Act declared that English criminal law was to be in force, it was only stating (as it acknowledged) what had been the case in practice since 1760, and in law since the automatic reception of English criminal law in 1763.[13] Finally, the powers and structure of the Legislative Council established by the Quebec Act differed little from those of the previous council established under the commissions and instructions to governors since 1764, maintaining the authoritarian system set up at the Conquest and which echoed pre-Conquest structures of colonial domination.[14]

Other apparently novel provisions, however, reflected instead the Quebec Act's enactment de jure of de-facto situations in the colony. For example, the Quebec Act explicitly recognized the right of the Catholic clergy to "hold, receive, and enjoy, their accustomed Dues and Rights," of which the most important was the right to collect the tithe; this in opposition to the refusal of this right in the 1760 Articles of Capitulation of Montreal. As might be expected, the measure provoked considerable debate and opposition during the adoption of the Quebec Act, because, among other reasons, the tithe was seen as a tax that profited the Catholic Church, and was backed up by the legislative might of the colonial government.[15] In fact, this did not represent any major change. As contemporary observers and later historians have long pointed out, most Canadiens continued to pay the tithe between the capitulation and 1775, and there are even examples of priests who before 1775 hauled refractory parishioners before the civil courts and successfully prosecuted for the payment of tithes.[16]

Another such provision, of utmost importance for the Canadiens, concerned the Test Oaths. It is still very often suggested, even today, that Catholics were excluded from all positions in the colonial administration, through the imposition of the Test Oaths.[17] But as I have shown elsewhere, the Test Oaths, in practice, were in fact applied to only a very limited range of positions. Essentially, it was only members of the governor's council, along with the judges and justices of the peace, who were constrained to swear the Test Oath and follow the other anti-Catholic provisions laid out in the penal acts. This was still an important disability for Canadien elites, but very far from the total exclusion postulated by many writers. Limited British immigration meant that the colonial administration had no choice but to rely on Catholics for a wide range of paid public duties that would have been denied them elsewhere in the Empire, from bailiffs and court clerks to grand voyers (chief roads officials) and even two of the judges of the prerogative court. If we add the non-imposition of criminal measures against Catholics, Canadiens enjoyed an almost complete civil emancipation long before the Quebec Act came into force in May 1775. There was of course British domination of lucrative government positions, but this was little different from what had been experienced in the colony before the Conquest: the dominance of metropolitans over colonials.[18]

The same sort of de-facto practices of forced accommodation can be found in the realm of civil law. A persistent historiographical myth postulates, first, the radical imposition of English common law by the Royal Proclamation of 1763 and the 1764 ordinance establishing the courts, and second, the existence of legal chaos between 1764 and 1775.[19] As summarized in Michel Morin's essay in this collection, the exact status of English and French law in Quebec before the Quebec Act was certainly the subject of considerable debate. But on the ground, as judge Dominique Mondelet put it succinctly as early as 1851, "From the period at which Canada became a British Province, up to the Quebec Act, justice would appear to have been administered according to both the English and French laws indifferently ... This is abundantly proved by the judicial records of those times."[20] Indeed, Canadian civil law (the law in force in the French colony of Canada before the Conquest) was never abandoned, and continued to be used by the legal system. Notaries continued to practice much as they had before the Conquest, following the same practices and using the same forms as under the French regime. In the courts, judges and lawyers had constant recourse to Canadian law. There was nevertheless a pluralism of law, in which procedures were a mixture of French and British influences and the parties, Canadiens as well as British, argued Canadian law or English law, according to what best suited their case. This legal pluralism anticipated both the "restoration" of Canadian civil law in 1775 and the pluralism that many see as having been established under the Quebec Act, including its territorialization of law (lands granted in free and common socage were potentially excluded from some or all of French civil law) and the inclusion of English practices, such as freedom of willing.[21] The same can be said of the use of French before the courts. The Quebec Act has sometimes been portrayed as re-establishing the linguistic rights of the Canadiens before the courts, or at least before the civil courts. However, the Quebec Act said nothing at all about language, whether in the courts or elsewhere; and at any rate, even before 1775, court proceedings in most courts, criminal as well as civil, were in both French and English, according to the language of the parties involved.[22]

One other continuity in governance of particular importance to the Canadien population as a whole, and especially the rural *habitants*, was the seigneurial system. It is a common trope, especially among non-historians writing about the past, that the Quebec Act confirmed the maintenance of the seigneurial system in Quebec.[23] Strictly speaking, the Quebec Act did nothing of the sort, since it said nothing explicitly about the seigneurial system, and, indeed, this was little discussed during the debates. At most, the preservation of the system was encompassed in the more general provisions on the protection of property rights and the recourse to the laws of Canada concerning property. However, property rights, including seigneurial property, had already been guaranteed by the 1760 Articles of Capitulation of Montreal,[24] while, as we shall see, it is far from certain that Canadian civil law was truly abrogated between 1764 and 1775. Further, as of 1771, the imperial government had already explicitly recognized seigneurialism by instructing the governor of Quebec to grant lands thereafter under seigneurial tenure.[25] As such, the most that can be said is that the Quebec Act simply left in place existing arrangements that had already confirmed the maintenance of the seigneurial system. The practice of seigneurialism did change significantly in the century after the Conquest, with for example an increasing interest in the seigneury as a liberal form of investment on the part of both British and Canadien merchants, and seigneurial exactions becoming increasingly harsh. But these changes were linked to more general changes in the social and economic structure of Quebec and of the British world more generally, rather than to specific legislation such as the Quebec Act.[26]

During the debates on the Quebec Act, the maintenance of the seigneurial system was attributed to the guarantee of seigneurial property in the Articles of Capitulation of Montreal.[27] But a useful parallel can also be drawn with the civil functions of the network of Catholic parishes in the colony, which were mentioned not at all in the Quebec Act or in the debates. Like the seigneuries, the colony's Catholic parishes had been established under the French regime, in this case, by the Church, but ratified by the colonial administration. Also like the seigneurial system, parishes structured rural life, and served not only religious but also civil administrative purposes, though less so than in seigneuries. After the Conquest, the Catholic parish system, like the seigneurial system, was not only tolerated by the British colonial administration, but even actively relied on. Thus, the new British rulers adopted the Catholic parish wholesale, as the basis for a whole range of administrative functions, ranging from census divisions to the appointment of local officials. Indeed, local administration in rural Quebec in the first decades of British rule was organized almost entirely around the parish, with the seigneury largely disappearing as a local unit of administration. This was a discordant note for a supposedly fiercely anti-Catholic empire, but no different in this respect than the maintenance of feudal land-holding under the seigneurial system, which can be attributed as much to practical necessity as to a desire to respect the Articles of Capitulation.[28]

CHANGES

I would not however argue that the Quebec Act changed nothing at all. It did bring very real changes, but they were fewer than is often suggested. Some of these concrete changes were explicitly effectuated by the Quebec Act. The most evident is the annexation of Labrador and the Great Lakes basin to Quebec. The latter in particular severely restricted the existing Indian Territory and hemmed in the American colonies. This was of potentially great import for Indigenous peoples; and it was of course at the heart of American resentment of the Quebec Act.[29] It was also significant for the Canadiens who lived in the small western settlements, such as Detroit or in the Illinois country, who in theory moved from military to civilian rule.[30] The territorial provisions of the Quebec Act, along with the duties on alcohol imports from the American colonies under the companion Quebec Revenue Act, also profoundly affected the Canadien merchants who continued to operate in the Montreal-based fur trade. These provisions effectively removed the competition from American-based fur traders, which should have been a positive development for them. But, as Dale Miquelon has shown, this in fact encouraged many deep-pocketed American fur traders to move to Quebec, overwhelming the remaining Canadien merchants and leading to a sharp decline in their place in the fur trade. However, this decline was already under way well before the Quebec Act, which simply sealed the Canadien merchants' fate.[31] As well, the effects of the Quebec Act on the bulk of the Canadien population, which was living in the St Lawrence Valley, were more marginal: the main contact of this group with the West was through fur-trade labour, and this in itself was little affected by the Quebec Act.

The exemption from the Test Oaths for Catholics is another example of an explicit change whose impact was less profound than is usually maintained. It did allow some members of the Canadien elite access to the Legislative Council (which now included about a third of Catholic Canadiens, almost all seigneurs) and to the judiciary. Members of the Canadien elites even rapidly came to dominate the ranks of the justices of the peace in the eighteenth century.[32] But as we saw, this change meant little for the vast majority of Canadiens, who could never aspire to such positions: the low-level state positions they might find themselves in, such as court bailiffs or other petty functions, had never been affected by the Test Oaths.

The non-recognition of the property rights of religious orders and communities was certainly a more significant change, particularly in comparison with the 1760 Articles of Capitulation of Montreal, which had granted them these rights.[33] Religious communities thus had every reason to be concerned. However, their position was already precarious: the apparent guarantees in the Articles of Capitulation were no bar to the colonial administration effectively seizing the property of two male communities, the Jesuits and the Recollects, well before 1775. Furthermore, in the longer term, the omission of the property rights of religious communities turned out to be of little real significance for the other communities. The fate of the Sulpicians of Montreal, who were responsible for the city's seminary, and also owned lucrative seigneuries, such as that of the Island of Montreal, is a case in point. The Sulpicians' property rights remained uncertain, and were regularly questioned by colonial administrators right up until the order was finally incorporated in 1840. This placed the Sulpicians constantly on the defensive and provided imperial authorities with a potent tool to ensure their loyalty. However, the Sulpicians also found ways to avoid outright confiscation, for example by transferring all their Canadian property from their mother house in Paris to the Canadian Sulpicians. Their revenues also increased steadily across the period, despite the fact that their property rights were not absolutely guaranteed. Similarly, despite the provisions of the Quebec Act, the Seminary of Quebec was confirmed in its possession of its lucrative seigneuries in 1781. As for the female religious communities, such as the Ursulines or the Congrégation de Notre-Dame, their property also remained in their hands.[34]

Other changes came about implicitly or indirectly through various provisions in the Act. Two that provoked great debate at the time and since were the Quebec Act's apparent revocation of two fundamental British "liberties," habeas corpus and trial by jury. Indeed, much of the Commons debates regarding the effects of the "reintroduction" of French civil law (or rather, the "laws of Canada") for "property and civil rights" concentrated on these two issues, as did the bitter complaints of the colony's British inhabitants when they learnt that what they considered inalienable rights had apparently been taken away.[35] This extended also to the Canadiens: as one slightly later critic put it, "the Canadians [are] themselves deprived of the two greatest Blessings an Englishman enjoys so far off; the Trial by Juries, and of the Habeas Corpus Act totally."[36]

In fact, the situation was far more complicated than a simple denial of basic British rights by the framers of the Act. Take the right to habeas corpus. This was assumed to have been introduced into Quebec with English criminal law in 1763, under the Royal Proclamation. Habeas corpus proceedings for countering unwarranted imprisonment had indeed been used in criminal cases in Quebec before 1775, although very infrequently.[37] Critics of the Quebec Act argued that its restoration of Canadian law for civil rights implied the abrogation of habeas corpus,[38] and their fears were apparently justified when habeas corpus was indeed effectively suspended in the colony between 1777 and 1784, during the conflict with the former American colonies. Several political dissidents were jailed on the orders of the colony's authoritarian governor, Frederick Haldimand, and then denied habeas corpus when they applied to the superior criminal court, the King's Bench, for redress, at a period when the court was held not by a legally trained chief justice, but by three commissioners, two of whom had no formal legal training.[39]

But was this really a result of the Quebec Act? True, when the commissioners rejected one application for the writ, in favour of Pierre Du Calvet, they apparently justified their decision on the grounds that "since the establishment of the French laws in the province in all matters of property and civil rights by the [Quebec Act], the English laws, concerning the writ of Habeas Corpus, were not in force in the province with respect to such persons as were imprisoned by the order of the Governor." In another case, in favour of Charles Hay, they apparently argued "that the writ of Habeas Corpus is not introduced into the province by the Quebec Act."[40] However, their position was doubtful. The colony's former chief justice, the far-more-educated Peter Livius, whom the commissioners had replaced, had earlier considered that the writ was at least available in Quebec, which led him into a conflict with the colony's military administrators that eventually contributed to his being dismissed from the bench.[41] Furthermore, the commissioners also grounded their rejection of habeas corpus on a series of other justifications, including imperial statutes which suspended habeas corpus for treason and sedition cases during the American rebellion and procedural issues. Clearly, the commissioners were seeking to keep the military governors' prisoners in jail on whatever shaky legal grounds they could find.

Instead, the suspension of habeas corpus in Quebec was an eminently political decision, which might well have been taken even had the Quebec Act explicitly introduced the writ – just as was the case in the American colonies, and also in Quebec and Lower Canada itself in the decades following the explicit introduction of the right to habeas corpus in 1784.[42] In short, the Quebec Act itself changed little in respect to the availability of habeas corpus in the colony. Indeed, as early as 1765, there were also doubts as to whether the Royal Proclamation of 1763 had in fact introduced habeas corpus into the colony, suggesting that, even without the Quebec Act's reference to civil rights, colonial judges eager to please powerful military governors would likely have been able to find the legal justification they needed to refuse the writ.[43]

Trial by jury was another matter. Unlike habeas corpus, juries were clearly established and regularly used in civil cases before 1775, and then became unavailable as a direct result of the Quebec Act. However, once again, the Act itself was only partially to blame. It certainly reintroduced French civil procedure, as part of French civil law, and although it said nothing explicitly on the matter of juries, this was taken to exclude them. However, while juries were not part of French procedure in civil cases, nothing prevented the colonial legislature from reintroducing juries immediately, as pointed out by one of the Quebec Act's main apologists, the undersecretary of state, William Knox.[44] Indeed, the colony's Legislative Council soon proved itself perfectly capable of reintroducing some English-civil-law procedures, such as English-style imprisonment for debt, when it adopted an ordinance regulating civil procedure in 1777; as others have argued, the Quebec Act was no bulwark against the introduction of English procedure.[45] As in the case of habeas corpus, the decision not to reintroduce juries in civil cases immediately was thus once again eminently political, although the Quebec Act, in wiping the slate clean, had provided the majority in the Legislative Council (including most of the Canadien seigneurs who were members) with the opportunity to do away with them passively rather than actively, and thus avoid any oversight of their actions from London.

Even more importantly, as far as most Canadiens were concerned, the abolition of trial by jury in civil cases was of relatively limited importance. First, even before 1775, juries were rarely used in civil cases: overall, juries were used in about 5 per cent of cases in the Court of Common Pleas, and far more frequently in cases involving British rather than Canadien parties. Further, the complete abolition of juries in civil matters was only temporary, as they were restored in commercial cases and in those involving personal damages a decade later, in 1785.[46] Finally, juries were not abolished in criminal cases, where their role in protecting the rights of individuals against arbitrary state decisions was seen as most important (even though, in fact, few criminal cases were decided by juries); and the representative function of grand juries was also fully maintained before and after the Quebec Act.[47] The issue of the abolition of juries under the Quebec Act was thus far more a rhetorical tool used by those who opposed the Act.

Other important changes wrought by the Quebec Act in the relationship between the Canadiens and the colonial state came about even less directly, stemming not from any provisions in the Act itself, but from its revocation of the ordinances passed by the governor and his council before 1775 – in essence, the same sort of wiping clean of the administrative slate as had aided the abolition of juries in civil cases. The ordinances adopted in the first decade of British civil rule of Quebec had set out a whole set of administrative provisions that regulated large parts of everyday governance in the colony, and were thus of great importance to the daily lives of its majority Canadien population. By sweeping them away, the Quebec Act upended significant parts of that governance.

In some cases, the disruption was only temporary, with some of the local legislative measures soon replaced by new ordinances. Thus, pre-1775 ordinances concerning markets (1764); the sale of bread (1764, 1768, 1769); legal interest (1764); road repairs (1766), and fire safety (1768, 1773), all in force up to 1775 and then abrogated by the Quebec Act, were replaced at the first productive session of the Legislative Council in 1777 with others of roughly the same nature, while a previous ordinance on tavern licensing (1768) was folded into the Quebec Revenue Act (1774).[48] But in other cases, measures adopted before 1775 were replaced only later, or never at all. One key example was the system of parish bailiffs, established in 1764 as part of the ordinance setting up the courts. These local officers, who replaced the pre-Conquest militia captains and filled more or less the same functions as parish constables in England, were elected among the essentially Canadien inhabitants of the rural parishes of the colony. It was, in fact, a system of very local democracy, which foreshadowed the establishment of parliamentary democracy thirty years later and even the systems of local elections installed by the Americans during their invasion in 1775–76. The Quebec Act abolished this system in 1775; in its aftermath, the bailiffs were replaced once again by militia captains appointed by the colonial administration, in a return to pre-Conquest authoritarianism, and local elections of state officials would not begin again until the 1790s.[49] Another example is the abolition of mandatory registration of deeds, which had been introduced in 1764, although only partially followed. Its abolishment in 1775 soon became a major bone of contention in Lower Canada and remained so right through to the early 1840s.[50] Or again, regulation of weights and measures by the colonial government, which made a brief appearance in 1764–75, did not reappear again until 1799; in the interim, there was at best piecemeal regulation by urban justices of the peace in Quebec City and Montreal.[51] The Quebec Act's abrogation of the previous ordinances even affected the age of majority: set at twenty-one years by an ordinance in 1764, it rose back up to the twenty-five years specified under pre-Conquest Canadian civil law in 1775, where it remained until 1782.[52] In short, it was in the Act's impact on these everyday matters, essentially ignored in contemporary debates around the adoption of the Act and neglected by later historians, that we can see its most significant impact on the Canadiens and their relationship with the colonial state.

CONCLUSION

The main thrust of this article has been that we must be careful with claims that the Quebec Act was a seminal moment in the history of the Canadiens. The empirical observation of the actual situation on the ground in Quebec, which was often quite different from what was advanced by commentators at the time, shows something quite different. At least in regard to the Canadiens, many of the apparently radical changes that the Act made were not changes at all, but rather the confirmation of pre-existing conditions. In this, the Canadiens were not unique. For Indigenous peoples as well, the Quebec Act did not necessarily represent radical change. As Alain Beaulieu shows, later in this volume, the Act's apparent abolition of the Royal Proclamation of 1763 within the vastly expanded territory of Quebec led to no significant break in British imperial policy towards Indigenous peoples. And as I and others have suggested, despite its apparent extension of French civil and English criminal law westwards, Indigenous people for the most part continued to be treated separately under the colony's justice system.[53]

However, arguing that the Quebec Act was not a seminal moment is not the same as affirming that it was unimportant. Aside from its evident discursive and ideological impact, it was also, like all declaratory acts, a synthesis of what its drafters thought was and should be. It set out the basic outline of how the British colonial government thought Quebec society should function and what the place of Canadien institutions, Canadien culture, and Canadiens themselves should be in the new colony. Whether this view was positive or negative, benevolent or Machiavellian; whether it was based on a desire to solve the problems of governance in Quebec, or in response to the rising tide of American discontent; whether it was subsequently (or even immediately) subverted by secret instructions, governors' political leanings, local political factions, or mutual British and Canadien mistrust and dislike, are another series of questions altogether, addressed by many of the other essays in this collection.

Emphasizing local conditions allows us to relativize the emphasis that is often put on imperial decision-making structures in a significant portion of imperial or transnational historiography. In law, for example, it was not decisions made in London that shaped the functioning of the judicial system or the nature of legal culture. Instead, legal change was mainly effectuated through decisions made on the ground in Quebec, by local actors such as judges, lawyers, or notaries. The Quebec Act followed these changes, rather than being the motor for them. At the same time, as many of the essays in this collection suggest, the broader imperial context was key. As Christian Burset shows, the receptivity towards a legal system other than the common law would have been difficult if not impossible without an imperial climate that favoured, at least in part, legal pluralism. One could say the same with respect to the apparent toleration of Catholicism. The setting aside of the penal provisions against Catholics, and their integration into many positions within the colonial administration well before May 1775, were measures clearly dictated by pragmatic local requirements. But they would have been impossible without the less fiercely anti-Catholic climate in the mid-eighteenth century, inspired by a large part of the British elite, though not necessarily ordinary Britons, as Brad Jones shows; or without the recognition of the failure of assimilationist policies in Ireland, explored by Aaron Willis. It is this dialectical relationship between local situation and pan-imperial ideologies which gave rise to the Quebec Act and its confirmation de jure of that which had already largely been adopted de facto, making it without doubt a structuring event, although perhaps not a seminal moment.

NOTES

1 "Quebec Act," https://en.wikipedia.org/wiki/Quebec_Act, accessed 29 May 2020. The French version of the page is less categorical.

2 Francois-Albert Angers, "Le dossier de L'Acte de Québec," *L'Action nationale* 64, no. 1 (1974): 872; Peter H. Russell, *Canada's Odyssey: A*

Country Based on Incomplete Conquests (Toronto: University of Toronto Press, 2017), 4; Paul-André Linteau, *Histoire du Canada*, updated 6th edition (Paris: Presses universitaires de France, 2016), 33–4. My translations.

3 The best overview of the historiography of the Quebec Act through to the 1960s remains Hilda Neatby, *The Quebec Act: Protest and Policy* (Scarborough: Prentice-Hall, 1972), though it omits two important works: Michel Brunet, *Les Canadiens après la Conquête, 1759–1775: de la révolution canadienne à la révolution américaine* (Montreal: Fides, 1969) and Neatby's own *Quebec: The Revolutionary Age, 1760–1791* (Toronto: McClelland and Stewart, 1966). More recent substantial published treatments of the Quebec Act include Philip Lawson, *The Imperial Challenge: Quebec and Britain in the Age of the American Revolution* (Montreal: McGill-Queen's University Press, 1989); Jacques-Yvan Morin and José Woehrling, *Les constitutions du Canada et du Québec: du régime français à nos jours*, 2nd. ed. (Montreal: Éditions Thémis, 1994): 42–121; Peter M. Doll, *Revolution, Religion, and National Identity: Imperial Anglicanism in British North America, 1745–1795* (Madison, NJ: Fairleigh Dickinson University Press / Associated University Presses, 2000), 92–154; Karen Stanbridge, *Toleration and State Institutions: British Policy Toward Catholics in Eighteenth-Century Ireland and Quebec* (Lanham: Lexington Books, 2003), 69–140; and Anne Trépanier, "La parade d'une seconde Conquête: l'Acte de Québec comme moment refondateur," in Anne Trépanier, ed., *La rénovation de l'héritage démocratique: entre fondation et refondation* (Ottawa: Presses de l'Université d'Ottawa, 2009), 178–219. The Quebec Act is also discussed at length in several unpublished or largely unpublished doctoral theses, including Pierre Tousignant, "La genèse et l'avènement de la Constitution de 1791" (PhD diss., Université de Montréal, 1971); Karl David Milobar, "The Constitutional Development of Quebec from the Time of the French Regime to the Canada Act of 1791: A British Perspective" (PhD diss., University of London, 1990); Mary Ann Fenton, "Petitions, Protests, and Policy: The Influence of the American Colonies on Quebec, 1760–1776" (PhD diss., University of New Hampshire, 1993); and Amy Noel Ellison, "'Reverse of Fortune': The Invasion of Canada and the Coming of American Independence, 1774–1776" (PhD diss., Boston University, 2016).

4 This was the perspective of much of the older imperial historiography, as well as those who take a "jovialist" view of the British Conquest. For a critical perspective on the latter, see Donald Fyson, "The Canadiens and the Conquest of Quebec: Interpretations, Realities, Ambiguities," in Stéphan Gervais et al., eds, *Quebec Questions: Quebec Studies for the Twen-*

ty-first Century, 2nd ed. (Toronto: Oxford University Press, 2016), 19–36.

5 This is the perspective taken by nationalist and neo-nationalist historians of Quebec, as part of the broader "miserabilist" take on the effects of the Conquest (on which see Fyson, "The Canadiens and the Conquest of Quebec"). For recent examples, see Jean-Pierre Wallot, "L'acte de Québec, ses causes, sa nature et 'l'Ancien Régime britannique'" and Claude Bariteau, "L'Acte de Québec. Assises de l'*Indirect Rule* toujours d'actualité," both in *Cahiers du Programme d'étude sur le Québec* 21(2001): 1–8 and 8–12.

6 Séraphin Marion, "L'Acte de Québec: concession magnanime ou intéressée?" *Cahiers des Dix* 28 (1963): 147.

7 Apart from the essays in this collection and the work cited above, recent examples on these themes include Mark D. Walters, "The Continuity of Aboriginal Customs and Government under British Imperial Constitutional Law as Applied in Colonial Canada, 1760–1860" (PhD diss., Oxford University, 1995), 159–79; Vernon P. Creviston, "'No King Unless It Be a Constitutional King': Rethinking the Place of the Quebec Act in the Coming of the American Revolution," *Historian* 73, no. 3 (2011): 463–79; Paul Langston, "'Tyrant and Oppressor!' Colonial Press Reaction to the Quebec Act," *Historical Journal of Massachusetts* 34, no. 1 (2006): 1–17; Stephen Conway, "The Consequences of Conquest: Quebec and British Politics, 1760–1774," in Phillip A. Buckner and John G. Reid, eds, *Revisiting 1759: The Conquest of Canada in Historical Perspective*, 141–65 (Toronto: University of Toronto Press, 2012); Heather Welland, "Commercial Interest and Political Allegiance: The Origins of the Quebec Act," in Buckner and Reid, *Revisiting 1759*, 166–89; Aaron Lukefahr Willis, "The New Laboratory for Empire: Quebec and the Reformulation of British Imperial Practice, 1760–1775" (PhD diss., University of Notre Dame, 2015); and Hannah Weiss Muller, *Subjects and Sovereign: Bonds of Belonging in the Eighteenth-Century British Empire* (New York: Oxford University Press, 2017), 121–65.

8 Elizabeth M. Arthur, "French Participation in the Government of Canada, 1775–1785," *Canadian Historical Review* 32, no. 4 (1951): 303; Neatby, *The Quebec Act*, 140. The same argument was also advanced later by Jean-Pierre Wallot: "L'acte de Québec," 5. For a recent example, see Lawrence A. Uzzell, "James Murray: A Forgotten Champion of Religious Freedom," *Catholic Historical Review* 104, no. 1 (2018): 57–91.

9 Much of the discussion in this essay of the nature of colonial governance before 1775 summarizes more-detailed work I have published elsewhere, in both English and French, which is referenced in the notes.

For a historiographical overview of governance in general in pre-Confederation Quebec, with a particular emphasis on the law, see Donald Fyson, "Between the Ancien Régime and Liberal Modernity: Law, Justice, and State Formation in Colonial Quebec, 1760–1867," *History Compass* 12, no. 5 (2014): 412–32.

10 As pointed out by Hilda Neatby (*The Quebec Act*, 138–40).

11 Donald Fyson, "The Conquered and the Conqueror: The Mutual Adaptation of the Canadiens and the British in Quebec, 1759–1775," in Buckner and Reid, eds, *Revisiting 1759*, 194–5 (Toronto: University of Toronto Press, 2012). For a recent overview of early policies regarding the Catholic Church, see Uzzell, "James Murray," although I would disagree with the centrality accorded to Murray himself.

12 There was never any serious suggestion of confiscating the property of Canadiens in general, even that of the seigneurs. Even the Protestant members of the 1764 Quebec Quarter Session Grand Jury, who launched a frontal assault on the right of Catholics to serve on juries, in government positions, and as attorneys and doctors, made no such demand (*At the First Court of Quarter-Sessions of the Peace, Held at Quebec, in October 1764* [Quebec: Brown & Gilmore, 1765]); S. Morley Scott, "Chapters in the History of the Law of Quebec, 1764–1775" (PhD diss., University of Michigan, 1933), 152–8; Lawson, *The Imperial Challenge*, 51–2; Donald Fyson, "Jurys, participation civique et représentation au Québec et au Bas-Canada: Les grands jurys du district de Montréal (1764–1832)," *Revue d'histoire de l'Amérique française* 55, no. 1 (2001): 87–66.

13 Donald Fyson, *Magistrates, Police, and People: Everyday Criminal Justice in Quebec and Lower Canada, 1764–1837* (Toronto: Osgoode Society for Canadian Legal History and University of Toronto Press, 2006), 15–23.

14 Christian Blais, "Aux sources du parlementarisme dans la Province de Québec, 1764–1791" (PhD diss., Université Laval, currently under evaluation), chapters 2–3; Fyson, "The Conquered and the Conqueror," 199–200.

15 Henry Cavendish, *Debates of the House of Commons in the Year 1774, on the Bill for Making More Effectual Provision for the Government of the Province of Quebec* (London: Ridgway, 1839), 55, 60–71, 216–21, 224–7, 294–5; R.C. Simmons and D.G. Thomas (eds), *Proceedings and Debates of the British Parliaments Respecting North America, 1754–1783*, vol. 5 (New York: Kraus, 1985): 5, 22–23, 27, 29, 119, 125–38, 164, 222–5. For the Quebec Act debates, I have chosen to cite both the nineteenth-century

initial publication of Cavendish's diaries (most often cited by historians) and the more-recent definitive edition.

16 Cavendish, *Debates*, 103–4 / Simmons and Thomas, *Proceedings*, vol. 5 (testimony of Carleton) and Cavendish, *Debates*: 130 / Simmons and Thomas, *Proceedings*, vol. 5, 22–3 (testimony of Maseres, although he also affirmed that some had stopped paying the tithe); Georges-Étienne Proulx, "Les Canadiens ont-ils payé la dîme entre 1760 et 1775?" *Revue d'histoire de l'Amérique française* 11, no. 4 (1958): 533–62; Lucien Lemieux, *Histoire du catholicisme Québécois*, vol. 2, *Les XVIII*[e] *et XIX*[e] *siècles.* Tome 1: *Les années difficiles (1760–1839)* (Montreal: Boréal, 1989), 126. A complete study of the payment of tithes between 1764 and 1775 remains to be carried out.

17 Take for example what is currently the most widely-sold popular history of Quebec, Éric Bédard, *L'histoire du Québec pour les nuls* (Paris: First, 2012), 91: "The Test Oath, thus, effectively excluded all Catholics from public service." Even as careful a historian as Jean-Pierre Wallot repeated this in his overview of the Quebec Act, Wallot, "L'acte de Québec," 2–3.

18 On the Test Oaths and the Test Acts, see Fyson, "The Conquered and the Conqueror," 194–9, and "Les Canadiens et le Serment du Test," in Laurent Veyssière, Sophie Imbeault, and Denis Vaugeois, eds, *1763: Le traité de Paris bouleverse l'Amérique* (Quebec: Septentrion, 2013), 272–7. On Canadiens in public positions before and after 1775, see also Donald Fyson, "Judicial Auxiliaries across Legal Regimes: From New France to Lower Canada," in Claire Dolan, ed., *Entre justice et justiciables: les auxiliaires de la justice du Moyen Âge au XX*[e] *siècle* (Sainte-Foy: Presses de l'Université Laval, 2005), 383–403; Fyson, "Domination et adaptation: les élites européennes au Québec, 1760–1841," in Claire Laux et al., eds, *Au sommet de l'Empire. Les élites européennes dans les colonies (XVI –XX*[e] *siècle)* (Berne: Peter Lang, 2009), 167–96; and Fyson, *Magistrates, Police, and People*, 83–5, 113–17, 141–50. This relaxation of the Test Oath requirements did not apply to imperial institutions such as the British army, from which Canadien elites were essentially excluded. Carleton had proposed raising a few companies of regular Canadien volunteers, officered by former Canadien officers, but this was rejected in London. The Quebec Act changed little in this regard. See *A History of the Organization, Development, and Services of the Military and Naval Forces of Canada from the Peace of Paris in 1763, to the Present Time*, vol. 1 (Ottawa: Department of Militia and Defence, 1919), 49–52, 109–113, 119–20; Roch Legault, *Une élite en déroute: les militaires canadiens après la Conquête* (Outremont: Athéna, 2002).

19 For classic statements of this older view, see André Morel, "La réaction des Canadiens devant l'administration de la justice de 1764 à 1774: une forme de résistance passive," *Revue du Barreau* 20, no. 2 (1960): 55–63; Jacques L'Heureux, "L'organisation judiciaire au Québec de 1764 à 1774," *Revue générale de droit* 1, no.2 (1970): 303–4, 329; and Luc Huppé, *Histoire des institutions judiciaires du Canada* (Montreal: Wilson & Lafleur, 2007), 152–3.

20 In *Stuart v. Bowman* (Montreal Superior Court, 1851), Michel Mathieu, *Rapports judiciaires revisés de la province de Québec*, vol. 3 (Montreal: C.O. Beauchemin, 1892), 306. For the context of the ruling, which involved deciding whether Section 9 of the Quebec Act exempted soccage land from Canadian civil law as a whole, see J.E.C. Brierley, "The Co-existence of Legal Systems in Quebec: Free and Common Soccage in Canada's Pays de Droit Civil," *Cahiers de Droit* 20 (1979): 277–87.

21 See, among others, Jean-Philippe Garneau, "Droit et 'affaires de famille' sur la Côte-de-Beaupré. Histoire d'une rencontre en amont et en aval de la Conquête," *Revue juridique Thémis* 34, no. 2 (2000): 515–61; John A. Dickinson, "L'administration chaotique de la justice après la Conquête: discours ou réalité?," in Giovanni Dotoli, ed., *Canada: Le rotte della libertà* (Fasano: Schena, 2005), 117–27; Arnaud Decroix, David Gilles, and Michel Morin, *Les tribunaux et l'arbitrage en Nouvelle-France et au Québec de 1740 à 1784* (Montreal: Éditions Thémis, 2012), 231–89; David Gilles, *Essais d'histoire du droit, de la Nouvelle-France à la province de Québec* (Sherbrooke: Éditions de la revue de droit de l'Université de Sherbrooke, 2014), 337–462; and Donald Fyson, "De la common law à la Coutume de Paris: les nouveaux habitants britanniques du Québec et le droit civil français, 1764–1775," in Florent Garnier and Jacqueline Vendrand-Voyer, eds, *La coutume dans tous ses états* (Paris: La Mémoire du Droit, 2013), 157–72. Hybridization also characterized parts of the criminal law and criminal justice: see Donald Fyson, "Legal Pluralism, Hybridization, and the Uses of Everyday Criminal Law in Quebec, 1760–1867," in Manon van der Heijden, Griet Vermeesch, and Jaco Zuijderduijn (eds), *The Uses of Justice in Global Perspective, 1600–1900* (London: Routledge, 2019), 198–218.

22 For the traditional view, see for example Francois-Albert Angers, "La langue française au Québec (1774–1974)," *L'Action nationale* 63, nos 8/9 (1974): 618–28; Danièle Noël, "Une langue qui ne capitule pas (la justice et les tribunaux)," in Michel Plourde, ed., *Le français au Québec: 400 ans d'histoire et de vie* (Montreal: Fides / Publications du Québec,

2000), 72–4; or Michael Dorland and Maurice Charland, *Law, Rhetoric, and Irony in the Formation of Canadian Civic Culture* (Toronto: University of Toronto Press, 2002), 89–95. For a more recent study, based on archival research, see Jean-Philippe Garneau, "Gérer la différence dans le Québec britannique: l'exemple de la langue (1760–1840)," in Lorraine Derocher et al., eds, *L'État canadien et la diversité culturelle et religieuse, 1800–1914*, 21–48 (Quebec: Presses de l'Université du Québec, 2009). On language in the criminal courts, see Fyson, *Magistrates, Police, and People*, 249–53.

23 See, for example, James Tully, *Strange Multiplicity: Constitutionalism in an Age of Diversity* (Cambridge: Cambridge University Press, 1995), 145–6; David Chennells, *The Politics of Nationalism in Canada: Cultural Conflict since 1760* (Toronto: University of Toronto Press, 2001), 563; or Alain-G. Gagnon and Luc Turgeon, "Managing Diversity in Eighteenth and Nineteenth Century Canada: Quebec's Constitutional Development in Light of the Scottish Experience," *Commonwealth & Comparative Politics* 41, no. 1 (2003): 1–23.

24 Adam Shortt and Arthur G. Doughty, *Documents Relating to the Constitutional History of Canada, 1759–1791*, 2nd ed. (Ottawa: J. de L. Taché, 1918), 26–7.

25 Ibid., 422–3.

26 For a synthesis and overview of the historiography, see Christian Dessureault, "L'évolution du régime seigneurial canadien de 1760 à 1854: essai de synthèse," in Alain Laberge and Benoît Grenier, eds, *Le régime seigneurial au Québec 150 ans après: bilans et perspectives de recherches à l'occasion de la commémoration du 150e anniversaire de l'abolition du régime seigneurial*, 23–37 (Quebec: CIEQ, 2009). Tellingly, Dessureault does not mention the Quebec Act at all.

27 Cavendish, *Debates*: 133 / Simmons and Thomas, *Proceedings*, vol. 5, 24 (testimony of Maseres).

28 Donald Fyson, "La paroisse et l'administration étatique sous le Régime britannique (1764–1840)," in Serge Courville and Normand Séguin, eds, *Atlas historique du Québec: La paroisse* (Sainte-Foy: Presses de l'Université Laval, 2001), 25–39.

29 For a basic description and discussion of the legislative changes with regards to territory, see Henri Brun, "L'évolution du territoire du Québec," in his *Le territoire du Québec: six études juridiques* (Quebec: Presses de l'Université Laval, 1974), 13–31. For a more detailed study of the effects of territorial expansion of Quebec under the Quebec Act,

and especially its reception in the American colonies, see the essay by Jeffers Lennox in this collection.

30 In practice, the transition was more difficult, and in some cases impossible. On Detroit, see Guillaume Teasdale, *Fruits of Perseverance: The French Presence in the Detroit River Region, 1701–1815* (Montreal: McGill-Queen's University Press, 2018); on the Illinois Country, Robert Englebert, "The Legacy of New France: Law and Social Cohesion between Quebec and the Illinois Country, 1763–1790," *French Colonial History* 17 (2017): 35–66.

31 Dale Miquelon, "The Baby Family in the Trade of Canada, 1750–1820" (MA, Carleton University, 1966), 134–58; and "Le commerce des fourrures dans la vallée du Saint-Laurent après 1763," in Laurent Veyssière, ed., *La Nouvelle-France en héritage* (Paris: Armand Colin / Ministère de la Défense, 2013), 81–101; José Igartua, "The Merchants and Négociants of Montreal, 1750–1775: A Study in Socio-Economic History" (PhD diss., Michigan State University, 1974).

32 Fyson, *Magistrates, Police, and People*, 83–5, 113–17; more generally, Fyson, "Domination et adaptation."

33 Shortt and Doughty, *Documents Relating to the Constitutional History of Canada*, 34. This was also recalled by Attorney General Thurlow during debates on the Quebec Act, although he appears to have mistakenly attributed it to the Treaty of Paris (Cavendish, *Debates*, 28 / Simmons and Thomas, *Proceedings*, vol. 4 (1984), 455).

34 John A. Dickinson, assisted by Angélique Da Silva-Gauthier, "Les Sulpiciens au Canada," in Dominique Deslandres, John A. Dickinson, and Ollivier Hubert, eds, *Les Sulpiciens de Montréal: Une histoire de pouvoir et de discrétion, 1657 –2007* (Saint-Laurent: Fides, 2007), 42–6, 54–5; John A. Dickinson, "Seigneurs et proptiétaires: Une logique ecclésisastique de l'économie," in ibid., 179–89; Noël Baillargeon, *Le Séminaire de Québec de 1760 à 1800* (Quebec: Presses de l'Université Laval, 1981), 46–7, 199–203; Colleen Gray, *The Congrégation de Notre-Dame, Superiors, and the Paradox of Power, 1693–1796* (Montreal: McGill-Queen's University Press, 2007), 46–54. For contrasting overviews of the fate of religious communities in the post-Conquest period, see Guy Laperrière, *Histoire des communautés religieuses au Québec* (Montreal: VLB, 2013), 48–57; Denis Vaugeois, "Le sort de l'Église et des communautés religieuses au lendemain de 1760," in Veyssière et al., *1763: Le traité de Paris bouleverse l'Amérique*, 349–61; and Uzzell, "James Murray."

35 Cavendish, *Debates*, and Simmons and Thomas, *Proceedings*, *passim*; Fran-

cis Maseres, *An Account of the Proceedings of the British, and Other Protestant Inhabitants, of the Province of Quebeck* (London: B. White, 1775), 240, 247, and 257.

36 *Observations and Reflections, on An Act Passed in the Year, 1774, for the Settlement of the Province of Quebec ... By a Country Gentleman* (London: J. Stockdale, 1782): 16.

37 Seaman Morley Scott claims there were "numerous instances of its employment" before 1775, but cites only a few high-profile cases: "Chapters in the History of the Law of Quebec," 246 n96. Extant criminal court records suggest that recourse to *habeas corpus ad subjiciendum* before 1775 was infrequent: between 1765 and 1774, only three such writs subsist (Bibliothèque et Archives nationales du Québec, Centre d'archives de Québec, TL18,S1,SS1). A full study nevertheless remains to be done.

38 For example, Maseres, *An Account of the Proceedings of the British*, 236–7.

39 See notably Hilda M. Neatby, *The Administration of Justice under the Quebec Act* (Minneapolis: Minnesota University Press, 1933), 20–1, 67–73, 196–7; F. Murray Greenwood, *Legacies of Fear: Law and Politics in Quebec in the Era of the French Revolution* (Toronto: Osgoode Society for Canadian Legal History and University of Toronto Press, 1993), 24–7; Jean-Marie Fecteau and Douglas Hay, "'Government by Will and Pleasure Instead of Law': Military Justice and the Legal System in Quebec, 1775–83," in F. Murray Greenwood and Barry Wright, eds, *Canadian State Trials*, vol. 1, *Law, Politics, and Security Measures, 1608–1837* (Toronto: Osgoode Society for Canadian Legal History and University of Toronto Press, 1997), 145–59; and Paul D. Halliday, *Habeas Corpus: From England to Empire* (Cambridge: Harvard University Press, 2010), 274–80.

40 Francis Maseres and Peter Livius, *The Case of Peter Du Calvet, Esq. of Montreal in the province of Quebeck* ... (London, 1784), 240–1; petition of Mary Hay to the Commissioners for exercising the office of Chief Justice, 1 May 1781, reproduced in Greenwood and Wright, eds, *Canadian State Trials*, vol. 1, 628.

41 This was also the position of government apologists of the Quebec Act and of English judges (Halliday, *Habeas Corpus*, 275–6, 278).

42 On later suspensions of habeas corpus in Quebec and Lower Canada, see notably Greenwood, *Legacies of Fear*; Jean-Marie Fecteau, F. Murray Greenwood, and Jean-Pierre Wallot, "Sir James Craig's 'Reign of Terror' and Its Impact on Emergency Powers in Lower Canada, 1810–13," in

Greenwood and Wright, eds, *Canadian State Trials*, vol. 1, 323–78; F. Murray Greenwood, "The Montreal Court Martial, 1838–9: Legal and Constitutional Reflections," in F. Murray Greenwood and Barry Wright, eds, *Canadian State Trials*, vol. 2, *Rebellion and Invasion in the Canadas, 1837–1839* (Toronto: Osgoode Society for Canadian Legal History and University of Toronto Press, 2002), 326–9; and Halliday, *Habeas Corpus*, 278–81.

43 Shortt and Doughty, *Documents Relating to the Constitutional History of Canada*, 242–3; Lawson, *The Imperial Challenge*, 70.

44 William Knox, *The Justice and Policy of the Late Act of Parliament, for Making More Effectual Provision for the Government of the Province of Quebec ...* (London: J. Wilkie, 1774), 57–62.

45 Evelyn Kolish, "Imprisonment for Debt in Lower Canada, 1791–1840," *McGill Law Journal* 32, no.3 (1987): 604–9; on the reintroduction of English procedures more generally, see Jean-Maurice Brisson, *La formation d'un droit mixte: l'évolution de la procédure civile de 1774 à 1867* (Montreal: Éditions Thémis, 1986).

46 Neatby, *Administration of Justice*, 208–12; Decroix, Gilles, and Morin, *Les tribunaux et l'arbitrage*, 291–309; Fyson, "The Conquered and the Conqueror," 206–7; and Fyson, "De la common law à la Coutume de Paris."

47 Fyson, *Magistrates, Police, and People*, 243–5, and "Jurys, participation civique et représentation."

48 The text of most ordinances adopted between 1764 and 1791 is available in the *Report on Canadian Archives*, 1913 and 1914–15 (*Sessional Papers* 1914 #29b and 1916 #29a); for the sake of brevity, I have not cited the titles/chapter numbers of individual ordinances.

49 Donald Fyson, "The Canadiens and British Institutions of Local Governance in Quebec, from the Conquest to the Rebellions," in Nancy Christie, ed., *Transatlantic Subjects: Ideas, Institutions, and Social Experience in Post-Revolutionary British North America* (Montreal: McGill-Queen's University Press, 2008), 58–66; Fyson, "La paroisse et l'administration étatique." The 1775–77 re-establishment of the militia itself, however, and of compulsory militia service, had little to do with the Act as such, and does not seem to have been a primary goal of local administrators such as Guy Carleton who helped frame the Quebec Act. Hence, the militia is essentially not mentioned in the Quebec Act debates (Cavendish, *Debates*; and Simmons and Thomas, *Proceedings*, passim). Instead, its restoration was a direct result of the American invasion of 1775. See Gerard M.F. Hartley, "Years of Adjustment: British

Policy and the Canadian Militia, 1760–1787" (MA, Queen's University, 1993), 18–65, and Luc Lépine, "La milice du district de Montréal, 1787–1829: essai d'histoire socio-militaire" (PhD diss., Université du Québec à Montréal, 2005), 66–71.

50 Scott, "Chapters in the History of the Law of Quebec," 162–4; Evelyn Kolish, *Nationalismes et conflits de droits: le débat du droit privé au Québec, 1760–1840* (LaSalle: Hurtubise HMH, 1994), 273–98; Sylvio Normand and Alain Hudon, "Le contrôle des hypothèques secrètes au XIXe siècle: ou la difficile conciliation de deux cultures juridiques et de deux communautés ethniques," *Recueil de droit immobilier* (1990): 171–201. The actual operation of the registry system in place between 1764 and 1775 has never been studied.

51 39 George III c.8. For a broad overview, see Bruce Curtis, "From the Moral Thermometer to Money: Metrological Reform in Pre-Confederation Canada," *Social Studies of Science* 28, no. 4 (1998): 556, 559–62, although he ignores the period from 1775 to 1799. The actual impact of the abrogation of the 1764 ordinance by the Quebec Act, and the regulation of weights and measures up to 1799, remains to be examined. The Montreal justices legislated regulation of weights used on the city market from 1777 (and fined three Canadiens in 1780 for selling meat with unregulated weights), and extended this regulation to the small towns of L'Assomption and William Henry in 1791 (*Quebec Gazette*, 12 June 1777, 3 May 1781; Bibliothèque et Archives nationales du Québec, Centre d'archives de Montréal, TL32,S1,SS11, Quarter Sessions registers, 15 January 1780, 19 April 1780, 14 November 1782, 12 July 1791 and 11 October 1791; Library and Archives Canada RG1 E15A, accounts of fines remitted by the Clerk of the Peace). The Quebec City justices also regulated weights and measures between 1780 and 1783 at least (*Quebec Gazette*, 11 May 1780 and 28 August 1783). On the nature of the justices' regulatory power, see Fyson, *Magistrates, Police, and People*, 23–32.

52 The actual impact of this measure in Quebec in general remains to be studied, but Jean-Philippe Garneau's study of the Côte-de-Beaupré suggests that notaries respected the changing norms, which could thus have a significant impact on young adult Canadiens, for example in the case of those subject to guardianship after the death of their parents: "Droit, famille et pratique successorale: les usages du droit d'une communauté rurale au XVIIIe siècle canadien" (PhD diss., Université du Québec à Montréal, 2003), 140–4, 240–3.

53 On Indigenous peoples in general, see the essay by Alain Beaulieu in this collection; on Indigenous people and the law, see Donald Fyson, "Minority Groups and the Law in Quebec, 1760–1867," in G. Blaine Baker and Donald Fyson (ed.), *Essays in the History of Canadian Law*, vol. 11, *Quebec and the Canadas* (Toronto: Osgoode Society for Canadian Legal History and University of Toronto Press, 2013), 281–290.

3

Choosing between French and English Law: The Legal Origins of the Quebec Act

Michel Morin

In 1774, the Quebec Act revived laws pertaining to "property and civil rights" in New France. It made an exception for testamentary freedom, which had been severely restricted prior to the Conquest, and for lands that had been or would be granted in free and common soccage, an English concept tantamount to full ownership. The Act retained English criminal law, however, and allowed Catholics to hold high-level public positions.[1] Finally, it created a Legislative Council, whose members were appointed by the crown and which could not for this reason impose taxes; furthermore, ordinances prescribing severe punishments or concerning religious issues required the King's approval. This decision was made after extensive reflection on the best way to reform the legal system of "Canada," which France had ceded to Great Britain in 1763. The former French subjects (called Canadiens), nearly all Catholics, considerably outnumbered British-born Protestants. For about three years, the British government hoped that immigration would correct this imbalance. Therefore, as in Ireland or Acadia, only Protestants were allowed to hold important public positions, although practising the Catholic religion remained legal. By way of comparison, the Spanish legal system was preserved in Minorca, which had very few British-born settlers.[2]

Ten years earlier, when the crown promulgated the Royal Proclamation of 1763 as part of the right of Conquest, it created four colonies in territories acquired from France or Spain: Quebec, East and West Florida, and Grenada.[3] Initially, it was assumed that Protestant settlers would rapidly represent the majority of the population.[4] Therefore, the governor was required to convene an elected House of Assembly "so soon as the state and circumstances ... will admit" in each new colony, to encourage its "speedy settling." The House of Assembly, along with the governor and council, would make laws that were as far as possible "agreeable to the Laws of England." The King promised the "Benefit" of these laws, ordering the courts to apply "Law and Equity, as near as may be agreeable" to English laws. The governor's commission required that he enforce English laws, excluding Catholics from the council and other important positions, such as judicial office or assembly membership.[5]

However, since Catholics represented about 95 per cent of the population, governors deemed it inexpedient to hold elections restricted to Protestant candidates. This policy aroused the hostility of newly established British subjects, most of whom were traders or craftsmen.[6] In their view, Protestant subjects were entitled immediately to elect their representatives. They believed that other fundamental rights were being denied to them, such as trial by jury and protection against arbitrary detention through habeas corpus.[7] Meanwhile, members of the military rarely settled in the province and tended to support stronger executive powers and to disdain colonial legislative assemblies. Their relationship with British-born civilians was strained at best.[8] For their part, Francophone elites (seigneurs, lawyers, notaries, merchants, etc.) emphasized their loyalty to the King as new British subjects and complained of religious discrimination in appointments to public positions, high litigation costs, and the apparent repeal of the laws of New France. As Hannah Weiss Muller points out in this volume, these two competing visions of subjecthood were mobilized to achieve specific results; for his part, Christian R. Burset emphasizes that, for colonies in which the majority of the population was not of British descent, "authoritarian Whigs" in London espoused legal pluralism to nip political dissent in the bud, and to ensure economic domination by Great Britain.[9]

From 1763, the British government received numerous reports written by colonial officers, London merchants, and the legal advisers of the crown. Each author had a particular way of addressing problems plaguing Quebec's legal system.[10] Obviously this required a comparison between the laws of New France and England. At first blush, the authors of these reports appear to have taken a positive view of the law of New France, save for some aspects of its criminal law, and to have promoted its continuance. Historians generally assume that the British government expected its decision to maintain the laws of New France would be long-term or permanent.[11] By relying as much as possible on original documents, some hitherto unknown, this essay will show that, up to the final stages of the drafting of the Quebec Act, it was assumed that the most important parts of French law would be repealed or rewritten, and that the laws in force prior to the Conquest would eventually disappear.

Many reports sought to break the attachment of Francophone judges, lawyers, and notaries to French legal culture; for these authors, relying on French judicial precedent before the courts or in judicial decisions should be forbidden. However, the English attorney general vetoed that idea in 1774. Throughout these discussions, writers always considered seigneurial rights and privileges untouchable; instead, they sought to overhaul family law, contract law, and extra-contractual liability (akin to torts). Some attempted to combine substantial rules of French law with common-law procedural rules, such as trial by jury. It soon appeared that mixing different legal systems risked creating untold problems and further resentment among the peoples of Quebec. Given the need to immediately secure the support of the local population in the event of a confrontation between Great Britain and its American colonies, the metropolitan government directed the Legislative Council established by the Quebec Act to introduce English private law for specific matters. The projected introduction of these rules stands in stark contrast with the magnanimous image of tolerance generally associated with the Quebec Act.

This essay will examine the various combinations of French and English law that were discussed prior to the adoption of the Quebec Act, and their eventual discarding. It will commence with a review of the problems that followed the implementation of the Royal Proclamation (I). Next, it will examine various recommendations made between 1766 and 1769, mostly by Quebec officials (II). It will then present the opinions of law officers of the crown in London (III) and various drafts of the bill read before parliament in May of 1774 (IV).[12] In conclusion, much like the contribution of Christian R. Burset in this volume, we will argue that, apart from securing the support of the majority of the population in Quebec, the British government wanted to discourage turbulent freeholders from establishing themselves in the Great Lakes area, and to channel the fur trade through a colony that would remain firmly under its control.

I. UNCERTAINTIES FLOWING FROM THE ROYAL PROCLAMATION OF 1763

The Royal Proclamation of 1763 and the court system established in 1764 generated much uncertainty in Quebec.[13] Courts, especially the King's Bench, generally applied English law. However, if the amount in dispute exceeded ten pounds, the plaintiff could at his discretion elect to sue in the Common Pleas, which relied on "Equity." In practice, this term was considered synonymous with the law of New France; a full-blown Court of Chancery was also created to apply the technical rules of English "Equity." Yet, contrary to what has been assumed until recently, litigants did not boycott courts, not even in family matters.[14]

The terms of the Capitulation of Montreal (1760) further complicated the situation. Although Amherst refused to guarantee the continuance of the "Laws and usages" of New France, he did promise to respect the "property and possession" of individuals, including their seigneurial rights.[15] In 1763, the Treaty of Paris expressly authorized French subjects to sell their property to British subjects, some of whom subsequently bought seigneuries.[16] Among the buyers were military officers who, coming from a country where landed property was a source of both prestige and wealth, had obvious cultural affinities with many Canadian seigneurs.[17] At the time, a well-established legal principle held that "articles of capitulation [...] and treaties are sacred and inviolable, according to their true intent and meaning."[18] British lawyers and political thinkers generally believed that property was an inalienable right that governments were required to honour.[19] In the case of Quebec, these principles warranted recognizing an implicit exception to the Royal Proclamation for seigneurial property.

In 1764, the grand jury of Quebec denounced the new regime, although the jury's Francophone members soon declared that they did not understand the presentment they had been asked to sign, because it was written in English. In a separate section, Protestant members referred to the English laws that barred Catholics from all public positions and professions. Subsequently, they claimed that they had simply wished to ensure that Protestant litigants be judged by jurors of the same religion.[20] In 1766, a new ordinance provided that jurors should be of the same religious persuasion as the litigants, or, if they differed, that there should be an equal number of Catholics and Protestants. This ordinance also authorized Canadien lawyers to appear before any court.[21] In Grenada as well, around this time, the religious issue turned explosive when the government decided to grant Catholics entry to the assembly and the council. Newspapers throughout the empire fervently denounced this innovation.[22]

Further reforms included the abolition of the much-criticized civil jurisdiction of the justices of the peace, the streamlining of judicial fees, and the curtailing of imprisonment for debt.[23] In addition, almost all judges, as well as the attorney general, were to understand French from 1766 onwards.[24] These reforms alleviated many of the concerns raised by the Francophone population, though the memory of these problems lingered on. Furthermore, the absence of an elected legislature created financial problems, since no taxes could be imposed. The government attempted to collect duties that had been imposed by the French king, arguing they were now due to the new sovereign, but Anglophone juries dismissed the proceedings.[25]

From 1764 to 1773, residents of Quebec sent numerous petitions to London.[26] Anglophones demanded a House of Assembly. Francophones protested religious discrimination, the high cost of justice, and the repeal of the laws of New France. Some initially supported the request for an assembly, but changed their minds when it became clear that Catholics would not be allowed to sit. On this basis, Carleton argued that an assembly was not a priority for them.[27] It can therefore be seen that public debates in Quebec centred on the administration of justice, the absence of an assembly with taxing powers, and the preservation of the laws of New France. From 1766 onward, many reports addressed these issues.

II. THE REPORTS OF 1766–69

Fowler Walker, a London lawyer and lobbyist for Quebec merchants, soon defined the terms of the debate pertaining to the colony's legal system. For him, the Royal Proclamation had introduced English law in its entirety; only colonial legislation could change the situation.[28] From 1764, the Governor's Council adopted ordinances without having overtly received the power to do so.[29] In March 1766, Walker made certain suggestions to the chancellor, Robert Henley, Earl of Northington.[30] Walker argued that English law was not suitable for a population whose spirit, education, and religion differed so completely from those of the British people.[31] Yet in light of the Proclamation, the colony was entitled to their "Benefit," which included lenient rules of criminal law and effective protection of personal liberty and property. Therefore, the administration of justice in the province and the rules concerning inheritance and land law needed to be as beneficial as those of England.[32]

Walker considered that a new "code" should specify how "far the laws of Canada run."[33] As for English criminal law, the "justice & equity of its general principles," the limited grounds for pre-trial detention, and the impartiality observed in the infliction of punishment would inspire "reverence" in the minds of Canadiens.[34] For other subjects, "the laws of Canada" should be collected, digested, and classified "under the heads of the laws of England." For personal property, the two systems probably differed more "in the mode of bringing litigation to a decision" than in their substantial principles.[35] For real property, those parts of the ancient laws compatible "with the genius and spirit of the English laws should perhaps be adopted"; the rest "should not be wantonly abrogated but rather corrected & alter'd with much care & deliberation." In this regard, it was "difficult to determine" whether English rules of procedure should be introduced "in all cases without any exception."[36] Though Canadiens might object to their "tediousness" – especially for small claims – they needed to consider, in Montesquieu's words, that these delays were "the price which they pay for & the Criterion of their Liberty."[37] According to Walker, the continuance of Canadian laws needed to remain quite limited, if not exceptional.

Prior to sailing for the province in April 1766, the newly appointed attorney general for Quebec, Francis Maseres, had determined that the British parliament should either declare which parts of Canada's laws would remain in force or empower a legislative council to "revise and reduce them into writing, and enact such of them as shall be found beneficial."[38] That same month, an opinion written by Attorney General Charles Yorke and Solicitor General William de Grey challenged the view that the "usages and Customs of Canada" had been entirely abrogated by the Royal Proclamation. In their view, such reasoning erroneously assumed that the King had intended to impose "with the rough hand of a Conqueror […] new, unnecessary and arbitrary Rules, especially in the Titles to Land" and in matters of successions to, or alienation of, immovable property; this would "tend to confound and subvert rights" instead of simply securing "Lives, Libertys [*sic*] and propertys [*sic*] with more certainty than in former times."[39]

They believed that for contracts and "*wrongs* proper to be compensated by damages [...] the substantial *maxims* of Law and Justice are every where the same," though procedural and evidentiary rules might vary. Therefore, if they relied on these maxims, Quebec judges could not "materially err, either against the Laws of England, or the antient Customs of Canada."[40] Introducing the technical "English Law of real Estates," however, would "occasion infinite confusion and Injustice." Instead, British subjects who purchased lands ought to conform to local rules, "as they do in particular parts of the Realm. [*sic*] or in the other Dominions of the Crown."[41] In 1766, the cabinet decided that a local ordinance should restore New France's law of immovable property. However, Chancellor Northington believed that this change necessitated the intervention of parliament and that a code of the relevant laws should be available before such a decision could be made.[42] His successor, Charles Pratt, Earl of Camden, took the same position. On 28 August 1767, the cabinet ordered that Governor Guy Carleton, Chief Justice William Hey, and Attorney General Francis Maseres prepare reports on the administration of justice and the complaints of Canadiens.

These reports have been summarized many times, with the exception of Maseres's initial draft, which contained a nuanced and penetrating analysis of New France's legal system.[43] The authors agreed on many points. The law of New France concerning immovable property, successions, and matrimonial regimes needed to continue in force, but only temporarily. As a first step, these reports advocated that other rules of private law be modified gradually by local ordinances and rendered similar to English law. Next, property and family law would be reformed. At that point, citing French judgments or law books before the courts would be prohibited, so as to avoid the perpetuation of "Sentiments inconsistent with the Idea of British Subjects in General," such as "the intrinsic excellence" of the French laws and the "Happiness" enjoyed under the French government.[44] Otherwise, Canadiens would "be inclined to think *that* government to be best, under which those laws could most ably be administered, which is that of the French King."[45]

Though Governor Carleton wanted to restore the private law of New France in its entirety, he agreed that it should be severed from its French roots after having been restated and revised by local ordinances.[46] As for criminal law, Carleton and Hey insisted on entirely retaining English law, while Maseres recommended adopting a code combining elements of both systems, notably the procedural guarantees of the common law. These arguments are generally similar to those made by Yorke and De Grey and differ strikingly from those of Fowler Walker, probably because the latter failed to appreciate the difficulties that marked the introduction of English private law in Quebec. In any event, the debate soon moved back to London, where Maseres returned in 1769, followed by Carleton in 1770 and by Hey in 1773.

III. THE LONDON PROPOSALS AND REPORTS, 1771–74

Back in England, Maseres wrote and arranged the printing of various draft bills or documents dealing with religious issues, the official creation of a legislative council composed of Protestant members, the law of succession, and similar matters. Through his works, we learn that François-Joseph Cugnet, an influential lawyer and seigneur who translated legal documents for the government, believed that the introduction of English criminal law was unavoidable and Canadiens approved of habeas corpus.[47] This comment – coming from a Francophone jurist – certainly lent support to those ideas.

In 1771, the crown's legal officers were required to recommend changes to Quebec's judicial system. The final version of a report by Solicitor General Alexander Wedderburn, dated 6 December 1772, no longer survives, but a transcript remains extant.[48] In Wedderburn's opinion, allowing Catholics to sit in the assembly "would be an inexhaustible source of dissension and opposition" between them and the old British subjects.[49] Furthermore, enfranchising every landowner would "be disgusting and injurious to every men [*sic*] of condition in the Province, who are accustomed to feel a very considerable difference" between them and their tenants. "Nor would it be beneficial to men of inferior rank; for [...] raising them above the level of their superiors, except by the efforts of their own industry, is pernicious."[50] None of the reports disagreed with this view, though the attorney general expressed no opinion on the matter.

Wedderburn believed that the "prejudices" of Canadiens and of newly established British subjects could not be "entirely disregarded," considering that the customs of the former had "become a part of their nature." Hence, they had a "claim in justice" to their "ancient laws regarding private rights" to the extent that it "is not inconsistent with the principles of the new government."[51] Yet many of these rules differed little from English law, so their replacement would hardly be noticed.[52] The same was not true of immovable property and intestate successions; local rules could very well be preserved for purposes of dealing with such issues, as was the case with English manors. But other rules were outdated and needed to be reformed by parliament or the provincial council. Examples included allowing lands held directly from the crown to be commuted into freehold tenure and imposing English law on spouses and their children, unless their marriage contract expressly provided for the application of the old law. Ideally, a restatement of the law of New France should be the only text recognized by the courts, but if its authority was doubtful, then selected articles should specify which "usages" in force prior to the Conquest should be observed.

Wedderburn believed that French criminal law was composed of "arbitrary and uncertain" definitions and procedures that were "incompatible with an English Government of any sort." Indeed, the difference between the "Arbitrary Severity" of this system and the "certainty and Mildness" of English criminal law made up for "the necessary Evils of Conquest."[53] Wedderburn therefore harboured the "national prejudice" denounced earlier by Maseres: he was "persuaded of the excellency" of his system over the laws "of all other nations."[54] But he agreed that some standard punishments, such as burning the hands and confiscating the personal property of persons who had been exempted from the death penalty after receiving "benefit of clergy" were clearly unsuitable for Quebec; similarly, theft below the value of five pounds should not remain a capital crime.[55] Furthermore, until one could be "better assured" of the "fidelity and attachment" of Canadiens, the writ of habeas corpus should not be reinforced by the procedural guarantees introduced by English legislation adopted in the 1679 Habeas Corpus Act.[56]

In view of the widespread criticism of civil procedure in France, Wedderburn refused to admit that the administration of justice in New France was less costly and speedier than in England.[57] For contracts and the reparation of civil injuries, the "principles of Natural Justice – adopted in the Law of England and common to the Law of all countries" – could substitute for French law.[58] As for trial by jury in civil matters, no one could complain if it was granted at the request of either party.[59] In the end, the courts should apply "the Customs of the Province, together with the Laws of England, the principles of natural Justice and Equity in those cases which do not depend upon local

Institutions" (i.e., customs) – a far cry from a full restoration of the private law of New France.[60]

The report of Advocate General James Marriott, written in 1773, generally agreed with Wedderburn on the fate of the province's old laws.[61] For him, criminal law automatically applied after the Conquest, a questionable statement to say the least.[62] Combining substantive and procedural rules taken from different systems seemed absurd to him.[63] Following the English example, he argued that tax cases in Quebec should not be tried by "interested juries" who would "suffer to escape" persons who defrauded revenue collection.[64] An act of parliament should restore the law of New France with respect to immovable property, successions, matrimonial regimes, and contracts, but the parties would then be allowed to adopt English law in their agreements. Furthermore, an abstract of the "custom of Canada" would be annexed to the Act, becoming the "sole rule" of decision, in order to "erase from the minds of the Canadian subjects, their ideas of veneration for the edicts of their late sovereign, and for the *arrêts* of the tribunals of France."[65] The usefulness of an "act of habeas corpus" would be doubtful during a future war against France, for the governor and its council would probably be authorized to suspend it in the event of armed conflicts.[66]

Attorney General Edward Thurlow's report, dated 22 January 1773, shattered this consensus.[67] In a section not yet published, he recalled the decision of the British government to collect some duties that it considered to have survived both the Conquest and the Royal Proclamation.[68] He confessed to being unable to understand how any part of the "laws of Canada" could have survived the latter document.[69] In his view, however, a "conqueror" would be well advised to leave his new subjects "in the habit of obedience of their accustomed laws," instead of demanding "a new obedience to laws unheard of before." This was true for criminal as well as civil laws.[70] Some changes to prior laws were "essentially necessary" to establish the authority of the new sovereign, for instance those concerned with "crimes against the state, religion, revenue."[71] Yet "creating a harmony and uniformity in the several parts of the empire" was an "unattainable" and "useless" goal, as was the attempt to strip "from a lawyer's argument all resort to the learned decisions of the Parliament of Paris, for fear of keeping up the historical idea of the origin" of the laws of New France. Thus the ultimate goal identified in previous reports – the gradual elimination of French legal culture – was called into question. Indeed, it was not even mentioned during the drafting of the Quebec Act.

IV. DRAFTING OF THE QUEBEC ACT, 1773–74

Following the Boston Tea Party (16 December 1773), the British parliament adopted five so-called "Intolerable Acts" that were intended to subdue the American colonies, and these included the Quebec Act, passed on 22 June.[72] The expansion of the province's boundaries (from Labrador to the Ohio River), the creation of an appointed legislative council, the official recognition of the Catholic religion, and the repeal of English property law and civil law created a firestorm.[73] In both Houses of Parliament, opposition members asserted that the government's true objective was to attract Catholic immigrants to Quebec in order to raise a powerful army that would be used against rebellious colonies.[74] The debate has raged ever since.[75]

The opinion of Lord Lyttleton seems to capture the cabinet's thinking: if a revolt did occur, Lyttleton declared that he would be happy to see "the loyal inhabitants of Canada ... co-operate with the rest of the Empire" and act as a "check to those fierce fanatic spirits" whose true purpose was "the demolition of regal authority" and "the setting up an absolute independent Republic.[76] Similarly, in 1775, Lord North declared before the Commons that, even though he "had not the least doubt this dispute would end speedily, happily and without bloodshed," if it became necessary to use force against the "refractory colonies," it would be "right, proper and necessary" to arm and employ in that service "the Roman Catholicks of Canada."[77] However, if one considers that work on the Quebec Act began in the summer of 1773, the events in America do not appear to have inspired its adoption, although they may have hastened it; overall, military considerations appear to have played only a minor role.[78]

How did the Act take shape? In 1773, creating a House of Assembly was out of the question, with or without Catholic members.[79] This meant that a legislative council needed to be created, though the imposition of taxes would be left to parliament; indeed, legislation to that effect was enacted soon after the adoption of the Quebec Act.[80] Various undated documents provide a general idea of how the remaining issues were gradually solved.[81] A memorandum cursorily listed the changes required "to restore the old Law and Constitution" of New France: the court system should as far as possible imitate the former one; capital offences should be tried by juries; torturing the accused to extract confessions, and execution by breaking wheel, ought both to be abolished; the "Privilege of the Common Law Writ of Habeas Corpus" was to be granted. Essentially, the former law would be revived, except for some revolting aspects of the criminal law, with the addition of some common-law procedural guarantees for the accused.[82]

A first draft would simply let the future council decide which part of the former laws should be restored, but this idea seems to have been rapidly abandoned.[83] The second draft, completed on 2 March 1774, repealed the Royal Proclamation and every ordinance or commission made or granted under its authority, a provision repeated in subsequent drafts and in the Quebec Act.[84] All the subjects "of and in" the Province of Quebec were granted the right to enjoy the "Property, Laws, Customs and Usages" recognized prior to the Conquest, to the extent that this was consistent "with their allegiance" to the King "and subjection to the Crown and Parliament of Great Britain." Chief Justice Hey objected strenuously to such vague wording and pointed out that the consequences would be unclear for British subjects newly established in the Province.[85] The reformation of the former laws was left to the council.

This draft also attempted to implement Thurlow's rather vague suggestion that laws on religion or on crimes against the state needed to be adapted to British sovereignty; it also reflected Maseres's criticism of both French and English criminal law.[86] Thus "the use of torture and those severe punishments to which the Inhabitants were formerly exposed" were formally abolished. Cases of High Treason or Misprision of High Treason were to be judged according to the "Laws and Statutes of Great Britain." For capital crimes recognized in New France, the accused would be "tried and acquitted or convicted and punished according to the Laws of England," including benefit of clergy, but without burning of the hand.[87]

Wedderburn found "very strange" the idea of "a Criminal Code in which for Treason the Law of England is followed; for other capital offences the Law of France (which avoids all definition) is to define the Crime, and the Law of England to prescribe the punishment and the mode of Trial," and, for misdemeanours, French rules on the "Crime [...] Trial and punishment" applied, including the "arbitrary punishment of cutting out Tongues, slitting noses &^{ce} [*sic*]."[88] Defending such a proposal before parliament must have sounded nightmarish, and no more was heard of French criminal laws afterwards. This may explain why Thurlow declared before the House of Commons that his own inclination would have been to consult "the French habit to a much greater extent."[89] For his part, Wedderburn frequently relied on the opinion of Chief Justice Hey, who believed that Canadiens were "in general very sensible to the advantages they derive" from the new system of criminal law.[90] Before the House of Commons, Hey stated bluntly: "I cannot conceive them so stupid as to wish for the French [criminal] law."[91] For Wedderburn, as for Hey, restoring this system was simply unthinkable.

This third draft also granted to Canadiens the right to "hold and enjoy" their property, possessions, customs, and usages as if the Royal Proclamation had not been enacted – again, to the extent that this was compatible with their allegiance to the king and subjection to the crown and parliament. But all cases concerning the "Property & Civil Rights" of either the new or the old subjects were to be decided solely according to Canadian law and ordinances made by the new legislative council.[92] At this point, Hey criticized a provision the exact wording of which seems to have disappeared, but which might have exempted newly arrived British subjects from Canadian law.[93] This tended to create an "Exception as large as the Rule; and leave still in doubt, whether in a matter of civil Right the Canadian or the English Law where they differ together with the form & mode of Proceeding, shall have the preference."[94]

Hey buttressed his argument with an example taken from a case he had heard in Quebec. It involved a "mortgage" granted by the Custom of Paris to masons, carpenters, and artificers, which was enforceable despite a "hundred mesne assignments," notwithstanding prior or subsequent encumbrances. An action of this kind was heard in the Court of Common Pleas in 1767, but subsequently reviewed by the King's Bench on a writ of certiorari. The plaintiffs then obtained an injunction from the Court of Chancery forbidding the latter court to hear the case.[95] The ultimate result is unknown, but because of this jurisdictional quagmire, plaintiffs were in dire straits. Lacking funds and being ignorant of the English language and of English law, they were unable to pursue their claims, although they had entered into a contract in French, according to the usages and customs of the colony. Meanwhile, they were threatened with imprisonment for debt.[96]

Relying on the same provision he had earlier criticized, Hey imagined that the owner of the house, who was being sued by the artificers, could raise the following objection:

> Every *Privilege Protection & advantage of what Nature soever or kind* that I am intitled to by the Laws & Constitutions of [...] England, are expressly reserved to me, amongst which I reckon the Tryal by Jury as an Eminent One. Let these men bring their Ejectment upon their mortgage Title & let the trespass be enquired into by a Jury according to the good old forms & usages of the realm of England, & not by Laws & in a mode of Proceeding unknown & not used there & which derogate from the Rights of a british subject.[97]

According to Hey, there was no way to escape this dilemma. The intent of the provision seemed to be that Canadian law would become "the general law of the country" and "govern british as well as canadian property." Therefore "any reservation with respect either to the Laws" or their administration "in favour of british subjects" needed to be "clearly ascertained." The proposed clause, however, would "either operate nothing, or go to the destruction of the whole."[98] Pursuant to these arguments, the government abandoned the idea of combining the fundamental rights of British subjects and the private law of New France. As Hannah Weiss Muller points out in this volume, the two were not considered incompatible. Indeed, the prime minister, Lord North, mentioned in the Commons in 1775 that "he did not approve of juries in civil cases."[99]

Hey's example showed that, whether or not the principles of the law of contract or extra-contractual liability were identical in civilized countries, the outcome of a case could well depend on differences between procedural and evidentiary rules. Here was a case where the enforcement of an immovable real right created by a contract could be thwarted by an English mode of trial (assuming jurors would sympathize with a merchant who had no way of knowing about the privilege held by tradesmen on the house he bought). Was the issue about property, contract, or procedure? Using any of these categories to determine the applicable law would obviously create practical problems.

Like its predecessors, the third draft was silent on habeas corpus, which was considered a civil remedy. This omission is not surprising considering the vigorous opposition of Wedderburn and Marriott to its recognition. During parliamentary debates, opposition members argued that this omission would allow the revival of the infamous *lettres de cachet* (a document signed by the French King that ordered the detention of a person without specifying cause).[100] This draft also maintained English criminal law in its entirety, despite the objections voiced by some seigneurs.[101] Again, the arguments of Wedderburn and Hey seem to have carried the day, with the support of Carleton and François-Joseph Cugnet, who sent various documents on the subject to Blackstone, and he in turn forwarded them to the minister in 1774.[102]

Cugnet also asserted that Canadiens greatly favoured testamentary freedom.[103] This probably explains why the third draft recognized this principle.[104] Undoubtedly this solution was considered preferable to a system in which a choice made in a marriage contract or upon the alienation of land would determine the applicable legal system.[105] Cugnet also requested the creation of an Assembly in which Catholics could sit; otherwise, the Legislative Council should be denied the power to modify the private law of New France. This shows that he understood the threat posed by such a power to the preservation of French legal culture in the colony.[106] He also provided a list of fourteen law books that would provide common-law judges with a working knowledge of the laws applicable to property and civil rights.[107]

Finally, the third draft restored the right of Catholic curates to collect tithes. A letter written by Lord Mansfield also convinced the cabinet at the last minute that a special oath of allegiance should be adopted for Catholics to dispense with the Test Acts, which effectively excluded them from public positions.[108] Prior to this change, the drafts would have let the government decide the issue when granting the governor's commission. This prompted the City of London to denounce the establishment of an "idolatrous and bloody" religion.[109]

Trial by jury was bound to disappear in civil and commercial matters because of the restoration of French law – but also to avoid having juries adjudicating tax claims.[110] Like the suppression of habeas corpus and the recognition of the Catholic religion, this proved to be a contentious issue, both before parliament and in the colonies.[111] The "British merchants trading to Quebeck" requested sufficient time to withdraw their effects and to have their claims adjudicated by a jury, should English law be repealed.[112] The City of London protested the suppression of this "sacred part" of English law,[113] which it considered a "wonderful effort of human wisdom."[114] According to this view, British subjects were being denied the benefit of English law as promised in the Royal Proclamation. But in the House of Commons, Lord North retorted that the legislative council would be in a much better position to decide the extent to which English modes of trial could be combined with the rules of French substantive law.[115]

CONCLUSION

The bill finally introduced in parliament in 1774, having undergone very few substantial modifications, gave precedence to two different national legal systems, one for private-law and one for criminal-law issues. This set the stage for reforms that would be undertaken by the Legislative Council. The government abandoned the idea of restoring only the property and family law of New France, as well as various attempts to combine French substantive rules with common-law procedural rights. Following Thurlow's strong protest, it viewed severing the links between the private law of New France and French legal literature as unnecessary and illusory; until then, this had been considered an essential component of future reforms. An exception was made to guarantee testamentary freedom, on the assumption that it enjoyed widespread support in Quebec.

In January 1775, instructions to the governor requested the council to consider whether Quebec's new legal system should include habeas corpus and the English law of contracts and torts, in whole or in part.[116] Thus the government still intended to merge parts of the two systems, though doing this from across the Atlantic appeared impracticable. Only through the vagaries of history did this legal dualism become an essential feature of Quebec's distinct identity. Difficulties continued until the 1960s; legislation often employed English models or terminology in civil-law matters, while some judges relied on common-law concepts or precedents, especially in respect of contracts and extra-contractual liability.[117] Yet, as we have seen, these two subjects were hardly discussed prior to the adoption of the Quebec Act.

In the end, the government prioritized the commercial interests and security of the British Empire, most notably by eliminating habeas corpus and trial by jury in civil matters, withdrawing its promise to create an assembly and imposing taxes through parliament.[118] Apparently the interests of Quebec merchants did not carry much weight, given the imminent confrontation with their counterparts in other colonies. However, the new boundaries of the province served the interests of those involved in whale or seal hunting on the North Shore of the St Lawrence River, and in the fur trade in the northern and western parts of the province. At the very least, proximity to the seat of government represented an advantage over southern competitors, especially Albany merchants, who imported New England rum.[119] Moreover, in 1774 the British parliament imposed a tax of three pence per gallon for brandy or spirits manufactured in England, six pence for rum or spirits imported from the British West Indies, nine for rum or spirits imported from other British colonies in America, and one shilling for foreign liquor.[120] This clearly encouraged the fur trade in Quebec and curtailed the production of rum by southern neighbours. As Christian R. Burset reminds us in this volume, Great Britain still believed that colonies should export staples and refrain from producing commodities.[121]

A similar point can be made about the seigniorial regime. British officials prided themselves on respecting property rights held before the Conquest. In their view, however, this tenure also ensured "Subordination, from the first to the lowest."[122] Though he would later be extremely critical of Quebec seigneurs, Maseres shared this view in 1766. His praise of seigniorial jurisdictions no doubt applied to the whole system. For him, they "preserved a reasonable and moderate subordination of the freeholders to their respective Seigniors, productive of respect on the one side, and affection on the other, and which is extremely consonant to the constitution of every species of monarchical Government."[123] He continued:

> The levelling spirit, which is the effect of a total want of distinction of ranks in the State, or a confusion of them [...] has a natural tendency to produce envy, avarice, luxury, and faction [...] The former of these causes seems at present to produce these unhappy consequences in the English plantations in North America, and the latter in Great Britain itself.

Carleton made the point clearly. The "British Form of government, never will produce the same Fruits as at Home, chiefly, because it is impossible for the Dignity of the Throne to be represented in the American Forests"; "a popular Assembly, which preserves it's full Vigor, and in a Country where all Men appear nearly upon a Level, must give a strong Bias to Republican Principles."[124] In 1771, the British government espoused those views when it authorized Carleton to grant lands "in Fief or Seigneurie."[125]

In 1774, Lord Hillsborough objected to a clause of the Quebec Act that authorized the granting of lands in free and common soccage. For him, the French mode of tenure was "the most fit" in the circumstances.[126] He convinced the government to suppress the clause that would have allowed seigneuries held directly from the crown to be commuted into free and common soccage.[127] As Carleton explained, this "Tenure [...] gives the Crown great power over the Seigneur," which would no longer be the case after such commutation. This regime was still considered preferable to freehold tenure in the 1780s. Much to their astonishment, the Loyalists who had resettled within the Province of Quebec, mostly near lakes Ontario and Erie, discovered that they held lands directly from the British king under a French seigneurial tenure.[128]

Lord Dartmouth, the secretary of state for the colonies, believed that, in the areas situated west and north of the Ohio River, "nothing can more effectually tend to discourage" British settlements than this form of tenure.[129] In 1775, Lord Camden criticized the creation of "an eternal barrier [...] intended to be placed, like the Chinese wall, against the further extension of civil liberty and the Protestant religion."[130] Apart from ensuring the subordination of Canadiens, then, this tenure was expected to close off the territories of Indigenous peoples to settlement. Unable to get rid of freeholders, the government decided to eliminate freehold tenure. Controlling land regimes and access to territories was accordingly the overarching concern of the Quebec Act; the legal system governing criminal, civil, and commercial trials paled in comparison and could be tinkered with at a later date.

NOTES

This chapter summarizes Michel Morin, "Les débats concernant le droit français et le droit anglais antérieurement à l'adoption de l'*Acte de Québec* de 1774," *La Revue de droit de l'Université de Sherbrooke – RDUS* 44 (2014): 259–306. The author would like to thank for their comments Mr Arnaud Decroix, Professors Jean Leclair and Han-Ru Zhou, and the contributors to the current volume who participated in the 2014 workshop organized by the editors. Remaining errors or omissions are his own.

1 Freedom of worship was also guaranteed, as was the obligation of Catholics to pay tithe to their curates. However, important issues concerning the bishop and religious communities remained: Michel Morin, "De la reconnaissance officielle à la tolérance des religions: l'état civil et les empêchements de mariage de 1628 à nos jours," in Jean-François Gaudreault-Desbiens, ed., *Le droit, la religion et le "raisonnable"* (Montreal: Éditions Thémis, 2009), 53–91. For the complex history of lands granted in free and common soccage, see J.E.C. Brierley, "The Co-existence of Legal Systems in Quebec: 'Free and Common Soccage' in Canada's 'Pays de Droit Civil,'" *Cahiers de Droit* 20 (1979): 277.

2 See Peter Marshall, "The Incorporation of Quebec in the British Empire," in Virginia Bever Platt and David Curtis Skaggs (eds), *Of Mother Country and Plantations: Proceedings of the Twenty-seventh Conference in Early American History* (Bowling Green: Bowling Green State University Press, 1971), 43–63; Pierre Tousignant, "L'incorporation de la province de Québec dans l'Empire britannique, 1763–91 – Ire partie de la Proclamation royale du Canada à l'Acte de Québec," in George Brown, Marcel Trudel, and André Vachon (eds), *Dictionnaire biographique du Canada*, vol. 4 (Sainte-Foy/Toronto: Presses de l'Université Laval/University of Toronto Press, 1980), xxxiv; Stephen Conway, "The Consequences of the Conquest: Quebec and British Politics, 1760–1774," in Philip Buckner and John G. Reid (eds), *Revisiting 1759: The Conquest of Canada in Historical Perspective* (Toronto: University of Toronto Press, 2012), 141–65; Heather Welland, "Commercial Interests and Political Allegiance: The Origins of the Quebec Act," in *Revisiting 1759*, ed. Buckner and Reid, 166–89; Hannah Weiss Muller, *Subjects and Sovereigns, Bonds of Belonging in the Eighteenth-century Empire* (New York, Oxford University Press, 2017), chapter 3.

3 *Campbell* v. *Hall*, 1 Cowp. 204, 98 ER 1048 (KB, 1774); Adam Shortt and Arthur G Doughty (eds), *Documents Relating to the Constitutional History of Canada, 1759–1791*, 2nd ed. (Ottawa: J. de L. Taché, 1918 [hereafter *CD. I*]), 522.

4 *Proclamation royale*, 1763, in LRC (1985), App. II, no. 1, or *CD. I*, 163.

5 *CD. I*, 173, at 174–5. Many lower-ranked positions could be held by Catholics: Donald Fyson, "Les Canadiens et le Serment du Test," in Sophie Imbeault, Denys Vaugeois, and Laurent Veyssière (eds), *1763: Le traité de Paris bouleverse l'Amérique* (Quebec: Septentrion, 2013), 272.

6 See for instance Karl David Milobar, "The Origins of British-Quebec Merchant Ideology: New France, the British Atlantic, and the Constitutional Periphery, 1720–1770," *Journal of Imperial and Constitutional History* 24, no. 3 (1996): 264–390.

7 See David Milobar, "Quebec Reform, the British Constitution, and the Atlantic Empire,1774–1775," in *Parliamentary History: Parliament and the Atlantic Empire*, ed. Philip Lawson, 65–88 (Edinburgh: Edinburgh University Pretss, 1995); P.J. Marshall, *The Making and Unmaking of Empires: Britain, India, and America c.1750–1783* (Oxford: Oxford University Press, 2005); Jack P. Greene, *The Constitutional Origins of the American Revolution* (New York: Cambridge University Press, 2010), 50–5; Jack P. Greene, "1759: The Perils of Success", in Buckner and Reid, *Revisiting 1759*, 95–114; Paul D. Halliday, *Habeas Corpus: From England to Empire* (Cambridge, MA: Belknap Press, 2010).

8 Douglas Hay, "Civilians Tried in Military Courts: Quebec, 1759–1764," in *Canadian State Trials. Law, Politics, and Security Measures, 1608–1837*, ed. F.M. Greenwood and B. Wright, 114–28 (Toronto: University of Toronto Press, 1996); Jean-Marie Fecteau and Douglas Hay, "'Government by Will and Pleasure Instead of Law': Military Justice and the Legal System of Quebec, 1775–1783" in ibid. at 136.

9 See also H. Weiss Muller, *Subjects and Sovereigns*, chapter 4, n3.

10 On the various political factions in Great Britain at the time, see Christian Burset's chapter in this volume.

11 The issue has often been studied, but the literature seldom looks at private and criminal law issues simultaneously: André Morel, "La réception du droit criminel anglais au Québec (1760–1892)," *RJT* 13 (1978): 449–541; Jean-Marie Fecteau, *Un nouvel ordre des choses: La pauvreté, le crime, l'Etat au Québec, de la fin du XVIIIe siècle à 1840* (Outremont: VLB Éditeur, 1989), 88–97; Evelyn Kolish, *Nationalismes et conflits de droits: Le débat du droit privé au Québec, 1760–1840* (Ville LaSalle: Hurtubise, 1994), 29–43. On the Quebec Act, see among others Pierre Tousignant, "La genèse et l'avènement de l'acte constitutionnel de 1791" (PhD diss., Université de Montréal, 1971); Hilda Neatby, *Quebec: The Revolutionary Age, 1760–1791* (Toronto: McClelland and Stewart, 1966); Philip Lawson, *The Imperial Challenge: Quebec and Britain in the American Revolution* (Montreal and Kingston: McGill-Queen's University Press, 1989); Karl David Milobar, "The Constitutional Development of Quebec from the Time of the French Regime to the Canada Act of 1791" (PhD diss., University of London, 1990); Jacques-Yvan Morin and José Woehrling, *Les constitutions du Canada et du Québec du régime français à nos jours* (Montreal: Thémis, 1992). On the transformation of the legal system in the aftermath of the Conquest, see the thoughtful synthesis of Donald Fyson, "Legal Pluralism, Hybridization, and the Uses of Everyday Criminal Law in Quebec, 1760–1867," in *The Uses of*

Justice in Global Perspective, 1600–1900, ed. Manon van der Heijden, Griet Vermeesch, and Jaco Zuijderduijn, 198–218, at 201–6 (London, Routledge, 2019).

12 In the eighteenth century, the attorney general represented the crown in important cases and gave it legal advice; the solicitor general seconded him in his duties. Both were members of parliament and kept a private practice. The advocate general represented the king before admiralty and ecclesiastical courts and provided him with legal advice as well. John Baker, *Introduction to English Legal History*, 3rd ed. (London: Butterworths, 1990), 188 and 194; Paul Romney, *Mr Attorney: The Attorney General for Ontario in Court, Cabinet, and Legislature, 1791–1899* (np: Osgoode Society, 1986), 14–16. For a recent discussion of the reports analysed in this paper, which largely coincides with the views expressed in M. Morin, "Les débats concernant le droit français et le droit anglais," see David Gilles, "Quand comparaison juridique n'est pas raison politique: Les juristes Britanniques et Canadiens-Français comme analystes des systems de common law et de droit civil en amont de l'Acte de Québec (1774)," *Clio@Themis* 13 (2017): online, https://www.cliothemis.com/Quand-comparaison-juridique-n-est.

13 *CD. I*, 163 and 229; see H. Neatby, *Quebec: The Revolutionary Age* (Toronto: McClelland and Stewart, 1966), 51–2, 97–9; Evelyn Kolish, "The Impact of the Change in Legal Metropolis on the Development of Lower Canada's Legal System: Judicial Chaos and Legislative Paralysis in the Civil Law, 1791–1838" *Canadian Journal of Law and Society* 3 (1988): 1–25; Arnaud Decroix, David Gilles, and Michel Morin, *Les tribunaux et l'arbitrage en Nouvelle-France et au Québec de 1740 à 1784* (Montreal: Éditions Thémis, 2012); Donald Fyson, "The Conquered and the Conqueror: The Mutual Adaptation of the Canadiens and the British in Quebec, 1759–1775," in *Revisiting 1759*, ed. Buckner and Reid, 190–217.

14 A. Decroix et al., *Les tribunaux et l'arbitrage* ; D. Fyson, The Conquered and the Conqueror" ; see André Morel, "La réaction des Canadiens devant l'administration de la justice de 1764 à 1774, une forme de résistance passive," *La Revue du Barreau de la province de Québec* [hereafter *R. du B.*] 20 (1960): 53.

15 *CD I*, 25 (art. 37 and 42). The original expression, *Biens seigneuriaux* (see *CD I*, 19), is translated as "noble [...] goods" (*CD I*, 32); "seigneurial property" is more accurate.

16 *CD I*, 115–16, art. 4; Alain Laberge, "Le régime seigneurial après la Conquête: Propriété et privilège fonciers à l'époque du traité de Paris

(1760–1774)," in S. Imbeault et al., *1763: Le traité de Paris bouleverse l'Amérique*, 324.

17 See Michel Morin, "The Discovery and Assimilation of British Constitutional Law Principles in Quebec, 1764–1774," *Dal. L.J.* 36, no. 2 (2013): 581–616, at 606–10.

18 *Campbell* c. *Hall*, 1 Cowp. 204, 98 ER 1048 (KB, 1774), *CD I*, 526.

19 See for instance Michel Ducharme, *Le concept de liberté au Canada à l'époque des Révolutions atlantiques, 1776–1838* (Montreal and Kingston, McGill-Queen's University Press, 2010), 30–1 and 174–5 (referring among others to Locke, Blackstone, and De Lolme).

20 See *CD I*, 212–22; D. Fyson, "The Conquered and the Conqueror"; M. Morin, "The Discovery and Assimilation of British Constitutional Law Principles," 602–3.

21 *CD I*, 249; M. Morin, "The Discovery and Assimilation of British Constitutional Law Principles," 602.

22 See M. Morin, "Les revendications des nouveaux sujets, francophones et catholiques, de la Province de Québec, 1764–1774," in *Essays in the History of Canadian Law: Quebec and the Canadas*, ed. Blaine Baker and Donald Fyson, at 147–8 (Toronto: Osgoode Society, 2013); Hannah Weiss Muller, "Bonds of Belonging: Subjecthood and the British Empire," *Journal of British Studies* 53, no. 1 (2014): 29–58; H. Weiss Muller, *Subjects and Sovereigns*, at 147–8.

23 H. Neatby, *Quebec, The Revolutionary Age*, 51–2, 97–9; Francis Maseres, *The Canadian Freeholder*, vol. 1 (London: B White, 1776), 350–78; Jacques L'Heureux, "L'organisation judiciaire de 1764 à 1774," *Revue générale de droit* 1, no. 1 (1970): 266–331, 324–8; but see Seaman Morley Scott, *Chapters in the History of the Law of Quebec, 1764–1775* (PhD diss., University of Michigan, 1933), Appendix 6, 444–9.

24 Chief Justice Hey, Attorney General Maseres, the judges of the common pleas and many justices of the peace understood French: H. Neatby, *Quebec, The Revolutionary Age*, 49, Donald Fyson, *Magistrates, Police, and People: Everyday Criminal Justice in Quebec and Lower Canada, 1764–1837* (Toronto: Osgoode Society/ University of Toronto Press, 2006), 202–3; D. Fyson, "The Conquered and the Conqueror," 200–1.

25 Francis Maseres, *A Collection of Several Commissions, and Other Public Instruments, Proceeding from His Majesty's Royal Authority, and Other Papers, Relating to the State of the Province of Quebec in North America, since the Conquest of It by the Bristish Arms in 1760* (Toronto: SR Publishers, 1966 [first published in 1772]); see also D. Milobar, "Quebec Reform, the British Constitution, and the Atlantic Empire, 1774–1775."

26 See chapter 1 by Hannah Weiss Muller in this volume.
27 M. Morin, "The Discovery and Assimilation of British Constitutional Law Principles," at 609–16; see also Donald Fyson, "La réconciliation des élites britanniques et canadiennes (1759–75): Reconnaissance mutuelle ou rhétorique intéressée?" in S. Imbeault et al., *1763: Le traité de Paris bouleverse l'Amérique*, 262.
28 Letter of Fowler Walker, 17 October 1763, LAC, Dartmouth Collection, MG 23 A 1, vol. 2, folio 1616.
29 Most lawyers believed that confidential instructions, such as the ones given to the Governor of Quebec could not validly delegate legislative powers: see F. Maseres, *A Collection of Several Commissions*, 26–7; Francis Maseres, "Considerations on the expediency of procuring an act of Parliament for the Settlement of the Province of Quebec" [1766], in *Occasional Essays on various subjects, chiefly political and historical* (London, Robert Wilks, 1809), 327–64; J. L'Heureux, "L'organisation judiciaire de 1764 à 1774," 271–2; M. Morin, "The Discovery and Assimilation of British Constitutional Law Principles," 155.
30 "Considerations on the present State of the Province of Quebec," LAC, Hardwicke Papers Add. MSS. 35915, MG21 vol. 107, folios 5–48.
31 Ibid., folio 34
32 Ibid., folio 36.
33 Ibid., folio 34.
34 Ibid., folios 46–7.
35 Ibid., folio 47.
36 Ibid.
37 Ibid., folio 36. Charles Louis de Secondat Montesquieu, *De l'esprit des lois* (Genève: Barillot & fils, [1748]), Book VI, ch. 2 (http://dx.doi.org/doi:10.1522/cla.moc.del1).
38 F. Maseres, *Occasional Essays*, 335.
39 *CD I*, 252.
40 Ibid., 255.
41 Ibid.
42 R.A. Humphreys and S Morley Scott, "Lord Northington and the Laws of Canada," *Canadian Historial Review* 14, no. 42 (1933): 48.
43 [Francis Maseres], "A View of the Civil Government and Administration of Justice in the Province of Canada while it was Subject to the Crown of France," *Lower Canada Jurist* 1 (1857): 1–25 (Addendum with separate pagination); see M. Morin, "Les débats concernant le droit français et le droit anglais." We have located the original manuscript: *Extract of the proceedings of a committee of the whole Council : under the following order*

of reference relative to a conversion of the present tenures in the province of Quebec into that of free and common soccage, 1790 (Fonds ancien, Bibliothèque du Séminaire de Québec). The 1769 reports are collected in W.P.M. Kennedy and Gustave Lanctôt (eds.), *Reports on the Laws of Quebec, 1767–1770* (Ottawa: F.A. Acland, 1931), and discussed by, among others, H. Neatby, *Quebec: The Revolutionary Age*, and P. Lawson, *The Imperial Challenge*. M. Morin, "Les débats concernant le droit français et le droit anglais," is perhaps more detailed.

44 W.P.M. Kennedy and G. Lanctôt, *Reports on the Laws of Quebec*, 75 (William Hey).

45 Ibid. at 80 (Francis Maseres).

46 Ibid. at 71(Guy Carleton and William Hey): upon republication of the former laws, "neither French Law Books, or [*sic*] the Decisions of the Parliament of Paris" will be "heared [*sic*] of."

47 M. Morin, "The Discovery and Assimilation of British Constitutional Law Principles in Quebec, 1764–1774," 611.

48 *CD I*, at 423, contains excerpts first published in 1848. The transcript is entitled: "Report of the Solicicitor General 6 dece[r] 1772" (LAC, MG 30, vol. 14). In 1754, Alexander Wedderburn was called to the bar in Edinburgh, where the civil-law tradition applied, and in the Inner Temple, in 1757. Elected to the House of Commons in 1761, he supported Grenville, who was a member of the government that adopted the Stamp Act; he resigned to support him. After the latter's death, in 1771, he joined Lord North's government as solicitor general and approved his policy against the colonies (*Encyclopaedia Britannica*, http://www.1902encyclopedia.com; http://www.oxforddnb.com/view/article/28954?docPos=60679; https://www.historyofparliamentonline.org/volume/1754-1790/member/wedderburn-alexander-1733-1805).

49 *CD I*, 426.

50 Ibid.

51 Ibid., 430.

52 For the following ideas, see A. Wedderburn, "Report of the Solicitor General," folios 11–14; see also the abstracts prepared at the time (*CD I*, 432 and 434).

53 A. Wedderburn, "Report of the Solicitor General," folio 15.

54 [Francis Maseres], "A Plan for Settling the Laws and the Administration of Justice in the Province of Quebec," (1857) 1 *Lower Canada Jurist*, at 33 (Addendum with separate pagination); see A. Morel, "La réception du droit criminel anglais au Québec"; M. Morin, "Les débats concernant le droit français et le droit anglais," 33.

55 Ibid., folio 15.

56 *CD I*, 431.

57 *CD I*, 432.

58 A. Wedderburn, "Report of the Solicitor General," folio 20.

59 Ibid., folios 19–20.

60 Ibid., folio 22–23.

61 James Marriott became an advocate at Doctors Commons in 1757. In 1764, he became advocate general before admiralty and ecclesiastical courts. He was elected to the House of Commons in 1780 and supported North's government (http://www.oxforddnb.com/view/article/18091; https://www.historyofparliamentonline.org/volume/1754-1790/member/marriott-sir-james-1730-1803).

62 *CD I*, 453–4; Michel Morin, "Portalis v. Bentham? The Objectives Pursued by the Codification of the Civil and Criminal Law in France, England and Canada," in Law Commission of Canada, *Perspectives on Legislation* (Ottawa, The Commission, 2000), 125–99, at 156–9 (translation revised by the author; http://hdl.handle.net/1866/1468).

63 *CD I*, 465.

64 Ibid., 479.

65 Ibid., 473.

66 Ibid., 475. The rest of the report does not deal with issues of public or private law: [James Marriott], *Plan of a Code of Laws for the Province of Quebec reported by the Advocate-General*, London, 1774.

67 *CD I*, 437; in 1758, Edward Thurlow was called to the bar at the Inner Temple. Elected to the House of Commons in 1765, he supported the more authoritarian positions of the day. He became solicitor general in 1770 and attorney general the following year. (*Encyclopaedia Britannica*, http://www.1902encyclopedia.com; http://www.oxforddnb.com/view/article/27406?docPos=1; https://www.historyofparliamentonline.org/volume/1754-1790/member/thurlow-edward-1731-1806).

68 This manuscript, available online, seems to have escaped scrutiny: "Rapport d'Edward Thurlow, procureur général de Grande-Bretagne, sur les lois, les cours de justice et le mode défectueux du gouvernement dans la province de Québec", Musée de la civilisation, collection du Séminaire de Québec, P-29-Fonds Georges-Barthélémy Faribault, Documents Faribault, no. 296, online, https://collections.mcq.org/objets/282910, folio 22

69 *CD I*, 442.

70 Ibid., 443–4.

71 Ibid., 444.

72 An Act to discontinue, in such manner, and for or such time as are therein mentioned, the landing and discharging, lading or shipping, of goods, wares, and merchandise, at the town, and within the harbour, of Boston, in the province of Massachuset's Bay, in North America, (1774 (G.–B.), 14 Geo. III, c. 19); An Act for the impartial administration of justice in the cases of persons questioned for any acts done by them in the execution of the law, or for the suppression of riots and tumults, in the province of the Massachuset's Bay, in New England (1774 (G.–B.), 14 Geo. III, c. 45); An Act for the better regulating the government of the province of the Massachuset's Bay, in New England (1774 (G.–B.), 14 Geo. III, c. 39); An Act for the better providing suitable quarters for officers and soldiers in his Majesty's service in North America; (1774 (G.–B.), 14 Geo. III, c. 54).

73 See D. Milobar, "Quebec Reform, the British Constitution, and the Atlantic Empire,1774–1775," and the chapters by Jeffers Lennox and by Brad A. Jones in this volume.

74 Henry Cavendish, *Debates of the House of Commons in the year 1774 on the Bill for making a more effectual provision for the Government of the Province of Quebec* (New York: SR Publishers; Johnson Reprint, 1966 [1839]), 228–9 (see also 62, 214); in the House of Lords, Lord Lyttleton dismissed the same objection, raised by William Pitt: "Motion to Agree to the Amendments Made by the House of Commons, Debate," in *American Archives*, 4th series, vol. 1, ed. Peter Force (Washington: M. St Clair Clarke and Peter Force), 212–14. (https://digital.lib.niu.edu/islandora/object/niu-amarch%3A97923).

75 See for example Hilda Neatby, *The Quebec Act: Protest and Policy* (Scarborough: Prentice-Hall, 1972; P. Lawson, *The Imperial Challenge*.

76 P. Force, *American Archives*, 214; at the time, many authors also assumed that a Quebec army would be used if the colonies revolted: [William Meredith], *A letter from Thomas Lord Lyttelton to William Pitt, Earl of Chatham on the Quebec Bill*, New York, Reprinted by James Rivington, 1774, 19; [Anonymous], *A letter to Sir William Meredith, Bart., in Answer to his late letter to the Earl of Chatham*, London, 1774, 39; [Anonymous], *Thoughts on the Quebec Act for making more Effectual Provision for the Government of the Province of Quebec* (London, T. Becket, 1774), 27–8; D. Milobar, "Quebec Reform, the British Constitution, and the Atlantic Empire,1774–1775." Carleton also mooted the idea in 1768 (*CD I*, 326.)

77 R.C. Simmons and P.G.D. Thomas (eds), *Proceedings and Debates of the British Parliaments Respecting North America*, vol 6, April 1775 to May 1776 (White Plains, NJ: Kraus International Publications, 1987), 66.

78 *CD I*, 533–4, n3.

79 See F. Maseres, "Considerations on the expediency of procuring an act of Parliament," at 341–2; Wedderburn and Marriott's report (*CD I*, at 426 and 455–6); Carleton to Shelburne, *CD I*, 295–6; Maseres to Dartmouth, *CD I*, 486–7 (4 January 1774); John Marr, "A few Remarks on the Province of Quebec" (RG4 B17 vol. 2, 1723, folios 1794–8).

80 An Act to establish a fund towards further defraying the charges of the administration of justice and support the civil government within the Province of Quebec in America, 1774 (G.–B.), 14 Geo. III, c. 88; *CD I*, 576 [hereafter "Quebec Revenue Act"].

81 They are found in the Dartmouth Collection (LAC, R9370-0-5-E, formerly RG4 B17); *CD I* has all the important parts.

82 *CD I*, 533–4.

83 *CD I*, 535.

84 *CD I*, 536.

85 *CD I*, 539–40, n3.

86 See text corresponding to footnote 71, and F. Maseres, "A Plan for Settling the Laws and the Administration of Justice in the Province of Quebec," 27–38.

87 *CD I*, 540.

88 *CD I*, 537, n1.

89 H. Cavendish, *Debates of the House of Commons*, 37.

90 *CD I*. 537, n1; for another quotation of Hey's opinion, see 539–40, n3.

91 H. Cavendish, *Debates of the House of Commons*, 158.

92 *CD I*, 546.

93 *CD I*, 549. Since the author mentions "A Case that came before me" in Quebec, the author can only be Chief Justice Hey, and not Lord Mansfield, as supposed by Shortt and Doughty (*CD I*, 549, n1).

94 *CD I*, 549.

95 On the Chancery Court of Quebec, see J. L'Heureux, "L'organisation judiciaire de 1764 à 1774"; Michel Morin, "La compétence *parens patriae* et le droit privé québécois: Un emprunt inutile, un affront à l'histoire," *R. du B.* 50 (1990): 831.

96 See their statement in LAC, RG4 B17, vol 2.

97 *CD I*, 550.

98 Ibid. (all quotations in this paragraph).

99 R.C. Simmons and P.D.G. Thomas, *Proceedings and Debates of the British Parliaments Respecting North America*, 66; see also the chapter of Christian R. Burset in this volume.

100 H. Cavendish, *Debates of the House of Commons*, 21–3 and 133–6; speech of the Earl of Chatham, in P. Force, *American Archives*, 212; see also Francis Maseres, *An Account of the Proceedings of the British and other Protestant Inhabitants of the Province of Quebeck in North-America, in order to obtain An House of Assembly in that Province* (London: B. White, 1775), 228, 279–82; Francis Maseres, *Additional papers concerning the province of Quebeck: Being an appendix to the book entitled, "An account of the proceedings of the British and other Protestant inhabitants of the province of Quebeck in North-America in order to obtain a house of assembly in that province"* (London: B. White, 1776), 229–21. In New France, only one *lettre de cachet* was signed by the king, and it was subsequently annulled: Josianne Paul, *Exilés au nom du roi, les fils de famille et les faux-sauniers en Nouvelle-France, 1721–1749* (Sillery, Septentrion, 2008), 44–5.

101 *CD I*, 546; see the opinion of Chartier de Lotbinière, *CD I*, 564; A. Morel, "La réception du droit criminel anglais au Québec," 469–73 and 494–500; Douglas Hay, "The Meaning of the Criminal Law in Quebec, 1764–1774," in *Crime and Criminal Justice in Europe and Canada*, ed. Louis A. Knafla, 77–111 (Waterloo: Wilfrid Laurier University Press, 1981); J.L.J. Edwards, "The Advent of English (not French) Criminal Law and Procedure into Canada in 1771 – A Close Call," *Crim.L.Q.* 26 (1983–84): 464.

102 M. Morin, "The Discovery and Assimilation of British Constitutional Law Principles in Quebec," at 611–14.

103 Michel Morin, "Blackstone and the Birth of Quebec's Distinct Legal Culture, 1765–1867," in *Re-Interpreting Blackstone's Commentaries: A Seminal Text in National and International* Contexts, ed. Wilfrid Prest, 105–24, at 111–12 (Oxford: Hart Publishing, 2014).

104 *CD I*, 546; see André Morel, *Les limites de la liberté testamentaire dans le droit civil de la province de Québec* (Paris: LGDJ, 1960); Jean-Maurice Brisson, "Entre le devoir et le sentiment: La liberté testamentaire en droit québécois (1774–1990)," *Recueils de la Société Jean Bodin*, vol 62: *Actes à cause de mort — Acts of Last Will* (Brussels: De Bœck, 1994), 277; Christine Morin, *L'émergence des limites à la liberté de tester en droit québécois: Étude sociojuridique de la production du droit* (Cowansville: Éditions Yvon Blais, 2009).

105 See text corresponding to n65.

106 M. Morin, "The Discovery and Assimilation of British Constitutional Law Principles in Quebec," at 613; M. Morin, "Les revendications des nouveaux sujets, francophones et catholiques, de la Province de

Québec," 154–65; Michael Dorland and Maurice Charland, *Law, Rhetoric, and Irony in the Formation of Canadian Civil Culture* (Toronto: University of Toronto Press, 2002), 94–7.

107 François-Joseph Cugnet, "Loix municipales de Québec, divisées en trois traités," Bibliothèque de l'Assemblée nationale du Québec, unnumbered folio following folio 301 [c. 1773]. (http://www.bibliotheque.assnat.qc.ca/DepotNumerique_v2/AffichageNotice.aspx?idn=36858).

108 *CD I*, 551, note 1 (Lord Mansfield to Lord Dartmouth, 28 April 1774).

109 "Petition of the City of London to the King, Against the Bill," P. Force, *American Archives*, 215.

110 See the letter of Lord Aspley, 15 May 1774, in LAC, Dartmouth Collection, MG 23 A 1, vol. 2, folio 2041.

111 See H. Cavendish, *Debates of the House of Commons*, 21, 97, 258; D. Milobar, "Quebec Reform, the British Constitution, and the Atlantic Empire,1774–1775"; David Schneiderman, "Edmund Burke, John Whyte, and Themes in Canadian Constitutional Culture," *Queen's Law Journal* 31 (2006): 578.

112 *CD I*, 515; H. Welland, "Commercial Interests and Political Allegiance: The Origins of the Quebec Act," 181–2; the chapter by Christian Burset in this volume.

113 "Petition of the Common Council of the City of London Against the Bill," P. Force, *American Archives*, 194.

114 "Petition of the City of London to the King, Against the Bill," P. Force, ibid., 215.

115 H. Cavendish, *Debates of the House of Commons*, 11–12, 235–6, and 256–7; Wedderburn insisted on the need to wait until Canadians were ready to accept trial by jury (56, 272–5); see also [William Knox], *The justice and policy of the late Act of Parliament for Making more Effectual Provision for the Government of the Province of Quebec Asserted and Proved* (London: J. Wilkie, 1774), 58–61.

116 *CD I*, 595, nos 12–13. This was partially done: the English law of evidence was introduced for commercial affairs in 1777, habeas corpus in 1784, and optional trial by jury was allowed between merchants and in claims for personal injuries in 1785 (*CD I*, 682, 780; J.-M. Fecteau and D. Hay, "'Government by Will and Pleasure Instead of Law': Military Justice and the Legal System of Quebec").

117 See Sylvio Normand, "An Introduction to Quebec Civil Law," in *Elements of Quebec Civil Law: A Comparison with The Common Law of*

Canada, ed. Aline Grenon and Louise Bélanger-Hardy, 25–47 (Toronto, Thomson-Carswell, 2008).

118 On the denial of habeas corpus in Quebec during the US War of Independence, see J.-M. Fecteau and D. Hay, "'Government by Will and Pleasure Instead of Law': Military Justice and the Legal System of Quebec."

119 Fernand Ouellet, *Histoire économique et sociale du Québec, 1760–1850*, vol. 1 (Montreal, Fides, 1971), 79–80 and 101–2. Furs were the main staple; there were not many lumber and wheat exports (ibid., 81–90).

120 *CD I*, 576. The following year, the Act was modified to eliminate, for those who were involved in the fur trade, the obligation to enter the province only through Saint John's (located south of Montreal) or Quebec City; this allowed inland navigations from New York to the Great Lakes (An Act for amending and explaining an Act, passed in the Fourteenth Year of His Majesty's Reign, intituled, An Act to establish a Fund towards further defraying the Charges of the Administration of Justice, and Support of the Civil Government within the Province of Quebec, in America, 1775 (G.-B.), 15 Geo. III, c. 40; *CD I*, 580.

121 See H. Welland, "Commercial Interests and Political Allegiance: The Origins of the Quebec Act."

122 *Carleton to Shelburne*, 24 December 1767, *CD I*, 288.

123 F. Maseres, "A View of the Civil Government and Administration of Justice in the Province of Canada," 11.

124 *Carleton to Shelburne*, 20 January 1768, *CD I*, 296.

125 *CD I*, 422.

126 *CD I*, 552.

127 *CD I*, 554.

128 *CD I*, 730.

129 *CD I*, 554; see the chapter by Jeffers Lennox in this volume.

130 R.C. Simmons and P.D.G. Thomas, *Proceedings and Debates of the British Parliaments Respecting North America*, 41.

4

Quebec, Bengal, and the Rise of Authoritarian Legal Pluralism

Christian R. Burset

In the 1770s and 1780s, many writers argued that, although English law was the best in the world, it was unsuitable for export to Britain's colonies. "Laws which are fit for a free country," they explained, "are, for that very reason, incompetent for a country where the government is arbitrary and despotical."[1] Jeremy Bentham disagreed, but he offered another argument for not sending the common law abroad:

> 1. That the English law is, a great part of it, of such a nature as to be bad every where. 2. but that it would not only be, but appear, worse in Bengal than in England. 3. that a system might be devised which, while it were better for Bengal, would also be better even for England at the same time.[2]

Bentham's collaborator John Lind made a similar point about Canada.[3] Supporters of the Quebec Act claimed that Canadiens would accept juries only if Britain changed their traditional size (Canadiens wanted an odd number of jurors) and requirement of unanimity.[4] "Instead of refusing them a jury on this account," Lind suggested, "some have thought it would have been wiser, and better to have modelled our own juries in the plan they held out to us."[5]

Bentham and Lind's observations suggest that the Quebec Act's restoration of French civil law emerged from a broader debate over the place of English law in the British Empire, in which developments in one jurisdiction might inform changes elsewhere.[6] These debates looked beyond Quebec to Minorca, Grenada, and especially Bengal, where the East India Company (EIC) administered Hindu and Muslim law, and England itself, where judges and legislators insulated courts martial from common-law review and explored ways to settle commercial disputes away from Westminster Hall.[7]

Rather than approaching Bengal and Quebec as radically novel legal situations, Bentham and Lind treated Britain's old and new colonies as commensurable.[8] Many of their contemporaries agreed, comparing Quebec, in particular, to England's earlier conquest of New York.[9] From this perspective, the retention of non-English law in Britain's new colonies was not the inevitable response to a new kind of colonial difference, but rather a political choice. Legal policies in Bengal and Quebec (including the Illinois Country) emerged from a debate between two visions of colonial development. Policy-makers generally agreed that granting English law to the new colonies would encourage the formation of commercial economies, vibrant civil societies, and political and economic integration with Britain. Because politicians disagreed about the desirability of those outcomes, they disagreed about the desirability of exporting English law. Their disagreement centred on English commercial law and civil juries, which were seen as particularly important mechanisms for shaping colonial development. Though questions of religious toleration and respect for local custom played an outsized rhetorical role in public debates, the core of the fight focused on the kind of institutions that would govern commercial transactions and public law.

Focusing on the politics of legal policy allows us not only to reframe the Quebec Act but also to refine our understanding of legal pluralism – situations in which multiple legal systems coexist.[10] Histories of legal pluralism have often focused on the unexpected ways in which colonial states emerged from social and political conflict, and on how the agendas of individual claimants ultimately shaped colonial legal orders.[11] Certainly that perspective can be productive in the context of the Quebec Act. For instance, Hannah Weiss Muller's contribution to this volume shows that petitions from the inhabitants of Quebec played a crucial role in rethinking imperial subjecthood. But the present chapter focuses instead on how the ambiguities and contingencies of local claim-making fit into an imperial story of partisan and ideological conflict, in which politicians and policy-makers deliberately constructed a plural legal order from the top down. Though local legal actors played crucial roles in refining and challenging the laws of Quebec, their efforts unfolded on a stage that was constructed by metropolitan politics.

This chapter also makes a second connection between the Quebec Act and our understanding of legal pluralism. Recent work on legal pluralism has highlighted the tension between its oppressive and liberating aspects.[12] The Quebec Act was no exception. It simultaneously offered unprecedented religious freedom to Catholic Canadiens and subjected them to a political economic regime that subordinated the province's development to broader imperial needs – an aspect of the Act sometimes underemphasized by scholars inclined to celebrate its liberality.[13]

BRITAIN'S PURSUIT OF LEGAL UNIFORMITY

British policy in Quebec and Bengal departed from earlier efforts to develop a unified imperial legal system. That is not to say English law had ever been uniform across the colonies – or even within England itself.[14] But the very heterogeneity of English law gave it the flexibility to accommodate new situations, so that colonial laws might differ from England's without being "repugnant" to its fundamental principles.[15]

Policy-makers treated the unity of imperial law as a political imperative, believing, in the words of Edward Coke, that "union of lawes is the best meanes for the unity of countries."[16] Accordingly, England imposed its law on Wales[17] and Ireland.[18] Until 1707, many Scots feared they were next,[19] and with reason: English statesmen accepted the survival of Scots law in the Union only because they thought it would disappear naturally.[20] England also extended its law overseas, including to New York, which England captured from the Netherlands in 1664.[21] Similarly, the EIC obtained a new charter in 1726 to anglicize its courts in India.[22] And in Britain itself, the 1745 Jacobite rebellion prompted a renewed interest in anglicizing parts of Scottish law.[23] If the British Empire of the 1740s was "Protestant, commercial, maritime and free," that "freedom found its institutional expression" in English law, diversely applied.[24]

That vision of legal uniformity came under attack in the 1740s, however, as some politicians sought to reduce the access of some subjects to common-law courts. Most controversially, Britain reduced the jurisdiction of common-law courts over courts martial, which threatened to make martial law into an independent legal system unaccountable to any civilian power.[25] Meanwhile, a coalition of Indian elites and EIC officials obtained a new EIC charter in 1753 that sharply limited Indians' access to English courts in India.[26]

This emerging interest in restricting the common law's jurisdiction emerged from an authoritarian Whig program to render British governance more disciplined and efficient.[27] Authoritarian Whigs were a loose ideological grouping more than a party; indeed, even contemporaries struggled to assign them party labels.[28] Nonetheless, they shared several beliefs about law's role in governing Britain and its empire. Like other Whigs, authoritarian Whigs considered the common law as an important pillar of Britain's revolutionary settlement. But they also saw social disorder as a growing threat to that settlement, both because disorder made Britain vulnerable and because mob-dominated juries compromised the Glorious Revolution's promise of impartial justice. Eventually, these concerns led many authoritarian Whigs to conclude that only by limiting the sphere of the common law could they defend the promise of English law more generally.[29]

The efforts of authoritarian Whigs alarmed two other groups – known as radical and establishment Whigs – who argued that only a universally accessible common law could protect constitutional rights. Like authoritarian Whigs, radical or "patriot" Whigs were an ideological group more than a party, though many clustered around William Pitt the Elder and John Wilkes.[30] In contrast to authoritarian Whigs' fear of social disorder, radicals worried primarily about tyranny, against which politically conscious juries were an essential defence.[31] Moreover, many radicals feared that legal pluralism in India and the military presaged efforts to circumscribe common-law jurisdiction elsewhere. (One writer wondered, only half-jokingly, whether gentry would use courts martial to collect rent and settle property disputes.[32])

These nascent divisions notwithstanding, legal pluralism remained a marginal political issue through the 1750s. Most politicians continued to believe that English law should govern most, if not all, British subjects.[33] At the capitulation of Montreal, General Jeffery Amherst rejected a request that Quebec "continue to be governed according to the custom of Paris, and the Laws and usages established for this country."[34] Canadiens were to "become Subjects of the King," which meant becoming subject to English law.[35] Britain acted accordingly after the war, giving Quebec a legal system "as near as may be agreeable to the Laws of England."[36] As in older colonies, administrators adapted English law to local circumstances,[37] such as by relaxing anti-Catholic penal laws.[38] But officials described these measures as temporary concessions to ease the eventual transition to English law. In the paradoxical formulation of Acting Governor Paulus Aemilius Irving, allowing courts temporarily "to adhere to the Coutume de Paris in their Decisions" would be "a certain, though moderate, method to introduce our Laws ... into the Province."[39] Temporary legal pluralism might be necessary to facilitate the transition to British rule – as it had been in New York[40] – but the ultimate goal remained legal uniformity.

AUTHORITARIAN LEGAL PLURALISM

In the 1770s, however, the traditional pursuit of legal uniformity yielded to a new commitment to legal pluralism. Under Warren Hastings, the EIC erected a court system that preserved Hindu and Muslim law in the newly acquired territories of Bengal, Behar, and Orissa, thus solidifying the separation between European and non-European litigants.[41] The Regulating Act of 1773 largely confirmed his policy.[42] The following year, the Quebec Act restored French civil law to Canada.

These policies reflected the new prominence of the authoritarian-Whig legal agenda. During the 1760s, the rise of radical politics generated a backlash that converted many establishment Whigs to the authoritarian cause,[43] including Lord Chief Justice Mansfield[44] and Solicitor General Alexander Wedderburn,[45] who curbed their prior commitments to common-law universalism and embraced legal pluralism as a tool of imperial and social discipline. Both men played key roles in forming legal policy for Bengal and Quebec.[46]

Though policies in Quebec and Bengal had important differences,[47] they reflected similar visions of imperial governance. Authoritarian Whigs wanted to ensure that colonies remained politically and economically subordinate to Britain. That meant limiting participatory politics, isolating colonies from each other, and encouraging economies that reinforced colonies' political dependence on Britain.[48] Radical Whigs rejected these goals, as did many establishment Whigs, a moderate group centred on the Marquess of Rockingham.[49] Radical and establishment Whigs opposed legal pluralism for different reasons and with different intensities. The former wanted the rapid and total anglicization of British colonies, often at the price of intolerance (particularly for Catholics); the latter were more interested in gradually integrating the colonies in a manner more sensitive to local customs and religious toleration.[50] But the two groups united in rejecting the political and economic consequences of the Quebec Act.[51]

Authoritarian Whigs embraced legal pluralism partly to divide colonial subjects. Keeping subjects under diverse laws would hinder alliances among colonial groups, thus fragmenting colonial politics and inhibiting resistance to metropolitan control. In India, this meant dividing Muslims from Hindus, castes from each other, and natives from Britons. In Quebec, it meant deterring the integration of Quebec with its southern neighbours.

Contemporaries agreed that dissimilar laws would divide colonial subjects.[52] As early as 1760, Benjamin Franklin had hinted at this consequence of legal pluralism by commenting on the Roman Empire's policy of using legal difference to segregate subjects.[53] Francis Maseres, too, recognized that if Quebec kept "laws and customs considerably different from those of the neighbouring Colonies," it would make it harder for Canadiens to "Join with those Colonies in rejecting the Supremacy of the Mother country."[54] But while Franklin and Maseres came to see this disunion as troubling, authoritarian Whigs embraced it as a tool of colonial discipline. Canada would be most useful to Britain, Governor Guy Carleton argued, if it remained "not united in any common principle, interest, or wish with the other Provinces."[55] Lord Lyttelton, defending the Quebec Act in parliament, noted with approval that the "political separation of Canada from the rest of America might be a means of dividing their interests" from their southern neighbours.[56] "[D]o you wish ... to combine the heart of the Canadian with that of the Bostonian?" asked Sir William Meredith of those who would unite Massachusetts and Quebec under a single law.[57] For authoritarian Whigs worried about rebellious New England, the answer was clearly no.

James Grant offered a similar argument against introducing English law to Bengal. Though he professed discomfort with creating "a most odious & invidious distinction" among British subjects, he insisted on the "necessity that all British subjects in India ... be separated from the native inhabitants," lest "the unaccustomed dangerous draught" of English law "produce intoxication & turn into a curse & our own destruction."[58] Luke Scrafton likewise noted that religious and caste divisions among Indians had facilitated their conquest and "prevent[ed] their uniting to fling off the yoke" of foreign rule.[59]

Opponents of legal pluralism, in contrast, argued that placing Canada and Bengal under English law would both acknowledge the equality of all British subjects and effect their further integration. William Bolts, for instance, insisted that Indians and Britons were equally "British subjects" and "members of the same body-politic," who deserved the protection of the same laws.[60] Similarly, an opponent of the Quebec Act, writing in response to Meredith, argued that, just as imposing English law on Ireland and Wales enabled their political integration with England, introducing English law to Quebec would "make the rising generation look upon themselves as Englishmen."[61]

For authoritarian Whigs, dividing colonial subjects was just one way in which legal pluralism would encourage obedience. The substance of non-English law would also reinforce Britain's political control. French law, wrote Carleton, "established Subordination, from the first to the lowest" and "secured Obedience to the Supreme Seat of Government from a very distant Province."[62] Attorney General Edward Thurlow agreed: under French law, "all orders of men habitually and perfectly knew their respective places."[63] Authoritarian Whigs hoped legal pluralism would operate similarly in India. An anonymous proposal to deploy African soldiers in Bengal advised that "[l]aws similar to those they were used to in their own Country ... will make them ... True, Faithful, and Obedient to Command."[64] English law, in contrast, would "instantly emancipate [Indian subjects] from subjection to" Britain[65] and "introduce[] a Levelling Principle among People accustomed to the most rigid Subordination of Rank and Character."[66]

The emancipatory power of English law derived partly from juries, which could take on representative functions in the absence of a colonial assembly. Quebec's grand jury, for instance, claimed, as "the only Body representative of the Colony," "a right to be consulted, before any Ordinance ... be pass'd into a Law."[67] Civil juries could also act politically, particularly in cases involving seditious libel or official misconduct.[68] As General Thomas Gage cautioned, it was too easy for an agitator motivated by "spite and malice" to "support[] and buoy[] up the People to commence frivolous and vexations Suits against the Officers, who were carrying on the King's Service."[69] In Bengal, EIC officials, too, worried that rambunctious juries would allow litigants to harass company agents.[70] The surest way to check juries' interference with government was to impose a juryless legal system – an impulse that also found expression in English law during this time.[71]

Finally, authoritarian Whigs believed that legal pluralism would encourage the development of economies conducive to the political dependence of colonies. [72] Authoritarian Whigs supported economic development in general; indeed, they were behind many of the period's major economic reforms.[73] But they also wanted to ensure that colonial economic growth did not undermine social and political order. That meant limiting what they perceived as excessive consumption and discouraging colonial manufacturing, which competed with British products and reduced colonies' dependence on the mother country.[74]

Authoritarian Whigs saw the suppression of manufacturing in North America as especially important for restoring political control – especially after Americans began using boycotts to protest imperial policies. Imperial officials realized that colonies' political resistance depended on their economic self-sufficiency, and particularly on their ability to substitute local manufactures for British imports.[75] It was essential, then, to end the efforts of Americans to "manufacture for themselves." "Surely ... the people in England can never be such dupes to believe that the Americans have traded with them so long out of pure Love, and Brotherly Affection," Gage wrote to Secretary at War Lord Barrington. "The disposition the Americans have shown, I think shou'd teach ... one instructive lesson, which is to keep them weak as long as they can, and avoid every thing that can contribute to make them powerfull."[76]

Though Quebec was less economically advanced than its southern neighbours, many observers thought that it was well on its way to developing manufacturing by the late 1760s.[77] Accordingly, authoritarian Whigs looked for ways to steer the colony away from manufacturing and towards resource extraction, which would ensure the colony's continued dependence on British markets.[78] "I am very concerned to find that the Manufacture of Linen & Woollen is carried on to a greater extent than I conceived the nature of that Country and Climate could have admitted of," Hillsborough observed in 1768. At the same time, he and Carleton both worried "that positive prohibition" of manufacturing was "equally impracticable and impolitic," and they looked for another "means of diverting the Peoples attention from employments less beneficial to this Kingdom."[79] Authoritarian Whigs soon found a solution in legal pluralism. "It is an object of great consideration ... that the returns to Great Britain are all made in raw materials to be manufactured here," observed Advocate General James Marriott. That purpose, he continued, "must direct the spirit of any code of laws" for Quebec.[80]

A related policy pertained in India. Though authoritarian Whigs were less concerned with suppressing manufacturing than raising revenue, the EIC was willing to sacrifice Bengal's thriving textile industry if necessary to secure greater short-term income and a stable political order.[81] Philip Francis, a member of the Supreme Council in Bengal and critic of the EIC's economic model, described the effects of company policy clearly: "Instead of supplying the rest of the World with the Manufactures of Bengal you will find e'er [*sic*] long that raw Materials make the Chief Article of Exportation."[82] As he complained to Lord North, "[E]very Consideration of prudence is absorbed in the Idea of unlimited Revenue, & immediate Returns."[83] In contrast, if Britain were to place India under English law, with English juries – "the palladium, and true security of Indian liberty and property" – then "arts, manufactures, and commerce" would immediately thrive, although perhaps at the cost of short-term revenue collections.[84]

Extractive colonial economies also promised to address another authoritarian Whig concern: Britain's ailing fisc. Authoritarian Whigs believed Britain's economic health and its national security required the nation "to reduce her unnecessary Expences to be extremely oeconomical."[85] By extracting as much wealth as possible from the colonies in the form of raw materials and taxes, authoritarian Whigs hoped to cure Britain's fiscal troubles while avoiding the political unrest higher taxation would cause at home.[86] Furthermore, an economy based on resource extraction would require less initial expenditure on colonial institutions than industrialization, which would have required a substantial state investment in improved infrastructure.[87]

These concerns pertained not only to Bengal and the old province of Quebec but also to the Illinois Country. Even before the signing of the Treaty of Paris, radicals in Britain and America had promoted the creation of new settlements in the American interior.[88] Though in the short term these settlements were expected to produce raw materials for Britain, radicals hoped eventually to transform the region into a vibrant consumer market funded by local manufacturing.[89] That was precisely the outcome authoritarian Whigs wanted to avoid: a self-sufficient colony far from metropolitan control.[90]

The best way to avoid such an outcome – in Quebec or Illinois – was to discourage new settlement, particularly by Protestant merchants likely to attract capital from other parts of the empire. "It is not the interest of Britain that many of her natives should settle" in Canada, Wedderburn argued.[91] Gage agreed: "It is really time to fall upon Means to stop the Emigrations" to North America.[92] But simply prohibiting settlement was insufficient, as demonstrated by the failure of the Proclamation of 1763 to stop migration across the Appalachian Mountains.[93] Instead, just as in their efforts to discourage manufacturing, authoritarian Whigs looked to legal pluralism to discourage activity that they were unable or unwilling to forbid directly. In Illinois, this took the form of delaying the creation of any civil government whatsoever. "I conceive the Establishment of a regular Government at the Ilinois, would be the most hurtfull of any, as it would tend to increase a Settlement, that it's more for our Interest to annihilate," Gage confided to Hillsborough.[94] Barrington agreed. English institutions like juries were necessary in the older colonies, "because without them Englishmen would not settle in the Country & make it populous & flourishing." But because "the interior parts of America ought to be a Desert, & all British Settlement discouraged," it would be better to have "no species of Civil Government whatever."[95]

Ultimately, Gage and his superiors decided that Illinois needed some civil government after all, if only to control its existing inhabitants. But authoritarian Whigs continued to refuse to introduce English law. Instead, they made the region part of Quebec – and thus subject to French law, "with the avowed purpose of excluding all further settlement therein."[96] The region's potential settlers understood the Act's purpose clearly. "[T]he designed Operation of that most execrable Quebec Act," Silas Deane wrote to Patrick Henry, was to halt "Settlements of True and well principled Protestants Westward."[97] The First Continental Congress explicitly linked the Act's population-control objectives to its legal policy, complaining that it "discourage[ed] the settlement of British subjects in that wide extended country," because colonists feared the "influence of civil [law] principles."[98]

Authoritarian Whigs hoped that French law would discourage investment as well as settlement. As early as 1765, merchants trading to Quebec had insisted on the need for English courts to protect their interests.[99] Any laws "contrary to the Establishment of all the other Courts of Law in the British Dominions," they warned, would have "the most ruinous consequence to every Person in Trade."[100] "[I]f we had supposed the French laws ... to be still in force there, or to be intended to be revived," the merchants complained after the Quebec Act's passage, "we would not have had any commercial connections with the inhabitants of the said province, either French or English."[101] Politicians in Britain understood these concerns. "No English merchant thinks himself armed to protect his property," Edmund Burke told parliament, "if he is not armed with English law."[102] Politicians would normally have taken these complaints seriously. "Merchants concerned in the Trade thereof must be the best Judges of the Advantages or Disadvantages likely to result to them from" any laws affecting Quebec, Carleton had once told the Board of Trade.[103] Now, however, authoritarian Whigs ignored merchants' assessment.

Radical and establishment Whigs opposed the Quebec Act's economic aims. Instead of subordinate colonies fit only to extract resources and revenue, radicals sought to develop anglicized, commercial colonies similar to existing North American settlements.[104] Because radical Whigs believed that Britain's economic health depended on colonial consumption of British goods, they insisted on creating conditions for the economic prosperity of the colonies.[105] Their plan depended on relatively free trade and, especially, population growth in the new colonies.[106]

The Quebec Act's opponents agreed with authoritarian Whigs that English law would encourage settlers to transfer their persons and property to the new colonies.[107] This, in fact, had been a central goal of the Proclamation of 1763 and subsequent instructions to Governor Murray.[108] Imperial officials knew that they could not achieve this goal without offering legal institutions similar to those in other colonies. Moreover, settlement, economic growth, and institutional development would be mutually reinforcing. More trade meant the colony could support more freeholders; and more freeholders "would increase that grand creative foundation of the state" by giving a broader base of representative government.[109] Over time, Quebec would lose its French character, turning "Canadian society" into "a near image of that of Britain."[110] One analyst, eager to accelerate the process, recommended founding a new capital (subtly named "British Town") to be settled primarily by Englishmen who would introduce "the English language, the English manners, & a Spirit of Industry, among the French Canadians."[111]

HOW THE LEGAL PLURALISM WORKED

Not all aspects of legal pluralism were equally controversial. In fact, politicians were willing to compromise on many of the Quebec Act's provisions. On one hand, most of its opponents were willing to tolerate Catholicism[112] and to allow Canadiens to retain their accustomed land tenures and inheritance laws.[113] On the other hand, some of the strongest supporters of legal pluralism agreed that Britain should introduce English criminal law[114] and freedom of testation.[115] The real disagreement over legal pluralism concerned commercial law and civil procedure, particularly civil juries.

Protests against the Quebec Act frequently asserted the importance of establishing English commercial law and civil juries. A group of merchants trading to Quebec, for instance, said they were "most especially anxious" to retain those parts of English law

> which relate to matters of navigation, commerce and personal contracts, and the method of determining disputes upon those subjects by the trial by jury, and likewise for those parts of it which relate to actions for the reparation of injuries received, such as actions of false imprisonment and of slander, and of assault, and whatever relates to the liberty of the person.[116]

The merchants, in other words, wanted English commercial law, civil procedure, and public law.

Private suits were the normal remedy against officers who abused their authority, so the merchants' request for common-law tort actions has something of a public-law flavour.[117] In contrast, the merchants were willing to accept French law regarding "tenures and descents of land."[118] Indeed, they argued that "the revival of the French laws in these particulars" would promote the eventual anglicization of the colony by encouraging the Canadiens to "acquiesce very cheerfully in the general establishment of the laws of England"[119] – the same argument Governor Irving had made a decade earlier.

This focus on commercial and procedural law was a frequent theme in discussions of legal pluralism in Quebec. John Lind warned his readers not to "confound[] two things perfectly distinct and independent": laws relating to inheritance and property, on one hand, and civil procedure, on the other.[120] The instructions to Governor Murray had proposed a similar distinction,[121] as did Britain's attorney and solicitor general,[122] Chief Justice of Quebec William Hey,[123] and Attorney General of Quebec Francis Maseres.[124] William Dowdeswell, MP, though a staunch defender of civil juries, likewise agreed that imposing English law related to "Descent of estates & conveyance of landed property, would be grievous."[125]

The differing treatment of commercial law and civil procedure persisted after the passage of the Quebec Act. Establishment Whigs who clamoured for the Act's repeal or revision often excepted property and inheritance law from their critique.[126] With a similar understanding of law, but very different political objectives, Governor Carleton strenuously resisted any effort to soften the Act's impact by introducing elements of English commercial law, despite receiving royal encouragement to do so.[127] Inhabitants of the new United States thought about legal pluralism in the same way.[128] The Northwest Ordinance of 1787, which covered some of the same territory as the Quebec Act, essentially codified the compromise the Act's opponents had offered. "French and Canadian inhabitants" of the American interior would continue to enjoy their own laws "relative to the descent and conveyance of property," but civil procedure would be "according to the course of the common law," including "trial by jury."[129]

This is not to say that property law was absent from the debates of the 1770s. Indeed, policy-makers in Bengal saw secure land tenures as fundamental to that colony's development.[130] But they also believed that substantive rights would be meaningless without a civil procedure capable of protecting property.[131] Furthermore, even with respect to Quebec, many radical Whigs attacked the retention of French property law as feudal and oppressive.[132] But these were truly radical demands that typically linked French property law with feudalism and popery, sometimes a little hysterically.[133] To be sure, many radical Whigs would have preferred the total abolition of French law (and, perhaps, Catholicism as well); but those more inclined to compromise saw English juries and commercial law as more fundamental than land tenure or religion.[134] By the late 1780s, even those merchants who wanted new lands granted in free and common socage accepted that seigneurs could keep their existing tenures.[135]

The preferences of Canadiens played an ancillary role in this debate. Although many anglophone and francophone subjects engaged in fervent campaigns for their preferred laws, imperial decision-makers proved adept at citing only those petitions that supported their preferred agenda. Carleton, in particular, tended to substitute the wishes of seigneurs for those of Canadiens more generally.[136] As a result, authoritarian Whigs were able to present the Quebec Act's elimination of civil juries as merely respecting Canadiens' wishes,[137] even though most francophone subjects had no objection to jury trials,[138] and sometimes even petitioned for them.[139] Similarly, authoritarian Whigs ignored the willingness of many Canadiens to accept English commercial law.[140] At the same time, authoritarian Whigs had no compunction about imposing English criminal law, despite evidence that some Canadiens disliked it.[141] The same was true to some extent in Bengal, where the introduction of English criminal law scandalized some local inhabitants, even as the EIC insisted on its desire to respect local sensibilities.[142] This is not to claim that policymakers did not sincerely wish to accommodate Britain's new subjects or that their claims carried no weight with decision-makers. But ultimately, legal pluralism depended more on the political and economic agenda of the party in power than local negotiation or petitioning from the periphery.

CONCLUSION: LEGAL PLURALISM IN A DIVERSE EMPIRE

Many historians have observed that the Quebec Act reflected a new vision of imperial governance – one that seemed less concerned with assimilation and anglicization than its predecessors. It is less frequently observed how far the Quebec Act's opponents were also willing to depart from the earlier paradigm. In opposing authoritarian Whigs' program of legal pluralism, moderate Whigs proposed a new institutional framework for reconciling the increasing diversity of Britain's subjects with its earlier commitment to a politically and economically integrated empire. Under that framework, conquered subjects would have retained their own laws governing religion, property, and inheritance, while uniform commercial and public laws would have drawn them closer to Britain and its older colonies. This was a new understanding of legal pluralism.[143] Earlier writers, such as Edward Coke and Matthew Hale, had emphasized the importance of a uniform property and inheritance law for economic and political integration.[144] By the 1770s, in contrast, many leading politicians argued that commercial and political institutions alone might be enough to unite a religiously and culturally diverse empire.

This moderate compromise lost, however, to the more complete form of legal pluralism backed by authoritarian Whigs – not because they were more tolerant of local customs than their opponents, but because they believed that mandatory legal pluralism would serve a particular political and economic agenda that was rooted fundamentally in the pursuit of colonial dependence. The authoritarian Whig victory of the 1770s in no way ended the debate over legal pluralism in the British Empire. In both Canada and India, discussion over the proper role of English law persisted through the 1790s and beyond.[145] What the Quebec Act did ensure, however, was that the old ideal of a legally uniform empire lost its appeal. From 1774, the question would no longer be whether to embrace legal pluralism, but how.

NOTES

This chapter draws on arguments made at greater length in Christian R. Burset, "Why Didn't the Common Law Follow the Flag?" *Virginia Law Review* 105, no. 3 (2019): 483–542. I thank Justin du Rivage, Steve Pincus, and my fellow conference participants for their feedback.

1 Jeremy Bentham, "Place and Time [1782]," in *Selected Writings*, ed. Stephen G. Engelmann (New Haven: Yale University Press, 2011), 180.
2 Ibid., 181. Bentham's position on law in India is beyond the scope of this paper. On one hand, he drafted a "Proposal for an East Indian Code," which called on Indians to accept British law; on the other, he ridiculed proposals to impose *all* of English law. See Stephen G. Engelmann and Jennifer Pitts, "Bentham's 'Place and Time,'" *The Tocqueville Review/La Revue Tocqueville* 32, no. 1 (2011): 43–66.
3 For Lind's friendship with Bentham, see W.P. Courtney and M.E. Clayton, "Lind, John (1737–1781)," *Oxford Dictionary of National Biography* [hereafter DNB], https://doi.org/10.1093/ref:odnb/16672.
4 [John Lind], *Remarks on the Principal Acts of the Thirteenth Parliament of Great Britain* (London: T. Payne, 1775), 473.
5 Ibid., 473–4.
6 For recent work connecting legal policies in different parts of the British Empire, see, for example, Richard Bourke, "Edmund Burke and the Politics of Conquest," *Modern Intellectual History* 4, no. 3 (2007): 403–32; Stephen Conway, "The Consequences of Conquest: Quebec and

British Politics, 1760–1774," in *Revisiting 1759: The Conquest of Canada in Historical Perspective*, ed. Philip Buckner and John G. Reid, 141–65 (Toronto: University of Toronto Press, 2012); Paul D. Halliday, *Habeas Corpus: From England to Empire* (Cambridge: Belknap Press of Harvard University Press, 2010), 274–90; Karen Stanbridge, "Quebec and the Irish Catholic Relief Act of 1778: An Institutional Approach," *Journal of Historical Sociology* 16, no. 3 (2003): 375–404; Robert Travers, *Ideology and Empire in Eighteenth-century India: The British in Bengal* (New York: Cambridge University Press, 2007), 49–50; and Heather Welland, "Commercial Interest and Political Allegiance," in Buckner and Reid, *Revisiting 1759*, 166.

7 See Christian R. Burset, "A Common Law? Legal Pluralism in the Eighteenth-Century British Empire" (PhD diss., Yale University, 2018), 178–288; see note 25 below, and accompanying text.

8 Cf. Arthur Mitchell Fraas, "'They Have Travailed into a Wrong Latitude': The Laws of England, Indian Settlements, and the British Imperial Constitution, 1726–1773" (PhD diss., Duke University, 2011), 2 (critiquing the assumption that "India represented a radically different place from Philadelphia or Gibraltar").

9 See, for example, *The Expediency of Securing Our American Colonies by Settling the Country Adjoining the River Mississippi, and the Country Upon the Ohio, Considered* (Edinburgh: np, 1763), 8; Notes on the Affairs of Quebec ([1767?]), Shelburne Papers, vol. 64, 471, William L. Clements Library, University of Michigan [hereafter WLCL] (recommending that reform of Quebec's laws follow "what was done in ... New York immediately after it was conquered from the Dutch"); Lord Shelburne to Board of Trade (17 May 1767), Shelburne Papers, vol. 64, 483, WLCL (suggesting that "civil government" in Quebec "might ... be regulated by the model of New York, Virginia, or any of the other Provinces").

10 Legal pluralism "is generally defined as a situation in which two or more legal systems coexist in the same social field." Sally Engle Merry, "Legal Pluralism," *Law & Society Review* 22, no. 5 (1988): 870. I use the term more narrowly to mean *mandatory legal pluralism* – a legal regime that (1) establishes hard boundaries between legal systems, so that litigants have little choice about what law applies; and (2) is state-centred (rather than emerging informally). For other definitions, see Lauren Benton, *Law and Colonial Cultures: Legal Regimes in World History, 1400–1900* (Cambridge: Cambridge University Press, 2002), 11–12; Paul D. Halliday, "Laws' Histories: Pluralisms, Pluralities, Diversity," in *Legal Pluralism and Empires, 1500–1850*, ed. Lauren Benton and Richard J.

Ross, 262–7 (New York: New York University Press, 2013); and Brian Z. Tamanaha, "The Promise and Conundrums of Pluralist Jurisprudence," *Modern Law Review* 82, no. 1 (2019): 159–79.

11 See, for example, Benton, *Law and Colonial Cultures*, 148–9; Michael Braddick, *State Formation in Early Modern England, c. 1550–1700* (Cambridge: Cambridge University Press, 2000), 47; Helen Dewar, "Litigating Empire: The Role of French Courts in Establishing Colonial Sovereignties," in *Legal Pluralism and Empires, 1500–1850*, ed. Lauren Benton and Richard J. Ross, 52 (New York: New York University Press, 2013); Linda M. Rupert, "'Seeking the Water of Baptism': Fugitive Slaves and Imperial Jurisdiction in the Early Modern Caribbean," in *Legal Pluralism and Empires, 1500–1850*, ed. Lauren Benton and Richard J. Ross (New York: New York University Press, 2013), 218.

12 See Lauren Benton and Richard J. Ross, "Empires and Legal Pluralism: Jurisdiction, Sovereignty, and Political Imagination in the Early Modern World," in *Legal Pluralism and Empires, 1500–1850*, ed. Lauren Benton and Richard J. Ross, 2–3 (New York: New York University Press, 2013); Halliday, "Laws' Histories," 262–7; Mitra Sharafi, "'Justice in Many Rooms' since Galanter: De-Romanticizing Legal Pluralism through the Cultural Defense," *Law and Contemporary Problems*, 71 (2008): 139.

13 See, for example, the works cited in Nancy Christie, "A Government Fit for British Subjects," this volume (noting historians' debate about whether the Act was an "unqualified liberal act of justice" or "authoritarian"); James Tully, *Strange Multiplicity: Constitutionalism in an Age of Diversity* (Cambridge: Cambridge University Press, 1995).

14 See Blackstone, *Commentaries on the Laws of England* 4: 411; Jack P. Greene, "'By Their Laws Shall Ye Know Them': Law and Identity in Colonial British America," *Journal of Interdisciplinary History* 33, no. 2 (2002): 253; Daniel J. Hulsebosch, *Constituting Empire: New York and the Transformation of Constitutionalism in the Atlantic World, 1664–1830* (Chapel Hill: University of North Carolina Press, 2005), 58.

15 See Mary Sarah Bilder, *The Transatlantic Constitution: Colonial Legal Culture and the Empire* (Cambridge: Harvard University Press, 2004); Joseph Henry Smith, *Appeals to the Privy Council from the American Plantations* (New York: Columbia University Press, 1950), 656.

16 Edward Coke, *The First Part of the Institutes of the Lawes of England* 141.b (1628; London: Garland Publishing, 1979); see also Matthew Hale, *The History of the Common Law* (London: James Moore, 1792), 58.

17 Laws in Wales Act, 1542, 35 Henry 8, c. 26; Laws in Wales Act, 1535, 27 Henry 8, c. 26. Robert Chambers, who succeeded Blackstone as Vinerian

chair at Oxford before joining the Supreme Court of Judicature at Calcutta, considered this legislation as a success. Robert Chambers, *A Course of Lectures on the English Law: Delivered at the University of Oxford, 1767–1773*, ed. Thomas M. Curley (Madison: University of Wisconsin Press, 1986), 1:276.

18 F.H. Newark, "Notes on Irish Legal History," *Northern Ireland Legal Quarterly* 7 (1947): 126–38.

19 A.J. MacLean, "The 1707 Union: Scots Law and the House of Lords," *Journal of Legal History* 4, no. 3 (1983): 67–8.

20 J.D. Ford, "The Legal Provisions in the Acts of Union," *Cambridge Law Journal* 66, no. 1 (2007): 117, 139–40.

21 Peter Charles Hoffer, *Law and People in Colonial America*, rev. ed. (Baltimore: Johns Hopkins University Press, 1998), 32; Hulsebosch, *Constituting Empire*, 48; Herbert A. Johnson, "The Advent of Common Law in Colonial New York," in *Essays on New York Colonial Legal History* (Westport, CT: Greenwood Press, 1981), 37–54; William E. Nelson, *The Common Law in Colonial America: The Carolinas and the Middle Colonies, 1660–1730* (New York: Oxford University Press, 2012), 43–5; David William Voorhees, "English Law Through Dutch Eyes: The Leislerian Understanding of the English Legal System in New York," in *Opening Statements: Law, Jurisprudence, and the Legacy of Dutch New York*, ed. Albert M. Rosenblatt and Julia C. Rosenblatt, 207–27 (Albany: Excelsior Editions/State University of New York Press, 2013). The contrast between the conquests of Canada and New Netherland is noted in Arnaud Decroix, David Gilles, and Michel Morin, *Les tribunaux d'arbitrage en Nouvelle-France et au Québec de 1740 à 1784* (Montreal: Éditions Thémis, 2012), 250 n853.

22 Fraas, "They Have Travailed into a Wrong Latitude," 12; Gagan D.S. Sood, "Sovereign Justice in Precolonial Maritime Asia: The Case of the Mayor's Court of Bombay, 1726–1798," *Itinerario* 37, no. 2 (2013): 50–1.

23 See Bob Harris, *Politics and the Nation: Britain in the Mid-Eighteenth Century* (Oxford: Oxford University Press, 2002), 168, 218; P.J. Marshall, "Empire and Authority in the Later Eighteenth Century," *Journal of Imperial and Commonwealth History* 15, no. 2 (1987): 112; Burset, "A Common Law," 59–63.

24 David Armitage, *The Ideological Origins of the British Empire* (Cambridge: Cambridge University Press, 2000), 8, 103. A few British possessions – Newfoundland, Gibraltar, and Minorca – did lack English law. Jack P. Greene, "1759: The Perils of Success," in *Revisiting 1759: The Conquest of Canada in Historical Perspective*, ed. Philip Buckner and John G. Reid, 97

(Toronto: University of Toronto Press, 2012). But these exceptions did not reflect a policy of accepting or encouraging legal pluralism. Newfoundland was officially "not a colony but rather a seasonal station for the migratory fishery"; even so, its blend of customary and maritime law "developed within the common law tradition." Jerry Bannister, *The Rule of the Admirals: Law, Custom, and Naval Government in Newfoundland, 1699–1832* (Toronto: Published for the Osgoode Society for Canadian Legal History by University of Toronto Press, 2003), 4, 15. Gibraltar and Minorca were essentially military garrisons, the latter "no more than a British fleet to which an island was appended." Peter Marshall, "The Incorporation of Quebec in the British Empire, 1763–1774," in *Of Mother Country and Plantations: Proceedings of the Twenty-seventh Conference in Early American History*, ed. Virginia Bever Platt and David Curtis Skaggs, 44 (Bowling Green, OH: Bowling Green State University Press, 1971). Minorca did have a civilian population, governed by Spanish law. But, into the 1760s, observers treated that situation as the regrettable consequence of its capitulation, rather than sound policy. See Conway, "Consequences of Conquest," 148; Desmond Gregory, *Minorca, the Illusory Prize: A History of the British Occupation of Minorca Between 1708 and 1802* (Rutherford, NJ: Fairleigh Dickinson University Press, 1990), 86; Queries Relating to Minorca [nd], Shelburne Papers, vol. 82, folio 399, WLCL. Furthermore, Minorcans could still invoke English law. Francis Maseres, *The Canadian Freeholder: Volume II* (London: Sold by B. White, 1779), 281–87; *Mostyn v. Fabrigas* (1773) 96 Eng. Rep. 1021, 1 Cowp. 161 (KB).

25 See Navy Bill, 1749, 22 Geo. 2, c. 33; *Barwis v. Keppel* (1766) 95 Eng. Rep. 831 (KB); Sarah Kinkel, *Disciplining the Empire: Politics, Governance, and the Rise of the British Navy* (Cambridge: Harvard University Press, 2018), 114–16; Richard D. Rosen, "Civilian Courts and the Military Justice System: Collateral Review of Courts-Martial," *Military Law Review* 108 (1985): 14–16. Nonetheless, officers remained amenable to suits for abuse of authority, and King's Bench continued to issue writs of habeas corpus for illegally impressed sailors. Halliday, *Habeas Corpus*, 34–8; Rosen, "Civilian Courts," 16 n78; Thomas M. Strassburg, "Civilian Judicial Review of Military Criminal Justice," *Military Law Review* 66 (1974): 4.

26 Fraas, "They Have Travailed into a Wrong Latitude," 14–15.

27 Historians have variously described this group as "authoritarian reformers," "authoritarian Whigs," or New Tories. Justin du Rivage, *Revolution Against Empire: Taxes, Politics, and the Origins of American Independence* (New Haven: Yale University Press, 2017); Kinkel, *Disciplining the*

Empire, 223 n33; James M. Vaughn, *The Politics of Empire at the Accession of George III: The East India Company and the Crisis and Transformation of Britain's Imperial State* (New Haven: Yale University Press, 2019). None of these labels is entirely satisfactory. "Authoritarian" is accurate insofar as the group was obsessed with establishing Britain's authority over its colonies, but it risks misleading comparisons to more recent authoritarian regimes. "Tory" or "neo-Tory" risks a different kind of anachronism: many of the group's members called themselves Whigs (even if many other Whigs would have disagreed). Cf. Norman S. Poser, *Lord Mansfield: Justice in the Age of Reason* (Montreal: McGill-Queen's University Press, 2013), 135 (quoting Henry Legge's description of Lord Mansfield as "the Tory head of a Whig body"). This chapter uses "authoritarian Whig" to emphasize that the movement's ideology grew out of orthodox Whig thought. See Christian R. Burset, "Merchant Courts, Arbitration, and the Politics of Commercial Litigation in the Eighteenth-Century British Empire," *Law and History Review* 34, no. 3 (2016): 635.

28 See Ian R. Christie, "Party in Politics in the Age of Lord North's Administration," *Parliamentary History* 6, no. 1 (1987): 59; Marshall, "Empire and Authority," 110. Many authoritarian Whigs followed the Duke of Bedford and Lord North. Cf. H.V. Bowen, *Revenue and Reform: The Indian Problem in British Politics, 1757–1773* (Cambridge: Cambridge University Press, 1991), 172–73; John Brewer, *Party Ideology and Popular Politics at the Accession of George III* (Cambridge: Cambridge University Press, 1976); David Bromwich, *The Intellectual Life of Edmund Burke: From the Sublime and Beautiful to American Independence* (Cambridge: The Belknap Press of Harvard University Press, 2014), 130.

29 Burset, "Merchant Courts," 635–6.

30 See du Rivage, *Revolution against Empire*; Steve Pincus, *The Heart of the Declaration: The Founders' Case for an Activist Government* (New Haven: Yale University Press, 2016).

31 See John Brewer, "The Wilkites and the Law, 1763–74: A Study of Radical Notions of Governance," in *An Ungovernable People: The English and Their Law in the Seventeenth and Eighteenth Centuries*, ed. John Brewer and John Styles, 128–71 (New Brunswick, NJ: Rutgers University Press, 1980); Kinkel, *Disciplining the Empire*, 166–7.

32 *The Preservation of Westminster-Hall the Concern of Three Kingdoms; or, a Slated Cover Lighter Than a Leaden One. Being a New Way to Turn Lead into Gold* ([London?]: np, 1749).

33 Indeed, some early authoritarian Whigs insisted on the need for greater legal uniformity between Britain and its colonies. Sarah Kinkel, "The

King's Pirates? Naval Enforcement of Imperial Authority, 1740–76," *William and Mary Quarterly* 71, no. 1 (2014): 9.

34 Articles of Capitulation (8 Sept. 1760), in Adam Shortt and Arthur G. Doughty, eds, *Documents Relating to the Constitutional History of Canada, 1759–1791*, 2nd ed. (Ottawa: J.L. Taché, 1918), 1:25, 34.

35 See ibid., 33.

36 Royal Proclamation of 1763, in Shortt and Doughty, *Constitutional History*, 1:165; see also Ordinance Establishing Civil Courts (1764), in Shortt and Doughty, *Constitutional History*, 1:205–6.

37 Cf. Hulsebosch, *Constituting Empire*, 16.

38 Ordinance Establishing Civil Courts (1764), in Shortt and Doughty, *Constitutional History*, 1:208; An Ordinance, To Alter and Amend an Ordinance of His Excellency the Governor and His Majesty's Council of This Province, Passed the Seventeenth Day of September 1764 (1 July 1766), in Shortt and Doughty, *Constitutional History*, 1:249.

39 Paulus Aemilius Irving to the Lords of Trade (20 Aug. 1766), in Shortt and Doughty, *Constitutional History*, 1:269–70.

40 See note 9, and accompanying text.

41 Travers, *Ideology and Empire*, 117–19.

42 The Regulating Act, 1773, 13 Geo. 3, c. 63, authorized the crown to establish a Supreme Court of Judicature, which was to have jurisdiction only over "British subjects" and others who submitted to its jurisdiction. After conflict erupted over who counted as a British subject and what law the court should apply, parliament passed another statute in 1781 clarifying that India would have a "dual judicial system" and limiting the reach of English law. M.P. Jain, *Outlines of Indian Legal History*, 3rd ed. (Bombay: N.M. Tripathi, 1972), 120–9; Travers, *Ideology and Empire*, 202; see also Hannah Weiss Muller, *Subjects and Sovereign: Bonds of Belonging in the Eighteenth-Century British Empire* (Oxford: Oxford University Press, 2017), 166–208 (describing conflicts over subjecthood in Calcutta).

43 See Marshall, "Empire and Authority," 110; Vaughn, *Politics of Empire*, 180.

44 Although Mansfield came from a Jacobite family (Paul Langford, *A Polite and Commercial People: England, 1727–1783* [Oxford: Oxford University Press, 1998], 222), he initially embraced a conventional Whig legal agenda: supporting the elimination of heritable jurisdictions in Scotland. W.S. Holdsworth, "Lord Mansfield," *Law Quarterly Review* 53 (1937): 228; advising the EIC in the 1740s that Hindus in India needed to follow English procedures in administering estates, Fraas, "They Have

Travailed into a Wrong Latitude," 312; and arguing that Hindus should be able to testify under oath in English courts – an argument that became a widely quoted defence of common-law jurisprudence, James Oldham, *English Common Law in the Age of Mansfield* (Chapel Hill: University of North Carolina Press, 2004), 9–10.

45 Wedderburn came to London in the 1750s "firmly opposed to the illiberal character of Tory political thought"; but in the 1760s, he became increasingly concerned about "popular radicalism" and grew attracted to authoritarian politics. Vaughn, *Politics of Empire*, 175. His conversion was gradual, however, and he maintained ties with the establishment Rockinghamites into the 1770s. Indeed, Wedderburn's 1772 report on Quebec was much closer to the moderate vision later articulated by Edmund Burke than the authoritarian bill Wedderburn defended in 1774. See Alexander Wedderburn, [Report on Canadian Law, 1772], Edmund Burke Fonds, R2903-0-4-E, National Archives of Canada (NAC). I thank Michel Morin and Aaron Willis for this reference. A version of the report is printed in Shortt and Doughty, *Constitutional History*, 1:424.

46 G.R. Gleig, *Memoirs of the Life of the Right Hon. Warren Hastings, First Governor-General of Bengal* (London: R. Bentley, 1841), 1:398–9; Philip Lawson, *The Imperial Challenge: Quebec and Britain in the Age of the American Revolution* (Montreal: McGill-Queen's University Press, 1989), 120, 173 n18; Mansfield to George Grenville (24 Dec. 1764), in William James Smith, ed., *The Grenville Papers* (London: J. Murray, 1852), 2:476; *infra* text accompanying note 91.

47 The Quebec Act, for instance, subjected all residents to English criminal and French civil law, while EIC regulations and the Regulating Act created separate jurisdictional rules for European and Indian litigants. The question of sovereignty in Bengal – crown, company, or Mughal – further complicated matters. See Travers, *Ideology and Empire*, 117–18. The difference between these different models of legal pluralism can have important implications for a colony's later development. For instance, Ronald Daniels, Michael Trebilcock, and Lindsey Carson argue that rule-of-law outcomes in former British colonies depend partly on the extent to which indigenous and English law were integrated into a single system. Ronald J. Daniels, Michael J. Trebilcock, and Lindsey D. Carson, "The Legacy of Empire: The Common Law Inheritance and Commitments to Legality in Former British Colonies," *American Journal of Comparative Law* 59, no. 1 (2011): 156–73.

48 Cf. Welland, "Commercial Interest and Political Allegiance."

49 For the Rockinghamite Whigs, see Brewer, *Party Ideology*, 77–95.

50 Cf. John Faulkner, "Burke's First Encounter with Richard Price: The Chathamites and North America," in *An Imaginative Whig: Reassessing the Life and Thought of Edmund Burke*, ed. Ian Crowe, 93 (Columbia: University of Missouri Press, 2005) (contrasting Rockinghamite and radical responses to the Quebec Act).

51 Cf. du Rivage, *Revolution against Empire*, 17–18 (noting the alliance of radical and establishment Whigs in opposing authoritarian Whig tax policy).

52 Cf. Benton, *Law and Colonial Cultures*, 12–15 (noting jurisdiction's power to reinforce cultural boundaries).

53 [Benjamin Franklin], *The Interest of Great Britain Considered, with Regard to Her Colonies, and the Acquisitions of Canada and Guadaloupe* (London: T. Becket, 1760), 39–42.

54 Francis Maseres to Richard Sutton (14 Aug. 1768), in *The Maseres Letters, 1766–1768*, ed. W. Stewart Wallace (Toronto: Oxford University Press, 1919), 110.

55 Guy Carleton to Lord Hillsborough (20 Nov. 1768), in Shortt and Doughty, *Constitutional History*, 1:325, 326.

56 William Cobbett, ed., *The Parliamentary History of England, from the Earliest Period to the Year 1803* (London: Printed by T.C. Hansard for Longman, Hurst, Rees, Orme & Brown, 1806–20), 17:1406.

57 William Meredith, *A Letter to the Earl of Chatham, on the Quebec Bill*, 2nd ed. (London: T. Cadell, 1774), 35.

58 James Grant to Lord Shelburne, State of the British Affairs in India at the Commencement of the Year 1780, & Continued to the 15th of October Following (30 Nov. 1780), Shelburne Papers, vol. 99, 340–1, WLCL.

59 Luke Scrafton, *Reflections on the Government of Indostan with a Short Sketch of the History of Bengal from MDCCXXXVIIII to MDCCLVI: And an Account of the English Affairs to MDCCLVIII* (London: 1763, reprinted by W. Strahan for G. Kearsley, 1770), 26.

60 William Bolts, *Considerations on India Affairs, Particularly Respecting the Present State of Bengal and Its Dependencies*, 2nd ed. (London: Printed for J. Almon in Piccadilly, P. Elmsly in the Strand, and Brotherton and Sewell in Cornhill, 1772), iii, 90.

61 *A Letter to Sir William Meredith, Bart., in Answer to His Late Letter to the Earl of Chatham* (London: G. Kearsly, 1774), 27; see also John Glynn, in Cobbett, *Parliamentary History*, 17:1362 (discussing the unifying power of law in Wales); Bourke, "Edmund Burke and the Politics of Conquest," 417; Willis, "Rethinking Ireland and Assimilation," in this volume.

62 Guy Carleton to Lord Shelburne (24 Dec. 1767), in Shortt and Doughty, *Constitutional History*, 1:288–9.

63 Edward Thurlow, "Report of Attorney General" (22 Jan. 1773), in Shortt and Doughty, *Constitutional History*, 1:437.

64 Observations Relative to Sending Negroe Soldiers to [India] (20 Apr. 1771), Add MS 38397, 166, British Library [hereafter BL].

65 Harry Verelst, *A View of the Rise, Progress, and Present State of the English Government in Bengal* (London: J. Nourse, 1772), 144.

66 *Observations upon the Administration of Justice in Bengal Occasioned by Some Late Proceedings at Dacca* ([London], 1778), 8.

67 Shortt and Doughty, *Constitutional History*, 1:213.

68 See Brewer, "Wilkites and the Law," 154; cf. Jerry L. Mashaw, *Creating the Administrative Constitution: The Lost One Hundred Years of American Administrative Law* (New Haven: Yale University Press, 2012), 63, 76 (noting that tort suits were the normal remedy for official misconduct).

69 Thomas Gage to Henry Bouquet (2 June 1765), Gage Papers, vol. AS 36, WLCL; see also John Wilkins to Thomas Gage (9 June 1771), Gage Papers, vol. AS 103, WLCL (complaining about "the Schemes that are laid to Engage me in Litigious Suits of Law").

70 See *The Present State of the British Interest in India: With a Plan for Establishing a Regular System of Government in That Country* (London: J. Almon, 1773), 46–7.

71 Lord Mansfield worked to curb juries' discretion, especially in political cases (though he accepted juries' utility in some respects). David Lieberman, *The Province of Legislation Determined: Legal Theory in Eighteenth-Century Britain* (Cambridge: Cambridge University Press, 1989), 99–121; Oldham, *English Common Law*, 12–70. Because the Quebec Act retained English criminal law, the province retained its grand jury – to the regret of some. James Marriott, *Plan of a Code of Laws for the Province of Quebec* (London, 1774), 62–4.

72 Cf. Benton, *Law and Colonial Cultures*, 22, 261–2 (discussing the relationship between legal pluralism and political economy); Willis, "Rethinking Ireland and Assimilation," in this volume (noting links between legal policy and political economy in Ireland and Quebec).

73 See, for example, Geoffrey W. Clark, "Insurance as an Instrument of War in the 18th Century," *Geneva Papers on Risk & Insurance* 29, no. 2 (2004): 247–57; Douglas Hay, "Moral Economy, Political Economy, and Law," in *Moral Economy and Popular Protest: Crowds, Conflict, and Authority*, ed. Adrian Randall and Andrew Charlesworth, 98 (New York: St Martin's Press, 2000); Poser, *Lord Mansfield*, 4.

74 du Rivage, *Revolution Against Empire*, 39; Kinkel, "The King's Pirates?" 9, 12.

75 See T.H. Breen, *The Marketplace of Revolution: How Consumer Politics Shaped American Independence* (New York: Oxford University Press, 2004), xviii.

76 Thomas Gage to Lord Barrington (10 Mar. 1768), Gage Papers, vol. ES 11, WLCL.

77 See, for example, "Sunday's and Monday's Posts," *York Chronicle & Weekly Advertiser* (8 Jan. 1773): 26; Maseres to Fowler Walker (19 Nov. 1767), in Wallace, *Maseres Letters*, 61–2.

78 See Lawson, *Imperial Challenge*, 113–14.

79 Lord Hillsborough to Guy Carleton (15 Nov. 1768), CO 43/8, 56, The National Archives, UK [hereafter TNA].

80 Marriott, *Laws for the Province of Quebec*, 47, 48.

81 See Vaughn, *Politics of Empire*, 242; John Darwin, *After Tamerlane: The Global History of Empire since 1405* (New York: Bloomsbury Press, 2008), 193.

82 Philip Francis to Welbore Ellis (13 Jan. 1777), MSS Eur E15, 467, BL.

83 Philip Francis to Lord North (14 Feb. 1777), MSS Eur E15, 521, BL.

84 *Present State of the British Interest in India*, 149–50.

85 William Knox, Hints Relative to Our Commerce (9 Nov. 1764), William Knox Papers, box 9, folder 4, WLCL.

86 du Rivage, *Revolution Against Empire*, 80; Vaughn, *Politics of Empire*, 242.

87 See Daron Acemoglu and James A. Robinson, *Why Nations Fail: The Origins of Power, Prosperity, and Poverty* (New York: Crown Publishers, 2012), 202; Vaughn, *Politics of Empire*, 203.

88 Clarence Edwin Carter, *Great Britain and the Illinois Country, 1763–1774* (Washington, DC: American Historical Association, 1910), 103, 107–9.

89 Phineas Lyman, Plan Proposed by Genl Phineas Lyman, for Settling Louisiana, and for Erecting New Colonies Between West Florida and the Falls of St Anthony ([1763 – 9]), Shelburne Papers, vol. 50, 170–1, WLCL; George Morgan, In Behalf of the Inhabitants at the Illinois, Some Reasons Why the Distillation of Spirits from Grain Ought to be Encouraged at the Illinois, Humbly Offer'd to the Consideration of His Excellency General Gage ([1769]), Gage Papers, vol. AS 88, WLCL.

90 Thomas Gage to Lord Hillsborough (10 Nov. 1770), Gage Papers, vol. ES 19, WLCL; George Turnbull to Thomas Gage (10 Jan. 1767), Gage Papers, vol. AS 61, WLCL; Representation of the Lords of Trade to the Principal Secretary of State (7 Mar. 1768), Gage Papers, vol. ES 11, WLCL.

91 Shortt and Doughty, *Constitutional History*, 1:424, 430.

92 Thomas Gage to Lord Barrington (2 Dec. 1772), Gage Papers, vol. ES 23, WLCL.

93 See Fred Anderson, *Crucible of War: The Seven Years' War and the Fate of Empire in British North America, 1754–1766* (New York: Vintage Books, 2001), 568–9.

94 Thomas Gage to Lord Hillsborough (6 May 1772), Gage Papers, vol. ES 22, WLCL.

95 Lord Barrington to Thomas Gage (1 Aug. 1768), Gage Papers, vol. ES 13, WLCL.

96 William Knox, *The Justice and Policy of the Late Act of Parliament for Making More Effectual Provision for the Government of the Province of Quebec, Asserted and Proved* (London: J. Wilkie, 1774), 42–3; see also Thomas Bernard, *An Appeal to the Public Stating and Considering the Objections to the Quebec Bill*, 2nd ed. (London: Sold by T. Payne and M. Hingeston, 1774), 55; Hilda Neatby, *Quebec: The Revolutionary Age, 1760–1791* (Toronto: McClelland and Stewart, 1966), 134.

97 Silas Deane to Patrick Henry (2 Jan. 1775), Schoff Revolutionary War Collection, box 1, WLCL.

98 Robert Joseph Taylor, ed., *Papers of John Adams* (Cambridge: Belknap Press of Harvard University Press, 1977), 2:397.

99 For example, The Memorial & Petition from the Merchants & Traders of the City of London Trading to Canada on Behalf of Themselves & Others (18 Apr. 1765), CO 42/2, 102, TNA; Memorial of Fowler Walker, Agent on Behalf of the Merchants, Traders, and Others the Principal Inhabitants of the Cities of Quebec and Montreal, 1765, CO 42/2, 113, TNA.

100 The Memorial of the Merchants and Other Inhabitants of the City of Quebec (10 Apr. 1770), CO 42/8, 7–8, TNA.

101 Case of the British Merchants Trading to Quebec, in Shortt and Doughty, *Constitutional History*, 1:515.

102 Edmund Burke, Commons Debates (10 June 1774), in *Proceedings and Debates of the British Parliaments Respecting North America, 1754–1783*, ed. R.C. Simmons and P.D.G. Thomas, 5:204, 208 (Millwood, NY: Kraus International Publications, 1982).

103 Guy Carleton to Board of Trade (21 Nov. 1767), CO 42/6, 204, TNA.

104 See, for example, John Campbell, *A Collection of Letters Relating to the East India Company, and a Free Trade* (London: W. Owen, 1754), 18, 24–5.

105 du Rivage, *Revolution Against Empire*, 60.

106 For example, William Johnson to Henry Seymour Conway, Shelburne Papers, vol. 48, folder 6, WLCL; ibid., 73 (connecting population to consumption of British manufactured goods); Objects To Be Attended to in Granting Lands in the Newly Acquired Islands, Shelburne Papers, vol. 74, folio 63, WLCL; Phineas Lyman to Lord Shelburne ([after Aug. 1766]), Shelburne Papers, vol. 50, WLCL.

107 See, for example, William Pulteney, Commons Debates, in Cobbett, *Parliamentary History*, 17:471–72 (discussing the likely effects if English law were extended to Bengal); Marriott, *Laws for the Province of Quebec*, 14–15 (noting that the 1763 proclamation establishing English law looked like an effort to attract immigrants to unpopulated regions).

108 Commission of Captain-General & Governor in Chief of the Province of Quebec (28 Nov. 1763), in Shortt and Doughty, *Constitutional History*, 1:173, 157–76; Board of Trade to George III (8 June 1763), in Shortt and Doughty, *Constitutional History*, 1:132–47; see also Marriott, *Laws for the Province of Quebec*, 14–15 (wondering whether the proclamation "had been copied inadvertently ... from ... some other unsettled British colony," as it seemed "that the reflection never entered the thoughts of the drawers up of this proclamation, that Canada was a conquered province, full of inhabitants, and already in the possession of a legal establishment").

Radicals especially emphasized Protestant settlement. Memorandum to the Board of Trade, Some Thoughts on the Settlement and Government of Our Colonies in North America (10 Mar. 1763), Shelburne Papers, vol. 48, folder 44, folio 523, WLCL. Accordingly, for many radical commentators, a major problem with the Quebec Act was that it would not only repel settlement by Protestants, but that it might also attract Catholic immigration. See, for example, Alexander Hamilton, "Remarks on the Quebec Bill" (22 June 1775), in Harold C. Syrett and Jacob E. Cooke, eds, *The Papers of Alexander Hamilton* (New York: Columbia University Press, 1961), 1:175.

109 *Letter to Sir William Meredith*, 5–6; see also Maurice Morgann, An Account of the State of Canada from its Conquest to May 1766 ([1766–7?]), Shelburne Papers, vol. 64, folios 525, 548–50, WLCL.

110 See Lawson, *Imperial Challenge*, 43.

111 Memorandum to the Board of Trade, Some Thoughts on the Settlement and Government of Our Colonies in North America (10 Mar. 1763), Shelburne Papers, vol. 48, folder 44, folios 523, 529, WLCL. The same memorandum recommended settling the American interior.

112 Even radical Whigs in the American colonies, who sometimes adopted the most extreme anti-Catholic language, were willing to accept Catholic freedom of worship. See, for example, Syrett and Cooke, *Hamilton Papers*, 1:169. Moreover, lawyers agreed that anti-Catholic penal laws did not extend to Quebec. For example, Fletcher Norton and William De Grey, Report of Attorney & Solicitor General Re. Status of Roman Catholic Subjects (10 June 1765), in Shortt and Doughty, *Constitutional History*, 1:236.

113 For example, [Francis Maseres], *An Account of the Proceedings of the British, and Other Protestant Inhabitants, of the Province of Quebeck, in North-America: In Order to Obtain an House of Assembly in That Province* (London: Sold by B. White, 1775), 135–7; [James Monk], *State of the Present Form of Government of the Province of Quebec, with a Large Appendix* (London: J. Debrett, 1789), 69.

114 This is perhaps because authoritarian Whigs treated criminal law as a less important means of shaping colonial development. Compare John H. Langbein, "Albion's Fatal Flaws," *Past and Present* 98, no. 1 (1983): 119 ("The criminal law is simply the wrong place to look for the active hand of the ruling classes. From the standpoint of the rulers, I would suggest, the criminal justice system occupies a place not much more central than the garbage collection system.").

115 Some Canadien proponents of the Quebec Act even claimed freedom of testation as a right. Michel Morin, "The Discovery and Assimilation of British Constitutional Law Principles in Quebec, 1764–1774," *Dalhousie Law Journal* 36 (2013): 62. The Act itself permitted property to be devised according to either Canadian or English law. See ibid., 58.

116 "Case of the British Merchants," in Shortt and Doughty, *Constitutional History*, 1:516–7; see also "To the Printer," *Public Advertiser* (19 May 1774), 6 ("[H]ow are Debts to be proved by People residing in Great Britain against People in Quebec?"). The merchants wished "most of all for the writ of habeas corpus, in cases of imprisonment." Ibid. The Quebec Act did not exclude the writ, although confusion about its availability persisted until the legislative council promulgated a habeas corpus ordinance in 1784. See Halliday, *Habeas Corpus*, 275–81.

117 See text accompanying note 68. See Mashaw, *Creating the Administrative Constitution*, 63, 76; James E. Pfander, *Constitutional Torts and the War on Terror* (New York: Oxford University Press, 2017), 4–13.

118 Maseres, *Account of the Proceedings*, 209.

119 Ibid., 212–13.

120 Lind, *Remarks on the Principal Acts*, 471.

121 Shortt and Doughty, *Constitutional History*, 1:181. Lord Hillsborough had interpreted the Proclamation of 1763 as retaining "the Laws and Customs of Canada, with regard to Property," but implementing English civil procedure. Lord Hillsborough to Guy Carleton (6 Mar. 1768), in Shortt and Doughty, *Constitutional History*, 1:297. His reading is textually implausible, but understandable in the broader context of English law; as he pointed out, this was precisely how English courts handled property in Kent and other locations where "particular customs prevail" regarding real estate. Ibid.

122 Charles Yorke and William De Grey, Report of Attorney and Solicitor General Regarding the Civil Government of Quebec (14 Apr. 1766), in Shortt and Doughty, *Constitutional History*, 1:251.

123 Neatby, *Quebec*, 106.

124 Francis Maseres to Sir John Eardley Wilmot (16 Aug. 1773), OSB MSS File, folder 9999, Beinecke Rare Book & Manuscript Library, Yale University.

125 [William Dowdeswell], Observations on Mr Maseres Letters to Mr T. Townshend (11 Nov. 1766), William Dowdeswell Papers, folder 10, WLCL; Cobbett, *Parliamentary History*, 17:43–4; Patrick Woodland, "Dowdeswell, William (1721–1775)," *DNB*, https://doi.org/10.1093/ref:odnb/7959.

126 For example, Maseres, *Account of the Proceedings*, 135–7; Monk, *State of the Present Form*, 69.

127 Instructions to Governor Carleton (1775), in Shortt and Doughty, *Constitutional History*, 1:594, 599 (suggesting that Carleton explore a local ordinance making "the Laws of England ... if not altogether, at least in part the Rule for the decision" for contracts and torts); Neatby, *Quebec*, 160. The instructions came via Lord Dartmouth, secretary of state for the colonies. Dartmouth had managed the drafting of the Quebec Act, but it is unclear to what extent he supported its underlying policy. Dartmouth had resisted other aspects of the authoritarian Whig agenda; for instance, at one point he supported an assembly for Quebec. Lawson, *Imperial Challenge*, 72. Accordingly, his efforts to introduce elements of English commercial law may have been an attempt to soften what he saw as the Quebec Act's less-desirable effects. Under Governor Haldimand in the 1780s, some elements of English procedure were introduced, though merchants continued to ask that civil juries and English commercial law be fully implemented. Edouard Fabre-Surveyer, "The Struggle for English Commercial Law in Canada," *Commercial Law League Journal* 34 (1929): 622–3.

128 Burset, "A Common Law," 381–3.

129 Northwest Ordinance of 1787, § 2 & art. II, 1 Stat. 51 n.(a).

130 See Ranajit Guha, *A Rule of Property for Bengal: An Essay on the Idea of Permanent Settlement* (Durham: Duke University Press, 1996).

131 *Present State of the British Interest in India*, 48.

132 See, for example, Continental Congress, Letter to the Inhabitants of the Province of Quebec (1774), in *Journals of the Continental Congress, 1774–1779* (Worthington Chauncey Ford, ed., 1904), 1:105; "From the London Gazette," *Pennsylvania Packet* (12 Sept. 1774), 2.

133 John Adams, for instance, wrote these agitated notes:

> CANADA BILL.
> Proof of Depth of Abilities, and Wickedness of Heart.
> Precedent. Lords refusal of perpetual Imprisonment.
> Prerogative to give any Government to a conquered People.
> Romish Religion.
> Feudal Government.
> Union of feudal Law and Romish Superstition.
> Knights of Malta. Orders of military Monks.
> Goths and Vandals – overthrew the roman Empire.
> Danger to us all. An House on fire.

John Adams, "[Notes of Debates in the Continental Congress]," in John Adams, *Diary and Autobiography of John Adams*, ed. L.H. Butterfield (New York: Atheneum, 1964), 2:154. See also chapter 8 in this volume.

134 For the contrast between the anti-Catholicism of radical Whigs and the more tolerant approach of establishment Whigs, see Faulkner, "Burke's First Encounter with Richard Price." The one place where establishment Whigs did focus on property law was the Debt Recovery Act, 5 Geo. 2, c. 7 (1732), which encouraged the use of land as collateral. Here, however, the concern was not with land tenures, but whether real property would be "answerable by the French Laws in Quebec for simple Contract Debts, as in other Colonies." "To the Printer," *Public Advertiser* (19 May 1774), 6. In other words, the concern was not with land per se but as an enabler of credit. (Imperial administrators believed that the Debt Recovery Act had been an important driver of colonial economic growth. Claire Priest, "Creating an American Property Law: Alienability and Its Limits in American History," *Harvard Law Review* 120, no. 2 (2006): 427–8.)

135 Report of the Merchants of Quebec by Their Committee to the Honorable Committee of Council on Commercial Affairs (5 Jan. 1787), CO 42/11, folio 44v, 51, TNA.

136 Neatby, *Quebec*, 127, 141.

137 For example, Meredith, *Letter to the Earl of Chatham*, 19–20.

138 Donald Fyson, "The Conquered and the Conqueror: The Mutual Adaptation of the Canadiens and the British in Quebec, 1759–1775," in *Revisiting 1759: The Conquest of Canada in Historical Perspective*, ed. Philip Buckner and John G. Reid, 205 (Toronto: University of Toronto Press, 2012); Notes on the Affairs of Quebec ([1767?]), Shelburne Papers, vol. 64, folio 471, WLCL.

139 Thomas Gage to John Wilkins (9 Mar. 1772), Gage Papers, vol. AS 109, WLCL; Gage to Lord Hillsborough (13 Apr. 1772), Gage Papers, vol. ES 22, WLCL; Gage to Hillsborough (2 Sept. 1772), Gage Papers, vol. ES 23, WLCL; Isaac Hamilton to Gage (8 Aug. 1772), Gage Papers, vol. AS 113, WLCL.

140 See Michel Morin, "Blackstone and the Birth of Quebec's Legal Culture, 1765–1867," in *Re-Interpreting Blackstone's Commentaries: A Seminal Text in National and International Contexts*, ed. Wilfrid Prest, 14 (Oxford: Hart Publishing, 2014); Francis Maseres, "Draught of an Intended Report of the Honourable the Governor in Chief and the Council of the Province of Quebec to the King's Most Excellent Majesty in his Privy Council; Concerning the State of the Laws and the Administration of Justice in That Province" (1769), in Shortt and Doughty, *Constitutional History*, 1:327, 347.

141 See Douglas Hay, "The Meanings of the Criminal Law in Quebec, 1764–1774," in *Crime and Criminal Justice in Europe and Canada*, ed. Louis A. Knafla, 77–110 (Waterloo, Canada: Published for Calgary Institute for the Humanities by Wilfrid Laurier University Press, 1981).

142 See Richard Bourke, *Empire and Revolution: The Political Life of Edmund Burke* (Princeton: Princeton University Press, 2015), 582; Travers, *Ideology and Empire*, 1056.

143 Scholars have generally not focused on the new importance of commercial law. See Bilder, *Transatlantic Constitution*, 10. Others have insisted on the centrality of land tenures. See Niall Ferguson, *Empire: The Rise and Demise of the British World Order and the Lessons for Global Power* (New York: Basic Books, 2003), xxii. This may be because most historians of this period have assumed that "property and value were defined exclusively with reference to land" – an assumption that recent scholarship seriously questions. See Steve Pincus, "Rethinking Mercantilism: Political Economy, the British Empire, and the Atlantic World in the Seventeenth and Eighteenth Centuries," *William and Mary Quarterly* 69, no. 1 (2012): 12. The different treatment of commercial law is

narrated in Fabre-Surveyer, "The Struggle for English Commercial Law in Canada," but that article does not explore why commercial law was treated differently. Paul Halliday notes that property law was more likely to vary than laws dealing with personal rights, though his focus is on habeas corpus. Halliday, *Habeas Corpus*, 263.

144 Bilder, *Transatlantic Constitution*, 32, 34; Hulsebosch, *Constituting Empire*, 27–8. Bilder points out that Francis Bacon offered a different view, in which uniform public law was more important than uniform land tenures; but, as she emphasizes, his position was marginal. See Bilder, *Transatlantic Constitution*, 33; see also Hulsebosch, *Constituting Empire*, 20 (discussing James I's proposal for a uniform Anglo-Scottish commercial law). But see MacLean, "The 1707 Union," 65 (noting the importance of property law in proposals for the 1707 Union).

145 See, for example, Karuna Mantena, *Alibis of Empire: Henry Maine and the Ends of Liberal Imperialism* (Princeton: Princeton University Press, 2010), 21–55; D.A. Washbrook, "India, 1818–1860: The Two Faces of Colonialism," in *The Oxford History of the British Empire*, ed. Andrew Porter, vol. 3, 395–421 (Oxford: Oxford University Press, 1999); Coen G. Pierson, *Canada and the Privy Council* (London: Stevens, 1960).

PART TWO

Religious and Ethnic Conflict

5

Rethinking Ireland and Assimilation: Quebec, Collaboration, and the Heterogeneous Empire

Aaron Willis

The French territories ceded to Britain in the Treaty of Paris (1763) created a number of difficult questions for British imperial administrators. In order to make sense of these challenges, and in an attempt to create solutions, contemporaries often looked to precedents of state formation within Britain and Ireland. In the case of Quebec and the Ceded Islands, Ireland stood out as an obvious guide.[1] Rhetorical links between Ireland and Quebec proliferated in the debate over the incorporation of seventy thousand new Catholic subjects in Canada.[2] A negative reappraisal of Irish history promoted a search for alternatives to previous practices of imperial incorporation. Over the course of the 1760s and 1770s, British imperial officials concluded that the penal laws, the imposition of English legal norms, and other means of coerced assimilation had failed to effectively incorporate non-Britons.[3] In response, they began searching for more effective means of incorporating new subjects, developing a more pluralist model of empire that moved it away from older mantras of "Protestant, maritime, and free."[4] In the service of imperial stability through collaboration with local elites, more flexible attitudes towards non-Britons and their traditions replaced strategies of assimilation based on state formation within Britain and Ireland.

Particular understandings of the "Glorious Revolution" of 1688 and the legal and ideological developments of the following decades enshrined the idea of Protestantism as a bulwark against despotism and disorder.[5] Legally and culturally, Protestantism defined Britain, and the values of reformed faiths stood as founts of British identity.[6] The two established churches in Britain, despite their marked differences, were both Protestant. In opposition to the stability and liberty offered by the principles of the established churches of England and Scotland, the Church of Rome offered only arbitrary and repressive control. For many Britons, therefore, allowing Catholics into public life and positions of power risked violence and arbitrary government.[7] In contrast to the relative uniformity in Britain, Ireland presented a more complicated picture.[8] Since the Reformation, despite their demographic disadvantage, English administrators had worked to redefine Ireland as a Protestant kingdom.[9] Assimilationist and exclusionist statutes, collectively known as the penal laws, defined the place of the Catholic "other" in both Britain and Ireland. The various Irish statutes attempted to eliminate Catholic military power and participation, severely restrict Catholic ecclesiastic structures, erect economic disabilities aimed especially at Catholic landowners, and ensure the complete exclusion of Catholics from political life. As expedient reactions to contemporary circumstances, the laws lacked any cohesive planning, yet the shared motivation and cumulative effect was the protection of Protestant interests.[10] Irish Protestants' understanding of their own history produced a deep distrust of Catholicism. They looked back and saw a past littered with violent Catholic plots, rebellions, and massacres. Through the penal laws they attempted to force Catholic elites and middling classes to adopt English religious, cultural, and political standards.[11] The solution to the Catholic question in the years prior to 1763 was either coerced integration, exclusion, or, where possible, as in Acadia, removal.[12]

What emerges in the debates over the Quebec and the Irish examples is the perceived instability generated by the removal of resident Catholic landowners and the resulting creation of a rudderless Irish Catholic population. According to the claims of politicians and administrators involved in formulating and defending the Quebec Act, many of them Irish-born, assimilationist policy in Ireland represented a significant failure. The Irish Catholic population was disconnected from both the Protestant Ascendency and British values. Ireland lacked a local elite, tied to the mass of the populace by cultural and religious affinity, who would ensure stability and encourage loyalty to British rule. The penal laws resulted in few meaningful conversions, pushed the majority of Catholics to hold their religion closer rather than rejecting it, and fostered instability that resulted in the need for a large body of troops to maintain order. If the penal laws were a failure, the Quebec Act and its underlying principles would offer a new way forward.[13] Rather than removing and replacing local elites or forcing the adoption of British norms, officials advocated for policies that fostered a symbiotic relationship between local collaborators and the British Empire. This movement towards collaboration in Quebec would define British strategies for incorporation of, and rule over, diverse populations well into the twentieth century.

I. RECREATING IRELAND

In the aftermath of the conquest of Canada and the cession of French territory to the British, older assimilationist strategies prevailed and attempts were made to implement practices utilized within the Irish context. Lord Egremont, the secretary of state for the Southern Department, contemplated the best means of incorporating the newly acquired territories. His papers contain a set of notes titled "Hints for the Division and Government of the Newly Conquered Territories." The document offered several recommendations for the incorporation of the new subjects. One of these highlighted Ireland's prominent place in the minds of many officials in London. The author suggested the crown "grant to such of the Canadians as may still adhere to popery, the same toleration and indulgence, as is allowed to his majesty's roman catholic subjects of Ireland, who by the capitulation of Limerick were in like circumstances."[14] For the author, and others, the terms of capitulation in Quebec and Montreal mirrored that of the Treaty of Limerick. Just as the terms promised in the Treaty of Limerick were effectively nullified by the penal laws, however, various factions concerned with Quebec did not expect the terms of capitulation to continue beyond the immediate future. Catholics in Quebec were eventually expected to face the same legal disabilities as those in Britain and Ireland.[15]

Egremont's successor, Lord Halifax, oversaw the development of a policy that many interpreted would extend anti-Papist laws to the colony. In the aftermath of the Seven Years' War, the Proclamation of 1763 represented the crown's initial attempt at organizing its new territories and subjects. The proclamation opened with assurances that it sought to support the king's Protestant subjects and encourage them to settle his new territories. In doing so, the policy attempted to structure the new colonies in line with British norms. They would have local representative bodies and operate under British legal standards: in short, their political culture would resemble that of the metropole. According to those who opposed conciliation towards the new Catholic subjects, the proclamation instantly established the laws of England in the colony and voided all prior concessions made to Catholics. It also set a line of settlement, much like the Irish Pale, meant to keep settlers within a boundary of civilized and organized society, with lands for the native population in the territory beyond. Both these strategies were based on the experience of state formation within Britain and Ireland.[16] Officials like William Petty, the Earl of Shelburne, born in Ireland and an important figure in shaping the Proclamation of 1763 and policies in Quebec, understood cultural progression in North America through the lens of Irish "savagery" and theories of stadial development. For many, the Canadiens and the indigenous peoples of North America, like the Irish in earlier centuries, required strenuous efforts to pull them further up the ladder towards British civility.[17] From this perspective, cultural continuity was a barrier to Canadiens, a people misshapen by their Catholicism and French culture, becoming full subjects and productive members of the British Empire.

The imposition of new legal and political structures was not the only way in which British authorities turned, first, to older models of imperial governance that had been used with the Irish. As in Ireland, the Board of Trade made the emigration of Protestant settlers a key strategy in shifting the demographic balance in the aftermath of the Treaty of Paris. In granting twenty thousand acres to a pair of merchants, the Board of Trade set several conditions, the first three of which directly addressed the religious makeup of the settler population.[18] The stipulations required,

> First, that the grantees be obliged to settle the said township with Protestant Inhabitants within ten years from the date of the grant, in the proportion of one person to every hundred acres. Secondly, That if one third of the township be not settled with protestant inhabitants in the abovementioned proposition within three years from the date of the grant, the whole will be void. Thirdly, That all such parts of the land, as shall not be settled with Protestant inhabitants in the said proportion at the expiration of ten years from the date of the grant, do revert to the crown.

Grants like this in the years after 1763 echoed settlement strategies in Ireland and were directed towards similar ends.[19] Focused on settling Protestants in the new territories, rather than on addressing the concerns of the new subjects, the Proclamation of 1763 and initial attempts to settle Quebec remained wedded to older models of empire. While such plans quickly proved woefully inadequate, this older vision of governance clearly retained its hold in the years following British conquest.

Projects like the above land grant and the desire to plan and settle a "British Town" were central to the assimilationist policies of those who envisioned exporting the Irish model to Quebec.[20] The Irish ideal of legal transfer and civil governance was predicated upon a large-scale demographic shift in favour of British Protestants. The transfer of English legal and political institutions and practices required a significant influx of settlers and a demographic swamping if Anglicization was going to take root.[21] In the absence of a significant transfer of Britons, especially along the densely settled St Lawrence River, there was little hope that the local populations would relinquish their cultural traditions.[22] Confessional assimilation faced barriers even when settlement reached the levels found in Ireland, where the Protestant population represented between 15 and 20 per cent of the total population.[23] The few examples of successful widespread conversion in early-modern Europe took place under Catholic monarchs who were willing to dedicate the military or the ecclesiastical resources necessary to compel widespread conversion. Even in Ireland, the British did not have the will or shared motivations to carry such a policy to its conclusion.[24] In Quebec, efforts to replace French legal and political structures led to confusion and resistance that undermined the legitimacy of British rule.[25] It would take almost five years before the demographic realities in Quebec were fully accepted in London.

Even in these early days of British control, however, key British officials were already articulating alternative models of imperial governance. In the months after his appointment in 1764 as the civil governor of Quebec, James Murray worried that the British settlers' expectations of an assembly and the imposition of English legal norms fostered instability within the colony and alienated the Catholic population. Several years after initially recommending a policy of mollification, Murray still found it the best way forward.[26] Far from seeing Ireland as a model to be copied, he expressly opposed the extension of penal laws into the province. As his conciliatory actions angered the British merchant population, Murray reached out for support. In writing to his brother Patrick, the 5th Baron Elibank, and Alexander Montgomerie, the Earl of Eglinton, Murray made the case for his policies.[27] In letters to both from 27 October 1764, he argued that, could the French "be indulged with a very few privileges, which the laws of England do not allow to Catholics at home, [they] must in a very short time become the most faithful and useful set of men in this American empire." He maintained that conciliation would create a body of loyal and productive subjects. Yet Murray feared that the reactions of the English public, stoked by misinformation from British merchants in Quebec, would undermine his goals. The continued complaints of the British merchants unhappy with his concessions to the French led to Murray's recall in 1765, reducing his influence on the policy for Quebec to one of an interested outsider.

Murray was not alone in promoting a more flexible attitude towards Catholics. In April 1764, the Archbishop of York, Robert Drummond, submitted his thoughts on the ideal ecclesiastical establishment to ensure "justice and sound policy" in Quebec.[28] Drummond devised a plan that drew inspiration primarily from two earlier British encounters with Catholics – those in Ireland and Minorca. He proposed a middle way between Catholicism's outlawed status in England and its open practice in France. Drawing on the restrictions enacted in the second year of Queen Anne's reign for Ireland and the orders to the governor of Minorca after the Treaty of Utrecht, the archbishop developed his "via media," with Murray's initial report on the colony as the basis for his understanding of the situation in Quebec.

For Drummond, Ireland under Anne served as one source of inspiration. Catholic priests were not to be affiliated with any religious order and were required to take the Oath of Allegiance. In addition, the number of priests would be fixed based on the needs of the parishes and each priest then registered by the governor.[29] Drawing on the experiences in Minorca, he suggested that all nominations to the benefices should pass through the governor of the colony. A Catholic "superior of the church" could be installed to tend to ecclesiastical matters, but no foreign ecclesiastical jurisdiction should hold sway over the Catholic Church in Canada, and ultimately the British crown should act as the head of the Catholic Church in the colony.[30] As was true for the Catholic Church in Ireland and Minorca, he cautioned against allowing the superior to have any outward sign of pomp or circumstance in public.[31] The Catholic Church would exist not as a vibrant part of an international church, but rather as a dour and well-regulated closed structure connected to wider Catholicism only through a shared dogma. This was meant to strip Catholicism of its symbolic and political power and ease the transition into a British identity. This initial treatment of the place of the Catholic Church in the colony underscores how policy decisions were not merely ad-hoc attempts at addressing the issues, but rather emerged from internal debates and a very English reliance on precedent. Quebec posed a problem that was not wholly new, but also could not simply be addressed using a single model.[32]

In June of 1766, John Pownall, the secretary for the Board of Trade, and Charles Yorke, the attorney general of Great Britain, drew up draft instructions for the governor of Quebec.[33] These instructions began as an attempt to address the growing crisis surrounding the system of judicature installed by Governor Murray in September 1764.[34] A striking feature of the instructions and the ensuing debate is the range of precedents and models suggested for various aspects of the new legal system. In the course of a few short paragraphs, the courts of grand session in Wales, the civil act in Ireland passed under George I, the circuit courts established in Scotland under George II, the continuation of the customs and usages of Normandy in the island of Jersey, the courts established in Virginia and North Carolina, the summary bench statutes in Barbados, and of course the courts and practices in England itself, were all offered as models for particular courts or practices that might be used in Quebec.[35] Such a list shows the range of source material in the minds of administrators, and their flexibility in working to formulate imperial policy.

It is perhaps not surprising to see such a broad range of solutions and a willingness to adopt a legal pluralism in Quebec. Legal authority, as Jack P. Greene's work has shown, was always the product of negotiations between metropolitan centres and colonial peripheries.[36] The controversy over the instructions, however, focused primarily on the nature of the subjects in Quebec. The subjects in Quebec were not Protestant Britons who were negotiating over the form and content of laws and authority from a position of shared tradition. The French Catholic population in Quebec represented the complete antithesis of Britishness.[37] The danger and controversy of these negotiations emanated not from "indifferent" laws, but rather from the Catholic "other" who would be in positions of power to shape and apply those laws.[38] The intellectual leap necessary to create room for "foreign" traditions and actors underscores why Quebec offers a multitude of meanings and legacies in disparate contexts. The principles enshrined in the Quebec Act are not solely an example of legal pluralism or negotiated authority, but serve as a critical example of religious and cultural pluralism within British imperial civil society. It is much easier to create space for negotiated authority and legal structures when the terms of those structures are based largely in the traditions of the metropole. The transformation occurs when those same practices are extended to "alien" traditions and cultures, an exercise far removed from the examples of Ireland and the early settler colonies.[39]

This change in approach held implications for more than just Ireland or Quebec. According to P.J. Marshall, incorporating the Catholics in Quebec and the other ceded territories "helped to break down inhibitions about bringing within an imperial framework Indians, people who were thought to be completely alien to all previous traditions of British rule."[40] Beyond bridging the intellectual gap between British and alien traditions, Quebec offered inspiration for the forms of collaboration and order that would allow Britain to maintain control over an empire where Britons would be a demographic minority and where rule would depend upon collaboration with local elites. Quebec was a critical site for the redefinition of British subjecthood towards a much more inclusive notion of the subject and the acceptance of non-English tradition and law.[41] This intellectual and constitutional expansion created room for non-British elites to share in the administration and benefits of British rule.

II. THE CASE FOR COLLABORATION

In the aftermath of his recall, Murray's allies kept him abreast of the latest developments. In August 1766, one of his staunchest allies on the colony's council, Dr Adam Mabane, wrote to inform him of recent events in Quebec. Despite resistance to juries in civil cases by the seigneurs, the ability to sit on juries still remained a critical point of interest for the Canadiens. This access, according to Mabane, opened their eyes to the benefits of English traditions.[42] "It is remarkable that in Ireland, when the English law was first introduced there, Trials by Juries were looked upon by the natives, as one of their greatest grievances. Perhaps the first English adventurers in that country resembled those we have at Quebec, full of national as well as religious prejudice." Prejudice undermined the validity of the English system for, "in a narrow country, where jurors are few and connected by passion and interest, the abuses are obvious, and no wonder strike forcibly the minds of the Canadians."[43] The Canadiens, like the Irish, rejected British actions that excluded them from civil society, but felt bonded to men and policies that sought to integrate them into public life. The attempt to avoid the problems evident in Ireland would shift from a broad consideration of Canadian desires to one focused on the seigneurs, a body of men considered critical for establishing and maintaining the legitimacy of British rule.

The shift in approach signalled by Murray and others gained its staunchest proponent in the form of his replacement as governor. Guy Carleton, officially appointed governor in 1768, did not grudgingly move towards a pluralist approach, but consistently and vocally advocated for its implementation. Carleton was born and raised in Ireland and was well-connected within elite Anglo-Irish circles.[44] While the destruction of his personal papers by his wife, at his request, means we are without his more candid thoughts on Quebec, we might read much of what he says as a commentary on the failings of the Irish model. At the very least, his case was built on the same arguments deployed by critics of the Irish model. He certainly did not argue for the creation of an Anglo-Canadian elite to mirror his Anglo-Irish roots.

In November 1767, Carleton wrote the Earl of Shelburne, the current secretary of state for the Southern Department, to make the case for a strong reliance on the Canadien seigneurs to maintain stability and the loyalty of the French population in Quebec.[45] This was the first in a series of three letters written over the course of several months. Taken as a whole, the letters appear as a linked effort by Carleton to make a sustained argument for his ideal approach to Quebec.[46] Carleton wanted to make Shelburne aware of the true standing of the colony in order to assure that deliberations in London were as productive as possible – especially since the colony presented "objects at so great a distance, and in themselves so different from what is to be found in any of His [Majesty's] other dominions."[47] Carleton realized new strategies were needed for an imperial possession where Britons would always be the minority within a dominant non-British culture. It was a situation he must have known was not so different from Ireland, but by presenting Quebec as a new challenge, he opened the door for strategic innovation.

Carleton believed it was foolish to assume that the colony would slowly become culturally or demographically British. He insisted to Shelburne that such a development was impossible. In looking at a demographic balance strongly favouring the Canadiens, he wrote, "it may not be amiss to observe, that there is not the least probability, this present superiority should ever diminish, on the contrary 'tis more than probable it will increase and strengthen daily."[48] The question was no longer how to assimilate the new subjects within a colony that would soon become peopled by significant numbers of Britons, but how to rule over a colony that would remain culturally distinct. Administrators had to develop new imperial practices to come to terms with the demographic realities of the expanding British Empire.

Carleton strategically built the case for maintaining a traditional French social structure in the colony as a means to ensure loyalty and stability. His second letter to Shelburne reinforced the case of the seigneurs as critical to the state of the colony. He reminded Shelburne that "they are not a migration of Britons, who brought with them the Laws of England, but a populous and long established colony, reduced by the king's arms, to submit to his dominion, on *certain conditions*."[49] These conditions were largely that the power of the king, especially his ability to raise revenue, depended on the maintenance of the seigneurs' status in society. According to Carleton, "this system of laws established subordination, from the first to the lowest, which preserved the internal harmony, they enjoyed until our arrival, and secured obedience to the supreme seat of government from a very distant province."[50] The British in the aftermath of the conquest, however, imposed new laws, upset the social order, and brought instability to the colony.[51] For Carleton, this level of disregard had "never before [been] practiced by any conqueror, even where the people, without capitulation, submitted to his will and discretion."[52] Carleton hinted that British actions to this point violated the Treaty of Paris, the capitulation agreements, and the principles of natural rights. He argued that a change in policy and a return to the pre-Conquest norms was the only proper solution.

To this end he ordered men in the colony to create the abridgement of the old laws to serve as a law code for the colony. The English legal system lacked any legitimacy in its current state, according to Carleton, who noted that the Canadiens continued "to regulate their transactions by their ancient laws, tho' unknown and unauthorized in the supreme court, where most of these transactions would be declared invalid."[53] Therefore, a return to the old system of laws offered the only answer to the problems plaguing the colony. If Canadiens refused to recognize British legal structures and codes as legitimate and opted not to use them for formal adjudication, then British rule proved a chimera and the stability of the state questionable. British power rested on its legitimacy within the local population. As Carleton told Shelburne, the body of laws must be "the Foundation of all, without which, other Schemes can be little better than meer Castles in the Air."[54]

Carleton pressed his case in the third, and final, letter of the triumvirate. He contrasted the value of instilling Canadiens with the rights to hold public office and the case made by the British merchants for an assembly.[55] Carleton suggested that people remained attached to the system of government and laws under which they grew up. The Canadiens sought a continuation of their old order, and so naturally it benefited the British to maintain continuity for the good of colonial stability. Legitimacy and authority, for Carleton, rested not in the British merchants but with the seigneurs. Unless Catholics were heavily represented, an assembly would hold no more legitimacy in Catholic eyes than the laws that they already refused to recognize. Carleton's fundamental objection to an assembly was its impracticability. Asked to provide "their scheme for an assembly, and to inform me, who they thought should be the electors, and who the representatives," the British merchants offered no workable solution. He then provided a portrait of the type of Briton agitating for an assembly. The latest leader of the cause, John McCord, "formerly kept a small ale house in the poor suburbs of a little country town in the north of Ireland, appearing zealous for the Presbyterian faith." Now residing in the colony, McCord sold alcohol to the troops in a ramshackle shed next to the barracks. When turfed out by the magistrates to prevent constant drunkenness among the troops he "commenced Patriot, and with the assistance of the late Attorney General [Maseres], and three or four more, egged on by letters from home, are at work again for an Assembly."[56] This clearly did not present a flattering picture of the true motivations for those seeking an assembly and subtly hinted at the possible spread of the same tensions and disorder plaguing Ireland.

Carleton reiterated his contention that the legal codes should remain intact as a means to bind the Canadiens to the crown. He argued that, even if the colony could be defended from an outside invasion, "I shall think the interests of Great Britain but half advanced."[57] He doubted that the oaths the Canadiens were willing to take fostered any guarantee of their loyalty. Here Carleton was arguing against the emphasis placed on oaths in contemporary British thinking. Oaths, in both their form and reliability, were a question of serious debate within the Irish context, and the same questions undoubtedly applied to the French Catholics in Quebec.[58] As papists, Catholics were seen as unreliable oath-takers, as the Pope could supposedly absolve them of oaths to their sovereign, making their loyalty suspect. Carleton suggests that, rather than concerning themselves with the reliability of oaths, officials should work to make being a subject of the British crown an attractive proposition. This was no less important in Ireland, as the crown increasingly depended on Irish soldiers to fill the expanding ranks of the imperial army.[59]

If the crown hoped to instill in the Canadiens a willingness to fight to remain under its dominion, something stronger than an oath had to bind them to British rule. Carleton used this uncertainty to further the case in favour of roles in public life for the seigneurs. Beyond the legal remedies, "as long as the Canadians are deprived of all places of trust and profit, they never can forget they no longer are under the dominion of their natural sovereign."[60] Carleton did not envision opening up public life to all Canadiens, just those of the seigneurial class. So, while this denial of their traditional role in society affected only seventy seigneurial households, "it affects the minds of all, from a national spirit, which ever interests itself at the general exclusion of their countrymen."[61] He recommended a few gestures which would ameliorate the problem. Without opening every office to Catholics, he suggested they could take up limited roles in the military and on the colonial council.[62] This policy would increase the bond between the Canadiens and the Empire, as the younger generation would know only loyalty to the king and the bonds of service to his rule. If the British were going to have loyal partners in a collaborative effort of imperial governance, they had to recognize the desires and practices of the Canadiens.

Carleton's case for cultural continuity and collaboration began to find support in the public sphere soon after his elevation to governor. In Grenada, where debates over Catholic participation in the local assembly raged in the late 1760s, supporters of toleration and legal flexibility continued to place Ireland and the penal laws in a negative light. The pamphlet *Audi Alteram Partem*, published in 1770, attacked the supposed benefits of the penal laws. In making their point, the authors proposed a question with only one sensible answer: "So say, my Lordship, had we submitted to the public consideration, whether the new subjects are most likely to be faithful and true to their allegiance, if treated by the old subjects as brethren embarked in the same cause; or as slaves to be kept only in subjection by the scourge of Penal Laws."[63] The author continued to mock the notion that harmony could be restored by removing the political and legal privileges of Catholic subjects. For "the French Roman Catholick subjects, are about two thirds of the inhabitants of the island; take away their right of voting at elections, render them incapable of holding the least share of legislation or executive offices, and you will secure perfect harmony to the island!"[64] As a policy, alienating the largest share of the landowners and largest number of inhabitants clearly appeared illogical.[65] Rather than creating a disaffected elite and a discouraged Catholic underclass, officials increasingly recognized the benefits of securing not the newly established Protestant interest, but the interests of an already-resident local elite. There were few barriers to the implementation of a policy of collaboration, rather than assimilation, once there was a widely accepted rhetoric and ideal that recognized seigneurs as rights-bearing subjects of the crown, albeit with their own cultural, legal, and religious traditions.

III. REJECTING IRELAND

The rhetoric of displacement and the importance of local propertied interests were not unique to Grenada or Quebec in the 1760s and 1770s. The discourse surrounding the negative influence of cultural distinctions, the resulting instability, and the alienation of Catholics mirrors the case for the removal of penal laws in Ireland. John Curry, a prominent member of the Irish-Catholic community, who was active in founding the Catholic Committee, a body established in 1757 to campaign for, among other causes, the repeal of the penal laws, wrote a number of pamphlets in favour of Catholic rights throughout the latter half of the eighteenth century. Curry's *Observations on the Popery Laws*, published in London in 1770, the same year as many of the pamphlets dealing with the crisis in Grenada, shows how a reappraisal of the Catholic question in Ireland was prompting a rethinking of policy in the ceded territories in North America. The shared discourse surrounding Quebec, Grenada, and Ireland signals the ways in which the questions asked about Catholics in the Americas merged with discussions about Catholics in Ireland.

Like the anonymous authors of the Grenadian pamphlets, Curry argued that the real benefits of the British constitution would be fully realized only when shared by all subjects. "Our real strength must arise from the soundness of our constitution, and from the circulation of its benefits. Should the principle of those benefits be forbid to the greater part of our laboring people, to the landholder, to the citizen, and to the yeoman; the hand of industry is actually and effectively cramped."[66] This restriction of industry threatened not only the productivity of the island itself, but also the stability of the civil government. Those excluded from participation and the rights of the constitution would become lazy and disengaged. The depressed situation of Ireland and "the great weakness incurred by the indiscriminate operation of our penal laws, call aloud for alternatives."[67]

For Curry, Ireland was perfectly suited to economic and civic health because of its natural bounty. Yet it was crippled by fallow fields. Were a traveller to compare the natural bounty of the island to the poverty and lack of cultivated lands, "he would have no hesitation in pronouncing, that *in a country so highly favoured by nature*, the inhabitants could not be miserable, *without some defect in our laws*."[68] The two major drains on Ireland were absentee landlords, who turned land into pasturage at the expense of the people and the productivity of Ireland, and the "wasting and wasted papists," who were not allowed to participate or add to the economic and civic health of the island. The first defect was not easily remedied and would remain a major challenge to the island, Curry believed. However, the penal laws could be quickly and easily removed, allowing the nation to tap the productivity of all levels of Catholic society. At present, the Catholic subjects were "cut off from the principal benefits of its free constitution, and they necessarily become a disease within its bowels, acting against it, from an incapacity to act for it."[69] The state would benefit more from collaboration with the local population, especially elites, than through the exclusion of those improperly deemed suspect in their allegiance.

The House of Commons debate over the Quebec Act further developed the link between Quebec and Ireland. Opponents of the bill defended the imposition of English legal norms based on Sir John Davies's *A discoverie of the true causes why Ireland was neverly entirely subdued*. Speaking in the Commons on 26 May 1774, John Glynn argued that it was the prerogative of parliament, and the soundest policy, to establish and enforce English law in Quebec. According to Glynn, history proved that all nations had the right to enforce their laws on a conquered people – a right they exercised. In British history, the best example lay in Ireland – and here Glynn expressly relied on Davies – where "they were subdued, they receive the laws of the conquerors to this day, [and] they are indebted for all the happiness they enjoy."[70] While we might question how much happiness the Irish felt as a result of English law, for many opposed to the bill the Irish model still held considerable legitimacy.

Edmund Burke similarly believed that extending English law was critical if parliament wished to bind the Canadiens to the British state. On 7 June, Burke rose to defend the imposition of English legal norms in Canada. Burke found much to criticize in the reversal of the Proclamation of 1763 and the continuation of French law in the colony. For Burke, the extension of English liberty trumped the continuance of the local traditions. Only by experiencing the full benefits of English law would French Catholics become loyal British subjects, a position that mirrored his view of Ireland.[71] Burke was not simply concerned with the benefits or harm to English subjects. In speaking on the proclamation and the decision to revoke the extension of English laws it promised, Burke argued that "the laws of England as they stand … they hold out a defence of the liberty of the person which other laws do not procure."[72] Denying these protections to the Canadiens was against their best interests and deprived them of the benefit of English liberty. Burke argued that, like supporters of the bill, his primary motivation was protecting the interests and liberty of the Canadiens. In the case of the colonies, Burke wished to "have English liberty carried into the French colonies; but not have French slavery brought into" them.[73] In the end, removing English law was "to the French a denial of a promise, to the Englishmen denial of law."[74]

Burke's opinions on the matter also signal that, where popular opinion might be shaped largely by anti-Catholic bigotry, elites often understood the Catholic question through the lens of political order and European conceptions of conquest and imperial strategy.[75] The debate over the rights of the conquered and conquerors drew on a long history within British and European thought.[76] Building on intellectuals such as Grotius, Montesquieu, and Pufendorf, contemporary commentators assumed broad and powerful rights of cultural imposition and absorption for the conqueror. For many contemporary figures, the opinions of British legal figures like Sir Edward Coke provided further support to the idea that, as in Ireland, the laws of Quebec were rightfully determined in London.[77] In British circles, the debate over Ireland exemplified by works like Sir John Davies's *A discoverie of the true causes* (1612) and William Molyneux's *The Case of Ireland … Stated* (1698), among others, served as critical source material in determining the right path forward.[78]

Yet Ireland's example did not offer a clear model, and its contested and complicated legacies presented only images of ambiguous identities and questionable political legitimacy.[79] Those who favoured the maintenance of local legal codes in Quebec drew more on contemporary thinkers, like the Physiocrats in France or Adam Smith in Scotland, who suggested that economic cooperation offered better long-term prospects than cultural imposition in the aftermath of conquest.[80] In addition, Britain's legal minds increasingly relied on European Natural Law theory as a means to work outside the English Common Law and traditional constitutional precedents. Natural Law theory allowed eighteenth-century British jurists outlets for pragmatic decisions with questionable validity within the Common Law.[81] The nature of conquest and the best means of steadying new territories and engendering loyalty among new subjects remained contested throughout the debate over Quebec. Yet for those who succeeded in having their vision enacted, the lessons from history and legal theory inspired a belief that conciliation of local traditions proved the best means for introducing stability, prosperity, and loyalty.

Many politicians and writers found little to admire in the strategies employed in Ireland. Robert Nugent, Lord Clare in the Irish peerage, was an active participant in parliamentary debate. In his defence of the bill in the Commons, Clare pointed out the misguided motivation behind the penal laws in Ireland, for "the laws are made in the heat of blood, and great provocation certainly after this infamous rebellion [1641]." Yet the policy, according to Clare, did not convert Catholics. In fact, as a result of the penal laws, Catholic elites either emigrated or became poor. This process left the Catholic population under the leadership of their priests, and more attached to their religion, not less. These laws made in the fit of fear proved counterproductive, especially as they forced the men of property, the natural leaders of Irish society, to go abroad. He asked, "what is the cause that miserable, ignorant, bigoted people the clergy of Ireland are looked up to. Because they have no men of landed property. Such has been the wisdom of the Irish laws, they have not only made laws that have driven the people of property out of the country, but they never can purchase."[82] While modern historians debate the full extent of the repercussions of the penal laws and the related redistribution of land, which saw only 5 per cent left in Catholic hands by 1776, for many contemporary critics this dispossession was the root of Ireland's problems.[83] In Ireland, the penal laws ensured opposition to the state, rather than the desired assimilation and loyalty. As a means of conversion, legal disabilities based on religious confession constituted a misguided policy. The obvious solution was to maintain the landed elite as a means to rule over non-Britons through collaboration that was beneficial to both sides.

Alexander Wedderburn, the solicitor general of Great Britain, also disputed the effectiveness of the imposition of English norms in Ireland, and suggested that the Quebec Act rested on stronger principles espoused by thinkers like Montesquieu and Grotius.[84] Wedderburn argued that the imposition of English law would prove ineffective and undermine the process of assimilation. "The inhabitants of Canada should acquire the mode of thinking of British subjects; as much as possible to adopt British manners. But if you alter the laws, it will be difficult. If you alter the manners, it will be more so. You should not attempt it by any violent, or sudden alteration; otherwise you put by that event into a greater distance, than if you let things take their own course."[85] Only through gradual change, facilitated by the seigneurs, would Canadiens eventually adopt British religious and legal traditions.[86] He presented historical evidence of his principal, "with respect to Ireland both instances [events in Ireland in the twelfth and fifteenth centuries] prove this, that all laws of the country must be the effect of time."[87]

After parliament passed the Quebec Act, the North government employed William Knox, the Irish-born undersecretary for the American department, to defend the act in print. Knox was not just a partisan used to produce propaganda for his employer; he played a central role in drafting and completing the Quebec Bill.[88] As a result, he was intimately aware and actively in favour of its underlying principles. In his 1774 pamphlet, *The Justice and Policy of the Late Act of Parliament*, Knox drew on the example of the Catholics in Ireland to defend the policy. Echoing Lord Clare, Knox argued that the framers of the penal laws created the legal regime not through sound reasoning and judgment, but rather because of "dread of their numbers, and resentment for the cruelties they had inflicted upon the Protestants while their rule lasted."[89] Readers could recognize that this rash and emotional motivation was a contrast to the decade of internal debate that gave birth to the Quebec Act. Knox spelled out the consequences of the resulting policies.

If the penal laws aimed to create stability and loyal subjects and convert Catholics to Protestantism, then "the effect of these measures, if we may believe the Irish Protestants, has not by any means answered these their avowed purposes, nor served in any degree to recommend them for our imitation in Quebec."[90] Instead, the Irish Protestants "think themselves in the utmost danger of being massacred by the papists, if, even in time of peace, there should happen to be a less number than twelve thousand effective troops remaining in the island."[91] In referencing the recent crisis in Ireland over the crown's desire to augment the number of troops raised in Ireland, Knox sought to highlight the Protestants' own sense of precariousness.[92] A stark contrast existed between the Protestant demands for assistance in maintaining order and their assertions of the beneficial impact of the penal laws and the imposition of English norms in Ireland. It seemed undeniable that, in Ireland, English norms were not willingly and successfully adopted. It was not, then, a model worthy of emulation. Accordingly, Knox hoped a new type of politician would arise in Ireland. He looked for one who recognized "men to be more disposed to support a government that protects them in all the rights of humanity, than one whose policy it is to extirpate them," and who realized that "men who invest their wealth in fixed property, are not the most apt to excite insurrections; and that to oblige men to transmit their property into foreign countries, is not the surest method of attaching them to the state they reside in."[93] In fact, he hoped Quebec would now act as an ideal for the further reform of Ireland.

CONCLUSION

In the years after 1763, Ireland looked like an increasingly poor model for Canada. The debate over Quebec suggests that for a critical mass of British officials the policies deployed in Ireland were ultimately ineffective. While the opposition presented Ireland as an example to be followed, the North ministry and those creating colonial policy, including many from past ministries, remained skeptical. The alienated Catholic population, which appeared rudderless after the loss of Catholic elites, created serious doubts about the underlying stability of the island. What emerges in the public and internal rhetoric of this period is a unified and sustained case in favour of the protection of law, property, and culture as a means to ensure loyalty and stability. For this growing number of elites, the policies developed in Quebec, especially structures of collaboration with local landholders, offered a new way forward for the empire.

Ultimately the Quebec Act was not simply a localized, pragmatic policy meant to address a specific set of problems. Imperial administrators, politicians, and countless others recognized that the decisions made with regard to incorporating this new Catholic population related to a host of other questions facing Britain at home and in its expanding empire. Efforts at Catholic relief began in Ireland in 1774 and continued in piecemeal fashion through the early nineteenth century.[94] Critically, reform in Ireland was geared towards addressing the concerns of the Catholic middle class, the body of subjects now expected to lead Catholic Ireland into a closer and more stable relationship with the British crown. The first major relief act in 1778 was primarily aimed at addressing the land question, in an effort to redress the growing imbalance and the underlying disruptions. In a language riddled with references to justice and humanity, defenders of the bill used many of the same cases for conciliation towards French Catholics that would be deployed in Ireland during what seemed, for a brief moment at the end of the eighteenth century, a comparatively rapid push towards Catholic emancipation.[95]

The language emerging around the crown's new and old subjects in Quebec, which treated difference as a mere distinction "between one description and the other" of the crown's subjects, presages in important ways Henry Dundas's attitude towards Catholic and Protestant subjects in Ireland.[96] In a letter to Lord Lieutenant Westmorland discussing the Catholic Relief Act of 1792, Dundas made clear that, for the king's ministers, "if it is a mere question if one description of Irishmen or another are to enjoy a monopoly of pre-eminence, I am afraid that it is not a question on which they would feel either their passions or their interests so naturally concerned."[97] The notion that the crown would not grant "pre-eminence" to one group of subjects opened the door to all kinds of strategies of rule that addressed the realities of the heterogeneous population in the wider empire.[98]

The reform of Irish political and legal structures emanated from many of the same motivations, especially the benefits of participation for all subjects, which drove policy in Quebec. Ultimately though, it was not the replication of a reformed Ireland that animated practice in the expanding British Empire, but a strategy of collaboration mirroring that developed in Quebec.[99] The concessions to the Canadien seigneurs were predicated on an imagined social structure that placed landholders at the top of a well-ordered hierarchy. Carleton's assumptions of order were based on ingrained attitudes towards French society that proved misguided and problematic.[100] While ostensibly less prejudiced against the French population than other imperial figures, he arrived in Canada with conditioned expectations of the feudal nature of French society. Not simply serfs, the habitants often expressed their independence in ways not clear to their social superiors.[101] The fact that they did not fit the expectations placed on them would not become clear until their neutrality – and at times outright hostility – during the American invasion of 1775.[102] The successful, though troubled, defence of the colony, however, convinced officials of the benefits of negotiating with elites in order to secure the imperial stability that would drive British policies in India and Africa.[103]

Authoritarian Whigs, like Alexander Wedderburn, supported a legal pluralism that held substantive value in dividing British colonial territories and ensuring that a cohesive levelling within the empire would not take place.[104] This pluralism also fostered legal systems with an authoritarian logic aimed at the internal structures of each individual colony. By choosing to construct legal regimes supposedly based on pre-Conquest norms, British officials were ensuring divisive hierarchal structures within colonies. To the benefit of local collaborators and imperial stability, British officials created structures that ensured that colonial societies throughout the empire were ordered from "the first to the lowest." This ordered, semi-feudal vision of places as disparate as Quebec and India was a defining aspect of British imperial imagination and rule until decolonization in the twentieth century.[105] Collaboration with indigenous elites necessitated cultural, legal, and religious pluralism alongside the imaginative creation of a well-defined social order in line with British needs.

C.A. Bayly has written on the authoritarian turn in the British imperial system in the period beginning around 1780, especially as it related to India. According to Bayly, "these colonial despotisms were characterized by a form of aristocratic military government supporting a viceregal autocracy, by a well-developed imperial style which emphasized hierarchy and racial subordination, and by the patronage of indigenous landed elites."[106] He recognized that Quebec, especially as it related to the patronage of landed elites, fit well within his definition of this system. Yet the repressive nature of empire and its ultimate dependence on inequalities of power does not mean that Quebec did not profoundly alter British ideals of empire and open spaces for pluralism. Bayly writes of the empire after 1780 that "constitution-making for the dependencies remained evolutionary and pragmatic; it rarely aspired to uniformity."[107] In fundamental ways, it would be difficult for him to write such a statement about the British officials dealing with an "alien" population of sizable proportion prior to Quebec, when they wished to believe the empire would remain largely British, "Protestant, maritime, and free." Local traditions were not simply wiped away, and assimilation did not prove the rule. Instead officials created hybrid systems of law and governance as they had in Quebec.

In South Asia, British officials faced many of the same questions raised by efforts to integrate French Catholics into the empire. A large population of non-Britons needed to be integrated in a way that would ensure loyalty and stability among a people that would forever remain the demographic majority. As the East India Company expanded its reach over South Asia, and British officials became more concerned and involved with events there, they relied on many of the same ideas, rhetorical devices, and ideological constructions to frame British intervention and governance. Under the governorship of Lord Cornwallis, the first governor to exercise civil and military control under the authority of the British government, reforms were introduced to stabilize the chaotic situation in Bengal. In establishing direct rule over Bengal in 1793, the British relied on several key strategies: the reformation of the criminal law, the use of the principle of "customs and usages," and the importance of the landed classes. These fundamental traits of British rule and reform offer a direct link to the languages, principles, and practices developed in Quebec.[108] The trade-off between imperial officials and local elites, in what became known as the Permanent Settlement, ensured that British rule was supported among key populations within the indigenous society.[109] The same strategies for colonial rule and incorporation were used as Britain expanded direct rule across India and in British Africa in the late-nineteenth and early-twentieth centuries.[110] This openness to "evolutionary and pragmatic" constitution-making emerged from the empiricist bent of the British official mind.

In the case of Quebec, Ireland presented a clear example of what happened within a conquered population when its native elite was removed. The Irish-Catholic population did not accept assimilation and, with its natural leaders driven out of Ireland, or into poverty, Ireland remained a problematic precedent. A partnership with the seigneurs, as imagined by figures like Carleton and supporters of the Quebec Act, avoided the disaffection so noticeable among Ireland's Catholic inhabitants. It also solved the tricky question of how to rule over a populace that would remain culturally distinct and a demographic majority. In imagining a Canadian landed elite with well-defined legal rights at the top of a hierarchy of power, British officials redefined the core strategies of imperial expansion and rule. The older Irish model, predicated upon assimilationist policies and the dispossession of pre-Conquest elites, was replaced by a system of collaboration and continuity within a heterogeneous imperial structure. By the end of the 1760s, Ireland was no longer the British imperial laboratory. Experiences and experiments in Quebec would lay the foundation of collaborative strategies deployed across the British Empire in the nineteenth and twentieth centuries.

NOTES

I would like to thank Richard Bourke, Jack Greene, Jim Smyth, and the editors and other authors in this volume for reading previous versions of this chapter. Their comments helped to sharpen the chapter, and all remaining flaws are entirely the fault of the author. I am grateful to the Keough-Naughton Institute for Irish Studies, the Nanovic Institute for European Studies, the Institute for Scholarship for the Liberal Arts, and the Graduate School at the University of Notre Dame for funding to carry out research that contributed to this article.

1 Dominica, Grenada, Saint Vincent, and Tobago comprised the Ceded Islands.

2 While being questioned in the House of Commons, Guy Carleton, the governor in 1774, estimated that, through immigration of Acadians and natural increase, the population was closer to 150,000 at the time of the bill's passage.

3 On British attempts at assimilation, see Jane Ohlmeyer, "A Laboratory for Empire? Early Modern Ireland and English Imperialism," in *Ireland and the British Empire* (Oxford: Oxford University Press, 2005).

4 For a treatment of British imperial ideology prior to this period, see David Armitage, *The Ideological Origins of the British Empire* (Cambridge: Cambridge University Press, 2000).

5 For two treatments of 1688, see Tony Claydon, *William III and the Godly Revolution* (Cambridge: Cambridge University Press, 1996); and Steven Pincus, *1688: The First Modern Revolution* (New Haven, CT: Yale University Press, 2009).

6 See, for instance, J.C.D. Clark, *English Society, 1660–1832* (New York: Cambridge University Press, 2000) and Linda Colley, *Britons* (New Haven, CT: Yale University Press, 2009).

7 For attachments to the Protestant constitution and the various forms of anti-Catholicism, see James Bradley, *Religion, Revolution, and English Radicalism* (Cambridge: Cambridge University Press, 1990); and Colin Haydon, *Anti-Catholicism in Eighteenth-Century England* (Manchester: Manchester University Press, 1993)..

8 For the pre-eminent synthesis of contemporary Ireland, see Ian McBride, *Eighteenth-Century Ireland* (Dublin: Gill and Macmillan, 2009).

9 S.J. Connolly, *Contested Island* (Oxford: Oxford University Press, 2007), and *Divided Kingdom* (Oxford: Oxford University Press, 2008). Connolly would also assert that Ireland does not fit into a colonial model, but rather is an example of an *ancien régime* society, see his, *Religion, Law, and Power: The Making of Protestant Ireland* (Oxford: Oxford University Press, 2002).

10 On the penal laws see, McBride, *Eighteenth-Century Ireland*, 194–214.

11 For the Catholic Question in Ireland, see Thomas Bartlett, *Fall and Rise of the Irish Nation*. (Dublin: Gill and Macmillan, 1992).

12 The Acadians, the previous French-Canadian population to find themselves under British rule, present a stark example of forced migration. On the Acadians, see John Mack Faragher, *A Great and Noble Scheme*. (New York: W.W. Norton, 2005), and Christopher Hodson, *The Acadian Diaspora* (Oxford: Oxford University Press, 2012).

13 Philip Lawson similarly pointed to a number of points of rhetorical and intellectual convergence between Ireland and Quebec, see Lawson, *The Imperial Challenge* (McGill-Queen's University Press, 1989).

14 The National Archives of the UK (TNA): Public Record Office (PRO), [hereafter PRO], 30/47/22/2, folio 70.

15 This opinion can be found throughout the material related to Quebec, but see, for instance, the Presentments of the Grand Jury of Quebec from October of 1764, which can be found in several locations: National Library of Canada, FC412 Q84 1765a, Cf. Tremaine 66, see especially pages 4 and 5; in Shortt and Doughty, *Documents Relating to the Constitutional History of Canada*, (1918), 153–6; and in the Canadian National Archives MG23 A1 vol. 4, 4510–18, with related material on pages 4519–30.

16 On the process of state formation in the four nations, see especially Michael Braddick, *State Formation in Early Modern England* (Cambridge: Cambridge University Press, 2000); Brendan Bradshaw and J.S. Morrill, eds, *The British Problem* (London: Macmillan, 1996); S.J. Connolly, ed., *Kingdoms United?* (Dublin: Four Courts Press, 1999); and Jim Smyth, *The Making of the United Kingdom, 1660–1800* (New York: Longman, 2001).

17 For a treatment of the relationship between practices and theories developed in the British Isles and the Proclamation of 1763, see Patrick Griffin, *American Leviathan* (New York: Hill and Wang, 2007), 19–45.

18 PRO CO 43/1, f. 143.

19 On the plantations of Ireland, see, Nicholas Canny, *Making Ireland British* (New York: Oxford University Press, 2001).

20 On the plan for settlement called "British Town," see CNA MG23 A4, vol. 10, 232.

21 The Québécois were spared the "Settler Revolution" that Anglicized so much of the globe, and they worked to resist Anglo settlement well into the nineteenth century. See, James Belich, *Replenishing the Earth* (Oxford: Oxford University Press, 2009), especially pages 288–92 on Quebec in the mid-nineteenth century.

22 For a comparative treatment of the transfer of legal and political systems in the Americas and the demographic reasons for the cultural continuity in Quebec, see Jack P. Greene, "The Cultural Dimensions of Political Transfers," *Early American Studies* (Spring 2008): 1–24.

23 S.J. Connolly, *Religion, Law, and Power*, 144–7.

24 McBride, *Eighteenth-Century Ireland*, 218–23.

25 On the legal and political disorder of this period, see Lawson, *The Imperial Challenge*, 43–84.

26 Murray, in his initial report back to London in the aftermath of the Conquest, signalled that conciliation of Catholic demands offered the best chance of stability and loyalty from the French population. This report from June 1762 can be found in Shortt and Doughty, *Documents*, 47–80.

27 The almost identical letters sent to his brother and Eglinton can be found in the CNA, MG23, GII 1, 170–4.

28 The full document can be found at CNA MG23 A4, vol. 14, 30–6.

29 CNA MG23 A4, vol. 14, 31.

30 Peter Marshall made the point that, while some aspects of Minorca offered a potential model for Quebec, it was really little more "than a British fleet to which an island was appended." As a result, few meaningful lessons could be drawn from it in developing policies for Quebec. See Marshall, "The Incorporation of Quebec in the British Empire," in

Of Mother Country and Plantations, ed. Virginia Bever Platt and David Curtis Skaggs, 42–61 (Bowling Green, OH: Bowling Green State University Press, 1971).

31 CNA MG23 A4, vol. 14, 31–2.

32 Stephen Conway argues that the debate over Quebec revolved around two models: Ireland and Minorca. While he is undoubtedly right that a vocal group resisted the shift away from the assimilationist policies of Ireland right up to the end, and many in this group continued to resist even after 1774, these voices were largely in the opposition. Yet his chapter seemingly represents this oppositional position as the predominant thinking within the debate. In addition, Minorca can at times be overemphasized as the direct source for the policies in Quebec. In practice it was never a binary choice between model A and model B in formulating policy for Quebec. For his discussion of the gradual and reluctant move away from the Irish model to the Minorcan, see Conway, "The Consequences of Conquest: Quebec and British Politics," in *Revisiting 1759*, ed. Phillip Buckner and John Reid, 141–65 (University of Toronto Press, 2012).

33 For a treatment of these instructions and the controversy they caused within the Rockingham ministry, see R.A. Humphreys and S. Morley Scott, "Lord Northington and the Laws of Canada," *Canadian Historical Review* 14 (1933): 42–61.

34 For Murray's ordinances, see Shortt and Doughty, *Documents*, 205–9.

35 See text and commentary in Humphreys and Morley Scott, 57– 60.

36 See Jack Greene, *Negotiated Authorities* (Charlottesville, VA: University of Virginia Press, 1994).

37 Colley, *Britons*.

38 In a report to the Board of Trade on the civil government of Quebec, Charles Yorke deemed local customs, especially regarding property and law, "in their own nature indifferent." See Shortt and Doughty, *Documents*, 255.

39 For a discussion of the development of legal regimes and forms of legal pluralism, see Lauren Benton, *Law and Colonial Cultures* (Cambridge: Cambridge University Press, 2002).

40 P.J. Marshall, *The Making and Unmaking of Empires* (Oxford: Oxford University Press, 2005), 196.

41 On how this redefinition and expansion of subjecthood took place in Quebec, see Hannah Weiss Muller's chapter in this volume.

42 It should be noted that civil juries did not find a place in the Quebec Act at the insistence of the seigneurs.

43 CNA MG23 A4, vol 16, 96. The mention of juries is directly related to the presentments of the Grand Jury of Quebec, which sought to exclude Catholics from public office.

44 For biographies of Carleton, see Paul David Nelson, *General Sir Guy Carleton* (Madison, NJ: Fairleigh Dickinson University Press, 2000), and Paul Revere Reynolds, *Guy Carleton* (New York: Morrow, 1980).

45 Letter dated 25 November 1767, Shortt and Doughty, *Documents,* 281. Both men were born and spent their early years in Ireland. While not wanting to make too much of the point, each would have been keenly aware of the tensions and realities within Ireland.

46 As the navigation of the St Lawrence proved impossible in winter, and his first letter would hardly have had time to reach Shelburne, the purpose of these letters was to underline his point through repetition in the packet of letters that would eventually make their way to Shelburne's desk. On the difficulty of winter and communication with Quebec, see Kenneth Banks, *Chasing Empire Across the Sea* (Montreal: McGill-Queen's University Press, 2002), 69–76.

47 Shortt and Doughty, *Documents,* 282.

48 Ibid., 284.

49 Ibid., 288. Letter dated 24 December 1767.

50 Ibid., 289. See Neatby, *Quebec: The Revolutionary Age* (Toronto: McClelland and Stewart, 1966).

51 For an example of similar debates in India, especially around the Bengal Court of Judicature, see Richard Bourke, *Empire and Revolution: The Political Life of Edmund Burke* (Princeton: Princeton University Press, 2015), 538–49.

52 Shortt and Doughty *Documents,* 289.

53 Ibid., 290.

54 As quoted in Neatby, *Quebec: The Revolutionary Age.*

55 Letter dated 20 January 1768. See Shortt and Doughty, *Documents,* 294–6.

56 Ibid., 295.

57 Ibid., 294.

58 See Patrick Fagan, *Divided Loyalties: The Question of the Oath for Irish Catholics in the Eighteenth Century* (Dublin: Four Courts Press, 1997), and Vincent Morely, "Catholic Disaffection and the Oath of Allegiance of 1774," in *People, Politics and Power: Essays on Irish History, 1660–1850,* ed. James Kelly, John McCafferty, Charles Ivar McGrath, 122–43 (Dublin: University College Dublin Press, 2009).

59 On Catholics in Ireland, the growth of toleration, and military service in this period, see R.K. Donovan, "The Military Origins of the Roman Catholic Relief Programme of 1778," *Historical Journal* 28, no. 1 (1985); and Bartlett, *Fall and Rise of the Irish Nation*, 82–92.

60 Shortt and Doughty, *Documents*, 294.

61 Ibid., 294. A similar case was, and is, made for the widespread effects of the penal laws in Ireland.

62 Ibid., 294–5.

63 *Audi Alteram Partem* (London, 1770), 40. Eighteenth Century Collections Online (ECCO).

64 Ibid., 44.

65 For more on the context in Grenada, see Willis, "The Standing of New Subjects: Grenada and the Protestant Constitution after the Treaty of Paris (1763)," *Journal of Imperial and Commonwealth History* 42, no. 1 (2014): 1–21.

66 *Observations on the Popery Laws* (Dublin, 1771) 8.

67 Ibid., 9.

68 Ibid., 12.

69 Ibid., 14.

70 R.C. Simmons and P.D.G. Thomas, *Proceedings and Debates of the British Parliaments Respecting North America, 1754–1783*, vol. 4 (Millwood, NY: Kraus International Publications, 1983), 464.

71 See, for example, Bourke, "Edmund Burke and the Politics of Conquest," *Modern Intellectual History* 4, no. 3 (November 2007): 403–32, and *Empire and Revolution: The Political Life of Edmund Burke* (Princeton: Princeton University Press, 2015), 460–70.

72 Simmons and Thomas, *Proceedings and Debates*, vol. 5, 121

73 Ibid., 122.

74 Ibid.

75 For a treatment of popular opinion, anti-Catholicism, and Quebec, see Brad Jones's chapter in this volume.

76 For a comparative history of the ideologies of conquest and empire in Europe, especially relating to Spain, Britain, and France, see Anthony Pagden, *Lords of All the World* (New Haven, CT: Yale University Press, 1995).

77 The question of who held the ultimate sovereignty to make the final decision, parliament or the crown, remained contested as it related to the validity of the Proclamation of 1763. By 1766, however, parliament seemed to hold the uncontested right to make such decisions. In this

regard the debate over Quebec fits well within contemporary politics, see John Brewer, *Party Ideology and Popular Politics at the Accession of George III* (Cambridge: Cambridge University Press, 1976).

78 See Bourke, "Edmund Burke and the Politics of Conquest," *Modern Intellectual History* 4, no. 3 (November 2007): 403–32, on the debate in parliament relating to theories of conquest and the links between Ireland and Quebec. Bourke highlights the implicit and explicit use of figures like Coke, Grotius, Montesquieu, and Davies.

79 One the legacies of conquest and identity in Ireland, see Jim Smyth, "'Like Amphibious Animals': Irish Protestants, Ancient Britons, 1691–1707," *The Historical Journal* 36, no. 4 (December 1993): 785–97.

80 For an account of a similar shift in emphasis in Ireland, see Jacqueline Hill, "Politics and the Writing of History," in *Political Discourse in Seventeenth- and Eighteenth-Century Ireland*, ed. D. George Boyce, Robert Eccleshall, and Vincent Geoghegan, 227–32 (London: Palgrave, 2001). The ideas of the Physiocrats played a similarly important role in shaping imperial policy in India; Ranajit Guha, *A Rule of Property for Bengal: An Essay on the Idea of Permanent Settlement* (Durham, NC: Duke University Press, 1996).

81 On this legal strategy, see D.J. Ibbetson, "Natural Law and Common Law," *Edinburgh Law Review* 5 (2001): 4–20.

82 Simmons and Thomas, *Proceedings and Debates*, vol. 5, 117.

83 McBride, *Eighteenth-Century Ireland*, 216–17 and 239–245.

84 See, Simmons and Thomas, *Proceedings and Debates*, vol. 4, 466, for his use of Montesquieu; vol. 5, 190, for his evocation of Grotius; and vol. 4, 465 and 470, for Wedderburn's comments on Irish history and his reading of Davies, Leland, and Coke.

85 Simmons and Thomas, *Proceedings and Debates*, vol. 4, 468–9.

86 On a similar realization within the French imperial system, which moved their position from one of assimilation to collaborative association, see Alice Conklin, *A Mission to Civilize: The Republican Idea of Empire in France and West Africa, 1985–1930* (Stanford, CA: Stanford University Press, 1997).

87 Simmons and Thomas, Proceedings and Debates, vol. 4, 470.

88 Knox was one of the first sub-ministers to combine the role of proposing and drafting legislation and acting as a ministerial apologist. Knox worked for almost a year on the Quebec bill and was a critical figure in much of the legislation emanating from the American department. This can be found in Jack Sosin, *Whitehall in the Wilderness* (Lincoln, NE: University of Nebraska Press, 1961), 239–55; and Franklin Wickwire, *Sub-*

ministers and Colonial America, (Princeton: Princeton University Press, 1966), 139–53.

89 *Justice and Policy of the Late Act*, 21.

90 Ibid., 22–3.

91 *Ibid.*, 23.

92 Tom Bartlett, "The Augmentation of the Army in Ireland, 1767–1769," *English Historical Review* 96, no. 380 (July 1981): 540–59.

93 *Justice and Policy of the Late Act*, 24–5

94 Bartlett, *Fall and Rise of the Irish Nation.*

95 On this trend, see Jack Greene, *Evaluating Empire and Confronting Colonialism in Eighteenth-Century Britain* (Cambridge: Cambridge University Press, 2013).

96 This phrase was used in a document produced by the Board of Trade in a plan for a Quebec assembly allowing a significant number of seats for Catholics in July 1769. Shortt and Doughty, *Documents*, 383.

97 As quoted in Jim Smyth, *The Making of the United Kingdom, 1660–1800* (New York: Longman, 2001).

98 For more on Quebec's role in the changing discussion over subjects see, Hannah Weiss Muller, "Subjecthood and the British Empire," *Journal of British Studies* 53, no. 1 (2014): 29–58.

99 On political reform aimed at the Protestant Ascendency, rather than the Catholic population, see Martyn J. Powell, *Britain and Ireland in the Eighteenth-Century Crisis of Empire* (New York: Palgrave Macmillan, 2003).

100 The various reactions of the Canadien population to British institutions, including the ambivalent reaction of the habitants to the continuation of the old order, is explored by Donald Fyson, "The Canadiens and British Institutions of Local Governance in Quebec from the Conquest to the Rebellions," in *Transatlantic Subjects*, ed. Nancy Christie, 45–82 (Montreal: McGill-Queen's University Press, 2008).

101 Neatby, *Quebec: The Revolutionary* Age, 24–5.

102 Neatby, *Quebec: The Revolutionary Age*, 144–7, and Ouellet, *Economic and Social History of Quebec*, 126–7.

103 The opinion of Reginald Coupland, who praised Carleton's conciliatory actions for ensuring Quebec remained part of the empire during the American Revolution, is an example of the lessons that contemporary supporters could draw from the outcome; Coupland, *The Quebec Act: A Study in Statesmanship* (New York: Clarendon Press, 1925).

104 See Christian Burset's chapter in this volume.

105 On this phenomenon and its importance for colonial rule, consult,

among other works, David Cannadine, *Ornamentalism: How the British Saw Their Empire* (Oxford: Oxford University Press, 2001); Nicholas Dirks, "Castes of Mind" *Representations* 37 (1992): 56–78; Guha, *A Rule of Property for Bengal*; Thomas Metcalf, *Ideologies of the Raj* (Cambridge: Cambridge University Press, 1994), especially chapters 3 and 4; D.A. Washbrook, "Law, State, and Agrarian Society in Colonial India," *Modern Asian Studies* 15, no. 3 (1981): 649 – 721.

106 C.A. Bayly, *Imperial Meridian* (New York: Longman, 1989), 9, and, on Quebec, 94.

107 Bayly, *Imperial Meridian*, 9.

108 See Hannah Weiss Muller's chapter in this volume on the language of "customs and usages."

109 On the "Permanent Settlement" and the reforms under Cornwallis, refer to Robert Travers, *Ideology and Empire in Eighteenth-Century India: The British in Bengal* (New York: Cambridge University Press, 2007), 207–49. Travers briefly touches on the place of Quebec in his narrative; see especially, 48–52.

110 See, for instance, Tomas Frederiksen, "Authorizing the 'Natives': Governmentality, Dispossession, and the Contradictions of Rule in Colonial Zambia," *Annals of the Association of American Geographers* 104, no. 6 (2014): 1273–90; and John Lonsdale and Bruce Berman, "Coping with the Contradictions: The Development of the Colonial State in Kenya, 1895–1914," *Journal of African History* 20, no. 4 (1979): 487–505.

6

London's Role in the Connection between the Holy See and North America, 1745–1812

Luca Codignola

The past generation of North American historians has devoted little attention, if any, to the political history of the era immediately following the British conquest of Canada in 1760.[1] Rejecting the nationalist and imperial preoccupations of previous generations, these historians were more attentive to social and economic concerns and emphasized long-term trends over catastrophic developments. One major victim of this lack of attention was the Quebec Act (1774), the timing and imperial motivations of which have been the object of only very sparse interest in the past thirty years.[2]

A second element missing in the recent debate on the post-Conquest era is the role of the Roman Catholic Church, although it powerfully shaped the attitude of the Canadiens towards the new British regime, as well as moderating the crown's policies. British historian and minister Peter M. Doll has recently examined the role of the Church of England in the context of the relationship between the Empire and British North America in the second half of the eighteenth century. For the Catholic Church, however, one must go back to the Canadian debates on the alleged servitude of Jean-Olivier Briand (1715–94), the first bishop of Quebec after the Conquest, or to the exchanges which took place in the 1960s. Both were overwhelmingly influenced by strong political opinions, federalist as well as nationalist.[3]

As for the United States, one must go even further back, to the works of the Jesuit historian Charles Metzger (1890–1972), conceived before the Second World War. Admittedly, the Catholic Church was still a minor player in the continental British colonies. Yet an ambitious synthesis such as that of the eminent American religious historian, Jon Butler, published in 2000 and entirely devoted to the years immediately preceding 1776, mentions the Quebec Act in a single line. In Butler's view, the act is significant merely because it "raise[d] fears about Roman Catholic sympathies in Britain." Evidently enough, he deemed the Act's consequences for North America negligible.[4]

Furthermore, the role and the presence of the Catholic Church has seldom, if ever, been placed in an international context for either the United States or for British North America. Several years ago, I described the profound change in the relations between the Holy See, France, and British North America, a consequence of the passage of the former Canada from the French to the British crown. I contended that, after 1760, Paris progressively lost its pivotal role in the network that linked Rome and North America. The Rome-Paris-Quebec connection was eventually replaced by a number of bilateral relations, mostly based on ethnic allegiances.[5] In this chapter I will examine how London, slowly but surely, began to take Paris's place in the concurrent network that linked the Holy See and British continental provinces from the mid-eighteenth century until the first decade of the nineteenth century. Undoubtedly, London's full-scale replacement of Paris took several decades and became fully evident only after 1812, during the administration of William Poynter (1762–1827) as vicar apostolic in the London district. However, some expressions of this trend already existed during the mandates of Poynter's three immediate predecessors, between 1758 and 1812.[6]

Although ecclesiastical authorities in London were largely uninvolved in the drafting of the Quebec Act, it nonetheless marked a milestone in the growing awareness and role of the British Church. Despite the fact that an aging vicar apostolic in London showed little interest in the new population of Catholics within the British Empire, the issues surrounding their governance would stretch from Rome to Paris, Minorca, Grenada, and Montreal, and eventually locate Church authorities in London at the centre of a vast Catholic network spanning the British Empire. Indeed, from the longest view, the Quebec Act foreshadows the growing importance of the British Church and the eventual policy of Catholic emancipation.

The Treaty of Paris (1763) sanctioned the passage of Canada to the British crown. Until then, a small number of Jesuits served the English-speaking Catholics of the British continental provinces. These men formally belonged to the English Province of the Society of Jesus.[7] The relationship was a bilateral relation – one that seldom, if ever, involved the Holy See. Outside of the Society of Jesus, no surviving documentation indicates any ongoing relationship between North American Catholics – French- or English-speaking – and the British Catholic community. Occasionally, as we shall see, the British upper hierarchy, in the person of the vicar apostolic in the London district, did speculate on its role towards the North American Catholics, and realized that such a role involved a number of spiritual duties. This realization originated not through solicitations coming from the American provinces, but through the impulse and the inspiration of the Holy See.[8] The earliest solicitation came from Rome in 1745 as part of a general request made by the Sacred Congregation de Propaganda Fide to be updated on the state of the English faithful. Propaganda Fide was the department of the Holy See in charge of mission territories, that is, countries that lacked an established Catholic hierarchy. At the time, the jurisdiction of the vicar apostolic in the London district included the West Indies as well as the British continental colonies, but did not extend to the diocese of Quebec, not even during the vacancy between the death of Henri-Marie Dubreil de Pontbriand (1708–60) in 1760 and Briand's appointment in 1766. Richard Challoner (1691–1781), who was vicar apostolic in the London district from 1758 to 1781, had no idea where this jurisdiction had originated, "tho' we ... always exercised jurisdiction there." Furthermore, Challoner was also keen to emphasize his lack of responsibility over places such as Nova Scotia and Newfoundland, ignoring the fact that they had formally been British colonies long before the Treaty of Paris.[9]

At any rate, Challoner was not particularly interested in colonial affairs. In his view, Catholicism needed to be more widely tolerated in Britain before it could expand in the British colonies. However, he dutifully answered Propaganda Fide's queries. Further solicitations reached Challoner in 1753, 1756, and 1759. He answered that, as far as he knew, five to seven thousand Catholics lived in Maryland, another two thousand in Pennsylvania, and a few more in Virginia and New Jersey. He was also aware of twelve Jesuit missionaries in Maryland

and four in Pennsylvania. Because the Society of Jesus was responsible for the spiritual needs of the Catholics living in the continental colonies, he suggested that Propaganda Fide approach one of its members, such as the Rector of the Venerable English College in Rome, for further information. Evidently grasping for more adequate solutions, at the very beginning of the Seven Years' War, Challoner suggested that a bishop be appointed for the continental colonies. However, he warned, the Jesuits would surely resent such a decision.[10]

In the period from the capitulation of Montreal (1760) to the Treaty of Paris (1763), the Canadiens of Quebec City and Montreal actively lobbied the British authorities in order to be guaranteed the free exercise of their religion.[11] The colony's restitution to France would entail the return of the Quebec church under the Gallican regime. Conversely, its cession to Great Britain would subject the colony to a regime in which the exercise of the Catholic religion was regulated by the Penal Laws, and hence proscribed both at home and in the colonies. Challoner was apparently unaware of such lobbying activities. After all, until then he had never entertained any relations with the French-speaking Province of Quebec. Nor had he felt any responsibility toward the old acquisitions brought in by the Treaty of Utrecht (1713), such as Newfoundland, Nova Scotia, and Rupert's Land, which he liked to believe were still included in the diocese of Quebec. Almost by default, however, Challoner continued to take some care of the British colonies on the continent as well as in the islands. In fact, his direct intervention was necessary with regard to certain spiritual powers (known as "faculties") that only a bishop could grant, and that the Jesuits – mere priests – were obliged to obtain from him. For example, he regularly granted matrimonial dispensations, probably for impediments linked to consanguinity, that the Jesuits used for the members of their Maryland community.[12]

Although Challoner was not especially informed about North American matters, when, in the immediate aftermath of the Treaty of Paris, Rome again asked him for a report on the state of the new British colonies, the bishop responded quickly. In 1763 and 1764 he drafted two major reports, one of which was addressed directly to Pope Clement XIII (1693–1769). He also had several exchanges on this question with Christopher "Kit" Stonor (1716–95), his agent in Rome, who often addressed Propaganda Fide on his behalf.[13] Challoner's sources are not known, except for some letters whose authors he did not identify and a visit to the superior of the English Province of the

Society of Jesus, Nathaniel Elliott (1705–80). Furthermore, some Jesuits, similarly unidentified, inquired about to whom they should apply for faculties over the newly acquired islands (Grenada, Dominica, Saint Vincent, and Tobago).[14] All in all, Challoner proved sufficiently well-informed on the West Indies, somewhat informed about the state of the continental provinces, but unaware and uninterested in new developments in the former French America, which he believed did not fall into his own jurisdictional responsibility.

Challoner was well aware that Article 4 of the Treaty of Paris had guaranteed the free exercise of the Catholic religion in all territories ceded by France, including the Province of Quebec, Upper Louisiana, Grenada, and the Grenadines. In the West Indies, Challoner believed that French-speaking priests would continue to serve the Catholic inhabitants of the newly ceded islands. As for the old British islands, where religion was at "a very low ebb," he knew that the three or four priests who were in Montserrat also served Jamaica, Barbados, St Christopher, and Antigua. Challoner had also been informed of the low moral standards of both the clergy and the faithful, all of them of Irish origin. The Catholics of Saint Vincent, Dominica, and Tobago, part of the newly acquired islands, were unfortunately not included in the stipulations of the Treaty of Paris. There, concluded Challoner, one could only "hope in the current moderation of the English Crown, that would not subdue their profession of faith."[15]

In the continental provinces, Challoner reported that there were sixteen thousand Catholics in Maryland, half of them reputedly of high moral standards, and six to seven thousand in Pennsylvania. They were respectively served by twelve and four Jesuits. (The number of the faithful was then three times larger than he had reported in the 1750s, whereas missionaries had remained the same.) In theory, he explained, these Catholics were subjected to Penal Laws. In practice, however, the exercise of their religion was tolerated. In fact, of the whole British Empire, Philadelphia was the place where Catholics enjoyed the most freedom. A new church (St Joseph's) was being built there. A few more Catholics lived in New Jersey and Virginia. None, however, were in the New England provinces, in New York, or in the southern provinces of North Carolina, South Carolina, and Georgia.[16]

According to Challoner, no new British acquisition was more important in terms of its vastness and territorial extension than Quebec. He was not worried by the recent events that had transformed the former French colony into a province of the British Empire. Although the last bishop of Quebec, Dubreil de Pontbriand, had died a few weeks before the Capitulation of Montreal (1760), he reported that the diocese was well in the hands of its rightful chapter. Moreover, Quebec's Catholic inhabitants continued to profess their religion and did so as publicly as they had done during the French regime. As for the rest of North America, Challoner restated his belief that Newfoundland and Nova Scotia were Quebec's responsibility and not his own. He also wondered about his own jurisdiction in Florida, another new acquisition, where the few Spanish-speaking inhabitants were also Catholics.[17]

Finally, Challoner suggested a new organization of the North American Catholic Church structured around three vicars apostolic, one for each linguistic community – one in Florida, one in Philadelphia (for the continent and the islands), and one in Quebec (including Nova Scotia and the Acadians). The apparent symmetry of this proposal, however, seems to have been grounded more in Challoner's wish to distance himself from the whole matter, rather than on careful appraisal. In his August 1763 report, he even put forward the unrealistic suggestion that the French-speaking bishop of Quebec be sent on a sacramental mission to the continental colonies. There the French-speaking prelate was supposed to administer the sacrament of confirmation to a minuscule English-speaking community dispersed in the midst of Protestant hostility. Over and over, Challoner emphasized that he was not "ambitious of engrossing to [himself] a jurisdiction over places so remote and where [he] can be of so little service."[18] One should recall that the vicar apostolic in the London district was eighty-two years old and already had enough on his hands.

The British crown made its crucial decisions regarding the status of the Catholic Church in the Province of Quebec between September 1763 and March 1764, around the time Challoner was drafting his last report. These decisions were neither hasty nor offhand. All interested parties – in Quebec City, Paris, Rome, and London – were obliged to modify their initial positions to reach a solution based on compromise. The Protestant crown confirmed the religious freedom of its new Catholic subjects in the Province of Quebec. It even accepted the presence of a bishop who formally based his jurisdiction on a foreign Catholic power. To be sure, the crown did so by acknowledging the bishop's role under the ambiguous title of "Superintendent of the Romish Church." It also allowed Briand to be appointed as bishop of Quebec, the first bishop of the British regime, an act that Clement

XIII officially formalized in his bulls of 11 January 1766. Undoubtedly, taken together these decisions were nothing less than revolutionary, and can be regarded as a fundamental step in the promulgation of the Quebec Act.[19]

Challoner had even less interest in the French colonies than he did in the American. In fact, his papers do not show any awareness of the negotiations that eventually led to the new episcopal appointment in Quebec. He certainly did not take part in them, although some information about events in Quebec must have come to his attention. For example, he knew that the military governor of the Province of Quebec, James Murray (1722–94), was unremittingly opposed to the first candidate that the clergy of Quebec had elected as prospective bishop, the Sulpician Étienne Montgolfier (1712–91). In fact, at the very moment Challoner was drafting his reports to Rome (1763–64), Montgolfier was in London hoping to be granted the crown's assent to his nomination. Challoner's mind revolved first and foremost around his Church's difficulties in England, where the Penal Laws were still in effect. As early as 1745, he had pointed to the fact that, without toleration at home, there was no room for any Catholic expansion in the British continental provinces. Almost twenty years later, the fact that his second and major report to Propaganda Fide (1763) went astray was most disquieting. He suspected that the report had been seized and opened along the way, even before it had a chance to leave England. This possibility was the source of significant anxiety, because, Challoner feared, some politicians might have been hostile to the opinions expressed in that report.[20]

Challoner's complex relationship with the Society of Jesus compounded his worries. When in 1756 he offhandedly suggested the appointment of a bishop in the British continental provinces, he had forewarned Stonor of the likely opposition of the English Province, the administrative branch of the Society of Jesus that was responsible for English-speaking North America. When a decade later he learned that the Holy See was assessing the option of a North America headed by two or three vicars apostolic, he emphasized the risks of such a move. The Maryland Jesuits, he explained, had for a long time enjoyed exclusive dominion over the continental provinces. Consequently, they would not accept the arrival of a priest who did not belong to their Society, let alone a bishop. According to Challoner, the English Jesuits had done their utmost to stop any move towards the establishment of a bishopric in the colonies. They had even engineered a petition signed by many lay people, which the English Province had asked their bishop to forward to the Holy See. At any rate, the needs of England still loomed larger among Challoner's preoccupations and remained an impediment to a more assertive approach to North America. In fact, Challoner emphasized, should any priests be needed for any North American project, the English clergy could not spare any from their midst.[21]

In the late 1760s and early 1770s, the political destinies of the continental provinces and the Province of Quebec diverged rapidly. In the former, new laws passed by the British parliament, such as the Stamp Act (1765) and the Townshend Acts (1767), combined with events such as the Boston Massacre (1770), contributed to a growing discontent. In the latter, the strict collaboration between Briand and the new governor, Guy Carleton (1724–1808), added to the Catholic population's growing loyalty towards the new regime. This loyalty was enhanced by the governor's decision to ensure the continuation of the episcopal hierarchy, thanks to an arrangement through which a coadjutor *cum futura successione* would have automatically replaced the bishop upon the latter's death. (This proviso recognized both the Church's right of presentation and the crown's power of veto.) In spite of several changes in government, crown and parliament demonstrated consensus on the necessity of a full and consistent act that would ensure the loyalty of the Province of Quebec. The Quebec Act, a new quasi-constitution for the Province, reformed and stabilized its ecclesiastical organization, together with its legal system and its parliamentary model.[22]

Challoner and his clergy did not take part in the debate on the future of the Province of Quebec or in the proceedings that led to the Quebec Act, in spite of its significance. Two clues, however, point to the fact that Challoner was not completely cut off from North American matters. The first is his suggestion that Briand be sent to those continental provinces to the south for a sort of sacramental tour. Given the prevalence of an anti-Catholic sentiment in those provinces, that proposal was awkward and unrealistic. Propaganda Fide, however, for lack of viable alternatives, embraced it and forwarded it to Quebec. The second clue is a memorandum, in Challoner's own handwriting, listing inhabitants and extant debts in a number of places in Maryland and Pennsylvania. This probably resulted from information coming from the Society of Jesus.[23]

Incidentally, in spite of their lack of official communication, a personal letter from a Philadelphia Jesuit to a Quebec confrere, dating from 1773, shows that the two communities were well aware of each other and of their different situations. Fr Ferdinand Farmer (born Steinmeyer, 1720–86) knew of the "far greater authority of law and freedom" enjoyed by the Quebec church. He was also well aware of Challoner's 1771 suggestion that Briand visit the continental provinces to administer confirmation. He admitted that the move had been stalled by the Maryland Jesuits, aware of the Americans' "incredible hate toward the very name of Bishop," Catholic or Anglican alike. At any rate, Farmer concluded, there was no way the crown would have granted Briand permission to exercise his spiritual powers outside the limits of the colony formerly belonging to the French.[24]

Around the time of the discussion leading to the Quebec Act, Challoner was much more interested and directly involved in an event of major importance for the Catholic Church worldwide. Via the pontifical brief *Dominus ac Redemptor* (21 July 1773), Pope Clement XIV (1705–74) suppressed the Society of Jesus. Throughout the world, its members were made into secular priests and placed under the direct jurisdiction of their territorial superior. The brief had immediate consequences for the ninety or so Jesuits of the English province. The brief was potentially even more significant for Maryland and Pennsylvania, whose sixteen missionaries were all Jesuit. About a month or so after its publication, Rome sent a copy of the brief to Challoner in London for its implementation. Asked about the nature, the size, and the allocation of the Jesuit possessions, the vicar apostolic was obliged to update his knowledge of the continental provinces.[25]

Once again, Challoner emphasized that his ecclesiastical authority was purely nominal, because those territories were far away and "almost in another world." In fact, he admitted to having access to only one source of information: the Jesuit provincial himself, Thomas More (1769–73). The two prelates met and agreed that it would have been impossible, let alone dangerous, to send a brief of suppression to every single American Jesuit, as requested by the Holy See. It was much simpler and safer, they suggested, to ask all of them to sign an individual act of submission. This is what they did, and in just a few months Challoner was able to send to Rome a document signed by the American Jesuits, all of them promising to comply with the brief of suppression. As for Challoner's view of the brief, he interpreted it as a rather beneficial move. The secularization of the English Jesuits (that is, their reduction to status of a simple parish priest), would have made clearer, once and for all, their jurisdictional dependence on the vicar apostolic in the London district. As for the continental provinces, the secularization of the American Jesuits would have provided a good opportunity to implement his old project of a vicar apostolic for the colonies, so far stalled by the Society of Jesus.[26]

The Quebec Bill was approved on third reading by the British parliament on 26 May 1774, it received the crown's assent on 13 June 1774, and was promulgated as the Quebec Act on 10 May 1775. Challoner and Briand did not exchange any correspondence on this issue, an issue that the Quebec church regarded as crucial. The bishop of Quebec was informed by Michel Chartier de Lotbinière, marquis de Lotbinière (1723–98), a Quebec seigneur who had been invited to London as a representative of the seigneurial order during the debate on the Quebec Bill. For his part, Challoner knew of the Quebec Act; about a month after its approval, he mentioned it in a general report on the missions under his jurisdiction, which he asked Stonor to forward to Propaganda Fide. This report was more original than those that had preceded it in the 1750s and 1760s, showing that his sources had gone beyond the English Province of the Society of Jesus.

With regard to the continental provinces, in his 1774 report Challoner was unusually comprehensive in describing the state of the Protestant churches. Presbyterians were the dominant sect in New England, whereas the Church of England ruled elsewhere. All colonies were under the "rather inattentive" authority of the Anglican bishop of London. The idea of establishing one or more Anglican bishops in the colonies was often debated, but never implemented, due to strong opposition. Pennsylvania granted full tolerance for anybody who recognized the existence of a God. The belief that the Bible was divinely inspired was the only religious requirement for public office. Catholics, then, were not excluded from such privileges.[27]

With regard to the Province of Quebec, Challoner recalled that the proviso "as far as the laws of Great Britain permit" could have nullified the good effects of Article 4 of the Treaty of Paris, which granted Catholics the "worship of their religion." The Quebec Bill, devised to "calm on this point the inhabitants of Canada," had indeed met with "strenuous opposition." Challoner's absence from any role in the negotiations leading to the Quebec Act shows that his main concern remained the state of Catholicism in England. However, his lengthy report also points to his growing interest in issues pertaining to North America. As early as 1745, he had expressed the view that there would have been no room for any expansion of the Catholic religion in the American colonies, unless a regime of religious tolerance was first approved for England. And yet he now acknowledged that the Quebec Act was the first example of such a freedom that parliament granted to "British subjects." After their "change of Religion," that is, the conquest of 1760, the Quebec Act now granted the new Canadian subjects "the full and free profession of the Catholic Religion, together with most of the same civil laws they had enjoyed under the French Crown." Somehow reversing his previous position that religious tolerance had to start in England, Challoner now interpreted the Quebec Act as an "example that, given some time, could lead to some change also in favour of the Catholic inhabitants of England" – a dream that would only be fulfilled over fifty years later with the passing of the final Catholic Relief Act of 1829.[28]

In view of developments that followed the American Declaration of Independence (1776), signed exactly two years after the Quebec Act, Challoner's feeble interest in North American matters is somehow startling. Yet his attitude can be understood in view of the minuscule size of the American Catholic community, of the traditional Jesuit opposition to outside interferences, and of his own age and slackening energy. The crucial element explaining Challoner's attitude, however, was his overall preoccupation with the status of the Catholic community at home. As early as 1763, he had praised the crown's moderation in matters of religion when negotiating the Treaty of Paris. Challoner's main concern was to avoid antagonizing the crown and pushing it towards enforcing the potentially lethal Penal Laws that regulated the life of the Catholic community at home.[29]

As far as North America was concerned, Challoner's cautious attitude had a number of negative consequences. He did not entertain any relationship with the American Jesuits, the Quebec Church, or the British politicians and crown bureaucrats who were in charge of British North America. Challoner was then conspicuously absent in the proceedings that led first to Briand's appointment and later to the Quebec Act. Furthermore, in spite of the several reports he sent to Rome, their limitations narrowed the scope of the Holy See's knowledge of the British North American provinces. Rome's ignorance of British North America directly contrasted to its attention to the Province of Quebec, whose events were followed closely by the Propaganda Fide bureaucrats from information that reached them via Paris or, increasingly, directly from Quebec itself.[30]

The Province of Quebec was not the only place where a Catholic community was ruled by a Protestant government, a fact that Challoner missed and consequently failed to convey to his correspondents. As British historians P.J. Marshall and Stephen Conway have shown, after the Treaty of Paris, British politicians and crown bureaucrats discussed at length whether and how to apply the Irish model to the Empire's new acquisitions in Quebec, Grenada, East Florida, and West Florida.[31] However, in the several conversations that he exchanged with Propaganda Fide on how best to provide for the spiritual needs of the West Indies, neither Challoner nor the Holy See showed any knowledge of the Irish model. Confronted with a matrimonial dispensation to be granted in Grenada, Clement XIII referred the issue to the vicar apostolic in the London district as the appropriate jurisdictional authority. Challoner took advantage of Benjamin Duhamel (d.1777), a French Capuchin who had autonomously moved from Martinique to Grenada and had self-appointed himself prefect apostolic. Challoner kept him as his vicar general in the island and, lacking a better alternative, Propaganda Fide approved. When eventually Propaganda Fide acknowledged Challoner's inadequacy and decided to ask Briand to send a superior to Grenada, the American War of Independence prevented the vicar apostolic from informing his Quebec colleague. France's decision to side with the American rebels had effectively closed any channel of communication between Quebec and Grenada.[32]

When Challoner died in 1781, at the age of ninety, he was automatically replaced as vicar apostolic in the London district by his coadjutor, James Robert Talbot (1726–90).[33] In spite of its coincidence with the Gordon Riots, the end of the American War of Independence, the establishment of an independent hierarchy in Newfoundland, and the beginning of the French Revolution, Talbot's mandate had little effect in North America. His substantive role was largely administrative. Although he was used by Quebec and Rome as a convenient conduit for their reciprocal correspondence, rarely, if ever, did he intervene in the conversation.[34] In 1781, Propaganda Fide renewed Talbot's faculties, only to reduce them three years later by carving Newfoundland and the United States out of his jurisdiction. In Newfoundland, the local Catholic community had requested and obtained the appointment of an independent prefect apostolic, the Irish Franciscan Observant James Louis O'Donel (1737–1811). The Irish Church, not London, had been instrumental in bringing this procedure to completion. As for the United States, because the American church made a point of distancing itself from London and corresponding directly with Rome, very few American matters crossed Talbot's desk.[35]

The Quebec clergy's efforts to circumvent the crown's prohibition on importing new French priests into the province did not appear in Talbot's correspondence. Nor did the predicament of four Savoy priests who in 1781–82 spent eight months in London waiting for a passage to Quebec; the 1783 arrival in London of the two Sulpicians who had been expelled from the province; the presence in London in the same year of a rather vociferous Quebec delegation, consisting of Jean-Baptiste-Amable Adhémar (1736–1800), the priest Jean De Lisle de La Cailleterie (1736–1814), and judge William Dummer Powell (1755–1834); or the 1779–84 intelligence activities of former Jesuit Pierre-Joseph-Antoine Roubaud (1724–*post* 1789). Furthermore, Talbot did not have any part in the surreptitious passage of three young clerics to Quebec, a move that had been engineered in Paris but was disclosed and stopped by the London crown bureaucrats in 1784.[36] On only one occasion was Talbot invited to substantively intervene in North American matters: he was asked to help provide new clergy to Nova Scotia, which was still under his jurisdiction. Rumours that the Penal Laws might be lifted in that province, a likely consequence of the first Catholic Relief Act of 1778, do not seem to have reached him. To be sure, Talbot declined to offer any assistance, pointing to the pitiful state of the ecclesiastical establishments in London, "torn down & demolished by the [Gordon] Rioters." These establishments were "so poor & low," he apologized, that "they [had] people abroad collecting & raising Subscriptions for them."[37]

It is most likely that the little interest Talbot had in North American matters waned even further with the 1784 appointment of Thomas Hussey as Quebec's vicar general in London. Hussey was an influential member of the Irish hierarchy and chaplain at the Spanish embassy in London. Louis-Philippe Mariauchau d'Esgly (1710–88), Briand's successor as bishop of Quebec, always corresponded with Hussey instead of Talbot. On the very day of his *prise de possession*, Mariauchau d'Esgly wrote to Hussey suggesting a revision of the Quebec Act. He recommended that the revised text excise any hint to royal supremacy in religious matters, as such wordings "frighten[ed] the Canadiens." Talbot's papers contain no mention of this suggested revision. Similarly, it was Hussey, not Talbot, who met with the Home

Secretary of State, Thomas Townshend, Baron Sydney (1733–1800), on the issue of the choice of a coadjutor for Mariauchau d'Esgly.[38] Furthermore, in spite of the suppression of the society, the Jesuit network that linked London and the United States continued to represent an alternative route which did not include Talbot. Toward the end of the decade, when a student of the English College of Douai, Robert Plunkett (d.1815), decided to go to the United States, he did so by addressing the pope directly, and did not inform Talbot at all.[39]

Talbot did not take any part in the 1786–88 exchange that went on between Propaganda Fide and François-Joseph Sorbier de Villars (1720–88) regarding ecclesiastical jurisdiction over the American West. At the time, the French referred to this region as Tamarois or Illinois, and the English as Mississippi or Upper Louisiana. Sorbier de Villars insisted that the region fell within the jurisdiction of the bishop of Quebec, Mariauchau d'Esgly. Propaganda Fide was not convinced. Was the region still under England, or had it become American, and as such fell under the archbishop of Baltimore? Propaganda Fide admitted to being "in the deepest darkness," though at least one thing was clear: the vicar apostolic in the London district was not part of the solution. The issue was finally solved by Mariauchau d'Esgly himself, who informed Propaganda Fide that the entire region south of the 45th parallel had been ceded to the United States and was no longer his responsibility. If Sorbier de Villars's pretensions had been the last attempt to regain some of the power that Paris had long lost with regard to North America, Talbot's absence from this exchange shows that London had not yet fully taken Paris's place.[40]

Of the very few items related to North America that reached Talbot, some had to do with individuals. There was, for example, a detailed report on the Roman conversion of the New England Congregationalist minister, John Thayer (1755–1815), but also a rather ironic commentary on the same Thayer, described as the "converter of Boston ... lurk[ing] in Navarre." William Hurst (*fl.* 1784), an Irish priest in Paris, reported on Thayer, but also on the misdeeds of another French priest, Claude-Florent Bouchard, known as abbé de La Poterie (1751–*post* 1790), soon to gain some celebrity in Boston for not getting along with John Carroll (1736–1815), the first bishop of Baltimore. America was also mentioned as one possible destination of Rome-born Henry Tourner (*fl.* 1785), a minor canon at St Peter's, who had suddenly disappeared, later to resurface in Dublin in the company of an Italian woman.[41]

By the time of Talbot's mandate, the Holy See had access to a variety of sources to inform its bureaucrats about North American developments. As shown by the Tamarois issue, Propaganda Fide also actively looked for better information by soliciting its sources whenever its knowledge was unclear or simply unavailable. The United States hierarchy, the bishop of Quebec (independently or via Hussey), some Nova Scotian missionaries, the Irish hierarchy, and Irish priests in Newfoundland were all in direct contact with Rome. Through these sources, the Holy See, and Propaganda Fide in particular, managed to become and remain somewhat more informed than they would have been had they relied on Talbot alone. Slowly but surely, the Holy See came to realize the extent of the fundamental changes that had been taking place in the North Atlantic area better than did the vicar apostolic in the London district himself.

The massive ecclesiastical migration set in motion by the French Revolution substantially changed Great Britain's attitude towards the Catholic Church. More than 150,000 French people, including some thirty thousand Catholic clergy, fled abroad. At least seven thousand French ecclesiastics went to Britain, where persecuted Catholics could regroup and wait for better times.[42] It was at this time that London definitively replaced Paris as centre of an Atlantic network that connected North America with the Holy See. However, whereas Paris's role had been unique, London became one of several connecting points in this network. Its primacy was the result of its being the seat of government and, after 1789, the residence of so many émigré priests. The year 1790 also began the mandate of John Douglas (1743–1812), who took over after Talbot's death. Like his predecessor, Douglas was involved in a number of administrative matters regarding North America, such as the promotion of O'Donel as vicar apostolic in Newfoundland. He also forwarded requests or decisions arriving from or destined to British North America.[43]

American preoccupations, however, constitute only a very small portion of Douglas's papers. Given the magnitude of the events that were taking place in Europe, it is no wonder that he, like his predecessor Talbot, was more concerned with matters at home than in North America. Douglas certainly did not meet with Carroll, who was in London from late July to early October 1790 and was consecrated bishop of Baltimore in Lulworth Castle, Dorset, on 15 August 1790. Carroll might have deliberately avoided the recently appointed vicar apostolic to keep his distance from the veto issue, a debate that was proving to be very divisive within the English and the Irish churches at the time.[44] The arrival in London of Charles Erskine (1743–1811), who was pontifical envoy to England from 1793 to 1801, may also have overshadowed Douglas the same way Hussey had Talbot.[45] Given Erskine's high diplomatic role – he was elevated to "envoy extraordinary" in 1795 – the new pontifical envoy certainly moved in higher governmental circles that Douglas. It was Erskine, for example, who in 1795 was charged with the Newfoundland file. He discussed it with the Home Secretary, William Henry Cavendish Bentinck, Duke of Portland (1738–1809), even before verifying Douglas's opinion on the matters at stake.[46]

The French émigré priests were such a massive presence in his vicariate apostolic that Douglas met with members of their community on a regular basis. Between 1793 and 1799 he was instrumental in sending or authorizing a number of them who wanted to proceed to the Province of Quebec or the United States.[47] One of them was the future bishop of Boston, Jean-Louis-Anne-Madelain Lefèbvre de Cheverus (1768–1836), who was most grateful for Douglas's assistance while in London. When, in 1798, he informed a number of friends of his satisfactory experience as missionary among the Penobscot and Passamaquoddy Indigenous nations, Douglas was among his addressees. Lefèbvre de Cheverus also took the opportunity to let Douglas know that public opinion in Boston favoured England and despised and abhorred "French principles & their abettors."[48] There is, however, little if any evidence of Douglas's relationship with the group of French émigré priests that had their home base in their King Street Chapel, at Portman Square. Denis Chaumont (1752–1819), Jean-Baptiste Le Vanier (1754–1823), Gabriel-François Le Héricy (1754–1844), Louis-Charles-Marie Lombard de Bouvens (1750–*post* 1830), and Adam Lymburner (*c.*1745–1836) variously acted as agents of the bishop of Quebec, whereas François-Emmanuel Bourret (*c.*1741–1807), founder and director of the chapel, was Quebec's vicar general in 1806–07. All these priests were at the centre of many letter exchanges between Quebec and Rome, where another émigré priest, Denis Boiret (1734–1813), was the Quebec agent from 1792 to 1813. Douglas, however, remained at best on the margin of these exchanges.[49]

Douglas developed a special interest in the Province of Quebec when a young nephew of his, Thomas Douglas (*fl.*1795), moved to Quebec City in the spring of 1795. T. Douglas had good connections with Bishop Jean-François Hubert (1739–97), and the Morrogh and McTavish merchant families. Unfortunately, nothing is known of him after that busy and eventful summer, in which he was involved in the wheat business.[50] At any rate, whatever interest Douglas had in North America subsided almost completely after his meetings with James Jones (*c.* 1743–1805). Jones had spent fifteen years in Halifax and was in London in September-October 1800. Undoubtedly the state of Catholicism in British North America, especially in Nova Scotia, was part of their conversations. Douglas, however, does not seem to have been cognizant of the London activities of the former Jesuits, who in the first decade of the nineteenth century tried to negotiate the passage to Nova Scotia of some of their members from Russia, one of the two kingdoms where the Society of Jesus had not been suppressed. (The other was the Kingdom of Naples.)[51]

On 29 April 1827, the secretary of Propaganda Fide, Pietro Caprano (1759–1834), asked Pope Leo XII (1760–1829) to bestow upon Poynter, then vicar apostolic in the London district, the title of bishop assistant at the pontifical throne. This was an honorific, yet extremely prestigious, ecclesiastical function, which ranked a bishop immediately after the cardinals. (Poynter, who was sixty-five at the time, was appointed, but died only a few months afterwards.) In supporting his petition, Caprano described Poynter as the most important channel of communication between Propaganda Fide and the Catholics of Great Britain, America, the East Indies, and the Pacific Sea.[52] Caprano was right. With regard to the international context, Poynter far surpassed his immediate predecessors, Challoner, Talbot, and Douglas. Through his active role he finally succeeded in placing himself at the centre of the Catholic networks that were active in the English-speaking world, including the United States, and in making London their main hub. Poynter was in constant touch with his French- and English-speaking colleagues in British North America and became the Holy See's trusted conduit for North American affairs. Whatever or whoever did not go directly to Rome, would pass through London – and land in Poynter's hands. Unlike his immediate predecessors, he was also in regular touch with British politicians and crown bureaucrats, whom he knew personally and met regularly in their offices.[53]

When Poynter took over as vicar apostolic in 1812, no less than half a century had gone by since the British conquest of Canada of 1760. Undoubtedly, all his immediate predecessors showed a pattern of minimal interest in North American matters, be they related to British

North America or to the United States. They manifested their unwillingness to extend their jurisdiction over territories that they deemed unfamiliar, distant, and of little import. The French language and traditions of the inhabitants of the new British acquisitions, such as the Province of Quebec, Upper Louisiana, Grenada, and the Grenadines, provided their rationale for not assisting them, in the hope that the bishop of Quebec or France would continue to do so.

If this attitude was particularly evident in Challoner's times (1758–81), it also emerged after the War of American Independence, when the new regions of the American West came to the fore. These were still mainly peopled by Canadiens, but were now included in the territories belonging either to the British crown or to the new United States. Challoner's attitude can be somewhat condoned. North American responsibilities hit him when he was already an old man. He was accustomed to living in a country where the Penal Laws, though relaxed, could be enforced at any time by a less-moderate crown minister or bureaucrat. Moreover, he lacked ecclesiastical personnel for his own district of London and felt he could not spare any of his priests for the colonies. There Catholics were, to say the least, a minuscule group that had always been managed by the Society of Jesus, a tight ecclesiastical community of which he had little knowledge and could hardly control. Among the consequences of Challoner's inaction in regard to North America, however, was his irrelevance in the negotiations that led to the appointment of the new bishop of Quebec, his lack of contacts with Briand, his unawareness of the lobbying activities that the Canadiens carried out in London over several years, and, finally, his absence from the debates that preceded the Quebec Act.

During Talbot's mandate (1781–90), a number of very significant events took place that had a direct influence over the Catholic communities of Newfoundland, Nova Scotia, the Province of Quebec, the United States, and the American West. However, the new vicar apostolic seemed even less interested than his predecessor. In fact, if anything, his administration is notable only for the sizable decrease in the territory that came under his jurisdiction. Furthermore, Talbot was probably unaware of a suggestion that the Quebec Act be revised in order to be made more palatable to the Canadiens. His lack of familiarity with the British politicians and crown bureaucrats kept his influence negligible.

The pattern of Douglas's administration (1790–1812) followed that of Talbot's. What made it different was the presence in London – and in Great Britain in general – of a massive number of émigré priests, some of whom developed an interest in North America and received Douglas's assistance for their passage. Furthermore, not only did their presence boost the overall number of Catholic priests, but the favourable attitude of the crown brought about a de facto tolerance for French and English priests alike, easing Douglas's work. Furthermore, the departure for the Province of Quebec of his nephew, Thomas Douglas, provided another incentive to improve his knowledge of North America and to extend a network of acquaintances around it, though this applies to the first decade of Douglas's mandate only. In fact, during its second decade the Douglas papers show almost no interest in matters relating either to British North America or to the United States.

As regards Poynter, aside from his opinions and advice, which the Holy See asked for often and weighed carefully, the Holy See treasured his role as a channel of communication between Rome and the Catholics of the British Empire. His immediate predecessors performed the same role, but, given their limited interest in and knowledge of North American matters, their impact engendered a number of contradictory consequences. Challoner narrowed the scope of the Holy See's knowledge of the British North American provinces, including the future United States, and failed to play any role in the developments taking place in the Province of Quebec. In spite of this, Propaganda Fide quickly learned about events in the former French colony. It did so, however, through sources that were still located in Paris, not in London. This dependence on French-speaking sources prevented Rome from noticing that the Province of Quebec was one among several where a Catholic community was ruled by a Protestant government – and that this phenomenon would soon become more and more common.

During Talbot's and Douglas's times, their lack of interest reduced the relevance of London's vicar apostolic in North American matters. Concurrently, in both British North America and the United States, a number of local communities defined by ethnic allegiances, such as the Germans, the Irish, the Scots, and the Acadians, challenged the leadership provided by Quebec City and Baltimore. Unity and uniformity were replaced by fragmentation and diversity. The Holy See now confronted direct relations with North American communities with leaders in places as far-flung as Halifax, St John's, Boston, New York, and the American West, in addition to Quebec City and Baltimore. Paris's role as the main channel of information between North America and the Holy See progressively diminished, until it abruptly ended once and for all with the French Revolution. London, however, did not immediately replace it. Rather, it became one among many vectors of communication. Its relevance very much depended on its leadership. Poynter provided such a leadership. Challoner, Talbot, and Douglas had other priorities, and did not.

The Quebec Act represented a major turning point in this lengthy process, which took place over half a century and directly involved three London vicars apostolic. The Catholics of Quebec immediately recognized the quasi-constitutional implications of the new law and, for the decades to come, would continue to use its legal protections. As for the English Catholics, even Challoner, who remained strongly Anglo-centric throughout his mandate, realized that the liberal provisos of the Quebec Act opened the way towards a similar liberalization, not only in the other colonial acquisitions, but also in England itself. "Given some time," he wrote a few days after its approval in 1774, the same could happen at home.[54] No fewer than forty-eight years were to pass between Challoner's death in 1781 and full Catholic emancipation via the Catholic Relief Act of 1829. But the door had been opened long before. As recalled by Aaron Willis in his chapter in this volume, efforts at Catholic relief began in Ireland concurrently with the Quebec Act. These efforts were soon thereafter extended to the Atlantic provinces. As early as 1782, religious liberty was brought to completion in Nova Scotia, and in Newfoundland in 1783. Furthermore, in 1784, O'Donel was permitted openly to take charge of the Newfoundland Catholics as their first prefect apostolic. Soon thereafter, the carnage of the French Revolution, Catholic migration into Great Britain, and the Napoleonic Wars made this new policy of tolerance almost inevitable.

NOTES

1 The author wishes to thank Terrence Murphy (Saint Mary's University, Halifax, NS), for his commentaries on an earlier draft of this chapter. He also is grateful to Kristina Bross (Purdue University) and Laura Stevens (University of Tulsa), co-chairs of the international conference of the

Society of Early Americanists, "London and the Americas, 1492–1812" (Kingston University, Kingston-upon-Thames, Surrey, United Kingdom, 17–21 July 2014), where an earlier version of this chapter was also presented.

2 For a classic examination of the Quebec Act, see Reginald Coupland, *The Quebec Act: A Study in Statemanship* (Oxford: Clarendon Press, 1925); Alfred L. Burt, *The Old Province of Quebec* (Toronto: Ryerson Press, and Minneapolis: University of Minnesota Press, 1933); Ian R. Christie, *Crisis of Empire: Great Britain and the American Colonies, 1754–1783* (London: Edward Arnold, 1966); Hilda Neatby, *Quebec: The Revolutionary Age, 1760–1791* (Toronto: McClelland and Stewart, 1966); Neatby, ed., *The Quebec Act: Protest and Policy* (Scarborough, ON: Prentice-Hall of Canada, 1972); Pierre Tousignant, "The Integration of the Province of Quebec into the British Empire, 1763–91," Part 1: "From the Royal Proclamation to the Quebec Act," in *Dictionary of Canadian Biography*, ed. Brown et al., 4: xxxii–xlix; Philip G. Lawson, *The Imperial Challenge: Quebec and Britain in the Age of the American Revolution* (Montreal: McGill–Queen's University Press, 1989); John A. Dickinson and Brian Young, *Brève histoire socio-économique du Québec* (Quebec: Septentrion, 2009 [1st ed. in English, 1988]), 76–9; Peter D.G. Thomas, *Tea Party to Independence: The Third Phase of the American Revolution, 1773–1776* (Oxford: Clarendon Press, 1991); Lawson, ed., *Parliament and the Atlantic Empire* (Edinburgh: Edinburgh University Press, 1995); David Milobar, "Quebec Reform, the British Constitution, and the Atlantic Empire, 1774-1775," in ibid., 65–88; Lawson, *A Taste for Empire and Glory: Studies in British Overseas Expansion, 1660–1800* (Aldershot: Variorum / Brookfield, VT: Ashgate Publishing Company, 1997). For a renewed attention, see Stephen Conway, *The British Isles and the War of American Independence* (Oxford: Oxford University Press, 2000); Karen A. Stanbridge, *Toleration and State Institutions: British Policy toward Catholics in Eighteenth-Century Ireland and Quebec* (Lanham, MD: Lexington Books, 2003); Nancy Christie, ed., *Transatlantic Subjects: Ideas, Institutions, and Social Experience in Post-Revolutionary British North America* (Montreal: McGill-Queen's University Press, 2008); Heather Welland, "Commercial Interest and Political Allegiance: The Origins of the Quebec Act," in *Revisiting 1759: The Conquest of Canada in Historical Perspective*, ed. Phillip A. Buckner and John G. Reid, 166–89, esp. 169, 181, 183 (Toronto: University of Toronto Press, 2012); Conway, "The Consequences of the Conquest: Quebec and British Politics, 1760–1774," in ibid., 141–65; Donald Fyson, "The Conquered and the Conqueror: The Mutual Adaptation of the

Canadiens and the British in Quebec, 1759–1775," in ibid., 190–217; Fyson, "La réconciliation des élites britanniques et canadiennes (1759–75): Reconnaissance mutuelle ou rhétorique intéressée?" in *1763: Le traité de Paris bouleverse l'Amérique,* ed. Sophie Imbeault, Denis Vaugeois, and Laurent Veyssières, 262–71 (Quebec: Septentrion, 2013); Fyson, "Les Canadiens et le Serment du Test," in ibid., 272–7.

3 Peter M. Doll, *Revolution, Religion, and National Identity: Imperial Anglicanism in British North America, 1745–1795* (Madison, NJ: Farleigh Dickinson University Press / London: Associated University Presses, 2000). For the Canadian debates and the role of Bishop Jean-Olivier Briand, see Marcel Trudel, *L'Église canadienne sous le régime militaire, 1759–1764* ([Montreal], Quebec: Les études de l'Institut d'Histoire de l'Amérique Française and Les Presses de l'Université Laval, 1956–7); Hilda M. Neatby, "Servant," in *The French Canadians, 1759–1766: Conquered? Half-Conquered? Liberated?* ed. James Cameron Nish, 107–12 (Toronto: Copp Clark, 1966), a shortened version of Neatby, "Jean-Olivier Briand: A 'Minor Canadien,'" Presidential Address. Canadian Historical Association, *Report* 42 (1963): 1–18; André Vachon, *Mgr Jean-Olivier Briand (1715–1794)* (Quebec: Les Éditions des Dix, 1979), also published, but without footnotes, as "Briand, Jean-Olivier," in *Dictionary of Canadian Biography*, ed. George W. Brown et al. (Toronto: University of Toronto Press, 1966–2005), vol. 4, *1771 to 1800*, ed. Francess G. Halpenny and Jean Hamelin, 94–103 (1979). The issue was recently examined in Luca Codignola, "Quoi de neuf sur la prétendue servitude de Monseigneur Briand (1760 à 1766)? Une nouvelle lecture historiographique de l'après -Trudel à partir des archives romaines," in *Le Saint-Siège, le Québec et l'Amérique française: Les archives vaticanes, pistes et défis*, ed. Martin Pâquet, Matteo Sanfilippo, and Jean-Philippe Warren, 109–31 (Quebec: Presses de l'Université Laval, 2013).

4 Charles H. Metzger, *The Quebec Act: A Primary Cause of the American Revolution* (New York: The United States Catholic Historical Society, 1936); Metzger, *Catholics and the American Revolution: A Study in Religious Climate* (Chicago: Loyola University Press, 1962); Jon Butler, *Becoming America: The Revolution before 1776* (Cambridge, MA: Harvard University Press, 2000), 242 ("fears").

5 Luca Codignola, "The Rome-Paris-Quebec Connection in an Age of Revolutions, 1760–1820," in *Le Canada et la Révolution française: Actes du 6e colloque du CIEC. 29, 30, 31 octobre 1987*, ed. Pierre H. Boulle and Richard A. Lebrun, 115–32 (Montreal: Centre interuniversitaire d'Etudes européennes / Interuniversity Centre for European Studies,

1989). With regard to the international context, Lucien Lemieux, *L'établissement de la première province ecclésiastique au Canada, 1783–1844* (Montreal: Fides, 1968); and Lemieux, *Les années difficiles (1760–1839)* (Montreal: Éditions du Boréal, 1989), represent a major exception. The two books, published more than twenty years apart, are very different, the former being a very institutional essay, the latter more socially oriented. Aside from their authors' thorough and original treatment of multiple sources, their overall interest resides in a pioneering North Atlantic perspective that takes into account British North America, Great Britain, and the Holy See at the same time, and shows their reciprocal and constant influences. For an even larger perspective, see also Codignola, "The Policy of Rome toward the English-speaking Catholics in British North America, 1750–1830," in *Creed and Culture: The Place of English-speaking Catholics in Canadian Society, 1750–1930*, ed. Terrence Murphy and Gerald J. Stortz, 100–25 (Montreal: McGill-Queen's University Press, 1993) (complementing the 1989 chapter, above). Centred on the United States, but placing American Catholicism in a larger international context, are Dale B. Light, *Rome and the New Republic: Conflict and Community in Philadelphia Catholicism between the Revolution and the Civil War* (Notre Dame, IN: University of Notre Dame Press, 1996); Michael T. Pasquier, *Fathers on the Frontier: French Missionaries and the Roman Catholic Priesthood in the United States, 1789–1870* (Oxford: Oxford University Press, 2010); Catherine O'Donnell, "John Carroll and the Origins of an American Catholic Church, 1783–1815," *William and Mary Quarterly*, 3rd ser., 58, no. 1 (January 2011): 101–26; Maura Jane Farrelly, *Papist Patriots: The Making of an American Catholic Identity* (Oxford: Oxford University Press, 2012); and Luca Codignola, *Blurred Nationalities across the North Atlantic: Traders, Priests, and Their Kin Travelling between North America and the Italian Peninsula, 1763–1846* (Toronto: University of Toronto Press, 2019), 80–140, 191–215.

6 Richard Challoner, titular bishop of Debra *in partibus infidelium*, was coadjutor *cum futura successione*, 1739–58, and vicar apostolic in the London district, 1758–81; James Robert Talbot, bishop of Birtha, was coadjutor, 1759–81, and vicar apostolic, 1781–90; John Douglas, or Douglass, bishop of Centuria, was vicar apostolic, 1790–1812; William Poynter, bishop of Alia, was coadjutor, 1803–12, and vicar apostolic, 1812–27. Given its chronological limits, Poynter's mandate is not part of this chapter, although the bishop is briefly mentioned towards its end.

7 On the early Jesuits in the United States, see the ponderous, but still useful, Thomas A. Hughes, *History of the Society of Jesus in North America*

Colonial and Federal: Text and Documents (London: Longmans, Green, 1907–17); James J. Hennesey, *American Catholics: A History of the Roman Catholic Community in the United States* (New York: Oxford University Press, 1981), 36–88; Thomas R. Murphy, *Jesuit Slaveholding in Maryland, 1717–1838* (New York: Routledge, 2001); and Thomas M. McCoog, ed., *"Promising Hope": Essays on the Suppression and Restoration of the English Province of the Society of Jesus* (Rome: Institutum Historicum Societatis Iesu, 2003).

8 In the period examined here, the Propaganda Fide top bureaucrats in charge of the North American files were: Giuseppe Spinelli (1694–1763), prefect from 1756 to 1763; Giuseppe Maria Castelli (1705–80), prefect from 1763 to 1780; Leonardo Antonelli (1730–1811), prefect from 1780 to 1795; the Barnabite Giacinto Sigismondo Gerdil (1718–1802), prefect from 1795 to 1801; and Stefano Borgia (1731–1804), pro-prefect from 1798 to 1800 and prefect from 1802 to 1804. At the time, an influential nuncio in Paris was Giuseppe Maria Doria Pamphili (1751–1816), who served from 1773 to 1785. In Paris, the French crown's missionary network, including North America, was managed by Pierre de La Rue, abbé de L'Isle-Dieu (1688–1779), who was vicar general of the bishop of Quebec from 1734 to 1777; he was replaced by François-Joseph Sorbier de Villars, who served in the same capacity from 1777 to 1788.

9 Archives of the Sacred Congregation "de Propaganda Fide (Vatican City) [hereafter APF], Acta, vol. 126, 352v–358r, Nicola Lercari to Propaganda Fide, 6 Dec. 1756 (Challoner officially granted jurisdiction, Benedict XIV's approval on 23 Jan. 1757).

10 Challoner replaced Benjamin Petre (1672–1758) as vicar apostolic in 1758, but before that date he had already been responsible for answering Propaganda Fide's questionnaires; Christopher "Kit" Stonor, his agent in Rome, was in charge of his relationship with Propaganda Fide. See APF, Scritture Originali riferite nelle Congregazioni Generali [hereafter SOCG], vol. 729, 47rv–48rv, Petre and Challoner to Propaganda Fide, 3 Sept. 1745 (missionaries only in Maryland, Pennsylvania, Antigua, Montserrat); ibid., Acta, vol. 116, 176rv–182rv, [Propaganda Fide internal memorandum], 4 July 1746 (ten thousand Catholics, eighteen missionaries); ibid., Congressi [hereafter C], America Antille [hereafter AA], vol. 1, 529rv–530rv, [Stonor] to [Propaganda Fide], [Feb. 1753] (Catholics in Maryland, Jesuit missionaries, toleration in Pennsylvania, St Mary's church, English College [the rector of the English College in Rome was then Henry Sheldon, 1686–1756]); Westminster Diocesan

Archives (London) [hereafter WDA], B, vol. 45, 135, 1rv, J. Fisher [*alias* for Challoner] to [Stonor], 14 Sept. 1756 (five to seven thousand Catholics and twelve Jesuit missionaries in Maryland; toleration in Pennsylvania, two thousand Catholics, four Jesuits; some Catholics in Virginia and New Jersey; origins of the vicar apostolic's jurisdiction unknown; after war, bishop of vicar apostolic should be sent, in spite of probable Jesuit resentment); APF, SOCG, vol. 767, 273rv–276rv, Stonor to Propaganda Fide, [Dec. 1756] (similar remarks); ibid., Acta, vol. 126, 352v–358r, Lercari to Propaganda Fide, 6 Dec. 1756 (Challoner granted jurisdiction); ibid., C, Missioni, Miscellanee [hereafter MM], vol. 14, 12rv–14rv, [Propaganda Fide's internal memorandum], [6 Dec. 1756] (de facto jurisdiction, renewed 25 March 1759); ibid., vol. 13, 26rv–29rv, [Propaganda Fide's internal memorandum], [6 Dec. 1756] (précis of Catholic expansion in the Americas); WDA, B, vol. 46, 25, 1rv–2rv, J. Fisher to Stonor, 31 Oct. 1758 (faculties expire in 1763); ibid., 31, 1rv–2rv, J. Fisher to Stonor, 6 Feb. 1759 (renewal of faculties following Petre's death); ibid., vol. 137, 9–10, Stonor to [Clement XIII], [March 1759] (renewal of faculties); APF, Udienze, vol. 8, 477rv, 480rv, Stonor to Clement XIII, March 1759 (renewal of faculties); ibid., 478rv–479rv. [Propaganda Fide's internal memorandum], [25 March 1759] (renewal of faculties); WDA, B, vol. 137, 10, Spinelli and Niccolò Antonelli to Challoner, 31 March 1759 (renewal of faculties); APF, Lettere, vol. 194, 117v–118r, [Spinelli] to Challoner, 31 March 1759 (renewal of faculties); WDA, B, vol. 46, 58, 1rv–2rv, J. Fisher to Stonor, 11 June 1762 (quotation); C, AA, vol. 2, 26rv–37rv, Challoner to Castelli, 2 Aug. 1763 (customary jurisdiction over colonies goes back to James II's times and made official only in 1757). For an overall assessment of Challoner, mostly from a spiritual point of view, see Ernest G. Rupp, *Religion in England, 1688–1791* (Oxford: Clarendon Press, 1986), 186–92.

11 The documents of American interest relating to Challoner's mandate have been partially examined and published in John D.G. Shea, ed., "Letter of Bishop Challoner to the Propaganda in 1763, Giving an Account of the American Missions under his Jurisdiction," *American Catholic Historical Researches*, 12, no. 1 (January 1895): 44–5; "The State of Religion in America. Report of Bishop Challoner of the London District to Rome in 1756," *American Catholic Historical Researches*, 13, no. 1 (January 1896): 35–40; Hughes, *History*; Edwin H. Burton, *The Life and Times of Bishop Challoner (1691–1781)*, 4 vols. (New York: Longmans, Green, 1909), esp. 2: 123–48; "Bishop Challoner," *Records of the American Catholic Historical Society*, 57, no. 4 (December 1946): 235–6. They have

also been calendared in Ivanhoë Caron, ed., "Mgr Jean-Olivier Briand. Inventaire de la correspondance de Mgr Jean-Olivier Briand, évêque de Québec, de 1741 à 1794," *Rapport de l'Archiviste de la Province de Québec* (1929–30), 45–136; Finbar Kenneally, ed., *United States Documents in the Propaganda Fide Archives: A Calendar. First Series* (Washington, DC: Academy of American Franciscan History, 1966–81); Luca Codignola, *Calendar of Documents Relating to North America (Canada and the United States) in the Archives of the Sacred Congregation "de Propaganda Fide" in Rome, 1622–1846* (Library and Archives Canada and Research Centre for Religious History in Canada of Saint Paul University, 2012), <http://ustpaul.ca/fr/centre – de – recherche – en – histoire – religieuse – du – canada – informations – generales_602_405.htm>.

12 APF, C, AA, vol. 1, 529rv–530rv, [Stonor] to [Propaganda Fide], [Feb. 1753] (Newfoundland and Nova Scotia probably under Quebec); WDA, A, vol. 40, 40, 1rv, [Challoner's memorandum], [before 11 June 1762] (payments made for Maryland and Pennsylvania); ibid., Z, vol. 71, 52, [Challoner's memorandum], [before 11 June 1762] (dispensations for Maryland mentioning George Hunter [1713–79], the Jesuit superior); ibid., B, vol. 46, 58, 1rv–2rv, J. Fisher to Stonor, 11 June 1762 (dispensation granted).

13 The first report is in APF, C, AA, vol. 2, 38rv, 41rv, Stonor to [Propaganda Fide], [June 1763] (original); ibid., C, America Centrale [hereafter AC], vol. 2, 425rv–430rv, [Stonor] to [Propaganda Fide], [June 1763] (original); WDA, B, vol. 137, 67–8, Stonor to [Propaganda Fide], [June 1763] (copy). The second and major report is in APF, C, AA, vol. 2. 36rv–37rv, Challoner to Castelli, 2 Aug. 1763 (original); ibid., C, AC, vol. 1, 290rv–291rv, [Challoner] to Clement XIII, 2 Aug. 1763 (copy); WDA, B, vol. 137, 417–23, [Stonor] to [Propaganda Fide], [2 Aug. 1763] (copy). Because the second report went astray, Challoner recalled and summarized it in early 1764. See ibid., vol. 46, 73, 1rv–2rv, Challoner to Stonor, 15 March 1764 (original); APF, C, AA, vol. 2, 42rv–43rv (copy); WDA, B, vol. 137, 70–1 (excerpts). Other exchanges are in ibid., vol. 46, 64, 1rv–2rv, Challoner to Stonor, 20 May 1763 (reference to a previous Stonor letter, now lost, dated 15 March 1763); ibid., 67, 1rv–2rv, Challoner to Stonor, 6 Sept. 1763; ibid., 70, 1rv–2rv, J. Fisher to Stonor, 17 Jan. 1764; ibid., 75, 1rv–2rv, J. Fisher to Stonor, 19 May 1764; ibid., 77, 1rv–2rv, Challoner to Stonor, 28 Aug. 1764; ibid., 79, 1rv–2rv, Challoner to Stonor, 2 Oct. 1764.

14 APF, C, AA, vol. 2, 36rv–37rv, Challoner to Castelli, 2 Aug. 1763 (letters); WDA, B, vol. 46, 70, 1rv–2rv, J. Fisher to Stonor, 17 Jan. 1764 ("visit"); ibid., 77, 1rv–2rv, Challoner to Stonor, 28 Aug. 1764 (Jesuits inquired).

15 APF, C, AA, vol. 2, 36rv–37rv, Challoner to Castelli, 2 Aug. 1763 (mentioning Art. 4; "sperare dalla moderazione presente del governo Inglese, che non saranno violentate in quella loro professione [di fede]"); WDA, B, vol. 46, 67, 1rv–2rv, Challoner to Stonor, 6 Sept. 1763 ("ebb"). On the Treaty of Paris and the West Indies, see also ibid., 64, 1rv–2rv, Challoner to Stonor, 20 May 1763; APF, C, AA, vol. 2, 38rv, 41rv, Stonor to [Propaganda Fide], [June 1763]. On the West Indies, see WDA, B, vol. 46, 77, 1rv–2rv, Challoner to Stonor, 28 Aug. 1764; ibid., 79, Challoner to Stonor, 2 Oct, 1764; ibid., vol. 137, 73–4, Stonor to Propaganda Fide [Dec. 1764], Art. 4 of the Treaty of Paris is in Zenab Esmat Rashed, *The Peace of Paris 1763* (Liverpool: At the University Press, 1951), 216; Grenada, the Grenadines, Saint Vincent, Dominica and Tobago are mentioned in Art. 9 (see ibid., 219).

16 On the continental provinces, see APF, C, AA, vol. 2, 36rv–37rv, Challoner to Castelli, 2 Aug. 1763.

17 On the Province of Quebec and the rest of North America, see WDA, B, vol. 46, 64, 1rv–2rv, Challoner to Stonor, 20 May 1763; APF, C, AA, vol. 2, 38rv, 41rv, Stonor to [Propaganda Fide], [June 1763]; ibid., 36rv–37rv, Challoner to Castelli, 2 Aug. 1763 (Florida "quasi deserta [almost desert]"); WDA, B, vol. 46, 73, 1rv–2rv, Challoner to Stonor, 15 March 1764; ibid., 77, 1rv–2rv, Challoner to Stonor, 28 Aug. 1764.

18 Suggestions are in APF, C, AA, vol. 2, 36rv–37rv, Challoner to Castelli, 2 Aug. 1763; WDA, B, vol. 46, 67, 1rv–2rv, Challoner to Stonor, 6 Sept. 1763; ibid., 73, 1rv–2rv, Challoner to Stonor, 15 March 1764. The refusal to extend his jurisdiction is in ibid., 64, 1rv–2rv, Challoner to Stonor, 20 May 1763; APF, C, AA, vol. 2, 38rv, 41rv, Stonor to [Propaganda Fide], [June 1763]; ibid., 36rv–37rv, Challoner to Castelli, 2 Aug. 1763; WDA, B vol. 46, 77, 1rv–2rv, Challoner to Stonor, 28 Aug. 1764; ibid., 79, 1rv–2rv, Challoner to Stonor, 2 Oct. 1764 ("ambitious"); ibid., vol. 137, 73–4, Stonor to Propaganda Fide, [Dec. 1764].

19 Legally, there is a most evident continuity in the field of Catholic recognition that starts with the Capitulation of Quebec (1759), the Capitulation of Montreal (1760), Jean-Olivier Briand's formal appointment (1766), and the Quebec Act (1774). The most thorough narrative of the six years between Henri-Marie Dubreil de Pontbriand's death (1760) and Briand's formal appointment (1766) is in Trudel, *L'Église canadienne*. The best biography of Briand is Vachon, *Mgr Jean-Olivier Briand*. The Capitulations of Quebec and Montreal, the Treaty of Paris and the Quebec Act are in Thomas Shortt and Arthur George Doughty, eds, *Documents Relating to the Constitutional History of Canada*,

1759–1791. 2nd and rev. ed. (Ottawa: J de L Taché, 1918), 1: 1–36, 91–163, 570–6 (the earlier edition of vol. 1, published in 1907, is less reliable than the 1918 edition).

20 APF, SOCG, vol. 729, 47rv–48rv, Petre and Challoner to Propaganda Fide, 3 Sept. 1745 (Catholicism to expand only if tolerated); WDA, B, vol. 46, 73, 1rv–2rv, Challoner to Stonor, 15 March 1764 (original report); Vatican Secret Archives, Fondo Missioni, not numbered, Étienne Montgolfier to abbé de L'Isle-Dieu, 21 May 1764 (renunciation). On the state and number of Catholics in the vicariate apostolic of London during Challoner's times, see David J. Butler, "The Catholic London District in the Eighteenth Century," *Recusant History* 28, no. 2 (2006): 245–68 (with a passing reference to the continental colonies, 252). On Montgolfier's presence in London, see Codignola, "Quoi de neuf," 113.

21 WDA, B, vol. 45, 135, 1rv, J. Fisher to [Stonor], 14 Sept. 1756 (probable Jesuit resentment); ibid., vol. 46, 81, 1rv–2rv, Challoner to Stonor, 15 Feb. 1765 (Jesuit opposition to the vicars apostolic idea, English clergy could spare no priests); ibid., 102, 1rv–2rv, R. Fisher to Stonor, 12 Sept. 1766 (Jesuit petition); APF, C, AC, vol. 1, 543rv–544rv, Challoner to Stonor, 4 June 1771 (Jesuit opposition); Archives de l'Archidiocèse de Québec (Quebec City) [hereafter AAQ], 7 CM, II, 124, 1rv, Ferdinand Farmer (born Steinmeyer) to Bernard Well, 22 Apr. 1773 (successful Jesuit opposition). Farmer's letter was translated into English in Martin I.J. Griffin, ed., "Letter of Father Farmer, of Philadelphia, to Father Well, of Quebec, Giving the Reasons Alleged by Bishop Briand of Quebec to the Sovereign Pontiff for not Executing the Order Received from Him to Visit the American Colonies for the Purpose of Giving Confirmation to the Catholics," *American Catholic Historical Researches* 21, no. 3 (July 1904): 118–22.

22 Lawson, *Imperial Challenge*, 110, describes the issue of the coadjutor from the crown's perspective.

23 APF, C, AC, vol. 1, 543rv–544rv, Challoner to Stonor, 4 June 1771 (suggestion on Briand in the context of general, but dated, information on the continental provinces); AAQ, 10 CM, III, 15, 1rv–2rv, Castelli and Borgia to Briand, 7 Sept. 1771, copy in APF, Lettere, vol. 218, 394v–395rv (sacramental tour suggested); WDA, A, vol. 41, 207, 1rv, [Challoner's memorandum], [early 1770s] (listing Charles County, St Mary County, Dr George's County, Eastern Shore, Baltimore City, Frederick, Philadelphia). For anti-Catholic ideology and background, see Colin Haydon, *Anti-Catholicism in Eighteenth-Century England, c.1714–80: A Political and Social Study* (Manchester: Manchester University Press, 1993); Francis D.

Cogliano, *No King, No Popery: Anti-Catholicism in Revolutionary New England* (Wesport, CT: Greenwood Press, 1995); Doll, *Revolution, Religion, and National Identity.*

24 AAQ, 7 CM, II, 124, 1rv, Farmer to Well, 22 Apr. 1773 ("longe alio jure & libertate," "Incredibile enim est, quantum sit ubique locorum in America apud Acatholicos odium vel ipsius nominis Episcopi").

25 APF, Lettere, vol. 222, 430rv–432rv, [Propaganda Fide] to Tommaso Maria Ghilini, 25 Aug. 1773 (brief to be forwarded); ibid., 432v–434rv, [Propaganda Fide] to Challoner, 25 Aug. 1773 (brief to be enforced in England and colonies).

26 WDA, B, vol. 137, 188–93, Stonor to [Borgia], [Sept. 1773] (ninety Jesuits in England, sixteen in Maryland and Pennsylvania, nominal jurisdiction, vicar apostolic project); ibid., A, vol. 41, 133, 1rv, Challoner to [Castelli], 10 Sept. 1773 ("qasi [*sic*] in alio mondo"); ibid., B, vol. 137, 198–200, Challoner to Stonor and [Borgia], 24 Sept. 1773 (Thomas More); APF, C, MM, vol. 5, 23rv, 26rv, Challoner to [Propaganda Fide], Oct. 1773 [*recte* 5 Oct. 1773] (brief forwarded by Ghilini, will write to American Jesuits); WDA, A, vol. 41, 208, 1rv, [Society of Jesus] to [Challoner], [early 1774] (list of sixteen Jesuits); APF, C, MM, vol. 5, 193rv, 200rv, George Hunter et al. to [Challoner], [early 1774] (twenty-one signatures, Jesuits accept brief). Challoner's 1773 report is briefly mentioned in D.J. Butler, "Catholic London District," 252. On the relationship between Challoner and the Society of Jesus, see T. Geoffrey Holt, "Bishop Challoner and the Jesuits," in *Challoner and His Church: A Catholic Bishop in Georgian England*, ed. Eamon Duffy, 137–51 (London: Darton, Longman and Todd, 1981); on Challoner's implementation of the brief, Joan Connell, *The Roman Catholic Church in England, 1780–1850: A Study in Internal Politics* (Philadelphia: American Philosophical Society, 1984), 128–30. The most recent work on the suppression is McCoog, ed., *Promising Hope*. It reprints several articles by the Jesuit historian, Holt (1912–2009), including "The State of the English Province on the Eve of the Suppression of the Society of Jesus" (originally published 1991), 27–35; "The English Ex-Jesuits and Jesuits and the Missions, 1773–1814," 177–90; and "The English Province: The Ex-Jesuits and the Restoration (1773–1814)," 219–58. The issue of the Jesuit possessions went unresolved for several decades in British North America, as well as in the United States. Hughes, *History*, gives the Society of Jesus's version with regard to the United States and is particularly interested in property issues. For more recent works on British North America, see Roy C. Dalton, *The Jesuits' Estates Question, 1760–1888: A Study of the Background for the Agitation of 1889*

(Toronto: University of Toronto Press, 1968); James R. Miller, *Equal Rights: The Jesuits' Estates Act Controversy* (Montréal: McGill-Queen's University Press, 1979).

27 AAQ, 90 CM, I, 5, 1rv, Michel Chartier de Lotbinière, marquis de Lotbinière, to [Briand], 12 May 1774 (Quebec Act). Contrary to Challoner, Farmer emphasized the limitations that the required oath imposed on the Pennsylvania Catholics with regard to public offices; see AAQ, 7 CM, II, 124, 1rv, Farmer to Well, 22 Apr. 1773.

28 WDA, B, vol. 137, 209–15, [Challoner to Stonor], [July 1774] ("non si ne piglia gran premura," "per quietare su questo punto gli abitanti del Canada," "quel popolo la piena e libera professione della Religione Catt[ca], ed insieme l'uso in gran parte delle stesse Leggi civili sotto le quali vivevano, quando erano sotto il Dominio del Re di Francia," "opposizioni gagliarde," "sudditi Britannici dopo la mutazione della Religione," "un simile esempio possa col tempo a poco a poco produrre qualche mutazione in favore anche de' cattolici abitanti in Inghilterra"); copy in ibid., vol. 48, 65, 3rv–8rv; and in APF, Miscellanee Varie, vol. I, 508rv–511r. For 1745, see APF, SOCG, vol. 729, 47rv–48rv, Petre and Challoner to Propagande Fide, 3 Sept. 1745.

29 Challoner's conservative attitude was not exceptional in the North Atlantic context of those years. See Codignola, "Roman Catholic Conservatism in a New North Atlantic World, 1760–1829," *William and Mary Quarterly*, 3rd ser., 64, no. 4 (October 2007): 717–56. A reference to Challoner's age is in WDA, B, vol. 137, 429–76, [Stonor] to [Propaganda Fide], [c.1771] ("Vecchio Venerando in eta di anni ottanta in circa"). The same memorandum makes reference to the role of J.R. Talbot, the brother of Charles Talbot, Earl of Shrewsbury (1753–1827), who had been Challoner's coadjutor since as early as 1759 (436).

30 It was actually Sorbier de Villars, who sent to Rome from Paris an excerpt of the Quebec Act, over three years after its approval; he also informed Rome of the departure for London of Charles-François Bailly de Messein (1740–94), whose prolonged stay there, from 1778 to 1782, does not find any echo in Challoner's papers. See APF, C, America Settentrionale [hereafter AS], vol. 1, 332rv, 335rv, Sorbier de Villars to [Propaganda Fide], 9 Nov. 1778 (Quebec Act, Bailly de Messein); ibid., 333rv–334rv, [Sorbier de Villars] to [Propaganda Fide], [9 Nov. 1778] (excerpt, including the translation into Italian of the required oath). On the Paris network, see Codignola, "The Rome-Paris-Quebec Connection."

31 On the Quebec analogy, see Conway, *British Isles*; Conway, "Consequences of the Conquest." On the overall framework of accommoda-

tion, see P.J. (Peter James) Marshall, *The Making and Unmaking of Empires: Britain, India, and America, c.1750–1783* (Oxford: Oxford University Press, 2005), 186–9.

32 On Grenada, see WDA, B, vol. 46, 64, 1rv–2rv, Challoner to Stonor, 20 May 1763 (France has priests in Grenada and should continue to supply them); ibid., vol. 137, 67–8, Stonor to Propaganda Fide, [June 1763], copy APF, C, AA, vol. 2, 38rv, 41rv (same); WDA, B, vol. 46, 73, 1rv–2rv, Challoner to Stonor, 15 March 1764 (a Dominican priest, one Devinish (*fl.* 1763–64), arrived in Grenada from Danish St Croix); ibid., 77, 1rv–2rv, Challoner to Stonor, 28 Aug. 1764 (dispensation, French Capuchin Benjamin Duhamel); ibid., Z, vol. 69, 88, Challoner to Duhamel, [March 1766]; ibid., B, vol. 137, 128–32, Challoner to Stonor, Jan. 1771 (Duhamel's appointment); ibid., 134–6, Castelli to Challoner, [6 Apr.1771] (Duhamel approved); ibid., 525–30, Challoner to Castelli [10 Sept. 1773] (Duhamel still in Grenada); APF, Fondo Vienna, vol. 37, 200rv–201rv, Challoner to Stonor, 7 Aug. 1778 (Briand and Grenada). Immediately after the Treaty of Paris, the procurator general of the French Capuchins had suggested that the bishop of Quebec be entrusted with jurisdiction over Grenada, the Grenadines, Dominica, St Vincent, and Tobago (APF, C, AA, vol. 2, 34rv–35rv, Aimé de Lamballe to [Propaganda Fide], 8 July 1763). Ironically, Propaganda Fide did not pursue this suggestion until 1778. On the most significant role of Grenada in the constitutional debate that took place in Great Britain, see Aaron Willis, "The Standing of New Subjects: Grenada and the Protestant Constitution after the Treaty of Paris (1763)," *Journal of Imperial and Commonwealth History*, 62, no. 1 (2014): 1–21. In this book, Willis's chapter rightly emphasizes the role played by the Ireland precedent in the devising of a new imperial framework for its Catholic subjects.

33 According to Mary D.R. Leys, *Catholics in England, 1559–1829: A Social History* (London: Longmans, Green / New York: Sheed and Ward, 1961), 137, when Challoner died "no other bishop had gained a comparable influence and independence." This judgment includes his successor, J.R. Talbot.

34 See WDA, A, vol. 42, 111, 1rv–2rv, [Talbot] to [L. Antonelli], [Oct. 1785]; APF, Lettere, vol. 252, 704rv, [Propaganda Fide] to Talbot, 1 Oct. 1788 (Talbot to use the Brook Watson firm).

35 For faculties, see APF, Udienze, vol. 19, 44rv, 49rv, [Stonor] to Pius VI, [March 1781] (asks for renewal); WDA, A, vol. 42, 9, 1rv–2rv, Borgia to Talbot, 4 March 1781 (granted); ibid., 10, 1rv, Stonor to [Talbot], 21 March 1781 (except Quebec). For Newfoundland, see APF, SOCG, vol.

867, 36rv– 7rv, James Louis O'Donel to Talbot, 31 Dec. 1783 (asks for approval); WDA, A, vol. 42, 44, 1rv–2rv, James Keating et al. to [Talbot], 14 Jan. 1784, copy in APF, SOCG, vol. 867, 32rv–33rv (ask for O'Donel's appointment); WDA, A, vol. 42, 59, 1rv–2rv, O'Donel to [Talbot], 19 Jan. 1784 (asks for permission); ibid., 47, 1rv–3rv, William Egan to [Talbot], 4 Feb. 1784 (recommends O'Donel); ibid., 54, 1rv–2rv, copy in APF, Lettere, vol. 244, 480rv–481r, L. Antonelli and Borgia to Talbot, 5 June 1784 (informed of O'Donel's new jurisdiction), WDA, A, vol. 42, 86, 1r–2rv, copy in APF, Lettere, vol248, 370rv–371r, L. Antonelli and Borgia to Talbot, 1 July 1786 (on O'Donel's jurisdiction). For the United States, see WDA, A, vol. 42, 55, 1rv–2rv, copy in APF, Lettere, vol. 244, 524rv–525r, L. Antonelli and Borgia to Talbot, 19 June 1784 (informed of John Carroll's new jurisdiction). Talbot acknowledged O'Donel's and Carroll's appointments in WDA, A, vol. 42, 52, 1rv–2rv, [Talbot] to [Propaganda Fide], [July 1784].

36 The four Savoy priests were Jean-Pierre Besson (1751–1836), Joseph-Vincent Bosson (1743–1819), Joseph-François Du Clot de La Vorze (1745–1821), and Joseph Masson (1746–1823). The two Sulpicians were Antoine Capel (*fl.* 1783) and François Ciquard (1754–1824). The three young clerics were François-Michel Aubert (1756–1804), a certain Gambier (*fl.* 1784), and Yves-François Duchesne (*ante* 1784–1812), the latter a nephew of Bishop Briand's, all members of the Séminaire du Saint-Esprit. On the Savoy priests, see Codignola, "Le Québec et les prêtres savoyards, 1779–1784: Les dimensions internationales d'un échec," *Revue d'histoire de l'Amérique française*, 63, no. 4 (Spring 1990): 559–68.

37 AAQ, 90 CM, I, 9, 1rv–2rv, William Meany to Edmund Phelan, 6 Dec. 1782 (reporting Talbot's answer). On the number of priests available to Talbot, see D.J. Butler, "Catholic London District," 266. On the first Catholic Relief Act and its consequences for Nova Scotia and Newfoundland, see Bernard N. Ward, *The Dawn of the Catholic Revival in England, 1781–1803*, 2 vols. (London: Longmans, Green, 1909), 1: 1–17; Angus A. Johnston, *A History of the Catholic Church in Eastern Nova Scotia* (Antigonish, NS: St Francis Xavier University Press, 1960–71), 1 (1960): 102–3; John Garner, *The Franchise and Politics in British North America, 1755–1867* (Toronto: University of Toronto Press, 1969), 144; John Bossy, *The English Catholic Community, 1570–1850* (London: Darton, Longman and Todd, 1975), 330–2; Hans-Josef Rollmann, "Richard Edwards, John Campbell, and the Proclamation of Religious Liberty in Eighteenth-Century Newfoundland," *Newfoundland Quarterly* 80, no. 2 (1984): 4–12, esp. 5–7; Murphy and Cyril J. Byrne, eds, *Religion and Iden-*

tity: The Experience of Irish and Scottish Catholics in Atlantic Canada. Selected Papers from a conference on Roman Catholicism in Anglophone Canada: The Atlantic Region, held at Saint Mary's University, 19–22 September 1984 (St John's: Jesperson Press, 1987), ii–iii; Richard Brown, *Church and State in Modern Britain, 1700–1850* (London: Routledge, 1991), 126–7; Codignola, "Policy of Rome," 34; Murphy, "The English-speaking Colonies to 1854," in Murphy and Roberto Perin, eds, *A Concise History of Christianity in Canada* (Toronto: Oxford University Press, 1996), 108–88, esp. 135–6; Jerry Bannister, *The Rule of the Admirals: Law, Custom, and Naval Government in Newfoundland, 1699–1832* (Toronto: University of Toronto Press / The Osgoode Society for Canadian Legal History, 2003), 218–19; Patrick Lacroix, "Popery and Tyranny: Catholicism as a Constitutional Issue, 1774–1778," *Historical Papers: Proceedings of the Canadian Society of Church History*, 2015, 27–45; S. Karly Kehoe, "Catholic Relief and the Political Awakening of Irish Catholics in Nova Scotia, 1780–1830," *Journal of Imperial and Commonwealth History* 46, no. 1 (January 2018): 1–20, esp. 9–14. See also in this volume Brad A. Jones, "The Quebec Act and Popular Patriotism in the British Atlantic," n103.

38 AAQ, 20 A, II, 3, 1rv 2rv, Louis-Philippe Mariauchau d'Esgly to Thomas Hussey, 2 Dec. 1784 ("effraye les Canadiens"). The bishop's reference was to Article V of the Quebec Act ("Les habitants de Québec peuvent professer la Religion Romaine, soumise à la suprématie du Roi ... jouir du libre exercice de la Religion de l'Église de Rome, soumise à la Suprématie du Roi"). On the meetings with Thomas Townshend, Baron Sydney, see APF, C, AS, vol. 1, 433rv, Hussey to Sorbier de Villars, 12 Apr. 1785; ibid., SOCG, vol. 870, 16rv–17rv, Hussey to Doria Pamphili, 19 Apr. 1785. In 1788 Hussey's appointment as vicar general was revoked on account of the crown's displeasure with him (AAQ, 210 A, I, 8–12, Jean-François Hubert to Sorbier de Villars, 20 Oct. 1788).

39 APF, C, AC, vol. 2, 535rv–536rv, Robert Plunkett to Pius VI, [1789]; ibid., Acta, vol. 159, f. 183v, Giulio Carpegna to Propaganda Fide, 20 Apr. 1789; ibid., Lettere. Vol. 255, 265v–266rv, [Propaganda Fide] to Carroll, 13 March 1789 [probably 13 May 1789].

40 APF, C, AS, vol. 1, 456rv–457rv, Sorbier de Villars to [Propaganda Fide], 10 Sept. 1786 (location of Tamarois); ibid., 464rv–465rv, Sorbier de Villars to [Propaganda Fide], 12 Dec. 1786 (report on former Canada, including Tamarois); ibid., Lettere, vol. 250, 36rv–37rv, [Propaganda Fide] to Sorbier de Villars, 13 Jan. 1787 (doubts on jurisdictions); ibid., 55v–56rv, [Propaganda Fide] to Leonard Neale, 20 Jan. 1787 (Challoner [*recte* Talbot] no longer responsible); AAQ, 10 CM, III, 49a, 1rv–2rv, L.

Antonelli and Borgia to [Sorbier de Villars], 13 Feb. 1787 ("dans la plus grande obscurité"); APF, C, AS, vol. 1, 468rv–469rv [Sorbier de Villars] to [Propaganda Fide], [12 March 1787] (Tamarois is under England); ibid., 472rv, Mariauchau d'Esgly to Sorbier de Villars, 15 Oct. 1787 (45th parallel); ibid., Lettere, vol. 252, 84rv–86r, [L. Antonelli and Borgia] to Sorbier de Villars, 1 March 1788, translation in AAQ, 10 CM, III, 49b, 1rv–2rv (addressee must accept Mariauchau d'Esgly's opinion). On the French presence in the American West, see the two most recent treatments in François Furstenberg, *When the United States Spoke French: Five Refugees Who Shaped the Nation* (New York: Penguin, 2014), 286–48; and Guillaume Teasdale and Tangi Villerbu, eds, *Une Amérique française, 1760–1860: Dynamiques du corridor créole* (Paris: Les Indes savantes, 2015).

41 On John Thayer, see WDA, A, vol. 42, 38, 3rv–4rv, [Stonor] to [?Talbot], 11 June 1783; ibid., 45, 1rv, Thayer to [Talbot], 18 Jan. 1784; ibid., 305, 1rv, William Hurst to [Talbot], 25 March 1784 ("converter"). On Claude-Florent Bouchard, known as abbé de La Poterie, see ibid., 304, 1rv, Hurst to Talbot, 19 Feb. 1784; ibid., 305, 1rv, Hurst to [Talbot], 25 March 1784. On Henry Tourner, see ibid., 58, 1rv–2rv, Stonor to [Talbot], 12 Jan. 1785; ibid., 70, 1rv–2rv, Stonor to [Talbot], 14 June 1785; ibid., 111, 1rv–2rv, [Talbot] to [L. Antonelli], [Oct./Dec. 1785].

42 For the refugees' waves, see Donald M. Greer, *The Incidence of Emigration during the French Revolution* (Cambridge, MA: Harvard University Press, 1951); Jacques Godechot, *La contre-révolution: Doctrine et action, 1789–1804* (Paris: Presses Universitaires de France, 1961), 152; Owen Chadwick, *The Popes and European Revolution* (Oxford: Clarendon Press, 1981), 448; Kirsty Carpenter, "London: Capital of the Emigration," in Carpenter and Philip Mansel, eds, *The French Émigrés in Europe and the Struggle against Revolution, 1789–1814* (Houndmills, UK: Macmillan, 1999), 43–67, esp. 61–2 n5. For the ecclesiastical refugees in Great Britain, see Dominic A. Bellenger, *The French Exiled Clergy in the British Isles after 1789: An Historical Introduction and Working List* (Bath: Downside Abbey, 1986); Bellenger, "'Fearless Resting Place': The Exiled French Clergy in Great Britain, 1789–1815," in Carpenter and Mansel, eds, *French Émigrés*, 214–29; Carpenter, *Refugees of the French Revolution: Émigrés in London, 1789–1802* (New York: St Martin's Press / Basingstoke: Macmillan Press, 1999).

43 For O'Donel, see APF, Lettere, vol. 268, 57rv–58r [Propaganda Fide] to Charles Erskine, 18 Apr. 1795; ibid., SOCG, vol. 902, 220rv–221rv, Erskine to Gerdil, 9 June 1795; ibid., C, Anglia, vol. 5, 470rv–473rv, Erskine to [Propaganda Fide], 23 June 1795; ibid., SOCG, vol. 902, 219rv, 222rv, Ersk-

ine to Gerdil, 21 July 1795; ibid., 226rv–227rv, [Propaganda Fide's memorandum], 23 Nov. 1795. For requests and decisions, see WDA, A, vol. 47, 205, 1rv–2rv, Neale to Douglas, 8 July 1798; ibid., 229, 1rv, Douglas to [Neale], 3 Oct. 1798; APF, Lettere, vol. 277, 178v–180r, [Propaganda Fide] to Erskine, 23 Sept. 1799; AAQ, 90 CM, I, 40, 1rv–2rv, François-Emmanuel Bourret to Joseph-Octave Plessis, 30 Sept. 1806; ibid., 59, 1rv–2rv, [Louis-Charles-Marie de Lombard de Bouvens] to [Plessis], 4 Nov. 1807. For the sending and receiving of mail, see APF, C, AS, vol. 2, 86rv–89rv, Pierre Denaut to Gerdil, 10 Sept. 1797; AAQ, 30 CN, I, 3, 1rv, O'Donel to Plessis, 28 Aug. 1798; WDA, A, vol. 47, 221, 1rv–2rv, Jean-Louis-Anne-Madelain Lefèbvre de Cheverus to Douglas, 31 Aug. 1798; AAQ, 30 CN, I, 6, 1rv–2rv, O'Donel to Plessis, 7 Aug. 1799; ibid., 90 CM, I, 27, 1rv–2rv, Gabriel-François Le Héricy to [Plessis], 6 Feb. 1805.

44 Archives of the Archdiocese of Dublin, AB2: John Thomas Troy Papers series, 116: Troy Correspondence, 1780–99, 5, no. 23, 1rv–2rv, Carroll to John Thomas Troy, 3 October 1790. On Carroll's London visit, see Annabelle M. Melville, *John Carroll of Baltimore Founder of the American Catholic Hierarchy* (New York: Charles Scribner's Sons, 1955), 115–21.

45 Hussey and Erskine seem to have been in frequent contact. See AAQ, 30 CN, I, 4, 1rv–2rv, O'Donel to Plessis, 12 May 1799. That Douglas resented Erskine's appointment is in Matthias Buschkühl, *Great Britain and the Holy See, 1746–1870* (Dublin: Irish Academic Press, 1982), 29–30.

46 APF, Lettere, vol. 268, 57rv–58r [Propaganda Fide] to Charles Erskine, 18 Apr. 1795 (verify the Newfoundland issue and consult with Douglas); ibid., C, Anglia, 5, 470rv–473rv, Erskine to [Propaganda Fide], 23 June 1795 (has already met with William Henry Cavendish Bentinck, Duke of Portland, and will consult with Douglas). Douglas, however, was able to confirm to Erskine that Newfoundland was not under the jurisdiction of the bishop of Quebec (APF, SOCG, vol. 902, 219rv, 222rv, Erskine to Gerdil, 21 July 1795).

47 AAQ, 90 CM, I, 13, 1rv, J. Douglas to Hubert, 28 Apr. 1793 (Candide-Michel Le Saulnier); WDA, B, vol. 16, folder VIII B, 1rv–2rv, Ange-François de Chalmazet to Mr Douglas [chemist in London, to be forwarded to J. Douglas], 12 June 1794 (Germain Bitouzé des Roqueries); WDA, A, vol. 46, 68, 1rv–2rv, Hubert to J Douglas, 18 July 1795, copy in AAQ, 210 A, vol. 2, 215 ("le vif interet que vous avez paru prendre au passage des pretres françois en Canada"); WDA, A, vol. 46, 106, 1rv–2rv, Thomas Douglas to J. Douglas, 19 oct 1795 (Claude-Gabriel Courtine, Jacques de La Vaivre, Joseph-Pierre Malavergne, Jean Raimbault); ibid., B, vol. 16/[ii], folder VIII D, ii, 1rv–2rv, Fleury to J. Douglas, 17 Dec.

1798; ibid., 1rv– rv, Jean-Mandé Sigogne to J. Douglas, 19 March 1799; AAQ, 90 CM, I, 18, 1rv–2rv, James Jones to Plessis, 5 Oct. 1800. For recent literature on French émigré priests in North America, see Thomas C. Sosnowski, "French Émigrés in the United States," in Carpenter and Mansel, eds, *French Émigrés*, 138–50, esp. 145–8; Bertrand Van Ruymbeke, "Refugiés or Émigrés? Early Modern French Migrations to British North America and the United States (*c.*1680–*c.*1820)," *Itinerario* 30, no. 2 (2006): 12–32. On the idea of a rebirth of a purer Catholicism in North America, see Codignola, "Roman Catholic Conservatism," 733–4.

48 WDA, A, vol. 47, 221, 1rv–2rv, Lefèbvre de Cheverus to J. Douglas, 31 Aug. 1798. For Lefèbvre de Cheverus's London acquaintance with J. Douglas, see Melville, *Jean Lefebvre de Cheverus, 1768–1836* (Milwaukee: Bruce Publishing Company, 1958), 30–1, 35, 39; for a reference to the letter dated 31 Aug. 1798, see ibid., 56–7.

49 AAQ, 90 CM, I, 40, 1rv–2rv, Bourret to [Plessis], 30 Sept. 1806 (accepts the appointment as vicar general without consulting J. Douglas); ibid., 59, 1rv–2rv [Lombard de Bouvens] to [Plessis], 4 Nov. 1807 (J. Douglas was able to appoint a temporary successor to the late Bourret as director of King Street Chapel, but on his own cannot appoint a full successor who could also be selected as Plessis's new vicar general). With the exception of these two instances, the émigré priests' correspondence, to be found in AAQ, APF, and WDA, does not mention J. Douglas's name, let alone his role. For an assessment (relating to 1820) of the impact of the émigré clergy on the overall number of the clergy, see Bossy, *English Catholic Community*, 356.

50 WDA, A, vol. 46, 65, 1rv–2rv, T. Douglas to J. Douglas, 9 July 1795; ibid., 66, 1rv–2rv, T. Douglas to J. Douglas, 17 July 1795; ibid., 68, 1rv–2rv, Hubert to J. Douglas, 18 July 1795, copy in AAQ, 210 A, vol. 2, 215; ibid., 71, 1rv–2rv, T. Douglas to J. Douglas, 9 Aug. 1795; ibid., 72, 1rv–2rv, Robert Morrogh to J. Douglas, 10 Aug. 1795; ibid., 106, 1rv–2rv, T. Douglas to J. Douglas, 19 Oct. 1795 and 25 Oct. 1795.

51 On Jones's visit, see AAQ, 90 CM, I, 18, 1rv–2rv, Jones to Plessis, 5 Oct. 1800. On the Russian Jesuits, see ibid., 210 A, III, 318, 186–7, Plessis to Jean-François de La Marche, 25 May 1802; ibid., 367, 215–17, Plessis to Jean-Louis de Leissègues de Rozaven, 12 Nov. 1802; ibid., 90 CM, I, 56, 1rv–2rv, William Strickland to Burke, 5 Oct. 1807; ibid., 70, 1rv–2rv, Strickland to Burke, 31 July 1808. On the issue of the Russian Jesuits, see Marek Inglot, *La Compagnia di Gesù nell'Impero Russo (1772–1820) e la sua parte nella restaurazione generale della Compagnia* (Rome: Editrice Pontificia Università Gregoriana, 1997); and Holt, "The English Ex-

Jesuits." J. Douglas's journal includes one item of American interest, yet an interesting one. In a conversation that took place on 5 Feb. 1798, a story was passed around that told of Benjamin Franklin's granting the free exercise of the Catholic religion in the future United States in exchange for France's intervention in the American War of Independence. See WDA, Z, vol. 72, 93, [J. Douglas's journal], [5 Feb. 1798].

52 APF, Udienze, vol. 68, 937rv–938rv, [Pietro Caprano] to [Leo XII], [29 Apr. 1827].

53 A hint of the extent of Poynter's activity and influence can be gleaned through the case of the Province of Quebec, as described in detail in Lemieux, *L'établissement*. To my knowledge, there exists no full-scale modern biography of Poynter. See, however, Peter Phillips, ed., *The Diaries of Bishop William Poynter, VA (1815–1824)* (London: Catholic Record Society, 2006).

54 WDA, B, vol. 137, 209–15, [Challoner to Stonor], [July 1774] ("col tempo a poco a poco").

7

A "Fit Instrument": The Quebec Act and the Outbreak of Rebellion in Two British Atlantic Port Cities

Brad A. Jones

In October 1774, an anonymous letter from Montreal appeared in John Holt's *New York Journal* and was thereafter exchanged in newspapers across the British Atlantic. It described the recent arrival of the province's governor-in-chief, Sir Guy Carleton. The governor was returning to the city after an unexpectedly long, four-year stay in London, where he had helped members of parliament craft the controversial Quebec Act. Welcoming ceremonies for governors, whether arriving for the first time or returning from a long trip, were common occurrences in the eighteenth-century British Atlantic, and were regularly reported on in newspapers. Such events played a crucial role in reinforcing ideas of civic authority, political allegiance, social harmony, and, more broadly, national identity and patriotism.[1] At times, however, these events could also bring to the surface latent political and social tensions within the community, region, or even empire.[2]

This was true of Carleton's arrival in Montreal, which, according to the writer, received little of the fanfare usually associated with such an event. There was no mention of soldiers parading, bells ringing, public toasts, or fireworks lighting the nighttime sky. Instead, the author reported only that Carleton and his "Lady and Family" were met at the landing by the lieutenant-governor, Hector Theophilus de Cramahé, "all of the French Clergy," and the colony's bishop, Jean-Olivier Briand. Local citizens, whose presence writers typically noted to confirm the authority of the governor and the widespread loyalty of the community, were conspicuously absent from the ceremony.

Their absence, and the apparent solemnity of what should have been a celebratory occasion, is perhaps best explained by what happened next. After the initial greetings from de Cramahé and the clergy, the writer stated that Carleton "had the Honour to be kissed by the Bishop, and afterwards very genteelly introduced to Popery, by placing him [Carleton] at his right Hand in his Chaise, in which Manner he [Briand] proceeded with him to the Castle." Seduced by the bishop's kiss, Carleton, a former war hero who served under James Wolfe in Britain's glorious victory at Quebec in 1759, willingly embraced arbitrary popish rule within moments of stepping foot in the colony he helped secure for his country a mere fifteen years earlier.[3] Over the following several days, according to the writer, the governor "has been visited by every Frenchman, down to the meanest People in the Place: – But very little by the *beggarly English* (as we hear he has been pleased to call them)." The writer explained that the English colonists were "incensed against [Carleton] ... on Account of the detestable Quebec Act, which is wholly ascribed to him, and said to have been framed under his Direction."[4] Even worse, claimed the author, "The French have said, '*That now all of their Laws will be made by the General, and the Bishop*' – and in Fact, if the General was a Roman Catholick, he could not shew them more Respect than he does."

Holt included two pieces of intelligence at the end of the letter to force readers to imagine the broader implications of one governor's embrace of popery. First, they were told that, ten days earlier, a "few English Merchants" – those "*beggarly English*" whom Carleton was now ignoring – "made up a Collection of Wheat for Bostonians, and have shipped them 1000 Bushels in a Brig belonging to Boston, Capt. Howes, who carries it Freight free." Readers also learned that Carleton recently received letters from officials in New York asking him to have several regiments "in Readiness, to embark at an Hour's Warning: We expect every Moment to hear of Vessels being taken up to carry them to Boston."[5] Such intelligence likely shocked New Yorkers and subjects elsewhere in the British Atlantic: Carleton and his Catholic allies were now prepared to use the army to further subdue Bostonians. Meanwhile, the few remaining Britons in Montreal desperately sought to retain their ties to a Protestant imperial identity by, of all things, opposing British rule in favour of their American brethren.

Stories such as this – and there were many more at this critical juncture in the imperial conflict – played upon one of the most persuasive and unifying fears of British subjects in the eighteenth century: the threat of French Catholicism. Britons throughout the North Atlantic had been reared for the better part of a century on the dangers that Catholicism posed to the stability and prosperity of their Protestant empire. An emerging transatlantic political culture of Loyalism regularly linked Catholic political rule with the perceived absolutism, tyranny, and brutality of the religion, an idea writers regularly referred to as popery. This stood in stark contrast to the celebrated post-1688 Protestant British imperial identity that celebrated economic prosperity, personal liberty, and religious toleration. The sheer simplicity of this rhetoric enabled Britons to identify themselves against their enemies in broad socio-political terms that transcended, to some degree, often more distinct local or regional identities.[6]

In the third quarter of the eighteenth century, however, the British union was only two generations old, and loyalty was remarkably dependent upon the presence of the familiar French enemy. Yet, when Carleton arrived in Montreal in the fall of 1774, Britons were not at war against France (at least, not yet). Instead, they found themselves on the verge of a civil conflict that called into question the very Protestant Whig ideals that were so fundamental to their sense of nation and national belonging.[7] For a decade or more, Britons on both sides of the Atlantic had been forced to debate the nature of consent, representation, and sovereignty, and the meaning of liberty and freedom, without reference to their standard lexicon of the dangers of Catholic tyranny.

This dynamic was certainly true of subjects living in New York City and Halifax, Nova Scotia, two port cities deeply tied to Britain's Atlantic empire and the crisis unfolding in the colonies. Since the early 1760s, residents of both cities were regularly required to engage with questions of national identity and loyalty in the absence of their traditional Catholic foes. What did it mean to be British? And, more crucially, why would it eventually become necessary to take up arms against their own brethren or to support such a conflict? Narratives of the growing crisis, written and exchanged in the many newspapers circulating the North Atlantic, played an essential role in answering these questions. Indeed, the act of making war required explanation. Reports and editorials that described the actions of the king and government, and the response of American colonists, led to the emergence of both Patriot *and* Loyalist common causes that made it possible for subjects to justify war against their fellow Protestant countrymen.[8]

The passage of the Quebec Act played a crucial role in this shift toward rebellion and war. The legislation revived age-old prejudices that had previously defined the loyalty of Protestant Britons across the empire.[9] For a nascent Patriot cause in both New York City and Halifax, the government's support of Catholicism simplified the complicated ideological debates of the previous decade by recasting political divisions in the far more familiar and frightening terms of popery. To do so was to reimagine proponents of such policies (like Carleton), not merely as political foes, but as dangerous and foreign enemies to the rights and liberties of Britons everywhere. Meanwhile, loyal Britons in both communities were left with a seemingly impossible task: they had to defend a king and government that had encouraged the spread of popery within the empire, while also opposing a growing movement in the colonies based on a Protestant Whig explanation of political and economic tyranny. Like their Patriot counterparts they too turned to a narrative of growing Catholic tyranny, describing the newly formed Continental Congress and the various local committees created to enforce the Continental Association as illegitimate, unrepresentative, and resembling popish rule. It seemed everywhere one looked in the winter of 1774–75, Catholicism threatened the security of free-born Protestant Britons.

The Quebec Act shattered a shared, transatlantic discourse of Loyalism. Yet the decision to remain loyal or to rebel depended on more than just popular fears of the spread of popery in the empire, whether these fears originated with the actions of the Crown or Congress. Choosing sides in the approaching conflict also came to depend on particular local conditions and political cultures that made loyalty or rebellion possible. In part, the local nature of the debate explains why Haligonians, though outspoken critics of the Quebec Act and largely supportive of the budding Patriot cause, were unable to break from Britain at the start of war. It also helps to make clear why radicals in New York City were able to use fears of popery to take control of the city in the spring of 1775, despite the presence of a sizable (and vocal) minority of loyal subjects. Choosing sides was complicated and contingent, depending as much on these broader ideological concerns as it did on more local circumstances.

News of the Quebec Act frightened many New Yorkers in the fall of 1774. Despite the city and colony's reputation as diverse and tolerant, New Yorkers, like Britons elsewhere, were reared in a virulent anti-

Catholic political culture that found meaning in real and imagined events. The ease with which people and armies could pass from Canada to New York prompted regular rumours of planned French and Native attacks on the city throughout much of the eighteenth century. Such fears prompted the colonial assembly at the start of the century to rid the colony of Catholics, though that did little to quiet the minds of the inhabitants.[10] Catholics were thought to have been behind both the 1712 and 1741 slave conspiracies, which did more than perhaps any other event in the first half of the century to shape white New Yorkers' understanding of freedom and liberty.[11] During the Seven Years' War, the city's printers filled entire columns of their newspapers with reports of the horrors of French Catholic rule in order "to keep alive," according to one writer, "a just Indignation against the treacherous bloody Religion of France."[12] The lurking Catholic, like the skulking Indian or plotting slave, terrified and excited subjects, who both understood and derived meaning from the threat that such groups posed to their cherished rights and liberty, their Britishness.[13]

What so concerned many New Yorkers in the fall of 1774 was that the threat came, not from their traditional Catholic enemies in Europe, but from their own king and government. Early reports in local newspapers suggested that the bill was the work of a corrupt ministry that sought to use French Canadians to subdue the rest of Britain's North American colonies. The extension of the province into the Ohio Country further incensed colonists, who now felt as though enemies to the Protestant faith surrounded them on three sides. In September, New Yorkers read that the true intention of the legislation was "to give a check to the rest of our colonies, and to keep them in awe." The writer warned readers that "there is no doubt but every Encouragement that can possibly be afforded to these licensed slaves, these children of Popery, supported by a Protestant court, will be given, in order to subdue these head-strong colonists who pretend to be governed by English laws."[14] The following month, when Carleton was supposedly "kissed by the Bishop," New Yorkers read a short soliloquy allegedly written by Lord North, who believed his best hope of restoring order rested on raising a "Popish army" in Canada that would be "glad to cut the throats of those heretics, the Bostonians."[15] New Yorkers were likely frightened by rumours thereafter that Carleton had received orders "to embody thirty thousand Roman Catholic Canadians immediately as a militia," to act "under the same military law as regular troops."[16]

If the Quebec Act appealed to colonists' innermost fears – the spread of popery – it also drew upon their more reasoned sensibilities. In giving assent to a bill that promoted Catholicism within the empire, George III betrayed one of his most important responsibilities as king: to act as the protector of the Protestant faith.[17] Doing so was a breach of his coronation oath, and, according to some colonists, a legal justification to absolve their allegiance to the monarch. Writers in colonial newspapers frequently denounced the king's actions in "giving his royal assent to the obnoxious Quebec bill, and thereby breaking his coronation oath."[18] In October, New Yorkers read an "EPIGRAM, on the QUEBEC BILL" that placed George III alongside two notorious British monarchs whose support of Catholic policies cost them the throne, implicitly suggesting that the former deserved a similar fate:

> COULD James the Second leave his Grave,
> Or Charles peep up, without his Head,
> How the two royal Knaves would rave
> To find a Parliament so bread!
> To join the King, and the Religion own,
> For which one lost his Head, and one his Crown![19]

Such reports were fuelled, in part, by the writings of the First Continental Congress. Delegates met in September, in hopes of finding a peaceful solution to the growing crisis, though their actions only intensified divisions. In their various petitions and addresses, many of which made their way into the pages of the newspapers of New York City and Halifax, the delegates repeatedly claimed that the real intention of the legislation was to use French Catholics as a "fit instrument" to violently suppress the rights and liberties of American colonists. In their *Declaration and Resolves*, which outlined colonists' opposition to the Coercive Acts and proposed a path towards opposing the legislation, delegates declared the Quebec Act to be of "great danger (from so total a dissimilarity of religion, law and government) ... [to] the neighboring British colonies, by the assistance of whose blood and treasure the said country was conquered from France."[20] The *Memorial to the Inhabitants of the British Colonies*, authored by William Livingston, warned readers "that the [French Canadians], deprived of liberty and artfully provoked against those of another religion, will be proper instruments for assisting in the oppression of such as differ from them in modes of government and faith."[21] The radical *Suffolk Resolves*, written in Boston in early September and endorsed by Congress a week later, argued for the arming of citizens, because, among other things, "the late act of parliament for establishing the Roman Catholic religion and the French laws in ... Canada, is dangerous in an extreme degree to the Protestant religion and to the civil rights and liberties of all America."[22] New York delegate John Jay wrote in an *Address to the People of Great Britain* that Canada was "daily swelling with Catholic emigrants from Europe, and by their devotion to Administration, so friendly to their religion, they might become formidable to us, and on occasion, be fit instruments in the hands of power, to reduce the ancient free Protestant Colonies to the same state of slavery with themselves."[23]

Congress's adoption of the Continental Association, a new, more expansive, boycott of British goods, was also motivated, in some measure, by fears surrounding the Quebec Act.[24] The association radically altered the political organization of the American colonies. It began the process of supplanting formal, constituted government with these various committees, which answered only to delegates in Philadelphia. It also threatened to undo Britain's prosperous Atlantic trade, which had done so much to define a shared imperial identity through the exchange of goods, print, and people. Congress defended its decision to enact such an aggressive boycott, because, among other reasons, the Quebec Act encouraged French Canadians "to act with hostility against the free Protestant Colonies, whenever a wicked Ministry shall choose so to direct them."[25]

These petitions and addresses helped to generate (as delegates had hoped) an incipient shared narrative – a Patriot common cause – among the growing number of opponents to British policies. Increasingly, many New Yorkers came to believe the unimaginable: their government was conspiring to use Catholics to destroy the rights and liberties of loyal Protestant subjects. It was at this moment, when New Yorkers were beset by the terror and uncertainty of their government's actions, that they learned of an even worse atrocity. General Gage and his troops had allegedly laid waste to Boston.[26] While the reports ultimately proved unfounded, some New Yorkers remained convinced that something sinister was afoot. One writer in Holt's *Journal* expressed disbelief at the reports coming from both Quebec and Boston. Though he admitted to having always considered "the King as politically impeccable ... [and] parliament [as] always composed of the bravest, wisest, and best men in the nation," he was alarmed by the recent passage of the Quebec Act. "What," he asked, "could ever induce men," to pass a bill meant "to rob, enslave and murder their fellow subjects at the expense of the *protestant cause*?" He warned readers that "the actual attack now made on the town of Boston, as well as recent accounts of orders being sent to Canada, for embodying the militia, who, in conjunction with the Indians, are to cooperate with a Roman catholic General, in carrying this infernal project into execution." In such alarming circumstances, he declared, it was "*an absolute necessity*" for colonists to "raise and maintain an army of observation ... to afford the speediest relief to the oppressed, as well as to support the frontiers against a winter invasion."[27] Five months before the outbreak of war at Lexington, fears of their king having abandoned the Protestant faith, and of a popish army descending upon their frontier, led some colonists to begin considering a war against their own country.

This was the narrative constructed by Patriot writers and delegates to Congress beginning in the fall of 1774. The threat posed by the Quebec Act did not replace decade-long concerns over the increasingly arbitrary policies of parliament. But it did shift the conversation away from the corruption of government officials to another, more dangerous, possibility. Parliament, and perhaps even the king, were no longer British. Tradition gave this narrative its heft. It was steeped in a century of British prejudice. Popery resonated because of how deeply it was embedded in the very notion of what it meant to be British in the eighteenth century. Long before Thomas Paine's *Common Sense*, some Britons were beginning to consider that their political opponents were no longer like them, and their system of government had given in to a form of tyranny with which they could not negotiate.

Moderate New Yorkers – many of whom would identify as Loyalists over the following several months – fought back, but with limited success. The city boasted the largest urban population of pro-British subjects in the colonies on the eve of fighting in Massachusetts, while Loyalists in some neighbouring communities formed a substantial majority over their radical Patriot counterparts.[28] Between a fifth and a third of the entire white colonial population remained loyal during the rebellion; in New York City and the surrounding region, that proportion doubled.[29] Historians have largely ignored the possibility that these Loyalists, like the American Patriots, were attracted to a shared cause, instead pinning Loyalists' political allegiances on a diverse range of personal interests that often predated the imperial crisis.[30] But these interpretations underestimate the extent to which a vibrant Loyalist press, like its opponents, could mobilize a populace.

This was especially evident in New York City, home to the influential Loyalist printer James Rivington. He was likely the most widely read printer in all of Britain's North American colonies, at least until the spring of 1775.[31] Through his press, Loyalist writers and pamphleteers gave meaning to a transatlantic political culture of Loyalism that was no less committed to eighteenth-century Whig ideals that celebrated political liberty, economic freedom, and Protestant virtue.

In the winter of 1774–75, these writers used Rivington's gazette to defend monarchy and legal, constituted government, and to rail against the tyranny of Congress and the violence of Patriot crowds and committees. But they struggled to articulate a unifying narrative capable of turning their opponents into dangerous enemies, a difficulty especially evident in their attempts to defend the unpopular Quebec Act. Some writers tried to argue that it would help to bring peace and stability to a region of the empire in crisis. In October, Rivington published Lord Lyttleton's response to William Pitt's attack on the Quebec Act, in which Lyttleton maintained that religious toleration was the surest way to secure the political loyalty of their former enemies. He did so, ironically, by playing on the very same age-old fears of lurking Catholics (and their Indian allies) employed by Patriot writers. He asked Pitt what was the point of acquiring Canada, "but that France might not have at her command a body of men, either to attack our American settlements in time of war, or harass them in time of peace, by inciting the native Indians to invade them?" Even worse, he feared that, should parliament have "to *coerce* America; do you wish in that melancholy event, to combine the Canadian with that of the Bostonian?"[32] Thomas Chandler agreed in a pamphlet Rivington published in November, arguing that to deprive these subjects of their faith "would probably have increased the number of his Majesty's disaffected American subjects; which appears to be too great without them."[33]

In other instances, supporters of the British cause used growing fears of popery against their political opponents. They frequently framed Congress and the various dependent committees as popish organizations that sought to deprive loyal Britons of their most cherished rights and liberties. In *The Congress Canvassed*, the Anglican minister Samuel

Seabury likened the enforcement of the Continental Association to a "*Popish* inquisition. No proofs, no evidences are called for. The committee may judge from *appearances* if they please – for when it shall be made appear to a majority of any committee that the Association is violated, they may proceed to punishment, and *appearances*, you know, are easily *made*."[34] In February, a Philadelphian reported in Rivington's newspaper that members of a local Patriot committee had entered one of the city's taverns to demand the name of a person who had anonymously printed a pro-British broadside. "I thought this *demand* favoured a little of a *popish inquisition*." He was even more surprised to find that those demanding the author's name "were the Committee, who had been chosen guardians of our liberties, but had instead of preserving them, introduced the worst species of tyranny, and the most dangerous kind of slavery that any country had ever experienced."[35]

Even New Englanders were susceptible to accusations of popery. Early in 1775, Rivington published John Lind's *An Englishman's Answer, to the Address from the Delegates to the People of Great-Britain*, which portrayed New Englanders – the supposed ringleaders of colonial resistance – as not all that dissimilar to their French counterparts. Lind reminded readers that, in the last century, they had "shed blood of the sovereign, and dispersed impiety, bigotry, superstition, hypocrisy, persecution, murder, and rebellion through every part of the empire!"[36] Lind's choice of descriptors was intentional. He sought to recast Patriot leaders as no longer British by likening them to the puritanical fanaticism of the Cromwellian era. Yet he did so by quoting from Congress's description of French Catholics in their *Address to the People of Great Britain*. As the colonies descended towards rebellion, both American Patriots and loyal Britons sought desperately to affix popish labels to their enemies to show that they themselves were the true defenders of Protestant British patriotism. If the king (or colonial governors like Guy Carleton) could become papists, so too could the heirs of Oliver Cromwell.

Rivington's press in the critical months of the winter of 1774–75 attempted to confuse an emerging Patriot cause by turning the language of Protestant British Loyalism against rebellious colonists. In various reports and editorials, Loyalist writers constructed an alternative path towards the imperial conflict by playing upon popular definitions of British loyalty and patriotism. Tyranny, according to these writers, came not from the actions of British imperial officials, but rather from the newly formed, extra-legal, and unrepresentative

Continental Congress. They argued that the Continental Association was passed without public consent and threatened to violently suppress the political and economic loyalties of American colonists. Though no less committed to a Whig defence of personal liberty, these writers and their readers were encouraged by the crisis to adopt a more moderate view of Loyalism. They celebrated the rule of law and legitimate, constituted government in the face of violent, subversive committees and crowds. Their writings also turned political labels – ones that have endured to this very day – on their heads by claiming that it was American Patriots who favoured popish submission to political authority (an illegitimate one no less) over a defence of their rights and liberties.

Loyal New Yorkers suffered at the hands of Patriot crowds for their willingness to defend a king who supported the spread of Catholicism in the empire. In March, for example, William Cunningham was beaten and robbed by a crowd for defiantly proclaiming, "God bless King George," rather than going "down on his knees and damn his Popish King George."[37] Weeks later in New Haven, Connecticut, a "loyal Constitutionalist" was "interrogated after the manner of the *Spanish* and *Portugal* inquisitions" for publicly criticizing Congress and refusing to "damn the King." "To this complexion is *American* liberty," claimed the writer, "through the influence of the King-killing Republicans, already arrived."[38]

John Case experienced something similar in early January 1775, when two well-known Patriots in the city, Alexander McDougall and Isaac Sears, invited him to a local tavern "to converse ... on politicks." Case, a known Loyalist from nearby Long Island, frustrated all of McDougall's attempts to prove his error in thinking. Sears then asked him point-blank, "whether the King had not violated his coronation oath?" (Yet another example of Patriot hostility to the Quebec Act.) Case "thought he had not." Incensed, Sears labelled the old man a "Tory, and told him, that if he was in Connecticut government he would be put to death." He then asked Case "whether, if Bostonians were to take up arms, he would fight for the King?" Case said he would, "as he conceived King George to be his lawful Sovereign." Growing angrier, Sears ordered Case to sit in a chair "in the chimney corner" and then ordered "a Negro boy, who belonged to the house ... to sit along with him." The boy "had too much understanding to comply," but Case sat in the corner for the remainder of the evening, while Sears and McDougall "ordered the rest not to drink with a Tory."[39]

Given the descent into violence that Loyalists all over the American colonies endured in these months before the war, Case – though socially humiliated – got off lightly.

Despite their commitment to defending monarchy, loyal New Yorkers struggled to explain away a piece of legislation so at odds with popular understandings of Britishness. The growing number of Patriots in New York City, on the other hand, embraced a narrative of the conflict that increasingly relied on the imagined threat of popery, which they used to assert greater control over the city's political culture. When some moderates threatened to block attempts by radicals to elect like-minded delegates to the Second Continental Congress in March 1775, the "Friends of Freedom" marched from the liberty pole to the city's exchange to ensure their victory in the contest. According to a report of the incident widely circulated in colonial newspapers, the crowd "carried a large Union Flag, with a blue Field, on which were the following Inscriptions: On one Side, GEORGE III. REX AND THE LIBERTIES OF AMERICA. NO POPERY. On the other, THE UNION OF THE COLONIES, AND THE MEASURES OF THE CONGRESS."[40] The words, "No popery," in this case, acted as the villain. They threatened to deprive New Yorkers of their liberties and their loyalty should they not join with the other colonies in supporting the decisions of their Congress.

Weeks later, New Yorkers were shocked to read of the fighting at Lexington and Concord and took to the streets in protest. Members of the Sons of Liberty raided the arsenal for weapons and ammunition, forced James Rivington to publicly renounce the British cause, and ordered the disarming of known Loyalists. All the while, Patriot crowds harassed their former friends, dragging some before the city's liberty pole, where they were "insulted and beaten in a Cruel manner if they refused to kneel down and Curse the King and his Government."[41] With the city teetering on the edge of rebellion, Isaac Low, then still joined with the Patriot cause, called a public meeting to announce the creation of a local association that would effectively turn control of the city over to the General Committee, which he chaired. Speaking in front of thousands of New York Patriots who gathered that day, Low "damned the King, [and] cursed the Ministry," before launching into a tirade against George III that was intended to inspire the crowd to action. He declared, of all things, that "the King was a Roman Catholic, nay, a Roman Catholic tyrant; that he had broken his coronation oath, had established the popish religion in

Canada, which was shortly to be extended to all the other colonies."[42] Fears of a popish king and army, not surprisingly, marked New York City's radical shift towards armed conflict with Great Britain.

A year later, Thomas Jefferson enshrined the Quebec Act in the nation's founding document, listing the legislation as one of the twenty-seven grievances against the king. He condemned George III "For abolishing the free System of English Laws in a neighbouring Province, establishing therein an Arbitrary government, and enlarging its Boundaries so as to render it at once an example and fit instrument for introducing the same absolute rule into these states." Jefferson's explanation of the bill reflected, in some ways, the public's fear about its intended purpose. The Quebec Act was ultimately dangerous because it served as "an example and fit instrument" to subject North American colonists to the same tyranny and arbitrary rule. That he intentionally placed the grievance directly preceding the ones that blamed the king for actually doing this (the 1774 Massachusetts Government Act and the 1767 New York Restraining Act, respectively) was meant to convince readers that such fears were legitimate.[43]

But it is also worth noting that Jefferson left out the more specific threat posed by the tens of thousands of French Catholics in Canada, which featured so prominently in popular responses to the legislation in the winter of 1774–75. In fact, residents of Quebec appear only as anonymous victims of British imperial policies, not as newly empowered subjects who were intending to invade their neighbours to the south. The placement of the text is also suggestive of how Jefferson and the committee viewed the Quebec Act. Rather than situate it among the final set of complaints, which were meant to elicit an emotional response from readers (the king had burnt their towns, armed slaves, Indians, and German mercenaries, and forced American seamen to kill their fellow countrymen), they placed it alongside the more reasoned set of political grievances against the king.[44] We can only speculate on the reasons for this placement, given that neither Jefferson nor any of the committee members explained their wording of the complaint, but it is likely they were motivated by pragmatic reasons. At the time, Congress was secretly courting an alliance with France, which saw the rebellion as an opportunity to weaken Britain's expanding influence around the globe.[45] Similarly, despite the failure of the Canada campaign, even in the late spring of 1776 Congress still hoped to persuade French Canadians to join their rebellion. It made little sense then to have listed their potential friends as dangerous enemies in the very document that justified American colonists' separation from Britain.

This reimagining of the Quebec Act in strictly political terms, absent fears of an invading Catholic army, was evident in how New Yorkers responded to the first public reading of the declaration. To celebrate the moment, the "Sons of Freedom" tore down the equestrian statue of George III in an act of symbolic regicide that was repeated in communities throughout British North America. Thereafter, New Yorkers reportedly melted the remains of their fallen king into 42,088 bullets, "to assimilate with the brain of our infatuated adversaries."[46] The numbers forty-two and eighty-eight harkened back to previous British monarchs whose pro-Catholic policies had also cost them the allegiance of their people. Just as important, though, these dates referred to moments when Englishmen overcame their popish oppressors in defence of their Protestant beliefs. In other words, Patriots in New York marked their turn towards independence by, of all things, acting the part of Protestant Whig defenders of liberty. They had not become American; their king had abandoned his Britishness.

Britons living in Halifax disliked the Quebec Act as much as their neighbours to the south. From its founding in 1749, anti-Catholicism defined the political culture of the remote North Atlantic port city. Haligonians were surrounded on three sides by Indian societies previously allied with France and a smaller French-Acadian population that still haunted the memories of many of the town's residents.[47] From the beginning, the Nova Scotia assembly sought to deny rights to known Catholics in the colony, refusing "popish recusants" suffrage, banishing all "priests of popish belief," and making it illegal for Catholics to own land.[48] In the 1760s as many as eight thousand New Englanders emigrated to the colony as part of a government plan to expand the presence of Protestant British subjects in the region. These new settlers, as we shall see, retained strong political and cultural ties to their former homeland. They were defiant in their support of self-government and personal liberty, and embraced a radical brand of Protestantism that was often framed against the perceived dangers of the Catholic faith.[49]

The colony's only newspaper, Anthony Henry's *Nova Scotia Gazette*, reflected in many ways the interests of these recent transplants. Henry frequently printed reports and editorials in defence of the rights of colonial subjects, and from as early as 1765, he used his press to promote resistance to imperial policies.[50] In the winter of 1774–75, the printer stoked reader's fears of the dangerous designs of the Quebec Act, printing every one of Congress's petitions and addresses, which still claimed to represent the interests of Nova Scotians.[51] Henry's gazette carried many of the rumours and reports coming from New York City newspapers alleging that the bill's true intention was to use French Canadians to subdue American colonists. He also reprinted essays intended to convince readers that the king had broken his coronation oath when he gave his assent to the "obnoxious Quebec bill."[52] Halifax's political culture was just as committed to a defence of Protestant British liberty as its neighbours to the south, and Henry's gazette was quick to amplify growing fears of the spread of popish tyranny occasioned by the passage of the Quebec Act.

However, in contrast to New York City, the public's opposition to the legislation failed to materialize into a sustained movement against British imperial rule. This was the result of the town and colony's unique political and economic circumstances, and not necessarily because the inhabitants espoused more moderate political beliefs than other American colonists. From its founding, political authority in the colony was centralized in the hands of a select few wealthy Haligonian merchants, whose interests were tied to the government in London. Additionally, the port town served as a base of operations for the British army and navy, which meant that soldiers were a constant – if not always welcome – presence in the town. Outnumbered by soldiers, and in the absence of a merchant community unwilling to put aside its own self-interest, Haligonians struggled to build a movement capable of resisting British rule in the colony.

In the winter of 1774–75, the city's merchants also stood to benefit from Congress's planned boycott, which would push New England merchants out of the North Atlantic and open up Halifax to the lucrative West Indian trade.[53] Their new governor, Francis Legge, petitioned parliament, unsuccessfully, to give Nova Scotia complete control over the North Atlantic fishing industry. By March, however, parliament passed the New England Restraining Act, excluding rebellious New Englanders from access to the fisheries, and the following month officials extended these restrictions to the remaining North American colonies. Congress's Association, long thought to have played a crucial role in drawing together colonists in opposition to British rule, likely tempered the political interests of some Haligonians. They could not reconcile their opposition to unpopular imperial policies with a desire to expand their colony's commercial interests.[54]

Some Haligonians did try to take a stand against their king and government, no doubt influenced by reports of popery spreading across British North America. While Henry was circulating stories of a possible third Jacobite rebellion unfolding on the continent, with the Young Pretender (who was anything but young in 1774) using the Quebec Act "to gain a Kingdom he so highly longs to govern," a group of Haligonians attempted, unsuccessfully, to stop the landing of East India Company tea in the city.[55] Governor Legge reacted harshly, arresting the alleged ringleaders and ordering a ban on unlawful assemblies that "promote illegal Confederacies, Combinations, public Disorders and the highest Contempt of Government."[56] One Haligonian believed Legge's aggressive tactics had "effectually cut the throat of Rebellious faction, in this Country & destroyed the seeds of Sedition, sewn among the People."[57] But reports circulating in colonial American newspapers contradicted these findings, suggesting instead that "subscriptions are opened" in Halifax to send relief to Bostonians.[58] On the eve of the delegates' meeting in Philadelphia, John Holt went so far as to claim in his *Journal* that "the provinces of New York, Philadelphia, South and North Carolina, Nova Scotia, and Halifax, have heartily entered into the American cause."[59]

Support for the Patriot cause grew in Halifax after news of fighting at Lexington and Concord arrived in early May 1775. Anonymous residents allegedly set two fires, one targeting the warehouses of local merchant and assemblyman Joseph Fairbanks, who had agreed to send a large quantity of hay to Gage's army in Boston, and the other the home of Richard Morris, a local justice of the peace and ally of the unpopular Governor Legge.[60] News of these fires excited Patriots in New York City, but Henry's gazette included only a brief report critical of both incidents and did not publish any additional essays or editorials.[61] Even the Halifax-dominated assembly hoped to use the growing crisis to weaken royal authority in the colony. In an address to parliament drafted weeks after the start of the war, they laid out a new plan of imperial-colonial relations that gave locally elected assemblies a greater degree of control over taxation and limited the authority of royally appointed governors and their council. The assemblymen believed such a plan would "preserve the inhabitants of this Province in duty and allegiance to our King."[62]

With the colony rising up with new political demands, Legge took even more aggressive steps to silence critics. He offered a reward for the capture of those behind the fires, and a week later he ordered recent immigrants from "any Parts of *America*" to give an oath of allegiance "to his Majesty's Sacred Person and Government."[63] In July, the governor prohibited Nova Scotians from "exporting gunpowder, arms, and ammunition, or Salt Petre out of the colony," and from aiding or abetting any rebel colonist. Legge also openly criticized the assembly's address, writing to Lord Dartmouth that it "contains some projection for the Alteration of Government upon the American System of Popularity."[64] By August, the situation had become so dire that Legge had all of the small arms and gunpowder in town moved to vessels in the harbour, and required *every person* to register an oath of allegiance to the king and parliament.[65] Haligonians, and Nova Scotians more generally, were to remain loyal to Great Britain – by force if necessary.

Many reasons likely pushed Haligonians to support the rebellion unfolding in the colonies, and popular opposition to the Quebec Act was certainly one of them. From the winter of 1774–75, Henry's gazette drew from a myriad of Patriot newspapers that increasingly framed the imperial crisis in broader, familiar terms, as a contest between a free Protestant society and an arbitrary Catholic one. Fears of popery running roughshod over Britain's Protestant colonies resonated with many of the city's residents who enjoyed close religious and cultural ties with their New England neighbours. That such fears focused on the actions of their own king and government, and not their long-standing enemies, likely pushed many of the city's residents toward rebellion.

This was certainly true of Timothy Houghton, a New Englander by birth, veteran of the Seven Years' War, and local magistrate in the nearby town of Chester. In August 1775, Houghton publicly objected to Governor Legge's proclamation that every resident swear allegiance to the king, because, according to Houghton, George III "had broke his Coronation Oath by establishing the Roman Catholic Religion at Quebec and that he could not in Conscience serve his Majesty." A friend and neighbour, William Harrison, claimed as well that Houghton had refused "to supply the King's troops then at Boston with any kind of relief or necessaries."[66] Another resident said that Houghton swore he could no longer serve as the town's magistrate, because "the King was a Papist," and his adviser, Lord Bute, was a

"Stewart," a term commonly used to describe a Jacobite. To prove his point, Houghton referred to a law book that showed "that no Protestant was bound in Allegiance to the King any longer than he continued protestant."[67]

Houghton's remarks might have earned him a place in New York City's Patriot leadership, but the situation was very different in Halifax. Over the previous year, officials there had resisted ceding control of the city to crowds or extralegal committees. Houghton's public criticism of the monarch required a similarly aggressive response. Officials arrested the war veteran in late 1776; he was found guilty of sedition the following February. He was ordered to pay a £50 fine and serve six months in jail, and was stripped of his government position. He returned to Chester to run his business, but only after he agreed to take the oath of allegiance he had rejected nearly two years earlier. The government in Halifax had effectually "destroyed the seeds of Sedition," which, at least in the case of Timothy Houghton, had found meaning in the king's decision to relieve Catholics in nearby Quebec.[68]

The British government's decision in 1774 to tolerate Catholicism in Quebec was widely criticized by Britons in both New York City and Halifax. Residents of these cities had been reared in a language of Protestant liberty that found meaning in its relationship to the perceived tyranny of the Catholic faith. To tolerate the faith at this moment, when Britain was mired in a political crisis that drew heavily upon popular understandings of Britishness, threatened to dissolve the tenuous bonds that previously bound together Britons across the North Atlantic. The Quebec Act, in fact, offered to some a reason to rebel. It raised questions about the right of George III to the throne and recast supporters of the crown as dangerous and foreign enemies. More generally, the Quebec Act reinvigorated a language of Protestant liberty, which inspired both rebellious and loyal subjects to act in new and far more aggressive ways towards one another.

In the contested streets of New York City, the Quebec Act radically altered popular understandings of loyalty among the city's diverse inhabitants. Congress's petitions and addresses, and the many published reports and editorials that appeared in local newspapers, fuelled an emerging Patriot cause that drew upon popular anti-Catholic prejudices to drive many New Yorkers towards rebellion. When news arrived in the city of fighting at Lexington and Concord, thousands of New Yorkers agreed to a war against their own country, in part, because they believed they were defending their rights as Protestant British subjects.

On the other hand, loyal New Yorkers struggled to make a counter-argument – a competing common cause – at the precise moment lines were being drawn. These loyal Britons were left to defend a king and government acting at odds with popular, transatlantic understandings of Britishness. While some writers tried to calm people's fears of the legislation, many others turned their focus to the writings and actions of the newly formed Continental Congress and the many committees created to enforce the Association. They argued that popery was deeply embedded in an emerging Patriot cause that sought to create consensus through the use of arbitrary violence and intimidation. In such circumstances, these loyal Britons concluded, it was far better to trust the crown and parliament to protect their rights than to support a dangerous political body that appeared every bit as popish as their traditional European enemies.

In Halifax, many of the town's residents appeared to support the growing Patriot cause in the American colonies, arguing that the Quebec Act represented a grave danger to the very values and ideals that defined eighteenth-century understandings of British loyalty and patriotism. Their local gazette drew heavily from the pages of Patriot newspapers, carrying many of the same stories that warned readers of the spread of popery in British North America. The conditions on the ground, however, made it all but impossible for these residents to act on their beliefs. In the crucial months of the winter of 1774–75, their governor demanded allegiance to the crown, arrested known agitators, and outlawed public meetings in an effort to secure the loyalty of the city and colony's inhabitants. In many ways, his actions paralleled the activities of Patriot committees in the streets of New York City, who had also reverted to violence and coercion to generate support for their cause. Despite repeated attempts to bring rebellion to Nova Scotia in the summer of 1775, the colony remained a part of the empire.

Ultimately, however, the Quebec Act proved to be just the first among several attempts by the British *and* American governments to tolerate Catholicism in the midst of a civil war premised on a defence of Protestant liberty. In 1778, the Americans formally negotiated an alliance with Britain's eternal enemy, France, and Spain joined the conflict a year later. While the alliance bolstered the American war effort, it also led to a dramatic upsurge in British patriotism throughout the empire, which rivalled the American response to the Quebec Act four years earlier.[69] For many loyal subjects, the alliance exposed the hypocrisy of the American rebellion and provided Britons with the more convincing and widely shared common cause they desperately lacked in 1774–75. From 1778 through the remainder of the war, loyal Britons everywhere, including those living in both Halifax and New York City, recast the Americans as French and Catholic and repeatedly questioned the legitimacy of a Protestant rebellion supposedly founded in opposition to the spread of popery.[70]

In the same year, however, parliament, needing to secure the loyalty of mainland Catholics and recruit additional soldiers to fight in the expanded war, proposed a series of Catholic relief bills for England, Scotland, and Ireland.[71] Mainland Britons, like many American colonists four years earlier, reacted bitterly to these bills, which they framed as a threat to their Protestant loyalties. They claimed that the legislation "would actually overthrow the *union*, dissolve the *claim of right*, renew the pretences of an abdicated, Popish family, to the crown, and break down the legal barriers against that arbitrary religion, so pernicious to the interest of Princes, as well as to the freedom of a brave and virtuous people."[72] Violent, deadly riots ensued in communities across Scotland and England, culminating in June 1780 with the infamous Gordon Riots in London.[73] In the final years of the war, renewed fears of the government encouraging the spread of popery nearly led to another rebellion, this time on the shores of mainland Britain.

Anti-Catholic rhetoric came to justify both rebellion *and* loyalty in communities throughout the British Atlantic during the American War for Independence. The threat of Catholic relief in Canada, mainland Britain, and even across the thirteen American colonies after 1778, radically altered popular understandings of Protestant loyalty by playing upon some of the most common fears of eighteenth-century British subjects. Yet, loyal and rebellious Britons in both New York City and Halifax, and elsewhere in the empire for that matter, confronted this narrative of the war from their own distinct local circumstances. This contentious relationship between subjects' broader, shared imperial identity – in which the threat of popery played a prominent role – and their more particular local interests ultimately decided their fate in the conflict.

NOTES

1 For examples of more typical entry ceremonies, see *The Newport Mercury*, 4 August 1766; *The New-York Gazette or the Weekly Post-Boy*, 22 October 1770. These ceremonies drew upon the more elaborate royal entry ceremonies common in Western Europe since the fourteenth century, especially in France. Neil Murphy, *Ceremonial Entries, Municipal Liberties and the Negotiation of Power in Valois France, 1328–1589* (Leiden, NL: Brill, 2016); Peter Borsay, "'All the Town's a Stage': Urban Ritual and Ceremony, 1660–1800," in *The Transformation of English Provincial Towns, 1600–1800*, ed. Peter Clark, 228–58 (London: Hutchinson, 1984); Patricia Seed, *Ceremonies of Possession in Europe's Conquest of the New World, 1492–1640* (Cambridge: Cambridge University Press, 1995), 41–68.

2 This was certainly the case in the summer of 1775, when George Washington, as the newly appointed commander-in-chief of the Continental Army, and William Tryon, the royally appointed governor of New York, both arrived in New York City on the same day. I.N. Phelps Stokes, ed., *The Iconography of Manhattan Island, 1498–1909*, 5 vols (1922; reprint, Union, NJ: The Lawbook Exchange, 1998), 4:894–5.

3 Fred Anderson, *Crucible of War: The Seven Years' War and the Fate of Empire in British North America, 1754–1766* (New York: Alfred A. Knopf, 2000), 344–68.

4 Carleton did advise members of parliament who were responsible for drafting the legislation. P.D.G. Thomas, *Tea Party to Independence: The Third Phase of the American Revolution, 1773–1776* (Oxford: Clarendon Press, 1991), 88–117.

5 *The New-York Journal; or, The General Advertiser*, 6 October 1774; *Rivington's New-York Gazetteer; or, The Connecticut, Hudson's River, New-Jersey, and Quebec Weekly Advertiser*, 6 October 1774. Rivington's newspaper went through several name changes during its existence. To avoid confusion, I will refer to it as *Rivington's Gazette* hereafter. *The Nova-Scotia Gazette; and the Weekly Chronicle*, 8 November 1774. See also *Dunlap's Pennsylvania Packet; or, the General Advertiser* [Philadelphia], 10 October 1774; *The Connecticut Courant, and Hartford Weekly Intelligencer*, 10 October, 1774; *The Connecticut Journal, and the New-Haven Post-Boy*, 14 October 1774; *The Boston Evening-Post*, 17 October 1774; *The New-Hampshire Gazette, and Historical Chronicle*, 21 October 1774; *Supplement to the Virginia Gazette* [Purdie and Dixon], 20 October 1774; *The Virginia Gazette* [Pickney], 20 October 1774. Several London newspapers included a shortened version of the story that referred to the widespread joy of

Catholics in Montreal upon receiving news of the passage of the bill. *General Evening Post*, 12 November 1774; *London Chronicle, or Universal Evening Post*, 12 November 1774; *Craftsman, or Say's Weekly Journal*, 12 November 1774.

6 This argument is indebted to the ground-breaking work of Linda Colley in *Britons: Forging the Nation, 1707–1837* (New Haven, CT: Yale University Press, 1992) and "Britishness and Otherness: An Argument," *Journal of British Studies* 31, no. 4 (October 1992): 309–29. Several historians have refined and challenged her argument. See Colin Kidd, *British Identities before Nationalism: Ethnicity and Nationhood in the Atlantic World, 1600–1800* (Cambridge: Cambridge University Press, 1999) and "North Britishness and the Nature of Eighteenth-Century British Patriotisms," *Historical Journal* 39, no. 2 (June 1996): 361–82; Kathleen Wilson, *The Sense of the People: Politics, Culture, and Imperialism in England, 1715–1785* (Cambridge: Cambridge University Press, 1995); Carla Gardina Pestana, *Protestant Empire: Religion and the Making of the British Atlantic World* (Philadelphia: University of Pennsylvania Press, 2009); Brendan McConville, *The King's Three Faces: The Rise and Fall of Royal America, 1688–1776* (Chapel Hill: University of North Carolina Press, 2006); Eliga H. Gould, *The Persistence of Empire: British Political Culture in the Age of the American Revolution* (Chapel Hill: University of North Carolina Press, 2000); Francis D. Cogliano, *No King, No Popery: Anti-Catholicism in Revolutionary New England* (Westport, CT: Greenwood Press, 1995); Jack P. Greene, "Empire and Identity from the Glorious Revolution to the American Revolution," in *The Oxford History of the British Empire*, vol. 2, *The Eighteenth Century*, ed. P.J. Marshall (Oxford: Oxford University Press, 1998), 208–30; Tony Claydon and Ian McBride, eds, *Protestantism and National Identity: Britain and Ireland, c. 1650–c.1850* (Cambridge: Cambridge University Press, 1998); S.J. Connolly, "Varieties of Britishness: Ireland, Scotland, and Wales in the Hanoverian State," in *Uniting the Kingdom? The Making of British History*, ed. Alexander Grant and Keith J. Stringer, 193– 07 (New York: Routledge, 1995); T.C. Smout, "Problems of Nationalism, Identity, and Improvement in Later Eighteenth-Century Scotland," in *Improvement and Enlightenment: Proceedings of the Scottish Historical Studies Seminar, University of Strathclyde, 1987–88*, ed. T.M. Devine (Edinburgh: John Donald Publishers, 1989), 1–21. For the ways in which anti-Catholicism informed early modern English politics and society, see Peter Lake, "Anti-popery: The Structure of a Prejudice," in *Conflict in Early Stuart England: Studies in Religion and Politics, 1603–1642*, ed. Richard Cust and Ann Hughes, 73–82 (London: Longman, 1989).

7 As John Murrin famously put it many years ago, "In a word, America was Britain's idea." "A Roof without Walls: The Dilemma of American National Identity," in *Beyond Confederation: Origins of the Constitution and American Identity*, ed. Richard Beeman, Stephen Botwin, and Edward C. Carter II, 333–48 (Chapel Hill: University of North Carolina Press, 1987). See also John Murrin, "1776: The Countercyclical Revolution," in *Revolutionary Currents: Nation Building in the Transatlantic World*, ed. Michael A. Morrison and Melinda Zook, 65–90 (New York: Rowman and Littlefield, 2004); Greene, "Empire and Identity," 227–9; Maya Jasanoff, *Liberty's Exiles: American Loyalists in the Revolutionary World* (New York: Alfred A. Knopf, 2011), 9; Dror Wahrman, "The English Problem of Identity in the American Revolution," *American Historical Review* 106, no. 4 (October 2001): 1236–62. Contemporaries regularly referred to the rebellion as a civil war. To cite just one example, see New Yorker John Thurman's letter to a friend in London in September 1774, in which he says "we dread the Consequences of Civil Warr & Fighting with our best friends," quoted in Stokes, ed. *Iconography of Manhattan Island*, 4:866.

8 Scholars have emphasized the power of print in shaping national identities. Jill Lepore, for example, argues, "the acts of war generate acts of narration ... [which] are often joined in a common purpose: defining the geographical, political, cultural, and sometimes racial and national boundaries between peoples." *The Name of War: King Philip's War and the Origins of American Identity* (New York: Vintage, 1999), x. See also Simon Newman, *Parades and the Politics of the Street: Festive Culture in the Early American Republic* (Philadelphia: University of Pennsylvania Press, 1999); David Waldstreicher, *In the Midst of Perpetual Fetes: The Making of American Nationalism, 1776–1820* (Chapel Hill: University of North Carolina Press, 1997); Robert Parkinson, *The Common Cause: Creating Race and Nation in the American Revolution* (Chapel Hill: University of North Carolina Press, 2016).

9 The act included four main provisions: it extended the province's territory into the Ohio Country; it reinstated French law in civil cases; it created a new colonial government that would be run by a royally appointed governor and council; and, finally, it tolerated Catholicism in the colony, though Catholics would be required to take an oath of allegiance to the crown. Hilda Neatby, *The Quebec Act: Protest and Policy* (Scarborough, ON: Prentice-Hall of Canada, 1972); Reginald Coupland, *The Quebec Act: A Study in Statesmanship* (Oxford: Clarendon Press, 1925). Philip Lawson, *The Imperial Challenge: Quebec and Britain in the*

Age of the American Revolution (Montreal: McGill-Queen's University Press, 1989); Peter M. Doll, *Revolution, Religion, and National Identity: Imperial Anglicanism in British North America, 1745–1795* (Madison, NJ: Farleigh Dickinson University Press, 2000), 146–53.

10 *An ACT against Jesuits and Popish Priests, Pass'd the 31st of July, 1700*, in *Laws of New-York, From the Year 1691, to 1751, Inclusive* (New York: Printed by James Parker, 1752), 37–8. In 1735, the assembly passed an act "for the better securing the Mahauk Indians in the British Interest," in an effort to render "their Inhabitants secure and safe from the Incursions of the French Indians." *The New-York Weekly Journal*, 15 December 1735.

11 For the 1712 slave conspiracy, see Jason K. Duncan, *Citizens or Papists? The Politics of Anti-Catholicism in New York, 1685–1821* (New York: Fordham University Press, 2005), 19–20. For 1741, see Jill Lepore, *New York Burning: Liberty, Slavery, and Conspiracy in Eighteenth-Century Manhattan* (New York: Vintage, 2005), 170–97.

12 *The New-York Gazette Weekly: or, The Weekly Post-Boy*, 17 January 1757. For similar reports, see *The New-York Gazette: or, The Weekly Post-Boy*, 2 May 1757; *The New-York Gazette: or, The Weekly Post-Boy*, 20 March 1758; *The New-York Mercury*, 1 October 1759. See also Peter Silver, *Our Savage Neighbors: How Indian War Transformed Early America* (New York: W. W. Norton, 2008), esp. chap. 4.

13 On the role that fears of Indians and slaves played in shaping the Patriot cause, see Parkinson, *Common Cause*; Silver, *Our Savage Neighbors*, esp. chap. 8.

14 *Rivington's Gazette*, 2 September 1774; *The New-York Journal; or, The General Advertiser*, 8 September 1774; *The Nova-Scotia Gazette; and the Weekly Chronicle*, 20 September 1774.

15 *Lord North's Soliloquy* (New York, 1774), Early American Imprints. Series 1, Evans 42633.

16 *The New-York Gazette; and the Weekly Mercury*, 31 October 1774; *Supplement to the Massachusetts Gazette*, 10 November 1774; *The Boston-Gazette, and Country Journal*, 7 November 1774; *The Essex Gazette*, 8 November 1774; *The New-Hampshire Gazette, and Historical Chronicle*, 11 November 1774; *The Newport Mercury*, 14 November 1774. Other reports suggested that the bill was actually part of a Jacobite plot to reinstate the Stuart dynasty on the throne. For example, see *The New-York Journal; or, The General Advertiser*, 7 July, and 3 November 1774; *Nova-Scotia Gazette, and the Weekly Chronicle*, 11 October 1774.

17 McConville, *King's Three Faces*, 288–90; Vernon Creviston, "'No King Unless It Be a Constitutional King': Rethinking the Place of the Quebec

Act in the Coming of the American Revolution," *The Historian* 73, no. 3 (Fall 2011): 463–79; Cogliano, *No King, No Popery*, esp. chap. 3.

18 *The Nova-Scotia Gazette, and the Weekly Chronicle*, 20 September 1774. A writer in Holt's newspaper described a Whig as someone who "thinks obedience [is] due to a King, *only while he adheres to his Coronation Oath* – and the moment he breaks that oath he absolves his subject from that allegiance." *The New-York Journal; or, The General Advertiser*, 9 February 1775.

19 *The New-York Journal; or, The General Advertiser*, 20 October 1774.

20 Peter Force, ed., *American Archives: A Documentary History of the English Colonies in North America*, 4th ser. (Washington, DC: M. St. Claire Clarke and Peter Force, 1837), 1:912

21 Force, ed., *American Archives*, 1:921.

22 *Rivington's Gazette*, 22 September 1774.

23 Force, ed., *American Archives*, 1:917. The address was reprinted in *Rivington's Gazette*, 3 November 1774; *The Nova-Scotia Gazette, and the Weekly Chronicle*, 10 January 1775.

24 The boycott on the importation of goods from Britain, Ireland, and the Caribbean began on 1 December 1774. The ban on exportation to Britain was to start on 10 September 1775.

25 Force, ed., *American Archives*, 1:913. The Association was reprinted in *The New-York Gazette; and the Weekly Mercury*, 31 October 1774; *The Nova-Scotia Gazette, and the Weekly Chronicle*, 22 November 1774.

26 T.H. Breen, *American Insurgents, American Patriots: The Revolution of the People* (New York: Hill and Wang, 2010), chap. 5.

27 *The New York Journal*, 10 November 1774.

28 At least six thousand New Yorkers, and likely more, refused to sign the Association, even after reports of fighting at Lexington and Concord. Half of the colony's fourteen counties either ignored or suppressed the implementation of the Association in the spring of 1775. Alexander Flick, *Loyalism in New York during the American Revolution* (New York: Macmillan, 1901), 47. See also Edward Countryman, "Consolidating Power in Revolutionary America: The Case of New York, 1775–1783," *Journal of Interdisciplinary History* 6, no. 4 (Spring 1976): 651–4; Carl Becker, *The History of Political Parties in the Province of New York, 1760–1776* (Madison: University of Wisconsin Press, 1960), 173. In February, the colony's assembly voted two to one to not recognize the proceedings of the First Continental Congress or endorse the Continental Association, while only the city and three county committees – Ulster, Albany, and Suffolk – actually came out in support of Congress. Carl

Becker, "Election of Delegates from New York to the Second Continental Congress," *American Historical Review* 9, no. 1 (October 1903): 73. For examples of communities where Patriots failed to gain a stronghold, see Sung Bok Kim, "The Limits of Politicization in the American Revolution: The Experience of Westchester County, New York," *Journal of American History* 80, no. 3 (December 1993): 868–89; Joseph S. Tiedemann, "Patriots by Default: Queens County, New York, and the British Army, 1776–1783," *William and Mary Quarterly* 43, no. 1 (January 1986): 35–63, and "A Revolution Foiled: Queens County, New York, 1775–1776," *Journal of American History* 75, no. 2 (September 1988): 417–44; Ruth M. Keesey, "Loyalism in Bergen County, New Jersey," *William and Mary Quarterly* 18, no. 4 (October 1961): 558–76. Philip Ranlet disputes claims of widespread Loyalism in the region. *The New York Loyalists* (Knoxville: University of Tennessee Press, 1986), 52–67.

29 For a useful summary of the debate over how many colonists were Loyalists, see Jasanoff, *Liberty's Exiles*, 364–5n16.

30 The list of those with such interests is extensive: wealthy merchants, local officials, Anglican ministers and their parishioners, recent immigrants, ethnic and religious minorities, tenants along the Hudson River Valley, and devotees of the more conservative De Lanceyite faction. Wallace Brown, *The Good Americans: The Loyalists in the American Revolution* (New York: Morrow, 1969), 44–81, and *The King's Friends: The Composition and Motives of the American Loyalist Claimants* (Providence, RI: Brown University Press, 1965); Robert McClure Calhoon, *The Loyalist in Revolutionary America, 1760–1781* (New York: Harcourt Brace Jovanovich, 1965), 370–81; William Nelson, *The American Tory* (New York: Oxford University Press, 1961), 85–115; Patricia U. Bonomi, *A Factious People: Politics and Society in Colonial New York* (New York: Columbia University Press, 1971), chaps, 7 and 8; Ranlet, *New York Loyalists*, 52–71; Joseph S. Tiedemann, Eugene R. Fingerhut, and Robert W. Venables, eds, *The Other Loyalists: Ordinary People, Royalism, and the Revolution in the Middle Colonies, 1763–1787* (Albany: SUNY Press, 2009). Maya Jasanoff does argue for a shared loyalist cause, what she calls the "Spirit of 1783," but it emerged only after the end of the revolution. At the outbreak of the war, she claims instead that "choices about loyalty depended more on employers, occupations, profits, land, faith, family, and friendships than on any implicit identification as an American or a Briton." *Liberty's Exiles*, 24. Ruma Chopra argues that Loyalists had a "deep ideological commitment and sentimental attachment to empire," but argues in the following paragraph that "more than ideological com-

mitments, the proximity of the British army and the threat of local coercion dramatically affected people's choices." *Choosing Sides: Loyalists in Revolutionary America* (New York: Rowman and Littlefield, 2013), 3. Mary Beth Norton similarly identifies Loyalists' arguments against their opponents but does not tie those arguments to broader understandings of what it meant to be British. *The British Americans: The Loyalist Exiles in England, 1774–1789* (Boston: Little, Brown, 1972), 16–24, 130–54. In her analysis of Southern Loyalism, Rebecca Brannon claims that Loyalists were not committed to a particular political ideology, but rather "understood loyalty viscerally." Rebecca Brannon, *From Revolution to Reunion: The Reintegration of the South Carolina Loyalists* (Columbia: University of South Carolina Press, 2016), 15. Donald F. Johnson admits that there existed "a rich literature of loyalism," by the early 1770s, but he contends that colonists living in British-occupied cities during the war held "flexible loyalties," and only turned to this language of Loyalism to advance their own political, economic, or social interests. "Ambiguous Allegiances: Urban Loyalties during the American Revolution," *Journal of American History* 104, no. 3 (December 2017): 610–31. Christopher Minty attributes political allegiances to the influence of local institutions, like the various committees of safety or the British military, and not to a set of competing ideas. "Mobilization and Voluntarism: The Political Origins of Loyalism in New York, c. 1768–1778," (PhD diss., University of Stirling, 2014), and "'Of One Hart and One Mind': Local Institutions and Allegiance during the American Revolution," *Early American Studies* 15, no. 1 (Winter 2017): 99–132. Finally, Edward Larkin claims Loyalists were motivated by "a variety of reasons that often had little to do with the politics and the grand ideals of the American Revolution." "Loyalism," in *The Oxford Handbook of the American Revolution*, ed. Edward G. Gray and Jane Kamensky, 291 (Oxford: Oxford University Press, 2013), and "What Is a Loyalist? The American Revolution as Civil War," *Common-Place* 8, no. 1 (October 2007), http://commonplace.online/article/what-is-a-loyalist/. For an exception to this thinking, see Janice Potter, *The Liberty We See: Loyalist Ideology in Colonial New York and Massachusetts* (Cambridge, MA: Harvard University Press, 1983), esp. 39–61; Timothy M. Barnes and Robert C. Calhoon, "Loyalist Discourse and the Moderation of the American Revolution," in *Tory Insurgents: The Loyalist Perception and Other Essays*, ed. Robert M. Calhoon, Timothy M. Barnes, and Robert S. Davis, 160–203 (Columbia: University of South Carolina Press, 2010); Mary Beth Norton, "The Loyalist Critique of the Revolution," in *The Development of a Revolutionary*

Mentality: Library of Congress Symposia on the American Revolution (Washington, DC: n.p., 1972), 127–50.

31 Rivington initially refuted Patriot claims that he was a tool of the ministry and changed the subheading of his newspaper to "Printed at his Open and Uninfluenced Press, fronting Hanover-Square." *Rivington's Gazette*, 12 May 1774. In the winter of 1774–75 there were only three other significant loyalist newspapers. Margaret Draper's *The Massachusetts Gazette and Boston News Letter*, Nathaniel Mills and John Hick's *Massachusetts Gazette, and the Boston Post-Boy Advertiser*, and James Humphreys's *Pennsylvania Ledger; or, the Virginia, Maryland, Pennsylvania, & New Jersey Weekly Advertiser*. None of them matched the reach or influence of *Rivington's Gazette*. Timothy M. Barnes, "Loyalist Newspapers of the American Revolution, 1763–1783: A Bibliography," *Proceedings of the American Antiquarian Society* 83, no. 2 (October 1973): 219–23, 232–3.

32 *A Letter from Thomas Lord Lyttelton, to William Pitt, Earl of Chatham, on the Quebec Bill* (New York, 1774), 19, Evans 13386.

33 Thomas Chandler, *A Friendly Address to All Reasonable Americans, on the Subject of our Political Confusions ... are Fairly Stated* (New York, 1774), 20, 53–5, Evans 13224.

34 Samuel Seabury, *The Congress Canvassed; or, An Examination into the Conduct of the Delegates, at their Grand Convention ... To the Merchants of New-York* (New York, 1774), 14–16, Evans 13601.

35 *Rivington's Gazette*, 23 February 1775.

36 John Lind, *An Englishman's Answer, to the Address from the Delegates to the People of Great-Britain ... in the Late Continental Congress* (New York, 1775), 21–3, Evans 14159. See also Philip Gould, *Writing the Rebellion: Loyalists and the Literature of Politics in British America* (Oxford: Oxford University Press, 2013), 144–67.

37 *Rivington's Gazette*, 9 March 1775.

38 Peter Force, ed., *American Archives: A Documentary History of the English Colonies in North America*, 4th ser. (Washington, DC: M. St. Claire Clarke and Peter Force, 1839), 2:252–3.

39 *Rivington's Gazette*, 12 January 1775. Ruma Chopra, *Unnatural Rebellion: Loyalists in New York City during the Revolution* (Charlottesville: University of Virginia Press, 2011), 32; Benjamin L. Carp, *Rebels Rising: Cities and the American Revolution* (Oxford: Oxford University Press, 2007), 62–3.

40 *The New-York Journal; or, The General Advertiser*, 9 March 1775; *The Pennsylvania Evening Post*, 11 March 1775; *The Connecticut Courant, and Hartford Weekly Intelligencer*, 13 March 1775; *Dunlap's Pennsylvania Packet; or,*

the General Advertiser, 13 March 1775; *The Connecticut Journal, and the New-Haven Post-Boy*, 15 March 1775. It was these "Friends of Freedom" that attacked William Cunningham and attempted to force him to "damn his popish King George."

41 "Colonel Marinus Willett's Narrative," in *New York City during the American Revolution: Being a Collection of Original Papers (Now First Published) from the Manuscripts in the Possession of the Mercantile Library Association of New York City*, ed. Abraham Tomlinson and Henry B. Dawson, 54–5 (New York: Privately Printed for the Association, 1861); Catherine S. Crary, *The Price of Loyalty: Tory Writings from the Revolutionary Era* (New York: McGraw-Hill, 1973), 45. See also Stokes, ed., *Iconography of Manhattan Island*, 4:881–2; Thomas Jones, *History of New York during the Revolutionary War* (New York: Printed for the New York Historical Society, 1879), 1:39–40; William H.W. Sabine, ed., *Historical Memoirs from 16 March 1763 to 9 July 1776 of William Smith* (New York: Colburn and Tegg, 1956), 1:221–3; Chopra, *Unnatural Rebellion*, 35–8.

42 Jones, *History of New York*, 1:42–3.

43 Pauline Maier, *American Scripture: Making the Declaration of Independence* (New York: Vintage, 1997), 116–19.

44 Maier, *American Scripture*, chap. 3.

45 William C. Stinchcombe, *The American Revolution and the French Alliance* (Syracuse, NY: Syracuse University Press, 1969), 1–13; C.H. Van Tyne, "French Aid Before the Alliance of 1778," *American Historical Review* 31, no. 1 (October 1925): 20–40.

46 *The New-York Journal; or, the General Advertiser*, 11 July 1776; *The New-York Gazette; and the Weekly Mercury*, 15 July 1776. The number is taken from an account current found in the papers of Oliver Wolcott, future governor of Connecticut. *Proceedings of the New York Historical Society for the Year 1843* (New York: Printed for the Society, 1844), 172–4.

47 Reports of French and Indian attacks on British settlements in Nova Scotia were commonplace in colonial newspapers. For example, see *Boston Evening Post*, 2 October 1749; *The Boston Weekly Post-Boy*, 22 January 1750; *The New-York Mercury*, 15 November 1756. See also Christopher Hodson, *The Acadian Diaspora: An Eighteenth-Century History* (New York: Oxford University Press, 2012), chap. 1.

48 John Garner, "The Enfranchisement of Roman Catholics in the Maritimes," *Canadian Historical Review*, 34, no. 3 (September 1953): 204. Robert Fletcher, *The Perpetual Acts of the General Assemblies of His Majesty's Province of Nova Scotia* (Halifax: Printed by Robert Fletcher, 1767), 2, 10–12.

49 Margaret Conrad and Barry Moody, ed., *Planter Links: Community and Culture in Colonial Nova-Scotia* (Fredericton, NB: Acadiensis Press, 2001); John G. Reid, "*Pax Britannica* or *Pax Indigena*? Planter Nova Scotia (1760–1782) and Competing Strategies of Pacification," *Canadian Historical Review* 85, no. 4 (December 2004): 669–82.

50 Anthony Henry lost his job as the king's printer in 1766 for his opposition to the Stamp Act. Much of the blame, however, lay with his outspoken young editor, Isaiah Thomas, who went on to an illustrious career as a printer in Massachusetts. Robert Fletcher replaced Henry, but Henry returned to printing his gazette in 1769. Isaiah Thomas, *The History of Printing in America, with a Biography of Printers and an Account of Newspapers* (Worcester, MA: From the Press of Isaiah Thomas, June 1810), 2:179–81; J.J. Stewart, "Early Journalism in Nova Scotia," in *Collections of the Nova Scotia Historical Society*, 6, 106–8 (Halifax: Nova Scotia Printing Company, 1888).

51 *The Nova-Scotia Gazette: and the Weekly Chronicl*e, 11 October, and 22 November 1774, 10 January and 28 February 1775.

52 *The Nova-Scotia Gazette: and the Weekly Chronicle*, 20 September 1774. For reports critical of the Quebec Act, see: *The Nova-Scotia Gazette: and the Weekly Chronicle*, 20 September,18 October, 25 October, 8 November, and 29 November 1774, and 3 January 1775. Henry also reprinted Congress's addresses: *The Nova-Scotia Gazette: and the Weekly Chronicle*, 22 November 1774, and 10 January, 31 January, and 28 February 1775.

53 Local merchants depended on New England traders and their ships to export goods to places elsewhere in the empire. In 1764, of the £64,790 in goods exported from Nova Scotia, £17,000 went through Boston. Viola F. Barnes, "Francis Legge, Governor of Loyalist Nova Scotia, 1773–1776," *New England Quarterly* 4, no. 3 (July 1931): 425.

54 Barnes, "Francis Legge," 428; W.S. MacNutt, *The Atlantic Provinces: The Emergence of Colonial Society, 1712–1857* (Toronto: McClelland and Stewart, 1965), 77–81; George A. Rawlyk, ed., *Revolution Rejected, 1775–1776* (Scarborough, ON: Prentice-Hall, 1968), 30–3; J.B. Brebner, *The Neutral Yankees of Nova Scotia: A Marginal Colony During the Revolutionary Years* (1937; reprint: New York: Russell and Russell, 1970), 303–5. Lewis R. Fischer, "Revolution without Independence: The Canadian Colonies, 1749–1775," in *The Economy of Early America: The Revolutionary Period, 1763–1790*, ed. Ronald Hoffman, John J. McCusker, Russell R. Menard, and Peter J. Albert, 94–123 (Charlottesville: University of Virginia Press, 1988).

55 "[Y]oung pretender," *The Nova-Scotia Gazette: and the Weekly Chronicle*,

11 October 1774. In a report of the event in Halifax, a writer in Boston admitted that the absence of "that great priviledge, Town-Meetings" in Nova Scotia prevented residents from taking a firmer stance. *The Boston-Gazette, and Country Journal*, 15 August 1774. See also Elizabeth Mancke, *The Fault Lines of Empire: Political Differentiation in Massachusetts and Nova Scotia, ca. 1760–1830* (New York: Routledge, 2005).

56 *The Nova-Scotia Gazette: and the Weekly Chronicle*, 20 September 1774. Legge wrote to Dartmouth in October that "the inhabitants have behaved with decorum; the East India Company's tea has been disposed of and dispersed through the country." Legge to the Earl of Dartmouth, 18 October 1774, quoted in *Report on Canadian Archives, 1894*, ed. Douglas Brymner (Ottawa, ON: S.E. Dawson, 1895), 322.

57 James Monk to the Earl of Dartmouth, 10 November 1774, quoted in Brebner, *Neutral Yankees*, 169.

58 *The New-York Journal; or, The General Advertiser*, 15 September 1774; *Dunlap's Pennsylvania Packet; or, the General Advertiser*, 19 September 1774; *The Providence Gazette; and Country Journal*, 24 September 1774; *The New-Hampshire Gazette, and Historical Chronicle*, 7 October 1774.

59 *The New-York Journal; or, The General Advertiser*, 15 September 1774.

60 *The Nova-Scotia Gazette: and the Weekly Chronicle*, 9 May 1775.

61 Ibid., 12 June 1775.

62 Peter Force, ed., *American Archives: A Documentary History of the English Colonies in North America*, 4th ser. (Washington, DC: M. St Claire Clarke and Peter Force, 1846), 6:61–4. Desserud asserts, correctly I believe, that this petition represents a very good, though largely ignored, example of British American constitutional thinking, which emphasized a mixed and balanced government. Donald A. Desserud, "An Outpost's Response: The Language and Politics of Moderation in Eighteenth-Century Nova Scotia," 29, no. 3 (Fall 1999): 379–405. See also J. Bartlet Brebner, "Nova Scotia's Remedy for the American Revolution," Canadian Historical Review, 15, no. 2 (June 1934): 171–81.

63 *The Nova-Scotia Gazette: and the Weekly Chronicle*, 27 June 1775; Executive Council Minutes, 23 June 1775, RG 1, 170: 166–7, Public Archives of Nova Scotia [hereafter cited as PANS].

64 Quoted in Desserud, "An Outpost's Response," 391.

65 Legge to Gage, 16 August 1775, quoted in Brebner, *Neutral Yankees*, 308.

66 William Harrison deposition, 19 December 1776, RG I, 342, 60, PANS.

67 Quoted in David Jaffee, *People of the Wachusett: Greater New England in History and Memory, 1630–1860* (Ithaca, NY: Cornell University Press, 1999), 185.

68 Barry Cahill, "The Sedition Trial of Timothy Houghton: Repression in a Marginal New England Planter Township during the Revolutionary Years," *Acadiensis* 24, no. 1 (October 1994): 35–58. Early historians downplayed the significance of the case. See, Brebner, *Neutral Yankees*, 341–42; W.B. Kerr, *The Maritime Provinces of British North America and the American Revolution* (Sackville, NB: Busy East Press, 1942), 83.

69 Stephen Conway, *The British Isles and the War for American Independence* (Oxford: Oxford University Press, 2000), chap. 9, and "From Fellow-Nationals to Foreigners: British Perceptions of the Americans, circa 1739–1783," *William and Mary Quarterly* 59, no. 1 (January 2002): 65–100; Colley, *Britons*, 132–45; Troy O. Bickham, *Making Headlines: The American Revolution as Seen through the British Press* (DeKalb: Northern Illinois University Press, 2009), chap. 5; Brad A. Jones, "'In Favour of Popery': Patriotism, Protestantism, and the Gordon Riots in the Revolutionary British Atlantic," *Journal of British Studies* 53, no. 1 (January 2013): 79–102.

70 An especially good example of this thinking is a Loyalist declaration of independence, which was printed in *Rivington's Gazette* in the fall of 1781. Modelled after Jefferson's declaration, the author(s) blamed Congress, not the king, for having deceived colonists into believing their lives were in danger with "the establishment of the Roman Catholic religion in Canada." Now, the writer argued, rebellious Americans were "leagued with the eldest son of this bloody, impious, bigoted, and persecuting church, to ruin the nation from whose loins we sprung." *Rivington's Gazette*, 17 November 1781; *The Nova-Scotia Gazette: and the Weekly Chronicle*, 22 January 1782; *The Gazette of Saint Jago de la Vega* [Jamaica], 31 January 1782; and the *Public Advertiser* [London], 12 July 1782.

71 Robert Kent Donovan, "Voices of Distrust: The Expression of Anti-Catholic Feeling in Scotland, 1778–81," *Innes Review* 30 (June 1979): 62–3; Robert E. Burns, "The Catholic Relief Act in Ireland, 1778," *Church History* 32, no. 2 (June 1963): 181–206.

72 *Transactions of the Eighty-five Societies, in and about Glasgow: United ... to Oppose a Repeal of the Penal Statues against Papists in Scotland* (Glasgow: Printed by William Smith, 1779), 7.

73 J. Paul de Castro, *The Gordon Riots* (London: Milford, 1926); Christopher

Hibbert, *King Mob: The Story of Lord George Gordon and the Riots of 1780* (1958; reprint, Stroud, UK: Sutton, 2004); George Rudé, "The Gordon Riots: A Study of the Rioters and Their Victims," *Transactions of the Royal Historical Society* 5th ser., vol. 6 (January 1956): 93–114; Jones, "In Favour of Popery," 79–102; Ian Haywood and John Seed, eds, *The Gordon Riots: Politics, Culture, and Insurrection in Late Eighteenth-Century Britain* (Cambridge: Cambridge University Press, 2015).

PART THREE
Indigenous Peoples and European Borders

8

Seeing Red: The Quebec Act and Its Geographic Implications

Jeffers Lennox

When Ezra Stiles, the scholar-theologian and future president of Yale University, first learned of the Quebec Act, he recorded his sentiments in a diary. It was the 23rd of August 1774, and he was upset. "The King has signed the Quebec Act," he wrote, "extending that Province to the Ohio & Mississippi and comprehending nearly two thirds of the territory of English America, and establishing the Romish Church & IDOLATRY over all that space." Stiles was "astonished" that leading imperial figures "should expressly establish Popery over three Quarters of their Empire."[1] For Stiles, the Act was "intolerable," not simply because Catholics could continue practising their religion in Quebec – an accommodation provided by the Proclamation Act of 1763 – but also because Quebec's territory had been extended along the back of the American colonies. While often listed among the other "intolerable acts" imposed on the American colonies after the Boston Tea Party, the Quebec Act was a unique piece of legislation that was years in the making and relied on established precedent for dealing with foreign subjects. In many ways the "Canada Bill," as the Act was often called, was the conclusion of a string of proclamations and treaties dating from the fall of Quebec in 1763. But its history went deeper than the capture of New France. British administrators had struggled to govern French subjects and their Indigenous allies since 1713, when French Acadia fell under de jure British control as Nova Scotia.[2] This experience provided British officials with lessons that could be applied in 1774.

Governing Quebec after 1763 provided specific challenges for king and parliament.[3] The majority of inhabitants in the province were French Catholics, with deep ties to the Indigenous fur trade extending through the Great Lakes and along the vast riverine networks that flowed south to the Gulf of Mexico. These new subjects had their own language, religion, customs, and laws. British experience governing French Acadians – a group defined by their neutrality during the seventeenth century, when Acadia switched hands several times – indicated that accommodations were necessary. Consequently, the Quebec Act provided a number of specific and nuanced responses to facilitate commercial, legal, and social relations. The Act's "intolerable" element was not the accommodations it offered French subjects, but rather the borders it provided for the province. Thus the Quebec Act inspired rebellion because its sweeping geographic scale blunted the sharper and more-focused policies it aimed to implement. The Act's specific benefits – recognition of the needs of a French population, better regulation of commerce, and protection of Indigenous alliances – were undone by the territorial expansion that rendered these policies unacceptable. An Atlantic approach depicts the Quebec Act as a process with planning, reception, and representation that drew upon experience, careful consideration, and precedent. But Quebec's size was an overwhelming element of the bill: it was a central component for the officials who drafted the Act; it worried legislators who debated the bill in parliament; it angered American colonists who considered it a betrayal; and it vexed geographers who struggled to incorporate Quebec into maps of the colonies. For all the answers the Quebec Act provided, the province's size offered British Americans yet another reason to resist imperial governance.

The Quebec Act should not be examined as a bill that emerged from parliament fully formed in the summer of 1774. It was the result of a process that took place over years (not months) and had its origins on both sides of the Atlantic (not in the private rooms of parliament).[4] When American patriots described the Quebec Act as despotic, they ignored the fact that many elements of the bill had their origins among colonists themselves.[5] Administrators, merchants, and officials who oversaw Indigenous relations were forced to deal with the legacy of 1763. In a perfect world, the French subjects of Quebec would have become loyal British subjects and, even better, Protestants. But for more than a century and a half of living in close quarters, British officials and settlers had demonized their French neighbours for their "Romish" religion and Indigenous alliances. For example, French traders more easily adopted Indigenous fashion and customs, creating the coureurs de bois who traversed the geographic and cultural boundaries that separated settlements and homelands.[6] For English settlers, "going Native" was unimaginable. English captives were martyrs who endured the "savage" lifestyle only by the grace of God, while their loved ones prayed for their return.[7] When Quebec fell to the British in 1763, officials faced the challenge of incorporating the French settlements, centred at Quebec but strung along lakes and river systems that cut through North America, into a British-American empire forged along the Atlantic littoral but increasingly influenced by agricultural and expansionist ideals.[8] Complicating this task was the need to appease powerful Indigenous nations that resisted English expansion and often remained allied with French traders.[9]

The Proclamation Act of 1763 attempted to address the issues of governing French and Indigenous territories. It was an expedient measure, meant to provide some regulations, but it failed to recognize the realities on the ground. The boundary dividing British and Indigenous territory – set at the height of land separating water that flowed into the Atlantic from that running towards the Mississippi – ignored those regions west of the boundary, in which British settlers already resided, and lands east of the boundary, under strong Indigenous control. It was left to the superintendents for Indian affairs – Sir William Johnson in the northern district and John Stuart in the southern – to craft acceptable boundaries between British and Indigenous lands.[10] Even these more realistic divisions, however, failed to prevent expansion into Indigenous homelands, and, with too few British forces stationed at trading posts, the administration was unable to control commercial interactions in Indigenous territory.[11] As Indigenous groups grew increasingly angry in the late 1760s, it fell to men such as William Johnson and his deputies to balance imperial demands with Indigenous concerns.[12] During a tour of the Illinois country in 1767, George Croghan, William Johnson's deputy superintendent, reported that the Shawnee, Delaware, and Huron peoples living "on the frontiers of our governments, and on the River Ohio" were greatly concerned about the murders of their people.[13] Additionally, the French had informed several Indigenous groups in the region that the English settlers "were coming with a numerous army, to cut them off, and by violence, to retain their country."[14] Easing these concerns and maintaining or winning Indigenous allegiance became a central goal for British officials on both sides of the Atlantic.

Pleas for regulations from agents who oversaw Indigenous affairs were often entangled with complications related to governing French inhabitants. Lands reserved for Indigenous peoples after 1763 were inhabited by French settlers who had established trading posts and settlements over the course of the eighteenth century. From the imperial perspective, then, reserving territory for Indigenous peoples also prevented the extension of British law to the French inhabitants south of the Great Lakes. In considering a new plan for governing the French subjects in Quebec, officials were required to keep in mind French subjects living in the heart of the continent. In 1773, Lord Dartmouth, the secretary of state for the colonies, wrote to Théophile-Hector de Cramahé, the lieutenant-governor of Quebec, and outlined his concerns for governing Quebec, particularly as they related to the province's boundary. "The Limits of the Colony will also in my Judgement make a necessary part of this very extensive Consideration," he wrote, adding, "there is no longer any Hope of perfecting that plan of Policy in respect to the interior Country, which was in Contemplation when the Proclamation of 1763 was issued."[15] The problem, according to Dartmouth, was that not enough was known about the French settlements in 1763, and thus the limits of Quebec set out in the proclamation (which reduced Quebec to a thin strip of land along the St Lawrence) were too narrowly prescribed. Extending the boundaries would thus encompass a greater number of inhabitants, while also, perhaps, protecting Indigenous territory.

The Indigenous nations who worked to assert control over their territory did not forget the promises made in 1763. Touring Quebec and reporting back to William Johnson, Daniel Claus recorded the concerns and complaints of many Indigenous peoples. In July 1773, Claus, who oversaw Indigenous affairs in Canada, attended a meeting with Hurons living at Lorette, who reminded him of the promises made by the king. A common complaint referred to the loss of traditional lands, even after they had relocated, with French encouragement, during the seventeenth century. The speaker, whose name was not recorded, lamented that priests sold away land that had been reserved for their settlement, and that warriors "were hemmed in by the white people with regard to their hunting grounds at Tadousack." "They beg," the minutes of the meeting state, "we may be supported in the right and privileges granted us by our present Royal Sovereign and father by his proclamation of 7th October 1763."[16] Claus was charged with providing a response to the Hurons, which he offered a few days later. Without a trace of irony, Claus simply informed them that, when a group moves to a new place, they have to follow the laws established by those already living there. "All I have to observe upon the subject," Claus explained, "is that whenever a Nation or people quit their Native Country in order to settle & abide in any other Nation or Government ... it is reasonably supposed & expected that they are to submit & conform themselves to the Laws Forms & Customs of that Nation or Government."[17] Put simply, the Hurons had moved from the Great Lakes to a region controlled by the French. The British now controlled that region, so new rules applied. That both the French *and* the British were settled on Indigenous land, with its own laws and customs, never crossed Claus's mind. At the very least, Indigenous nations could remind British officials of the promises made in 1763.

By 1773, however, few residents of Canada were happy with the state of affairs in the province – regardless of the regulations established a decade earlier – and calls for addressing Quebec's boundaries sprang from a variety of groups. While Indigenous nations were unhappy about land encroachment, merchants were concerned about the economic potential of such a spatially restricted colony. At the end of December 1773, a group of English merchants in Quebec drafted a memorial to Lord Dartmouth expressing their concern about the colony's prosperity.[18] Yet their focus was not the Ohio Valley, which British Americans at the time (and most historians today) considered paramount. Rather, the merchants looked east to Labrador and worried about the loss in trade and the behaviour of the Indigenous peoples in a region bereft of British control. These men complained that inhabitants "as well old as new subjects" have been "deprived of their personal property and even of their real estate" by the "sequestration" from the province of posts around Lake Champlain and the Coast of Labrador. "If the province is not restored to its antient limits," the merchants argued, "the morals of the Indians will be debauched, and the fur-trade as well as the winter seal fishery forever lost" for the province and Great Britain, because only the inhabitants of Canada were suited to oversee these tasks.[19]

The province's Roman Catholic inhabitants shared many of these sentiments. That same December, several French petitioners sent a memorial to Dartmouth, indicating their pleasure that so many French institutions had been maintained after 1763, and noting "this excess of kindness towards us we shall never forget." But they wanted confirmation that these allowances would continue: "vouchsafe, most illustrious and generous sovereign, to dissipate these fears and this uneasiness, by restoring to us our ancient laws, privileges, and customs, and to extend our province to its former boundaries."[20] A supporting memorial attached to the original dealt with the boundary issue in more detail. "The province, as it is now bounded by a line passing through the forty fifth degree of north latitude," the memorial argued, "is confined within too narrow limits. This line is only fifteen leagues distant from Montreal."[21] These restricted boundaries removed from Quebec much of the most fertile lands and stranded thousands of subjects outside any legal authority. Extending the province to its pre-1763 limits (including Labrador) would bring additional subjects and increased economic opportunities to Quebec.

Importantly, according to these leading French inhabitants, the province was in no state to govern itself through an assembly.[22] Both English and French inhabitants had requested an extended Quebec, but it was English merchants who pushed for an assembly. These requests were at odds; Quebec would be too big, and too sparsely settled, to provide for a functioning assembly. After the Act was passed, Frances Maseres, the former attorney general for Quebec, explained this paradox to Quebec's English residents who had petitioned the king: "an act of parliament has been passed which seems to put an end to all hopes of success in your endeavours to obtain an assembly, having erected a legislative council in its stead without any limitation of time, and enlarged the province to such a degree as to make an assembly an impracticable method of government."[23] But the calls for a more general reworking of colonial governance resonated in London. By late December 1773, Dartmouth informed the lieutenant-governor of Quebec that plans were in the works to address the specific demands in the colony.[24]

While merchants, officials, and settlers in Quebec and New York debated the need for a larger Quebec – for reasons both economic and paternalistic in nature – administrators in London and their subordinates in North America began crafting a plan to address the competing needs of English, French, and Indigenous peoples. In the decade after the Proclamation Act, reduced British forces at western posts, combined with anemic colonial governments, resulted in trading and settlement chaos along the proclamation line. In March 1774, before members of parliament met to debate the Quebec Act, Frederick Haldimand, who was acting commander-in-chief while Thomas Gage was in London, issued a proclamation from New York that echoed the 1763 proclamation. Such legislation was required to address confusion over who had the authority to grant lands in the west.[25] Haldimand reminded governors and settlers that Indigenous homelands lying beyond the boundaries set in 1763 (or, one could expect, beyond the boundaries established by Johnson and Stuart after 1763) could not be purchased or settled.[26] William Johnson worked to reassure Indigenous nations in the Ohio Valley that British officials would protect their territory, but concerns (and violence) were mounting in areas where settlers ignored royal instructions. Worse still, Johnson's failing health troubled the Iroquois, who feared his death would leave them without access to London. Iroquois leaders went so far as to relay a request to London through Johnson that his son-in-law/nephew Guy Johnson replace him.[27] It became apparent to Dartmouth that legislation was required to address the various concerns regarding Quebec, its limits, and the needs of those who lived in and around the province. He informed Lieutenant-Governor Cramahé in early May that a bill was before the House of Assembly.[28]

The bill presented to the House of Commons attempted to balance religion, law, and geography.[29] The parliamentarians who debated the Quebec Act were well aware of the impact that guaranteeing the free exercise of Catholicism, protecting French civil law, and introducing new boundaries would have on North America; consequently, they debated the bill and many challenged the government on a number of fronts.[30] The bill was introduced in the House of Lords and passed easily. Members of parliament at the time (and historians since) have viewed the fact that the bill originated in the Upper House as evidence of a mischievous government. In fact, it made sense for North to introduce the bill in the House of Lords, because it was there that discussion on the subject had ended in 1767, and it was members of that house who possessed the most detailed knowledge of Quebec.[31] The Act faced stiffer resistance from the Lower House, though the opposition was scattered and, for the most part, disorganized.[32] North had his detractors, including Rockingham, Chatham (William Pitt), and Charles Fox, each with several MPs in their corner. Yet, for all the dissent, little of it was marshalled effectively. On the other side, North had an imposing complement of witnesses to support the bill, none more effective than Governor Guy Carleton himself. One MP claimed that the governor was "the most valuable witness I ever heard in my life."[33] Opposition witnesses were less useful, and reflected the scattered nature of those who hoped to defeat the bill because of its religious or constitutional implications.[34]

Members who opposed the bill initially had some support from the public, which was undergoing a parallel assessment of the legislation. This wider discussion was not supposed to happen. Unlike the case earlier in the eighteenth century, when popular publications such as *Gentleman's Magazine* or the *London Magazine* published parliamentary debates (often to skewer and satirize assembly members), the sessions held in 1774 came at the end of the Thirteenth Parliament, commonly known as the "unreported parliament," during which members were sworn to the strictest secrecy. Yet the gallery during the Quebec Act debates was often full of spectators, many of whom scribbled notes furiously and later published their findings in the press. The threat of having to account for such actions, which would have included being called to apologize to the House or face imprisonment in the Tower of London, was evidently an insufficient deterrent. Neither did officials seem to mind, even if they found themselves misquoted.[35] Fortunately for historians, Sir Henry Cavendish, an active parliamentary diarist, who kept detailed notes in shorthand, was taking as factual an account of the proceedings as he could. He eventually published his records from the debates.[36]

On 6 June 1774, the House of Commons examined the first clause of the Act, which set out the new limits of Quebec.[37] There were many concerns regarding whether an extended Quebec would infringe upon any boundaries previously made, especially in the British colonies of New York and Pennsylvania. Lord North was cautious about the best way to draw such a boundary, readily admitting that officials in London had a poor grasp of the geography. "We are so much in the dark as to the situation of this country," North argued, "that it is not possible to do anything more safe, than saving the rights of the other colonies, leaving them to be settled on the spot by commissioners. Persons possessing local knowledge can act better than we can."[38] Such geographic caution did little to assuage the objections of those who felt the bill was completely wrong-headed. George Johnstone, a naval officer and colonial governor of West Florida, argued that the bill would "extend a despotic government over too large a surface," and that the new boundary line would also serve as a "line of justice."[39] Those within Quebec would be subject to Catholic laws, which would rob English men of

English justice. The boundary, then, was not only geographic and religious, but also juridical.

That line of argument continued with the objections of Edmund Burke. Burke called for the testimony of John Pownall, undersecretary of the American colonies, to help clarify geographic implications. Apparently, the members were meeting to discuss boundaries without bothering to collect maps. Upon being challenged by Lord North on this request, Burke replied: "if we had originated this measure above stairs, where maps might have been laid upon the table, no doubt the whole dispute of this day would have been avoided."[40] Burke explained that, when he learned that a new border was to be drawn by which British subjects would fall under foreign laws, religion, and language, he "thought it of the highest importance that we should endeavour to make this boundary as clear as possible."[41] Burke, acting as an agent for New York, argued that the boundary had been drawn in the wrong place, and offered to work with Alexander Wedderburn (the king's advocate) to put it right, which the two did.[42]

This attention to the boundary supports the claim that extending Quebec was not meant to infringe on existing colonies. The bill's second clause, which follows the description of the new boundary, states "that nothing herein contained relative to the boundary of the province of Quebec shall in anywise affect the boundaries of any other colony."[43] It became evident during his lengthy response to the Quebec Act that, for Burke, this was not simply a boundary that separated one British colony from another. Because of the legislation's legal, linguistic, and religious significance, this border was, in his words, "a line which is to separate a man from the right of an Englishman."[44] This extension and its implications were in many respects the heart of the bill, and some imperial administrators objected to them even before the bill was presented to the House of Commons.[45] For example, Lord Hillsborough, former secretary of state for the colonies, informed Dartmouth, who succeeded him in that post, that extending Quebec to the Ohio was dangerous because of the inducements made to Catholics to move into the region. It would be better, Hillsborough argued, for the crown simply to extend jurisdiction to the territory in question, rather than have parliament pass this bill.[46] Dartmouth's response explicitly explained why the Act and the extension of boundaries were necessary: "it provides for the establishment of civil government over many numerous settlements of French subjects, but does by no means imply an intention of further settling the Lands included within this extension,

& if it is not wished that British Subjects should settle that country nothing can more effectually tend to discourage such attempts."[47] For Dartmouth, an extended Quebec supported by an act of parliament could serve multiple purposes, not least of which was protecting the interior from British-American settlers.

After many drafts and much debate, the Quebec Act received royal assent on 22 June 1774. Its specific and nuanced elements attempted to improve relations with new French subjects, but reactions against the Act were swift in the British colonies. Ezra Stiles documented his disapproval, and his diary records that wider protests occurred. These protests were not always about the Quebec Act specifically, but rather served as an outlet for anger and frustration against the British administration more generally for the series of acts that imposed restrictions after the Boston Tea Party. In the late fall, Stiles recorded that "this afternoon three popes &c. paraded thro' the streets, & in the evening they were consumed in a bonfire as usual – among others were Ld. North, Gov. Hutchinson, & Gen. Gage."[48] Including popes in the procession – alongside leading British administrators – was a clear reference to the anger over the guarantee of Catholic faith in the extended Quebec. Popular images encouraged this kind of outrage. Paul Revere's image, published in October 1774, depicted Anglican bishops (to New Englanders, imperialist figures) dancing around the Quebec Bill as Lord North (with the devil on his shoulder) looked on approvingly (figure 8.1). On the heels of the "intolerable" acts, the Canada Bill added insult to injury. By early September, Haldimand reported to Amherst that, despite the best efforts of administrators to help them realize their best interests, Americans were upset by recent developments. "They do not approve here of the Act that set (wisely) the government and the boundaries of Canada," he reported, "the people here do not want to see a chain pulled along the backs of their settlements."[49]

Quebec's new borders were the problem. While few British Americans complained that Labrador was incorporated into a Catholic province with French laws, many Americans found Quebec's southern extension unacceptable, which made all parts of the bill that much more detestable. The bill's crafters might have hoped for a better reception; after all, 1774 was not the first time Roman Catholicism had been tolerated or French subjects had been welcomed into political institutions. For much of the eighteenth century, Catholic priests operated openly and with tacit British consent in Nova Scotia, serving both the Acadian and Mi'kmaq population. Governance in Nova Sco-

8.1 Paul Revere, "The Mitred Minuet," *The Royal American Magazine*, October 1774

tia similarly depended on the participation of Acadian deputies who would, in an unofficial capacity, represent their settlements, bring complaints to the council, and often enlist Acadian elders to help resolve a variety of disputes.[50] Elsewhere in the British-Atlantic world, accommodations and compromises with French inhabitants helped facilitate governance and incorporate new subjects into the British empire. In Grenada after 1768, French Roman Catholics were allowed to sit in the assembly, despite the Test Act.[51] As Pauline Maier argues, "in many ways, the government's efforts to establish regular government in Grenada by absorbing the old French settlers into public office, while making necessary alterations in traditional English procedure to accommodate them, forecast the Quebec Act of 1774, which became for many the strongest proof for despotism."[52] Accommodations, then, could be tolerated. However, what differentiated the Quebec Act from examples in Nova Scotia and Grenada was the province's geographic expanse and corresponding proximity to older British colonies.

Not long after the Quebec Act became the subject of debate and protest in the British-American colonies, leading colonial figures met at Philadelphia to discuss colonial tensions and perceived imperial overreach. The first Continental Congress debated colonial options and fielded complaints from representatives. In mid-September, the congress received the *Suffolk Resolves* (delivered to them by Paul Revere, who apparently had a knack for bearing important news), a list of suggested responses to deal with the "intolerable" acts. The tenth item on the list dealt with the enlarged Canada: "That the late act of parliament for establishing the Roman Catholic religion and the French laws in that extensive country, now called Canada, is dangerous in an extreme degree to the Protestant religion and to the civil rights and liberties of all America; and, therefore, as men and Protestant Christians, we are indispensably obliged to take all proper measures for our security."[53] Over the course of the following month, Quebec remained on the minds of members of the Continental Congress. During a session in the middle of October, John Adams jotted notes for his speech on the "Canada Bill," which compared the British Empire to the fall of Rome. It read almost like a poem:

> Proof of Depth of Abilities, and Wickedness of Heart.
> Precedent. Lords refusal of perpetual imprisonment.
> Prerogative to give any Government to a conquered People.
> Romish Religion.
> Feudal Government.
> Union of feudal Law and Romish Superstition.
> Knights of Malta. Orders of military Monks.
> Goths and Vandals – overthrew the Roman Empire.
> Danger to us all. A House on Fire.[54]

The "house on fire" metaphor perfectly combined the internal dangers men such as Adams believed were threatening their safety with the hellish imagery that linked Roman Catholicism with the devil.

Adams's scribbles reflected the sentiments of most members of the Continental Congress, who later expressed these ideas in an open letter to the people of Great Britain. Near the end of the letter, issued on 21 October, the congress turned to the Quebec Act and the dangers of Catholicism. "And by another Act the dominion of Canada is to be so extended, modelled, and governed, as that by being disunited from us, detached from our interests" that the settlement itself could endanger the older English colonies.[55] Such a claim, of course, was a complete fabrication. Congress imagined an extended Quebec that would soon be filled with French Catholics, ardent devotees to their faith and laws, who would become "instruments in the hands of power, to reduce the ancient free Protestant Colonies to the same state of slavery with themselves."[56] The population of Canada in 1774 was approximately seventy thousand people, compared to almost two and a half million British Americans. There was no chance of a Catholic invasion, but having territory under French law and religion was concern enough. Members of the congress expressed their dismay "that a British Parliament should ever consent to establish in that country a religion that has deluged your island in blood, and dispersed impiety, bigotry, persecution, murder and rebellion through every part of the world."[57] While the congress hoped such language would stir up support among the British, the letter itself only put more distance between British Americans and their French neighbours.

By the time the Continental Congress sent its open letter to Britons, publications in the colonies were discussing the impact of the Quebec Act in terms that would please the men meeting in Philadelphia.[58] Quebec's size was the problem, because it brought dangerous Catholics so close to good Protestant subjects. In July 1774, the *Pennsylvania Gazette* provided an abstract of the Quebec Act,[59] and it did not take long for contributors to argue against it. "As the spirit of liberty, in some of our colonies, has given so much trouble to the Government," one contributor noted, "it was resolved to cherish the spirit of slavery in others." French laws and popery would enslave the body and the mind and were consequently "adopted by our state movers behind the curtain."[60] By the fall, there were calls to resist the Act and rebalance the territorial adjustments that were threatening the Protestant colonies. One writer demanded action not for "greediness to enlarge our territories, or to enrich ourselves with spoils, at the expense of innocent and peaceable neighbours," but rather to preserve "what encroachment and usurpation would draw away: to assist in adjusting such a balance of Power, as may prevent ourselves and sister colonies becoming a prey to an insatiable devourer."[61] Few literate colonists would have mistaken the "insatiable devourer" for anyone other than the devil, who would be represented in their new French-Catholic neighbours.

South Carolina readers might have been surprised when Satan himself chimed in on the matter, though he predictably favoured the Quebec Act. In a letter signed by "Devil on Two Sticks," Quebec's new borders were lauded for preventing Americans in that region from governing themselves and "ruining themselves by their opposition to that power which protects them." What is more, an enlarged Quebec increased the value of land in the other colonies by preventing expansion. "Now this spirit of dispersion is confined," wrote the devil, "the happy consequences of which will be, that our fields will equal the well-cultivated Gardens of England."[62] In New England, opinions were rarely leavened with such humour. Rev. Ebenezer Baldwin, of Danbury, Connecticut, expressed the dangers of the Quebec Act in no uncertain terms. He thanked God that Americans had not "experienced the galling chains of slavery" – exempting, apparently, the experience of the slaver – and thus "few perhaps among us, realize the horrors of that slavery, which arbitrary and despotic government lays men under."[63] Now that a despotic government had been established at the back of the colonies, New Englanders had reason to be concerned. Most affected, according to Baldwin, were those English settlers who had already settled in Quebec on the promise that English laws would be established there.[64] Most troubling, however, was the new size of Quebec. Foreshadowing the language of the Continental Congress, Baldwin described how easily thousands of French Canadians might pour into the Ohio Valley. Quebec's geographic scope was, for Baldwin, simply unacceptable:

> And that this French arbitrary government may take in as much of America as possible, its limits are extended southward to the Ohio, and westward to the Mississippi: so that it comprehends an extent of territory almost as large as all the other provinces. When this vast extent of territory comes to be filled up with inhabitants, near half America will be under this arbitrary French government. So that upon the whole the Quebec Act doubtless wears as threatening an aspect upon Americans as any act that hath been passed by the British government.[65]

Tolerating Roman Catholics in specific places – Acadia, Grenada, Maryland, or a limited Quebec – was one thing. Reserving such a huge expanse for this "despotic" government was simply too much for British Americans.[66]

While newspapers and pamphlets circulating in the British colonies were largely critical of the Quebec Act, the legislation found more support in Britain itself. Strident defence of the Act came from Sir Thomas Bernard, the Harvard-educated son of a former Massachusetts governor. Bernard carefully addressed several of the popular complaints against the bill. He concluded that the Act intended to bring civil government to regions in which it had been wanting; it reorganized territory in a sensible manner by putting Labrador under Quebec's jurisdiction rather than the seasonal government of Newfoundland; and it reaffirmed territorial protection that had been promised to Indigenous groups in 1763.[67] All accommodations made to the French were "subject to the King's supremacy," which should have reassured Britons that no power was being surrendered. And Bernard stressed the democratic nature of the bill, flipping arguments about the need for an assembly on their head. The Act specifically did not "enable four hundred emigrants, because they are Protestants, to erect themselves into a constitutional aristocracy, and tyrannize over and oppress above an hundred thousand peaceable and dutiful subjects, who first settled the country; men of property, of rank, of character."[68] Citing Montesquieu, Bernard reminded his readers that "it is the folly of conquerors to wish to give to every people their own laws and customs," because all subjects are capable of obedience, regardless of the system of government.[69] The accommodations provided by the Quebec Act prevented oligarchy and tyranny and thus encouraged a conquest of liberty.

Over nearly a third of the pamphlet, Bernard offered an equally supportive analysis of the Act's geographic implications. Attaching Labrador to Quebec was reasonable, because, unlike Newfoundland, the Labrador fishery was fixed and sedentary, rather than seasonal. It required more oversight than could be provided by the "rule of the admirals" that operated in Newfoundland. Halifax, on the other hand, was not yet developed enough to extend its jurisdiction. Quebec was the best choice.[70] As for the interior, Bernard lamented the inability of British officials to enforce the Proclamation of 1763. The only defence against American encroachment was the superintendent, William Johnson, who had virtually no budget and could rely only on his good relations with the Indigenous nations.[71] "In this situation," Bernard posited, "what better can be done than to annex this country to Quebec, and subject the whole to the jurisdiction of that colony, to which the only lawful settlers in it were originally subject" and who shared common religion, laws, and language.[72] Bernard concluded his tract by reminding his readers that British-American settlers could hardly be trusted to oversee the interior, in no small part because they were likely to form a new colony at too far a distance from the Atlantic littoral for the British navy to control. The point of colonization, he argued, was to extend British commerce, resources, and wealth "upon our own terms. If this is not done, our title to America is but a vain name and nothing more."[73]

William Knox, an Irish government official and pamphleteer, also published a tract extolling the virtues of the Quebec Act. Knox, like Bernard, had some experience in America. He served as the provost marshal in Georgia for five years, beginning in 1756, and his time in the colony led him to question the power that legislatures had over their governors. In his mind, such power threatened imperial authority. He returned to England in the early 1760s and continued to search for an official appointment, a quest greatly facilitated by a marriage that brought him a sizable fortune. His capabilities as a writer attracted some attention, and he was soon commissioned to write in support of government legislation. By 1770, Knox had established enough of a reputation to receive an appointment as undersecretary in the American department. North's administration turned to Knox to write favourable tracts concerning imperial policies, including the Quebec Act.[74]

In *The Justice and Policy of the Late Act of Parliament*, Knox offered a comparative analysis to justify the Quebec Act. He looked to examples where Great Britain had governed a Catholic population: Ireland and Minorca. Knox found little to emulate in the Irish example. In 1774 many Irish still detested the Protestants, and Britain needed ten thousand troops there for security.[75] The severity imposed in Ireland had "so little served to attach these infatuated people to the English government and their fellow-subjects," what hope would there be in imposing similar methods in Canada, "where the Roman Catholic inhabitants are five hundred to one Protestant," and just ten years ago those inhabitants had raised arms for France against Britain?[76] Minorca, a small Spanish island in the Mediterranean, offered a much better example. Captured during the War of the Spanish Succession and ceded to Britain by the Treaty of Utrecht, Minorca became a site of accommodation, as residents "had been permitted the full enjoyment of their religion and properties."[77] Though Knox did not make the comparison, Acadia also served as a useful example for governing Catholics. Like Minorca, it had a tiny population, most members of which dealt with the British government as necessary, but largely hoped to remain independent in peace and neutral in war.

Knox spent several pages detailing the importance of Quebec's new boundaries, but his findings echoed those already circulating in Britain. He agreed that the Proclamation of 1763 was sound policy, but the administration had failed financially to support the territorial limits. Consequently, the region west of the boundary was left without a government (or, more accurately, without a European government). American settlers ignored the line, forcing Indigenous peoples to relocate farther west.[78] Whereas Bernard justified the extension of Quebec's authority in part because neighbouring colonies were either seasonal (Newfoundland) or not sufficiently mature (Nova Scotia), Knox took a more geographic approach. "The province of Quebec was preferred" as the source of government in these regions, Knox argued, "because the access by water is much easier from Quebec to such parts of this country as are the most likely to be intruded upon, than from any one other colony."[79] Given its riverine networks and existing connections to the interior via the Great Lakes and their tributaries, Quebec was the easy choice.[80] Expanding its boundaries simply made governing the interior an easier task.

While the British government employed men such as William Knox to publish pamphlets that bolstered their policy decisions, British Americans turned to their own representatives in Europe in the hopes that these policies could be altered or retracted. These hopes were pinned on Benjamin Franklin, who in 1774 was in London serving as a colonial agent. In the spring of 1774, as rumours of the Quebec Act were circulating in London, Franklin wrote Jonathan Shipley, the bishop of St Asaph in Wales and fellow critic of Lord North, outlining his opinions on the matter. "I apprehend that one view of the intended bill may be," Franklin opined, "the discouraging of emigrations."[81] This was, of course, exactly what Dartmouth had expressed to Hillsborough. But Franklin knew the true character of British Americans, and he was confident any such measures would fail. He believed officials were mistaken if they thought Americans would not go west without official land titles. "The Natives of America are those that settle new lands," wrote Franklin, "removing from those [lands] they have begun to cultivate as fast as they have an opportunity of selling them to new comers ... and this will go on," with or without government sanction.[82] Franklin's "Natives" were entrepreneurial British Americans. No legislation could prevent them from expanding into truly Indigenous territory.

After the Quebec Act passed, and as the situation grew more tense in British America, Franklin became involved in secret negotiations to resolve American affairs. While still in London, he was approached by David Barclay, a banker, and Dr John Fothergill, who was Franklin's former physician. The men, both Quakers, assured Franklin that they had

Dartmouth's ear and hoped that they could help to broker a peace between Whitehall and the colonies. Around the same time, Franklin was introduced to Caroline Howe, a socialite and the sister of a Royal Navy admiral with government connections. Soon he was negotiating through this channel as well.[83] These discussions lasted several weeks, and Franklin eventually offered Barclay and Fothergill his "Hints or Terms for a Durable Union" in early December 1774. He shared a list of suggestions that might ease tensions between Britain and the colonies, including returning duties paid and repealing certain acts (including the Tea Act) after the destroyed tea was paid for. Number eleven on Franklin's list of hints suggested "the late Massachusetts and Quebec Acts to be repeal'd, and a free Government granted to Canada."[84]

The response to Franklin's "hints" was mixed. While some articles were approved, many were modified or rejected. Franklin's suggestion that the duties collected be returned was refused, but all acts restraining manufacturing in the colonies could be repealed. The response to Franklin's eleventh point, dealing with the recent "coercive" acts, suggested that there might be some flexibility regarding Quebec's boundaries: "The eleventh refus'd absolutely," the response read, "except as to the Boston Port Bill, which would be repeal'd; and the Quebec Act might be so far amended, as to reduce that Province to its ancient Limits."[85] Ultimately these preparations for negotiations came to nothing. A few weeks later, Franklin embarked on a return voyage to the colonies, during which he collected his papers and wrote an account of his discussions. In this account, which took the form of a letter to his son, Franklin opined that Americans should have some say over the government of Quebec:

> I reply'd, that we having assisted in the Conquest of Canada, at a great Expence of Blood and Treasure, had some Right to be considered in the Settlement of it. That the Establishing an arbitrary Government on the back of our Settlements might be dangerous to us all; and that loving Liberty ourselves, we wish'd it to be extended among Mankind, and to have no Foundation for future Slavery laid in America.[86]

The existence of "arbitrary government" in North America troubled Franklin, especially since that government extended along the backs of several British colonies.

Once the Quebec Act had been debated, proclaimed, and eventually received by administrators and colonists alike, there was time to reflect on how the extension of Quebec would impact governance and colonial relations in North America. While the Act loomed large in the colonial mind – especially among those who invested the time and effort either to promote or denigrate the bill – it did not receive a sustained or thorough cartographic treatment. In fact, few maps depicted the Quebec Act at all. Several reasons account for this lacuna in the history of eighteenth-century map-making. The Quebec Act preceded the battles of Lexington and Concord by only a few months, so geographers did not have much time to produce and market maps. Moreover, the Quebec Act faded from political discourse as attention turned to the fighting in America. However, maps that were produced demonstrate just how difficult it was to incorporate an enlarged Quebec into the British imperial system via geographic depictions. During the eighteenth-century wars that raged in North America, British map-makers could chart the growth of their plantations as part of a zero-sum game in which any extension of territory was good for Britain because it was bad for France. Yet, after 1763, there was no common enemy to rally Britons and British Americans. Quebec came to represent a barrier against expansion, not a symbol of British strength or the increasing flexibility of imperial governance. Consequently, British imperial territory in North America was divided against itself. The specific policies meant to integrate new French subjects were engulfed by the province's size. The Quebec Act demonstrated just how difficult it was for British officials, geographers, and British Americans to map the internal divisions that, while meant to protect imperial territory, signalled the disintegration of British North America.

For those opposed to the Quebec Act, including Ezra Stiles, maps became an excellent medium for demonstrating the Act's nefarious nature. Stiles was a cartophile and amateur map-maker, and he would jot down his cartographic endeavours in his diary. For example, in February 1769 he made a map of Indigenous tribes in New England and copied a map of Connecticut.[87] His cartographic acquisitions were also recorded, such as his December 1773 purchase of a map of New England.[88] At times his geographic efforts were noted as simply matter of fact, little more than an indication of how he spent his day. "Making a map of Boston," he recorded in August 1775.[89] It is somewhat puzzling, then, that he made no record of what is perhaps his most remarkable map. With a simple title, "The Bloody Church" (figure 8.2), Stiles's

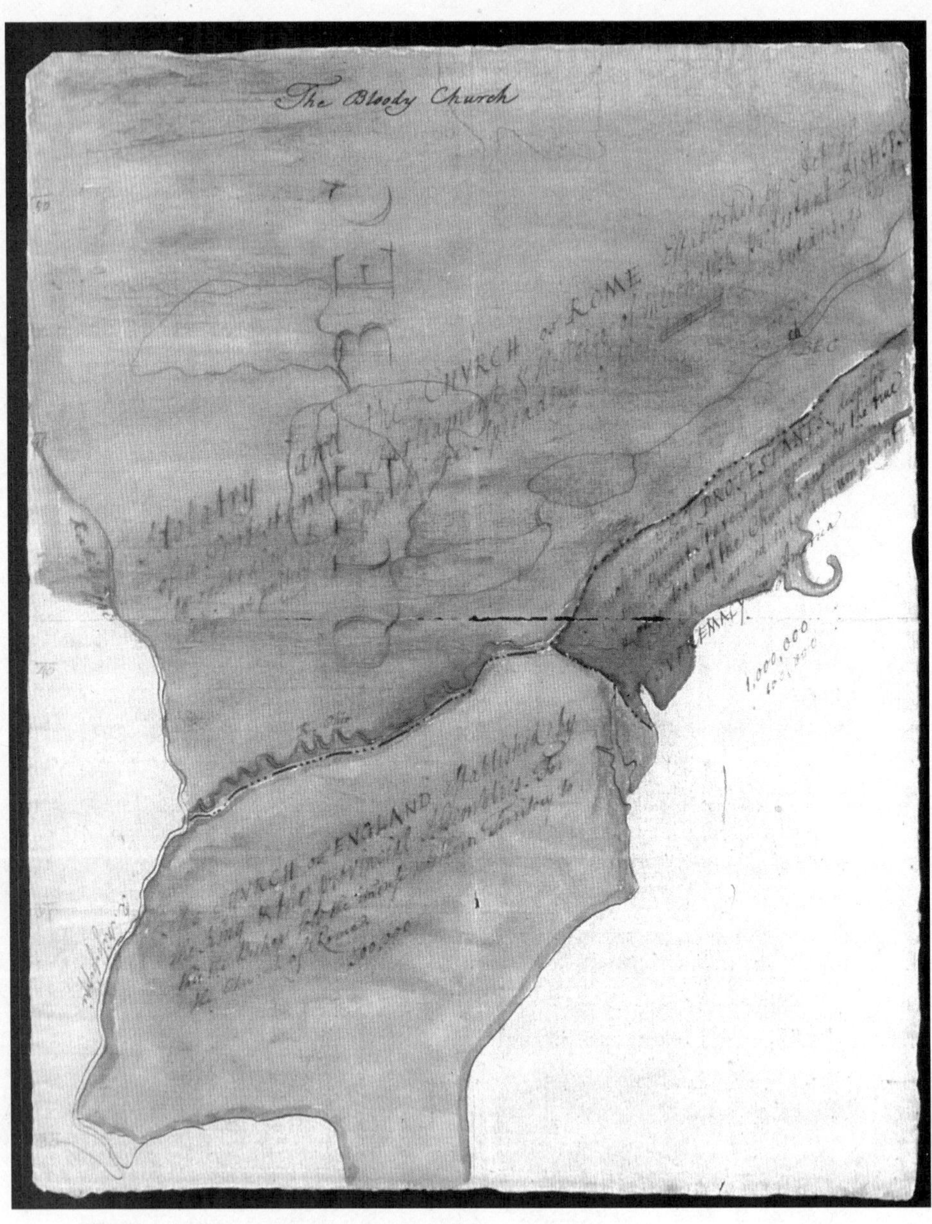

8.2 Ezra Stiles, "The Bloody Church," August 1774

map of the Quebec Act was presumably done around the time that he expressed his anger over the spread of idolatry across so much of the Protestant empire. The map depicted Quebec as blood red, like an open wound threatening to drown the light-green Protestant colonies as it enveloped them on all sides.[90] Stiles saw religion as a territorial barrier, writing across the province of Quebec "Idolatry and the Church of Rome established by Act of a Protestant Parliament and the Voice of the English Protestant Bishops to restrain and suppress the spreading of the ~~damn~~ Presbytians, as they are politely called." Of course, being a staunch and devout Protestant, Stiles dutifully crossed out his expletive. Across the southern colonies he wrote "The Church of England established by the King & the provincial assemblies. For this the Bishops sold the imense northern territory to the Church of Rome." Stiles used the map to depict a religious aversion in unmistakable terms. The new boundaries mattered because they expanded Catholic territory and a map was the ideal medium to illuminate such a threat.[91]

While Stiles could use a manuscript map to rail against the Quebec Act, map-makers in England struggled to chart an empire dividing against itself. Any reconfiguration of borders (or debate over the limits of a given province) usually increased the production of maps, as geographers hoped to take advantage of interest in any given region and boost imperialist sentiment. One excellent example of this kind of propaganda took place during the 1750s, when Thomas Jefferys and Jacques-Nicolas Bellin engaged in a public and heated debate over the extent of Acadia's boundaries, each accusing the other of using maps for imperial ends.[92] Yet surprisingly few maps published after 1774 featured Quebec's new borders. Aside from advertisements for maps that might feature Quebec, few maps appeared in the pages of American, British, or French popular newspapers and magazines.[93] However, maps published separately between 1774 and 1777 demonstrated a range of imperialist arguments. In 1776, Robert Sayer and John Bennett published Thomas Jefferys's *The American Atlas*, which included "A New Map of the Province of Quebec," featuring the province's 1763 limits (figure 8.3). Jefferys, one of Britain's most successful map-makers, who rose to prominence during the Seven Years' War, had died in 1771, and thus can be forgiven for not updating the boundary. Sayer and Bennett then published a second map, "The Theatre of War in North America," which included both the old province

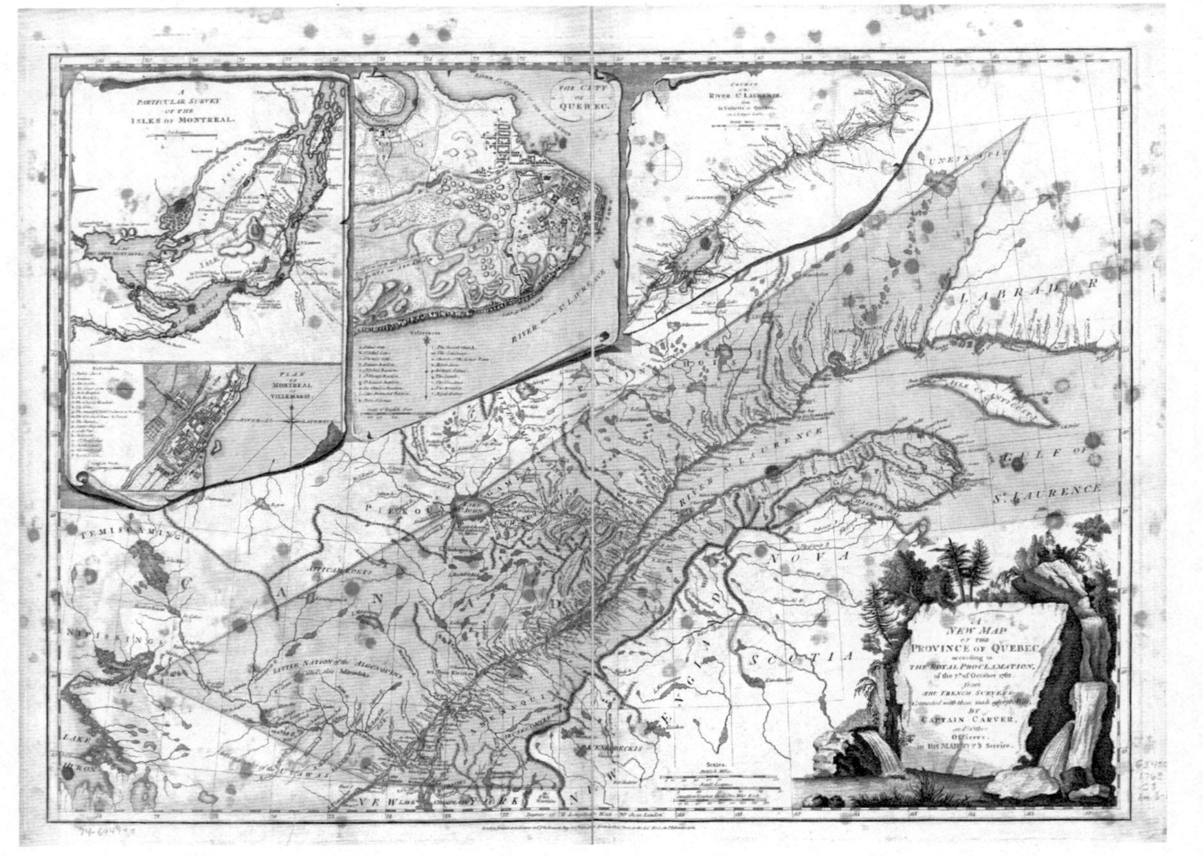

8.3 Thomas Jefferys, *A new map of the Province of Quebec, according to the Royal Proclamation, of the 7th of October 1776*

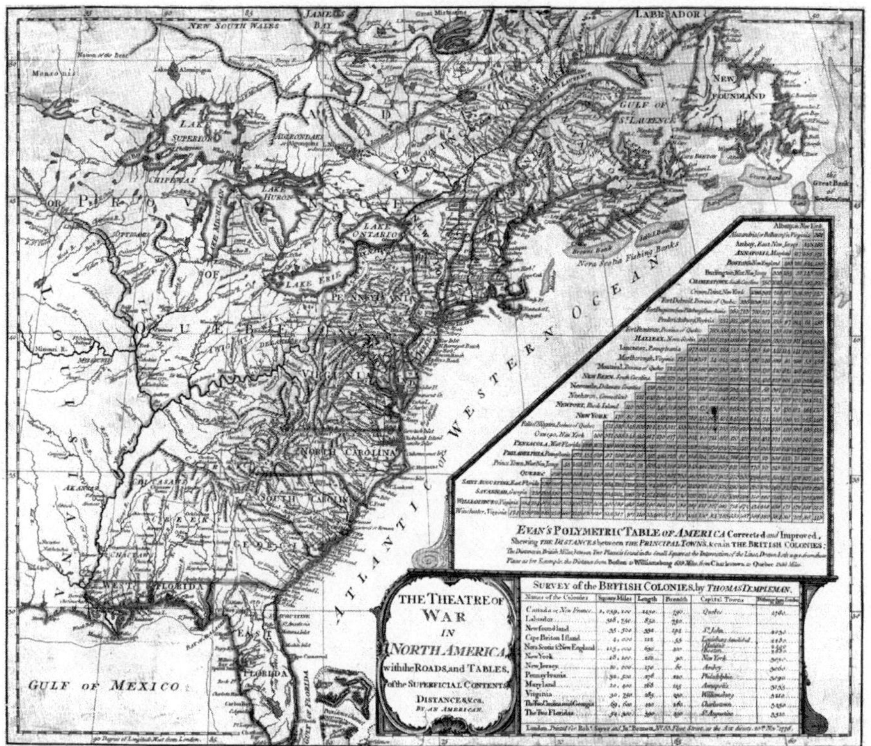

8.4 Robert Sayer and John Bennett, *The Theatre of War in North America*, 1776

(marked as "Province of Quebec") and its enlarged boundaries (marked as "Canada or Province of Quebec") (figure 8.4). The description of the province begins with listing its 1763 limits, but then informs the reader that the Quebec Act extended the boundaries "adding to its jurisdiction all the lands comprised between the northern bounds of New-York, the western line of Pennsylvania, the Ohio, the Mississippi, and the southern boundary of Hudson's-Bay company." By including both versions of Quebec, the map equivocates on where boundaries lie and exactly how large the province may be. It is up to the reader to favour one interpretation or another – hardly an endorsement of imperial cohesion.[94]

The Quebec Act was a difficult piece of legislation to depict geographically, which might account for why William Faden seemed to hedge his bets in "The British Colonies in North America, 1777"

8.5 William Faden, "The British Colonies in North America," in *The North American Atlas*, 1777

(figure 8.5). Faden rose to prominence in the last quarter of the eighteenth century. In 1773, two years after finishing an apprenticeship, Faden partnered with the son of the late Thomas Jefferys (also Thomas). These were both young men – Faden was twenty-four and Jefferys just eighteen.[95] What the Seven Years' War did for Jefferys the elder, the American Revolution did for Faden. His 1777 map, however, raises interesting questions about the limits of imperial cartography. "The British Colonies in North America" provided viewers with an excellent example of just how large Quebec had become. Yet this map depicted harmony among colonies already at war, rather than division between provinces such as Quebec and Nova Scotia (which had remained loyal to Britain) and the thirteen colonies, which had declared independence. Quebec, New York, Maryland, and South Carolina were coloured in a similar greenish hue, while Nova Scotia, New

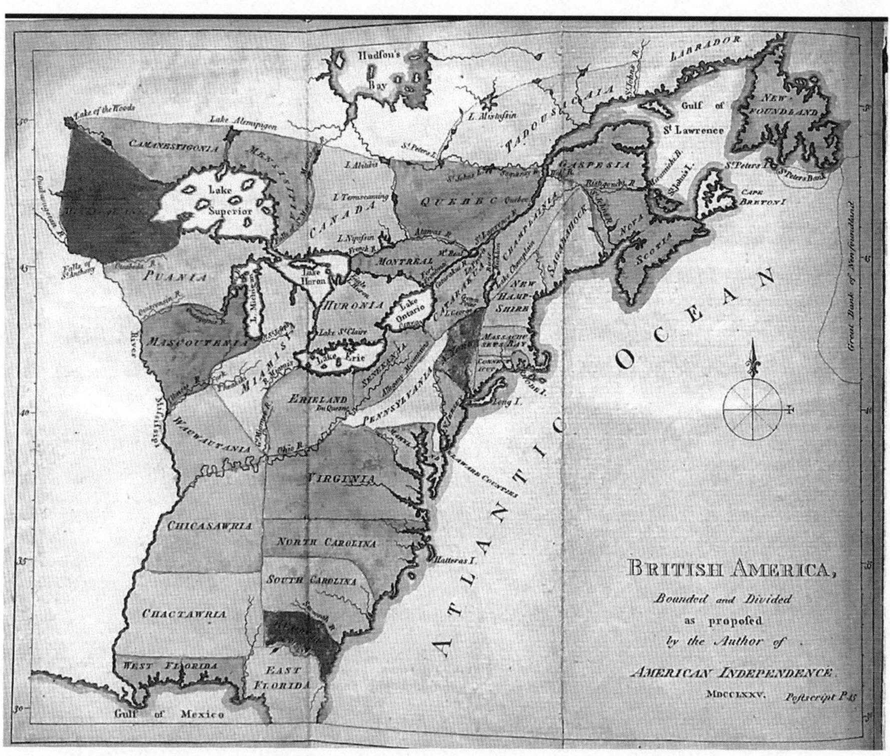

8.6 John Cartwright, "British America, Bound and Divided," in *American Independence: The Interest and Glory of Great-Britain.* 1775

Jersey, Virginia, and Georgia were pink. Faden's cartouche featured peaceful commerce rather than colonial conflict, even though 1777 was an important year in the Revolution; the American victory at Saratoga and the drafting of the Articles of Confederation signalled to the British that the Americans were not likely to reconcile with the empire. These complications prevented an easy geographic depiction of Quebec's place in British North America.

Ezra Stiles relied on his map the "Bloody Church" to express anger towards the Quebec Act; British geographers struggled to include an enlarged Quebec in a viable image of the British empire; however, at least one prominent British reformer used maps and borders to offer an alternative view of North America as a federation of independent states. John Cartwright, a prominent campaigner for parliamentary reform, believed he could resolve the American problem, which he outlined in his *American Independence* and its accompanying map (figure 8.6). The first edition of his work appeared as a series of letters in *The Public Advertiser* in the spring of 1774, all of which were later collected and published together. A second edition, with a postscript and an accompanying map, appeared in 1775.[96] His solution may not have been popular, as imperial officials were hardly willing to reorganize their empire as a federation. In the late summer of 1774, Cartwright expressed his anxiety surrounding the publication of *American Independence*. "My letters on American Independence are now in the press," he wrote, adding "as a republication of them may possibly be displeasing to Government, I do not wish at present to be known as their author. – I am not afraid of the law, but should be glad of advancement in my profession."[97] Cartwright's tract illustrated the entangled nature of French, English, and Indigenous concerns, and his geographic response attempted to create a federation that would address the needs of each group.

He quickly took aim at the product of the Canada Bill. "To begin then with Quebec," Cartwright argued, "I should not be content myself with reducing it to the same size as before its late enormous extension," but rather the province should be shrunk even further to make way for new colonies.[98] Cartwright saw the American colonies as independent states with the capacity for self-governance, and thus they were ill suited for parliamentary sovereignty.[99] However, categorizing all colonies in this fashion elided the variations within British settlements. Some colonies, such as Nova Scotia, Georgia, and especially Quebec, were the products of parliament. While colonies in New England could claim allegiance only to the king and dismiss the sovereignty of parliament – because parliament had no such power when the first English colonies were established – Quebec (and Nova Scotia and Georgia) were much younger colonies with stronger connections to the House of Assembly.[100] The Quebec Act guaranteed a colonial existence for a province that, despite the desires of a few hundred English merchants, was far from prepared to govern itself in the English model.

Equally challenging for Cartwright was the need to balance imperial reform with requisite protections for Indigenous lands. Reducing Quebec created space for new states in the Ohio Valley, which Cartwright created – in the quintessential imperial fashion, despite his status as a reformer – by carving up the map.[101] The division of the remaining territory resulted in new independent states, ostensibly to be filled with European settlers, but with names that reflected an

Indigenous presence. Cartwright noted that Great Britain's role would be to protect "the rights and independencies of the several tribes or nations of Indians in amity with or under the protection of the British crown, until these points shall be more particularly adjusted by treaty."[102] Cartwright consequently reversed the typical imperial geographic practice of marginalizing or removing the Indigenous presence.[103] While it is easy to point to the regularity with which European powers wiped Indigenous groups off colonial maps, we must also explore the role of Indigenous nations in their own geographic identity by simply remaining powerful enough to participate in spatial constructions.[104] Even after the American Revolution, certain Indigenous peoples – the Mi'kmaq in Nova Scotia, for example – exerted considerable influence on the process of settlement and expansion.[105] The years immediately preceding hostilities witnessed no shortage of violence in the Ohio Valley, and settlers quickly realized that Indigenous nations in that region represented a significant force.[106] Cartwright's map, intentionally or not, reflected that reality.

The map that accompanied *American Independence* is striking because it presents the reader with a complicated image of North America. Though Cartwright hoped to increase settlement in western regions, and he undoubtedly believed that British Americans would populate those new states, his map's toponymy reflects the Indigenous nature of much of North America. Several new colonies took their names from Indigenous groups, and thus infused the map with an identity that challenges British (or American) sovereignty. Maine became Sagadohock; above West Florida could be found Chocktawria and Chickasawria; Ohio and the Indian Reserve became Erieland and Miamisia; and the reduction of Quebec created room for Huronia. For Cartwright, it appears as though an Indigenous North America was preferable to a French one. Yet the geographic reduction of Canada, which answered so many complaints levelled at the Quebec Act, left room for new states founded on Indigenous nations. These new borders would be no easier for British Americans to penetrate. If anything, Cartwright's proposal was a more accurate reflection of the local geopolitics, though surely no more tolerable to anxious American settlers who hoped to push west. At the very least, Cartwright's cartographic efforts indicated how difficult it was to address the size of the Quebec Act. Removing or altering the province's extended limits could easily create new problems rather than offer solutions.

The Quebec Act was more than the sum of its parts, and that proved its ultimate undoing. While individual elements of the Act taken in isolation – guaranteeing practice of religion, allowing French Catholics to hold public office, securing French civil law and language – could be tolerated in a circumscribed place such as Acadia or Grenada, broadening these allowances by expanding the size of Quebec was simply too much for British Americans. Consequently, administrators in Quebec and London were put in an impossible position; the Act provided law and order for new subjects in old French settlements and fulfilled promises made to Indigenous groups by instituting laws, languages, and limits that the majority of British America could not tolerate in the aggregate. The Quebec Act was an Atlantic piece of legislation. The ideas that formed the Act, the reception the Act received, and the methods by which the Act was represented criss-crossed the ocean in ways that reveal just how entangled were the British, French, and Indigenous groups attempting to establish new regulations after the fall of New France. No one could know that attempts to create a new model of governing the British empire in North America would lead to its collapse. Those generally tasked with charting the growth of British settlements at the expense of its enemies were wholly incapable of depicting an empire dividing against itself.

NOTES

1 Franklin Bowditch Dexter, ed., *The Literary Diary of Ezra Stiles*, DD, LLD, vol. 1 (New York: Charles Scribner's Sons, 1901), 455.

2 For an overview of the negotiations required after 1713, see John G. Reid et al., *The "Conquest" of Acadia, 1710: Imperial, Colonial, and Aboriginal Constructions* (Toronto: University of Toronto Press, 2004); Jeffers Lennox, *Homelands and Empires: Indigenous Spaces, Imperial Fictions, and Competition for Territory in Northeastern North America, 1690–1763* (Toronto: University of Toronto Press, 2017).

3 S. Max Edelson, *The New Map of Empire: How Britain Imagined America before Independence* (Cambridge, MA: Harvard University Press, 2017), see chap. 2.

4 Administrative officials worked from at least seven reports concerning how to govern Quebec drafted in the 1760s and 1770s by officials in Quebec and London. See Hilda Neatby, *Quebec: The Revolutionary Age, 1760–1791* (Toronto: McClelland and Stewart, 1966), 126.

5 While it was possible for British Americans, especially those with Patriot leanings, to see the hand of the king in the creation of the Quebec Act, it was a bill influenced as much by colonists and administrators in Quebec as by officials in London. Many Patriots certainly did blame the king, however. See Vernon P. Creviston, "'No King Unless It Be a Constitutional King': Rethinking the Place of the Quebec Act in the Coming of the American Revolution," *Historian* 73, no. 3 (2011): 463–79.

6 David Hackett Fischer, *Champlain's Dream* (New York: Simon and Schuster, 2008), 294–6.

7 See *A Narrative of the Captivity and Restoration of Mrs Mary Rowlandson* (1682). Captivity was both an abstract idea that concerned Britons surveying their growing empire and a very real fear facing colonial settlers. For an overview, see Linda Colley, *Captives: Britain, Empire, and the World, 1600–1850* (London: Jonathan Cape, 2002); John Demos, *The Unredeemed Captive: A Family Story from Early America* (New York: Alfred A. Knopf, 1994).

8 Stephen Hornsby, *British Atlantic, American Frontier: Spaces of Power in Early Modern British America* (Hanover: University Press of New England, 2005), esp. chap. 6.

9 The post-1763 challenges facing British-Indigenous relations are thoroughly discussed in a number of excellent monographs. A few selections include Edelson, *The New Map of Empire*, chap. 4; Colin G. Calloway, *The Scratch of a Pen: 1763 and the Transformation of North America* (New York: Oxford University Press, 2006); Daniel K. Richter, *Facing East from Indian Country: A Native History of Early America* (Cambridge, MA: Harvard University Press, 2001); Colin G. Calloway, *New Worlds for All: Indians, Europeans, and the Remaking of Early America* (Johns Hopkins University Press, 1998); Richard White, *The Middle Ground: Indians, Empires, and Republics in the Great Lakes Region, 1650–1815* (Cambridge: Cambridge University Press, 1991).

10 Donald William Meinig, *The Shaping of America: A Geographical Perspective on 500 Years of History*. Vol. 1: *Atlantic America, 1492 –1800* (New Haven, CT: Yale University Press, 1986), 284–6.

11 Johnson and Stuart faced a formidable challenge, as their attempts to limit expansion and negotiate acceptable boundaries were ignored by settlers and speculators, especially from Virginia, who hoped to lay claim to territory around the Ohio River. See Matthew L. Rhoades, "Blood and Boundaries: Virginia Backcountry Violence and the Origins of the Quebec Act, 1758–1775," *West Virginia History: A Journal of Regional Studies* 3, no. 2 (2009): 1–22.

12 Johnson was particularly adept at engaging with Indigenous leaders, and he was not above using his diplomatic skills for personal gain. See "Johnson, Sir William," DCB; Calloway, *New Worlds for All: Indians, Europeans, and the Remaking of Early America*, 195; Fintan O'Toole, *White Savage: William Johnson and the Invention of America* (New York: Excelsior Editions, 2005).

13 Report of George Croghan, New York, 18 January 1767, in *The Papers of Sir William Johnson*, vol. 12, ed. Milton W. Hamilton, 406–7 (Albany: The University of the State of New York, 1962).

14 Ibid., 407.

15 Dartmouth to Cramahé, Whitehall, 1 December 1773, in *Documents Relating to the Constitutional History of Canada, 1759–1791*, ed. Adam Shortt and Arthur G. Doughty, 1st ed., 339 (Ottawa: Printed by S.E Dawson, Printer to the King's Most Excellent Majesty, 1907).

16 Journal of Daniel Claus, 19–27 July 1773, *The Papers of Sir William Johnson*, vol. 12, 625.

17 Journal of Daniel Claus, 28 July–10 August 1773, ibid., 628–9.

18 For an overview of merchant interests, see Stanley Brice Frost, *James McGill of Montreal* (Montreal and Kingston: McGill-Queen's University Press, 1995), chaps. 2 and 3.

19 Memorial from Quebec to Lord Dartmouth, Quebec, 31 December 1773, Shortt and Doughty, *Documents Relating to the Constitutional History of Canada*, 351. The memorial was signed by English merchants: Jenkin Williams, John Welles, John Lees, John McCord, Charles Grant, Malcom Fraser, and Zach Macaulay.

20 A Petition of divers of the Roman-Catholick Inhabitants of the Province of Quebeck to the King's Majesty, signed, and transmitted to the Earl of Dartmouth, his Majesty's Secretary of State for America, about the Month of December, 1773, and presented to his Majesty about the Month of February, 1774, ibid., 355–6.

21 Memorial of the Foregoing French Petitions in Support of their Petition, ibid., 358.

22 Ibid., 359.

23 Francis Maseres to the English Merchants of Quebec, Inner Temple, 22 August 1774, in Francis Maseres, *An Account of the Proceedings of the British, and other Protestant Inhabitants, of the Province of Quebeck, in North America, in order to obtain an House of Assembly in that Province* (London, 1775), 224.

24 Jack M. Sosin, *Whitehall and the Wilderness: The Middle West in British*

Colonial Policy, 1760–1775 (Lincoln: University of Nebraska Press, 1961), 238.

25 The confusion was a result of the 1757 Yorke-Camden opinion, which applied to the dispensation of lands in British India, but was misread by many to suggest that officials in the colonies could grant territory that the king had conquered. See ibid., 229–33.

26 Frederick Haldimand's Proclamation, New York, 10 March 1774, *The Papers of William Johnson*, vol. 8, part 2, 1074–6. Governors in several colonies had received similar reminders from the secretary of state for the southern colonies. See Rhoades, "Blood and Boundaries: Virginia Backcountry Violence and the Origins of the Quebec Act, 1758–1775," 10–12.

27 The Indigenous peoples "are unanimous in requesting I should express their wishes that his Majesty would be graciously pleased to nominate him." William Johnson to General Gage, 20 April 1774, 7, Folder 6, Box 1, Gen MSS 494, Guy Johnson Collection, Bieneke Library, Yale University.

28 Dartmouth to Cramahé, Whitehall, 4 May 1774, Shortt and Doughty, *Documents Relating to the Constitutional History of Canada*, 352.

29 For an overview of some of the main discussion points, see Sosin, *Whitehall and the Wilderness: The Middle West in British Colonial Policy, 1760–75*, 244–9.

30 Philip Lawson, *The Imperial Challenge: Quebec and Britain in the Age of the American Revolution* (Montreal and Kingston: McGill-Queen's University Press, 1989), 109–10.

31 Ibid., 131.

32 The opposition's inability to organize their efforts, despite the talents of leading politicians and pamphleteers, helps explain why Lord North was able to maintain power for as long as he did (though he continually threatened to resign, much to the annoyance of King George III, who threatened to abdicate rather than accept American independence). See Andrew Jackson O'Shaughnessy, *The Men Who Lost America: British Leadership, the American Revolution, and the Fate of the Empire* (New Haven, CT: Yale University Press, 2013).

33 Lawson, *The Imperial Challenge: Quebec and Britain in the Age of the American Revolution*, 133.

34 Ibid., 135.

35 Ibid., 138.

36 See "Cavendish, Sir Henry, second baronet (1732–1804)," *Oxford Dictionary of National Biography*, www.oxforddnb.com

37 *Debates of the House of Commons in the Year 1774, on the Bill for Making More Effectual Provision for the Government of the Province of Quebec. Drawn up from the Notes of the Right Honourable Sir Henry Cavendish, Bart.* (London: J. Wright, 1839), 183.

38 Ibid., 184.

39 Ibid., 186.

40 Ibid., 188.

41 Ibid., 189.

42 Lawson, *The Imperial Challenge: Quebec and Britain in the Age of the American Revolution*, 141.

43 14 Geo. III, c.83, *An Act for making more effectual Provision for the Government of the Province of Quebec in North America,* ii. http://avalon.law.yale.edu/18th_century/quebec_act_1774.asp. See also Alfred LeRoy Burt and Hilda Neatby, *The Old Province of Quebec*, vol. 1 (Montreal and Kingston: McGill-Queen's University Press, 1968 [1933]), 170.

44 *Debates of the House of Commons in the Year 1774*, 192.

45 Hilda Neatby notes that when members of the assembly requested the reports that informed the bill, none were presented because the final bill did not reflect the reports' suggestions. The final draft of the Quebec Act presented to legislators was based almost entirely on Governor Carleton's representation of the wishes of Canadians. Neatby, *Quebec: The Revolutionary Age, 1760–1791*, 127. Lawson, however, offers a convincing argument that Wedderburn's report was instrumental to the Act and that reports were not tabled in the Lower House to prevent unnecessary delays. See Lawson, *The Imperial Challenge: Quebec and Britain in the Age of the American Revolution*, 121.

46 Lord Hillsborough's Objections to the Quebec Bill in its Present Form, *Documents Relative to the Constitutional History of Canada*, 388.

47 Dartmouth's Reply to Hillsborough, 1 May 1774, ibid., 390.

48 Stiles, *Literary Diary*, 470. Entry for 5 November 1774. On the other side of the Atlantic, North's supporters tarred and feathered leading American figures. See Kathleen Wilson, *The Sense of the People: Politics, Culture, and Imperialism in England, 1715–1785* (Cambridge: Cambridge University Press, 1995), 244.

49 Haldimand to Amherst, New York, 7 September 1774, folios 356–7, B–1, MG21–Add.MSS, Haldimand Papers, Library and Archives Canada. "On n'approuve point icy l'Acte qui (357) fixe (si sagement) le gouvernement & les limittes du Canada, ces gens icy naiment point a voir cette chaine tirée sur leur derriere."

50 On the French, English, and Indigenous relations in Nova Scotia/Acadia, see Geoffrey Gilbert Plank, *An Unsettled Conquest: The British Campaign against the Peoples of Acadia* (Philadelphia: University of Pennsylvania Press, 2001); N.E.S. Griffiths, *From Migrant to Acadian: A North American Border People, 1604–1755* (Montreal: McGill-Queen's University Press, 2005); John Mack Faragher, *A Great and Noble Scheme: The Tragic Story of the Expulsion of the French Acadians from Their American Homeland*, 1st ed. (New York: W.W. Norton, 2005); William Craig Wicken, *Mi'kmaq Treaties on Trial: History, Land and Donald Marshall Junior* (Toronto: University of Toronto Press, 2002). Borders and boundaries were equally important in Nova Scotia. See Jeffers Lennox, "Nova Scotia Lost and Found: The Acadian Boundary Negotiation and Imperial Envisioning, 1750–1755," *Acadiensis* 40, no. 2 (2011): 3–31; Jeffers Lennox, "A Time and a Place: The Geography of British, French, and Aboriginal Interactions in Early Nova Scotia, 1726–44," *William and Mary Quarterly* 72, no. 3 (2015): 423–60.

51 See Hannah Weiss Muller's contribution to this volume, as well as Hannah Weiss Muller, *Subjects and Sovereign: Bonds of Belonging in the Eighteenth-Century British Empire* (Oxford: Oxford University Press, 2017), 122–65.

52 Pauline Maier, *From Resistance to Revolution: Colonial Radicals and the Development of American Opposition to Britain, 1765–1776* (New York: W.W. Norton, 1991), 185.

53 17 September 1774. *Journals of the Continental Congress, 1774–1789*, vol. 1, *1774*. Edited from the Original Records in the Library of Congress by Worthington Chauncey Ford Chief, Division of Manuscripts, (Washington: Government Printing Office, 1904), 34.

54 Notes of Debates in the Continental Congress, 17(?) October 1774. *Papers of John Adams*, vol. 2: Founding Families: Digital Editions of the Papers of the Winthrops and Adamses, ed. James Taylor (Boston: Massachusetts Historical Society, 2007) http://www.masshist.org/ff/

55 Address to the People of Great Britain, *Journals of the Continental Congress, 1774–1789*, vol 1, *1774*, 87–8.

56 Ibid.

57 Ibid. At the same time, Congress drafted a letter to the inhabitants of Quebec that took a much different tone. In this letter – the first of three sent between 1774 and 1776 – Congress encouraged the Canadiens to join the Patriot cause and assured them that their religion would not be a barrier to inclusion. See Jeffers Lennox, "Revolution Expected: The Invasion of Quebec and American Independence," in *Violence, Order, and*

Unrest: A History of British North America, 1749–1876, ed. Elizabeth Mancke et al., 95–116 (Toronto: University of Toronto Press, 2019); Amy Noel Ellison, "Montgomery's Misfortune: The American Defeat at Quebec and the March toward Independence, 1775–1776," *Early American Studies* 15, no. 3 (2017): 591–616. On Catholicism and the American Revolution, see Robert Emmett Curran, *Papist Devils: Catholics in British America, 1574–1783* (Washington, DC: Catholic University of America Press, 2014); Maura Jane Farrelly, *Papist Patriots: The Making of an American Catholic Identity* (New York: Oxford University Press, 2012).

58 Paul Langston, "'Tyrant and Oppressor!': Colonial Press Reaction to the Quebec Act," *Historical Journal of Massachusetts* 34, no. 1 (2006): 1–17.

59 *Pennsylvania Gazette*, 27 July 1774.

60 Ibid., 31 August 1774.

61 Ibid., 12 October 1774.

62 *South Carolina Gazette*, 1 November 1774.

63 Rev. Ebenezer Baldwin, "Appendix stating the heavy grievances that colonies labour under from several late acts of the British Parliament ... " in Samuel Sherwood, *A Sermon, Containing Scriptural Instructions to Civil Rulers, and all Free-Born Subjects* (New Haven, 1774), 48.

64 Ibid., 56.

65 Ibid., 67.

66 Elizabeth Fenton argues that anti-Catholicism in the British American colonies was a central element of developing an American national identity. She argues, "In imagining Canadian Catholics as subjects whose private lives were entirely dictated by papal rule, Anglo-Protestant colonists constructed themselves as freely private subjects capable of shaping a religiously plural – and therefore 'liberal' – nation that could accommodate diversity because it was 'not Catholic.'" See Elizabeth Fenton, "Birth of a Protestant Nation: Catholic Canadians, Religious Pluralism, and National Unity in the Early US Republic," *Early American Literature* 41, no. 1 (2006): 30.

67 Sir Thomas Bernard, *An Appeal to the Public, Stating and Considering the Objections to the Quebec Bill* (London, 1774), 11–12.

68 Ibid., 15. Bernard failed to recognize the fact that those who "first settled" the country were not French but Indigenous.

69 Ibid., 18–19.

70 Ibid., 38–40. On the development of a naval rule in Newfoundland, see Jerry Bannister, *The Rule of the Admirals: Law, Custom, and Naval Government in Newfoundland, 1699–1832* (Toronto: University of Toronto Press, for the Osgoode Society for Canadian Legal History, 2003).

71 Ibid, 48–50.

72 Ibid., 50–1. Even after the revolution, Americans faced challenges in taking control of the Illinois, which remained populated by French traders who could exploit their alliances with the Indigenous peoples. See Jay Gitlin, *The Bourgeois Frontier: French Towns, French Traders, and American Expansion* (New Haven, CT: Yale University Press, 2009).

73 Ibid., 53.

74 "Knox, William (1732–1810)," in *Oxford Dictionary of National Biography*.

75 English efforts to colonize Ireland and "civilize" the Irish were mirrored in early attempts to establish plantations in North America. See Jack P. Greene, *Pursuits of Happiness: The Social Development of Early Modern British Colonies and the Formation of American Culture* (Chapel Hill: University of North Carolina Press, 1988), chap. 5; Daniel K. Richter, *Before the Revolution: America's Ancient Pasts* (Cambridge, MA: Belknap Press / Harvard University Press, 2011), 107–12.

76 William Knox, *The Justice and Policy of the Late Act of Parliament for Making More Effectual Provisions for the Government of the Province of Quebec, Asserted and Proved; and the Conduct of Administration Respecting that Province, Stated and Vindicated* (London: 1774), 20–4. Quotation from 24.

77 Ibid., 26.

78 Ibid., 39–40.

79 Ibid., 43.

80 As Lauren Benton has argued, waterways and river systems influenced the exercise of imperial authority. Lauren Benton, "Spatial Histories of Empire," *Itinerario* 30, no. 3 (2006): 19–34. Stephen Hornsby notes how, after 1763, the British empire was able to integrate France's American settlements because they were maritime and riverine, which suited Britain's Atlantic and naval strengths. Hornsby, *British Atlantic, American Frontier*, chap. 6.

81 Benjamin Franklin to Jonathan Shipley, Cravenstreet, 10 March 1774, *The Papers of Benjamin Franklin*. (Sponsored by the American Philosophical Society and Yale University, Digital Edition by The Packard Humanities Institute. www.franklinpapers.org), vol. 21, 139.

82 Ibid., 140.

83 David Morgan, *The Devious Dr Franklin, Colonial Agent: Benjamin Franklin's Years in London* (Macon, GA: Mercer University Press, 1999), 241–2.

84 Benjamin Franklin, *Memoirs of the Life and Writings of Benjamin Franklin*, vol. 1 (Philadelphia: T.S. Manning,[1818]), 284.

85 Answers to Franklin's "Hints," before 4 February 1775, *The Papers of Benjamin Franklin*, vol. 21, 467–8. Sosin argues that any suggestion that the boundaries might be changed was a misunderstanding of imperial desires. Dartmouth was unwilling to alter Quebec's limits. Sosin, *Whitehall and the Wilderness: The Middle West in British Colonial Policy, 1760–1775*, 249 n21.

86 Benjamin Franklin to William Franklin, "Journal of Negotiations in London," 22 March 1775, ibid., 540.

87 Stiles, *Literary Diary*, 4.

88 Ibid., 424.

89 Ibid., 589.

90 The English had long defined themselves in relation to the French. See Linda Colley, *Britons: Forging the Nation, 1707–1837* (New Haven, CT: Yale University Press, 1992).

91 Many thanks to Matthew Edney for pointing me towards Stiles's map. See "The Irony of Imperial Mapping," in *The Imperial Map: Cartography and the Mastery of Empire*, ed. James R. Akerman (Chicago: University of Chicago Press, 2009), 11–45.

92 See Lennox, "Nova Scotia Lost and Found: The Acadian Boundary Negotiation and Imperial Envisioning, 1750–1755," 3–31.

93 French readers learned about Jefferys's "American Atlas" from the *Journal de politique et de littérature* in 1778.

94 See Edney, "The Irony of Imperial Mapping," 24.

95 Joel Kovarsky, "William Faden (1749–1836)" (Digital Scholarly Editions, Lehigh University Press), http://digital.lib.lehigh.edu.dse/atlas/4/ See also Worms, Lawrence. "Faden, William (1749–1836)," *Oxford Dictionary of National Biography*.

96 S. Max Edelson and Steve Sarson, "The Grand British League and Confederacy: John Cartwright and the Geographies of Sovereignty in Revolutionary America," Fourth Biennial Conference of the European Early American Studies Association (EEASA), Bayreuth University, Germany, 14 December 2012, 1–2. Many thanks to Max Edelson for sharing this paper.

97 August 1774, *The Life and Correspondence of Major Cartwright*, ed. F.D. Cartwright, vol. 1 (New York: Augustus M. Kelley, 1969 [1826]), 53.

98 John Cartwright, *American Independence: The Interest and Glory of Great Britain, A New Edition* (London: 1775), 44.

99 Edelson and Sarson, "The Grand British League and Confederacy," 17–18.

100 Elizabeth Mancke, *The Fault Lines of Empire: Political Differentiation in Massachusetts and Nova Scotia, ca. 1760–1830* (New York: Routledge, 2005), 5. Mancke offers a compelling argument for the political differentiation between Nova Scotia and Massachusetts, specifically the towns of Liverpool and Machias.

101 Edelson and Sarson, "The Grand British League and Confederacy," 27.

102 Cartwright, *American Independence*, 35.

103 J.B. Harley, *The New Nature of Maps: Essays in the History of Cartography* (Baltimore: Johns Hopkins University Press, 2001), 179–83.

104 As Karl Offen has argued in relation to the Mosquito of Central America, Indigenous spatial practices provided Indigenous peoples with an active role in mapping the region and allowed certain nations to "co-produce" colonial cartography. See Karl H. Offen, "Creating Mosquitia: Mapping Amerindian Spatial Practices in Eastern Central America, 1629–1779," *Journal of Historical Geography* 33, no. 2 (2007): 254–82.

105 John G. Reid, "Empire, the Maritime Colonies, and the Supplanting of Mi'kma'ki/Wulstukwik, 1780–1820," *Acadiensis* 38, no. 2 (2009): 78–97.

106 For a useful overview of eighteenth-century contests in the west, see Colin G. Calloway, *One Vast Winter Count: The Native American West before Lewis and Clark* (Lincoln: University of Nebraska Press, 2003), chap. 7. While Indigenous strength waned over the course of the century, western expansion was hardly a fait accompli in 1774.

9

"Our Concerns with Indians are now greatly extended": Cherokees, Westward Indians, and Interpreting the Quebec Act from the Ohio Valley, 1763–1774

Kristofer Ray

For British colonial expansionists, the 1774 Quebec Act represented a major problem: it pulled the rug from beneath western land speculation, a potentially lucrative exercise for "entrepreneurs" in Virginia, Pennsylvania, and the Carolinas (as well as most other colonies). Already they had endeavoured to overcome restrictions placed upon trans-Appalachian development by the Royal Proclamation of October 1763. Between then and 1774, the empire gradually had peeled back the proclamation's boundary, and speculators had proven adept at overcoming other colonial and imperial legal impediments. Parliament created a potentially formidable barrier, however, when it placed virtually all of the northern Ohio Valley under Quebec's jurisdiction.

Colonial expansionists' sense of injustice arose from the assumption that the Ohio Valley was the domain of Europeans – a place where the British empire had firm jurisdictional control because of its victory over France in the Seven Years' War. For Virginians like George Washington, Richard Henderson, or Fincastle County representatives, the only real issue in 1774 was whether they would perfect land titles despite the roadblocks thrown up by this "intolerable" statute. American Indians would have laughed at such an assumption. Despite over a century of drastic societal alterations, Indigenous polities firmly controlled the Ohio Valley and its riparian connections. The British certainly maintained a powerful imperial imagination, but they could do little either to project force into the valley or to subordinate the many Native societies making use of it.[1]

This latter point is crucial: mobility defined life in trans-Appalachia generally and in the Ohio Valley specifically. It had been that way throughout the eighteenth century, but after 1763 it became clear to British North American leadership that Indigenous movement limited their imperial options. Most notably, Anishnaabeg (Ojibwes, Odawas, and Potawatomis from the Great Lakes region) and Senecas (a member polity of the Haudenosaunee to the east) checked British expansion by laying siege to Fort Detroit and other trans-Appalachian posts in 1763.[2] Shawnees and Lenapes supported that attack from the upper Ohio Valley, while at the same time interfering with British efforts to descend the Ohio River and claim the *pays des Illinois*. Meanwhile, the "Illinois" – Caskaskias, Cahokias, and Peorias, along with Piankeshaws, Mascoutens, and Kickapoos – rejected British authority in and around their country and continued to trade with the French agents who remained in the area.[3]

This frenetic pace of economic, military, and diplomatic life extended well south of the territory subsequently identified in the Quebec Act. Illinois polities, Shawnees and members of the Six Nations, for example, regularly crossed the Ohio River to challenge coalescent societies along the Mississippi and Tennessee. Chickasaws often were targeted, although these raids focused forcefully upon the western towns of the Aniyunwiya. The reasons were self-evident to those on the offensive: Cherokees from their "Overhill" and "Valley" settlement regions had entered into and contested the *pays des Illinois*, Ohio Valley, and Wabash Valley at least since the 1710s. After 1730 they accelerated their western forays, and by 1763 the Cherokee presence was ubiquitous. As a result, violence escalated between them and their western counterparts.[4]

The cartographical boundaries that defined the western extension of the Quebec Act meant little in a fluid world where northern, western, and southern Indians interacted and competed with one another.[5] And try as they might, British imperial authorities could not assume jurisdictional control over that world. Men like Commander-in-Chief Thomas Gage, northern Indian superintendent, Sir William Johnson, and southern Indian superintendent, John Stuart, understood the point quite well. Between 1763 and 1774, they unsuccessfully "sabre-rattled" to pacify western Indians; Gage and Stuart encouraged a Cherokee–Six Nation alliance as a means of forestalling violence; and all three men insisted on limitations to colonial encroachment from the east. They grew frustrated that colonial governors and legislatures did little to stop intrusions into trans-Appalachia, despite crown mandates. And they lamented that the metropole undermined imperial North American authority over Indigenous affairs through economic retrenchment and by placing trade regulation in the hands of colonial leaders. To them, the thirteen seaboard colonies were utterly ill-equipped to deal with the palpable instability of Native affairs.[6] Ultimately parliament agreed, and in the Quebec Act imposed boundaries intended to stabilize a palpably unstable Ohio Valley.

In short, the Quebec Act represented an opportunity for the British empire "to correct the defective state of the hinterland."[7] Only centralized authority could advance unified Indigenous diplomatic initiatives, stop corrupt speculation and trade practices, and solidify jurisdiction in trans-Appalachia. The Quebec Act laid the groundwork for it.

CHEROKEES AND INDIGENOUS MOBILITY IN THE OHIO VALLEY

British and French North Americans long had understood that geopolitical fluidity defined Indian life in the Ohio Valley. Basic riparian realities explained why. South Carolina's governor, James Glen, pointed out in 1754, for example, that trans-Appalachia was the "bed principally of the three great Rivers": the Wabash, Ohio, and Tennessee. The three rivers came together, he observed, before ultimately draining into the Mississippi, in the process creating a massive riparian system.[8] One feature of this system particularly stood out to Glen: the Tennessee River – known to the Aniyunwiya as the "Long Man" for its spiritual significance – "has its rise in the Cherokee Nation and runs a great way through it."[9] They may physically have inhabited only five clusters of settlement extending 150 miles along the Appalachian Mountains, but to Britons the Cherokees had "undoubted" ownership over all land adjoining the Tennessee. It was a territory reaching from the edge of Carolina "quite to the Mississippi ... [and] stretching from east to west eight hundred miles."[10]

As early as the Yamasee War, European sources chronicle a Cherokee presence throughout this riparian system. In 1716, for example, they raided a Kaskaskia town, in the process killing nearly a dozen Frenchmen.[11] Louisiana officials saw it as a British-induced attack, and feared that Illinois polities were intimidated enough "to become reconciled to the English."[12] Those fears were reinforced a year later when a report surfaced that a raid led by men from Quanase and Tellico (a Valley and Overhill town, respectively) had killed French officers along the Wabash while searching for "Nottoways, Senecas, Caskaskias," and Cahokias.[13] When in 1726–27 Carolina officials encouraged Overhill men to slave raid among Lower Creek towns, the Long Warrior of Tanasee instead indicated his desire to "go against the French Indians."[14] Not surprisingly, many of his targets were in Illinois.

British North American leaders saw an opportunity in Cherokee mobility and "land ownership," and thus made them important elements in their evolving conception of empire. If they consented to becoming subjects of the crown, the argument went, then any area that Cherokees might claim would fall under British jurisdiction. It would give Carolinians direct access to Illinois and the Ohio Valley from the south. When combined with perceived authority over the Haudenosaunee – which also had interests in Illinois and the Valley – it would give Britons a two-pronged means by which to claim dominion over the entirety of trans-Appalachia.[15] Such an intoxicating imperial imagination directly informed British Carolina's encouragement of Overhill Cherokees to travel the Tennessee and into the Ohio Valley. In 1730, it led to efforts to establish an exclusive "Chain of Friendship," which, while suitable for British interests, was entirely fictive to Cherokees, because it created a subordinate and artificially singular nation.[16]

Despite subsequent misunderstandings by both parties, this Chain sustained decades of Anglo-Cherokee interaction. Its impact on European understandings of trans-Appalachia was similarly remarkable: between 1730 and 1763, Spanish and French sources chronicle an ever-increasing Cherokee presence, not only across the south but also in Illinois and the Ohio and Wabash valleys. They seemed to gather intelligence for Carolinians, alternately harassing and encouraging French trade and allies. To these other Europeans, the Anglo-Cherokee alliance was real.

Of less concern to them, but absolutely crucial to trans-Appalachian geopolitics, was the fact that Cherokee excursions produced palpable resentment among some Indigenous groups then settling in (or near) the Ohio Valley. Over the first half of the eighteenth century, Illinois-based Twightwees (Miamis) and Mascoutens resettled in western Ohio and the Wabash Valley.[17] As those two groups' presence diminished in Illinois, the Kickapoos and Piankeshaws moved into that space, while Anishnaabeg travelled south from the Great Lakes to reinforce links to the region.[18] After the 1720s, meanwhile, Shawnees, Lenapes, and Senecas began to move west from Pennsylvania and New York (among other regions) into the upper Ohio Valley. The more visible Cherokees became, the more they encountered these other polities. By the outbreak of the War of Jenkins's Ear in 1739, attacks, counter-attacks, and negotiations between Cherokees and "Westward" groups were becoming common. Historian Michael McDonnell, for example, has observed that, in 1741, "Several hundred warriors from Detroit, St Joseph's, and Michilimackinac sent out war parties against the Chickasaw and Cherokee."[19] Not long after the completion of Fort Loudoun in 1757, British officer Paul Demere revealed that "a Party of Tweektwees was in our neighbourhood," intent upon attacking Overhill towns.[20]

French defeat in 1763 exacerbated the situation. Although the Treaty of Paris officially ended the war, no Frenchman in the Ohio Valley immediately understood that they would have to vacate in favour of the British. The lack of clarity led to a number of questions: Should they continue as normal under the assumption that Versailles would protect them? Should they redouble fortifications at Forts Chartres and Massac in Illinois? Should they encourage friendly Indians to reject British jurisdiction? Only three years earlier, Louisiana's governor, Louis Billouart, Chevalier de Kerlerec, had feared that the loss of Fort Massac (at the mouth of the Tennessee River) could lead the British to use Illinois as a staging area for an attack on New Orleans. He thus sent orders to maintain "different bands of Indians and Frenchmen along La Belle Rivière in order to observe the maneuvers of the English," while simultaneously redoubling efforts to maintain links with the upper Creek towns, Overhill Cherokee towns, and Choctaw towns.[21] In 1762 Kerlerec reached out to "the Cherokees, Choctaws, Abekas, Alibamos, and other [Southern] Indian nations" to distribute supplies. He then ordered Antoine Lantagnac, a French trader in Overhill towns, to "bring him ... six respected Cherokees ... to New Orleans." His explicit purpose: "to discuss ways of protecting the Illinois by destroying all the English establishments in that area."[22]

Kerlerec's mindset helps explain why French officials did not vacate their Illinois posts until well after 1763, and why French traders continued to ply their wares throughout the Ohio Valley. The consequence was that no Indian group in trans-Appalachia accepted the permanence of British success. Cahokias, Caskaskias, Odawas, Kickapoos, Ojibwes, and Potawatamis in Illinois explicitly rejected British jurisdiction and continued to trade with the French. Wyandots, Shawnees, and Lenapes took similar positions further east in the Ohio Valley, and contributed to the 1763 Anishnaabeg attack upon Detroit. A British expedition under Major Arthur Loftus left New Orleans in 1763 to claim Illinois, but was abandoned before it reached Natchez because of Indigenous challenges and rumours of opposition from Louisiana's government.

The experiences of British officer Thomas Morris are particularly instructive. In August-September 1764, Morris travelled to the Miami River and upper Ohio Valley to deliver appeals for peace to Indigenous groups supporting attacks on Fort Detroit. He underwent significant trauma along the way, nearly losing his life several times at the hands of Indians who were fundamentally hostile to British interests. His description of these two months is revelatory. In a remarkable example of performative symbolism, unhappy Miamis dressed in uniforms given them by northern Indian superintendent, William Johnson, before informing Morris that the English were untrustworthy. Odawa headman Pontiac similarly proclaimed that "the English were liars," and suggested that the French empire was encouraging challenges to the extension of British jurisdiction. Shawnees and Lenapes, meanwhile, urged neutral Miami headmen to execute the British agent.[23]

Through it all, Morris observed a steady flow of Indigenous traffic through the Ohio country. Illinois groups such as the Kickapoos entered into and left Miami towns, no doubt taking their observations of Morris's expedition back to their leadership. Those observations would have been reinforced by Odawas loyal to Pontiac, who themselves spent time in Illinois in 1764 and 1765. When Shawnees and Lenapes departed Miami country, some went to Ouiatanon on the Wabash to encourage Weas to kill the English expedition. Others left to negotiate with St Joseph's River Potawatamis. Morris must have been astounded by the extent to which the British lacked a presence in this extremely mobile world.

A month after Morris finally managed to return to Detroit, British Ensign Gavin Cochrane reminded General Thomas Gage that unrest in the Ohio Valley extended south of the river as well. Cochrane resided in the fall of 1764 in Overhill Cherokee country, and in October he informed Gage that a Cherokee, lately a "prisoner" where "great Warrior [Oconostota] used to go for presents [Fort Massac]," had returned to Overhill country. This unnamed man explained that, while he was at Fort Chartres, "a great ffrench officer [was] very Assiduous in sending for different tribes of Indians in their Alliance to whom they gave talks, ammunition, guns, flints, tomahawks, & knives, desiring them to go to War against the English & their allies, to kill all & not trouble them with prisoners."[24]

For Gage, Cochrane's intelligence confirmed that "The French at the Ilinois" were furnishing Lenapes and Shawnees with a "Very Considerable Quantity" of arms and ammunition. It meant that the attacks on Fort Detroit could well extend into the foreseeable future.[25] Something would have to be done. On the one hand, he called upon William Johnson to procure Iroquois support in this British struggle with "props of the longhouse." On the other hand, he ordered southern Indian superintendent, John Stuart, to inquire whether "it may be possible to engage the Cherokees perhaps, to Seize the Persons & Goods of [French] Traders, as they go up the Ohio."[26] He further believed that "the Cherokees may be of service" in ensuring the safety of British soldiers taking possession of Illinois. "Understanding that Nation extends [to the mouth of the Ohio]," he wrote to Stuart, and that they were "almost the only Indians who trade at Fort Massiac," with the right gifts and diplomatic initiatives they could expedite British jurisdictional control.[27]

Gage's willingness to tap into trans-Appalachian geopolitical fluidity looked similar to Kerlerec's efforts of only a few years earlier. It also reveals a crucial point: Cherokee mobility – combined with their decentralized political identity – made diplomacy and alliance-building difficult for European empires. Historians long have argued that a post-1730 Cherokee nation uniformly supported the British, doing little more than occasionally "playing" their Anglo allies off against the French to ensure their independent status. A recent study summarizes the position well: some Cherokees "certainly retained suspicions about the English, but the larger part of the nation remained wary of the French and instead gave essential assistance to Great Britain during the Seven Years' War. For their part, the French had given Cherokees little reason to trust them. [That] empire provided little in the way of gifts that could have established an alliance."[28]

Archeologists Ted Gragson and Paul Bolstad offer a counter-argument. "The pre-1776 Cherokee literature," they note, "has often relied on interpretations that outrun evidence, which compounds the difficulties of making sense of a sparse and often ambiguous record. Grand narrative and evocative imagery have been used to present global generalities that apply neither any*where* nor any*time*."[29] Their observation is relevant for understanding mobility and its impact on political identity formation. The fact that Cherokees identified according to town or perhaps region for most of the eighteenth century meant that each of the five settlement areas could (and did) have unique political/economic/diplomatic dynamics. The Overhill towns were easily the most mobile in terms of the Tennessee River and Ohio Valley, and by consequence their geopolitical realities were rooted in the West in ways other Cherokee settlement areas were not. It made "Westward" Indians and affairs – as well as the French in Louisiana – a meaningful part of their calculations.

Put simply, eighteenth-century European notions of "alliance" were stilted. Native polities in the Ohio Valley engaged in acts of trade, war, and diplomacy to which Europeans were not privy. The latter were on the margins, recording only snapshots of situations first manipulated by Indigenous representatives and then filtered through the lens of imagined imperial extension. And their efforts to involve themselves invariably led to greater difficulties.

Gage's desire to involve Cherokees in Illinois affairs, then, placed the British in the middle of already-escalating tensions between Cherokees and their "Westward" counterparts.[30] When a 1765 expedition led by Alexander Fraser arrived in Illinois, skeptical (unnamed) Indians questioned who he was and whom he represented. He explained that he was "an English Chief come to acquaint their Nation that the Shawanese, Delaware, and all the Nations on the Ohio had made Peace." The Indian response was telling: "They said it was very well, that they thought we had been Cherokees."[31] Fraser's expedition unsuccessfully secured British jurisdiction, and in fact he was warned that any subsequent Briton in Illinois could face execution.

Not long thereafter, the deputy northern Indian superintendent, George Croghan, arrived from Fort Pitt. As Historian Gregory Evans Dowd has pointed out, Kickapoos and Mascoutens explained to Croghan that the French "had warned them that the English were leagued with the Cherokees, bent on enslaving all Illinois people and on taking Indian land." These men were so paranoid about an attack that they "said that they had mistaken Croghan's Shawnee and Delaware escorts for invading Cherokees."[32] Later that year, a French informant named Lagautrais informed British Major Robert Farmar that Potowatamis had "killed 21 Charaqui" in Illinois and feared that open war could result. He promised that he could "prevent this War & pacify them" by appealing directly to the "five Chiefs from the Illinois of different Villages." With the right inducements, he was sure that they would be "well disposed to make peace with the English Nation."[33] Even so, there was a risk. Had another war broken out, the British might well have had to concede jurisdictional control in Illinois for the foreseeable future.

In 1766 the valley became even more chaotic. In addition to Westward Indians, Cherokees also dealt with an increasing number of "Norward" invasions – that is to say, from the Six Nations. Chota headman Kittagusta explained the situation at a congress at Fort Prince George, South Carolina. "Our enemies from the Northward," he revealed, have "attacked us this year in all parts of our Country in greater Numbers & more frequent than we have ever known." He was at a loss to explain why, and wondered aloud "if they are Sett on by any Body & by whom." It was important, not just because "their Hatchets ... are very Sharp," but also because they "have been lifted up against White as well as Red Men in our Nation." Overhill Cherokee agent Alexander Cameron described one such confrontation between unnamed "Norwards & a hunting Party of the Cherokees down the Tenassie." In that event, four Norwards had been killed, along with three Cherokees "& several wounded on both sides." Cherokees had been vastly outnumbered, but protected themselves by securing a blockhouse constructed by Overhill headman, Attakullakulla, the previous winter "for his own defense in his hunting Camp."[34]

Cameron further described a "Norward attack" on white traders. An unidentified older man and his grandchild outside the Lower Cherokee Town of Toogaloo had had their brains knocked out "with a war club which was left by them with Shame Signs upon it." No legitimate trader, Cameron feared, would "Venture into this Nation if the Enemy are permitted to kill white people as well as Red." For that matter, he was increasingly fearful that Cherokees would respond by killing traders above the Ohio River, "which they already begin to insinuate."[35]

Cherokees were not averse to retaliating for "Norward" attacks, to be sure.[36] Yet, despite outward appearances, their options were limited by significant internal problems. In the late 1750s and early 1760s, Cherokee country was hit hard by a smallpox epidemic. It coincided with a two-year bloody confrontation with South Carolina, and the combination notably challenged the population and power of the Aniyunwiya. At that same moment they seemingly had to deal with an increasing stream of corrupt traders and encroachment by white settlers. Even as he feared Indigenous attacks on traders in Cherokee country, Alexander Cameron expressed shock at "the tearing cheating & horse stealing that have been committed among the Indians by the Traders and Packhorsemen." It was no surprise to him that Cherokee loyalty should waver "when we allow such villains to trade or reside amongst them."[37]

Land encroachment, corrupt trade, and escalating Westward and Norward confrontations were too much for Cherokees to handle alone. They seemed to calculate that Westward Indians represented the biggest immediate threat, so in 1766 they swallowed forty years of enmity and pushed for peace with their Norward adversaries.[38] The Six Nations were slow to agree. As early as the Tuscarora War they had come south to engage Catawbas and Cherokees.[39] They had also established diplomatic links with Creek towns, and by the 1720s were encouraging them to attack Cherokees.[40] Between then and the 1760s, the two Iroquoian-speaking groups repeatedly found themselves at odds, even as the British claimed alliance with both and put notable pressure on them to negotiate a peace. Anglo officials simply refused to accept that neither Cherokees nor the Iroquois marched "in step with the beat of the British drum." Although both groups "tried rapproachment ... [they struggled to meet] the demands of their own societies and cultures" and thus continued through decades of diplomatic and military contestation affecting trans-Appalachia.[41]

Their differences extended to western land issues. The Six Nations had long imagined their own jurisdiction over the Ohio Valley and Illinois country, and were displeased that Cherokees were so visible in both places. By the 1760s, the Overhill presence particularly – if implicitly – challenged Haudenosaunee jurisdiction over a critical swath of the valley that eventually would fall under the Quebec Act: the territory between the Great Kanawha and Tennessee rivers. The Haudenosaunee insisted that the territory belonged to them by (a fictional) right of conquest, and flatly rejected Cherokee claims that it was part of their extended hunting grounds. Despite William Johnson's assurances to the contrary, they could not have been happy when the British empire informed the Cherokees that Six Nations' "Claims have not been Suffered to extend beyond the Conhoway and its Confluence with the Ohio."[42] Working through these two competing claims factored directly into the land-cession negotiations at Fort Stanwix, New York, and Hard Labour, South Carolina, in 1768.[43]

By that point, however, the Cherokees and the Haudenosaunee had a major problem in common: Westward Indigenous polities. Six Nations claims to jurisdiction over the Ohio Valley implied that all Westward groups were subordinate to them within the covenant chain – and had no say, for example, in the large land cession to which the Six Nations agreed at Fort Stanwix. Anishnaabeg, Illinois, Mascoutens, Miamis, Weas, Shawnees, and Lenapes thought otherwise, and worked hard to achieve a greater level of inter-tribal cooperation at the expense of their Indian "uncles" – an effort that extended even into Cherokee country.[44] The result was that Westward confrontations continued well after the so-called "Pontiac's Uprising" and despite Iroquois condemnation. By 1768 it was clear to Onondaga that they could not control their supposed subordinates, and their power was at stake. This was embarrassing enough that, despite disagreements relative to the Kanawha and Tennessee rivers, they finally agreed to make peace with Cherokees in 1768.[45] William Johnson provided a telling description of the Iroquois position. "I must say," he wrote to George Croghan, "I never See the Six Nations so hearty in any thing, as in this Peace."[46] Less than a year later, Cherokees returned to Iroquoia to encourage their new allies "to join their Arms with yours against Several Tribes of Western & Southern Indians Enemies to both."[47] It seemed that Westward inter-tribal efforts were leading directly to another form of inter-tribal alliance.

Cherokees also pushed the British for greater support in challenging Westward attacks. At the Hard Labour Congress in October 1768 – where Cherokees ceded a large swath of land in return for firm promises that the new boundary would be secure from white encroachment – Overhill headman, Oconostota, informed John Stuart that Westward Indians represented the major Indian threat to Cherokee country.[48] They had "shut their Ears to the Talks of their Father Sir William Johnson," he explained, "and continue to strike us." Like Kittagusta and Alexander Cameron before him, Oconostota observed that "it is not us alone who they strike the white people's blood runs as well as ours they make no distinction." Only a few days before the Indian Congress at Hard Labour, in fact, "they killd a great man of our Nation and a white Trader near Great Telico." He finished with a rhetorical flourish: "Father," he said, "I am much beaten by those Western Indians the Piankashaws, Youghtanous, Twightwees, Kickapous, Meamis, Otowawas and other western Nations [and] you are struck by them also." Although he had agreed once before to "Sit still whilst a peace was Negotiating with them," now was the time for aggression.[49]

Stuart understood quite well that western Indians "were in an Hostile State with us, as well as [Cherokees], [an opinion] Confirmed by Intelligence of their Behavior on the Ohio, and at the Illinois."[50] Thus he told Oconostota what he wanted to hear: go on the offensive (albeit without direct British military support). Although William Johnson had the final say because of his "jurisdiction over the western nations," he nevertheless advised that Cherokees could not "remain passive and Suffer your people and Traders to be killed with Impunity."[51] Overhill headmen did not need another invitation. At a conference at Congarees, South Carolina, in 1770, Oconostota informed Stuart that Cherokees had sent parties to attack "Piankashaws and other Western Tribes." Stuart responded positively and reinforced his delight at the Cherokee–Six Nation alliance, telling Oconostota that "You are certainly right to strengthen Yourselves by Joining with the Northern Indians against them."[52]

The British also proved willing to use British-Iroquois-Cherokee diplomacy as a tool to threaten Westward polities. In 1769, Lieutenant John Wilkins explained to an Indigenous congress at Vincennes that the British had too long "endured the evil actions of a number of his ill disposed Children." They were tired, he said, of "their bad Conduct toward their Fathers in many different parts of the Country & particular … on the Wabash & Ohio Rivers." He informed his audience that Iroquois, Shawnees, and Lenapes, "as well as the Cherokees & Chikesaws to the Southward, are now but one People with their Fathers the English."[53] He then delivered an ultimatum: rein in Westward warriors and give immediate evidence of having done so. Otherwise, the British would interpret it "as an open Declaration of War, and shall directly send an Account thereof to the great King your Father, and to all the Indians with whom We are in Friendship, all of whom are now ready to join us in Extirpating you from the face of the Earth."[54] Wilkins and his military commanders were well aware that they were in no position to make such threats, and Westward Indians knew it. When they called their bluff, the British could do little about it.

Clearly, the British empire got a lot more than it bargained for when it signed off on the 1763 Paris Peace Treaty. Trans-Appalachia was an Indigenous world, and one Britons simply could not control.

EASTERN LAND ENCROACHMENT

Imperial North American leaders understood that Indian alliances were critical to whatever control they might eventually assert in the West, but were frustrated that said alliances continually were undermined by eastern colonials. Whites, it seemed, were not concerned with diplomatic balance. They wanted land, and they grounded their right to it in prevailing theories of natural law. The seventeenth-century philosophy of John Winthrop and John Locke certainly imparted foundational ideas, but eighteenth-century author Emmerich de Vattel spelled out their position. "The savages of North America had no right to appropriate all that vast continent to themselves," he wrote in the *Law of Nations*, "and since they were unable to inhabit the whole of those regions, other nations might without injustice settle in some parts of them, provided they left the natives a sufficiency of land."[55]

Colonial land speculators could not have agreed more. The boundary line established in the 1763 Royal Proclamation thus came under challenge almost as soon as it was announced. It put British officials on the defensive at precisely the moment when Ohio Valley Indian affairs grew beyond their jurisdictional ability to control. Indian congresses, such as those at Fort Stanwix, Hard Labour, and Lochaber, were convened to alleviate pressure, to be sure, by offering whites more land while simultaneously assuring Indians that encroachment would go no further. Much to the chagrin of North American officials, however, colonists promptly ignored the new boundaries in pursuit of individual interests.

By 1772, the situation was becoming dire, as General Thomas Gage made clear. "I am sorry you find Reason every where to complain of the fraudulent and bad Practices of the Traders, which I wish was in my Power to remedy," he wrote to John Stuart regarding Cherokee affairs.

> I have heard of those Complaints as long as I have heared of America, and tho' various schemes have been formed to put the

> Trade under proper Restrictions, the old Complaints continue, and I despair of seeing it upon a good Footing. You have had much Trouble as well as Sir Willm Johnson in settling the Boundarys throughout the Continent and a large Sum it has Cost the Government … The People in some Places have already passed the Boundarys, the Indians Complain of their Building and planting beyond the Line, and they talk of making Purchases of considerable Extent of the Indians beyond the Limits fixed in 1768.[56]

Western realities had further unravelled by the time parliament passed the Quebec Act in 1774. At that moment, Virginians led by Governor John Murray, Earl Dunmore, attempted to assert control over the area around the confluence of the Great Kanawha and Ohio rivers. In the process, they initiated a war with Shawnees that General Gage felt was nearly criminal. He insisted in early 1775 that northern Indian superintendent Guy Johnson inform Shawnees and Lenapes that it "was Intirely a War with that Province, [and] that none of the Kings troops had appeared against them." He also wanted it made clear that "his Majesty was not pleased with the Virginians for what they had done."[57]

Gage's headaches increased when word reached him that Virginian Richard Henderson's Transylvania Company had "purchased" twenty-seven-thousand square miles of the southern Ohio Valley from the Cherokees.[58] Although no Indians specifically lived on this land, the white settlement that resulted threatened to devastate hunting grounds by allowing free-ranging livestock to reduce canebreaks and grasses that indigenous animals used for shelter. A few years later Cherokee headman The Tassel informed United States commissioners that Henderson was a "liar," who had forged Cherokee names on the deeds to the purchase.[59] Although Virginia, North Carolina, and the British empire all rejected Henderson's purchase, the damage was done.

Confrontations between Cherokees, the Six Nations, and Westward Indians. Land encroachment and corruption from the east. By the time the Quebec Act became public knowledge in North America, the Ohio Valley was in flames. For people like Gage, Johnson, and Stuart, something had to be done.

INDIANS AND THE DEBATE OVER CENTRALIZED POWER IN BRITISH NORTH AMERICA

In Johnson's opinion, the root of these problems was easily identifiable: colonial oversight of Indian affairs. The provinces undermined the empire, he believed, because they focused too much on individual interests when "The General Interests of the Whole, & the Security of Peace on the Frontiers is what alone should be pursued."[60] It was hardly a new idea. Over the previous two decades several intellectuals had suggested that thirteen separate Indian policies were incoherent collectively. In 1754, Benjamin Franklin had even provided a blueprint for rectifying the problem. In his "Albany Plan of Union" he called for a North American "President General" with the power to "hold or direct all Indian treaties, in which the general interest of the Colonies may be concerned, and make peace or declare war with Indian nations." He proposed a legislative council, meanwhile, that would "make such laws as they judge necessary for regulating all Indian trade." Anticipating the powers asserted in the October 1763 Royal Proclamation, Franklin also called for a Grand Council to "make all purchases from Indians, for the crown, of lands not now within the bounds of particular Colonies, or that shall not be within their bounds when some of them are reduced to more convenient dimensions."[61]

Franklin's model created a North American governing body, to be sure, but the centralizing impulse is striking. It stripped significant control from the colonies by establishing an executive independent of local funding. It empowered a governing authority that was subject to crown oversight. And after its universal rejection, Franklin concluded that the colonies lacked the wherewithal to protect their – or imperial – interests. As he complained to Peter Collinson, "Every Body cries, a Union is absolutely necessary; but when they come to the Manner and Form of the Union, their weak Noddles are presently distracted. So if ever there be an Union, it must be form'd at home by the Ministry and Parliament."[62]

Imperial officials increasingly agreed. In 1757, the Earl of Loudoun bluntly asserted that "The King has seen that His Indian Interest has been lost in a great measure, by the management of the different Provinces, in whose hands it was originally placed." As a result, he explained to Pennsylvania governor, William Denny, the king had embarked on a new policy: he "appointed two persons with large Salarys for the Management of Indian affairs, one for the Northern Indians, and the other for the Southern, with Orders to the Commander in Chief to supply them with money, to Inspect into their Conduct and give Proper directions to them."[63] Imperial negotiators encouraged even greater centralization only seven years thereafter, at the Augusta Congress between Southern Indians and North and South Carolina, Virginia, and Georgia. At that point, the southern governors plus John Stuart insisted to the Earl of Egremont, secretary of state for the Southern Department, that the ministry had a golden opportunity "for ... establishing the Commerce with Indians upon a general safe equitable footing." As Franklin had suggested, however, it would have to come from above: such measures, they believed, "will never be done by respective Provinces."[64] Around that same moment, William Johnson informed General Gage that he was "much concerned at the backwardness of the Provinces, but 'tis no more than may be expected from their different Interests & Sentiments." It was a sad-but-true fact, he thought: the colonies would never make Indian diplomacy "a common cause."[65]

The 1763 Royal Proclamation provided a good launching point for reforming Indian policy. While it left room for subsequent boundary alterations, the language of the proclamation was clear: until the "Royal Pleasure be known," colonies were not to issue trans-Appalachian land grants. Colonial officials also were to ensure that Indians "not be molested or disturbed in the Possession of such Parts of our Dominions and Territories as, having been ceded or purchased by us, are reserved to them, or any of them, as their Hunting Grounds." The proclamation further outlawed individual land purchases, and to stabilize commerce it required that trade licences would have to come from royal governors.[66] Even if impermanent, the proclamation clearly intended that the colonies operate within imperial parameters.[67]

Pontiac's Uprising, Ohio Valley chaos, and abrogation of Indian Treaty rights further justified oversight. Greater power thus was granted to Indian superintendents to regulate and control trade (and migration) – which undermined the ability of individual colonies to hide behind laissez-faire attitudes. New boundaries were encouraged, but the ministry upbraided colonial leaders who did not do enough to stop fraudulent encroachments. A mid-1760s set of instructions from the king to North Carolina governor, William Tryon, for example, observed that "Indians ... make great Complaints that Settlements have been made and Possession taken of Lands the Property of which they have by Treaties reserved to themselves." Particularly galling to His Majesty's government was that the "Chief Officers of Our said Colonies, regardless of the Duty they Owe to Us and of the Welfare and Security of Our Colonies, have Countenanced such unjust Claims and Pretensions by passing Grants of the Lands so pretended to have been purchased of the Indians." Directly violating the proclamation in such a manner would have "fatal Effects [and] would attend to a Discontent amongst the Indians in the present situation of Affairs," the ministry informed Tryon. Understanding that danger, the crown had decided that it would "upon all Occasions ... support and protect the said Indians in their just Rights and Possessions, and keep Inviolable the Treaties and Compacts which have been Entered into with them." Translation: colonies had to stop exacerbating a western situation already beyond British control and respect the rule of law.[68]

Some colonial officials made attempts to fall into line. In 1765, for example, Virginia's Governor Francis Fauquier issued a proclamation offering a hundred-pound reward for the capture of a group of "villains" who had attacked and killed a Cherokee delegation on their way to Winchester. He argued that their actions were "in Violation of the Treaties ... between that Nation and us," and moreover that it destroyed Virginia's "Honour."[69] Three years thereafter, John Wilkins informed General Gage that the Pennsylvania Assembly had "passd an Act to make it a Capital Offence to any white man that shall Settle on the Indians lands."[70] And in 1774, East Florida governor, Patrick Tonyn, informed John Stuart that he had directed his attorney general "to take out a Writ against [a corrupt trader] for a Contempt of the Kings Prerogative and another for a Trespass on the Kings Land with ten Thousand Pounds damages."

Unfortunately for officials like Stuart and Gage, governors tended not to follow through, and the metropole chose not to sustain the momentum.[71] After five years of unsuccessful efforts to secure jurisdiction in the Ohio Valley, inconsistent diplomacy with trans-Appalachian Indians, spotty support from colonies, and the maintenance of fortifications of limited value, in 1768 Lord Hillsborough, secretary of state for American affairs, decided that Indian diplomacy and western garrisons drained too many imperial resources. They directly affected the already-contentious North American debate over debt, taxation, and constitutional liberty, so Hillsborough chose to retrench: garrisons deemed unnecessary were closed, those remaining open faced careful financial scrutiny, and limits were called for on diplomatic expenditures. Perhaps most ominously, Hillsborough scaled back superintendent support staffs and transferred significant authority over trade and Indian affairs back to provincial authorities.

Retrenchment reimposed greater colonial control at a moment when imperial power should have been consolidating, argued men like Gage, Stuart, and Johnson. A frustrated General Gage exclaimed to Johnson that "Our concerns with Indians, are now greatly extended by our acquisitions in the late war & we seem to have occasion, for some settled, uniform system, for the management of Indian Affairs. The number of your Deputies, Interpreters &c should be increased, and the several nations with whom they are to deal, allotted to them." Given its lack of stability, the Ohio Valley particularly needed support. "To begin at Detroit, and take in the whole Country," he observed, "and by the Illinois River to Fort Chartres, and from thence down the Mississippi, and up the Ohio to Fort Pitt, seems the best tract of Country immediately under our Consideration."[72] It is worth noting that his boundaries correspond to those established in the Quebec Act.

William Johnson's nephew Guy believed that retrenchment was hopelessly naive. "I cannot help observing," he remarked to Gage, "That the principle upon which [Hillsborough's order] seems founded, That the Colonies will manage better and be more cautious in preventing frauds in Trade at this day than formerly, when under greater Apprehensions from the Indians, does not seem to promise all that their Lordships Expect from it."[73] Inevitably, the policy would lead to a more corrupt and fraudulent – and thus far more precarious – relationship with the Indians.

As noted earlier, events on the ground bore out his fears. Indian diplomats understood quite well the implications of such overwhelming British imperial confusion, as an exchange between William Johnson and the Six Nations reveals. During a March 1768 conference, Iroquois delegates informed Johnson that, although he represented "a Government and Laws[,] you don't prevent [land fraud]." They found it ironic: "you often tell us we don't restrain our people, and that you do so with yours," they observed, but "your Words differ more from your Actions than ours do."[74] If an empire built on written laws could not make its "People do what they are desired [and] prevent all this, and if they wont let us alone you should shake them by the head." Or perhaps, suggested Six Nations delegates, the government had "no Mind to hinder them?" If so, they would do it on behalf of the British. After all, Haudenosaunee "Legs are long and our

Sight is good, that we can see a great way thro the Woods; We can see the Blood you have spilled and the Fences you have made, and surely it is but right that we should punish those who have done us all this Mischief."[75]

The Six Nations also expressed dismay on behalf of their new ally to the south, noting that provincial "boundary lines around Cherokees have surrounded and stifled them."[76] Cherokees agreed wholeheartedly. At the Hard Labour Congress, John Stuart had promised their delegates that, after the boundaries between Virginia and Cherokee Country were finalized, "you may rest satisfied that none of his Majesty's Subjects shall with Impunity violate the Treaty now entered into by invading your Rights."[77] Two years later, he had to admit the hollowness of that declaration. Virginians were undermining the Hard Labour boundary, and Stuart was outraged. "His Majesty's instructions render it my Duty to Endeavour to see justice done you," he insisted,

> and his Express orders prevent my Ratifying any other Boundary Line, than what he has been pleased to point out. I have humbly submitted to His Majesty's Ministers my Sentiments on the pretensions of the province of Virginia, and wait for further Instructions which as soon as I receive shall be Communicated to you in the mean Time the Line agreed upon at Hard Labour the 14 October 1768 remains valid & is the true Boundary.[78]

Stuart was equally frustrated with the Cherokees, however: by the 1770s some had begun selling land directly to individual colonists (such as Richard Henderson), which violated the 1763 Royal Proclamation, was contrary to the spirit of the Hard Labour Congress, and rendered "Ineffectual the orders given by the King to prevent Encroachment on your Hunting Grounds." Cherokees, he insisted, should deal only with imperial authority – not the provinces or locals. Otherwise, "If irregular people who settle on such Lands by your permission behave ill you are not to Complain or to expect any Redress from us."[79]

Oconostota did not disagree, but blamed "Virginians" for coveting land at the expense of fairness and diplomatic balance. "They are always renewing their Demands, and are never satisfied," he observed. And despite their promises, they never followed through on sharing "their Bounty." The remedy, he suggested, was for the empire to re-take control of the diplomatic ground.[80] Its representatives, after all, remembered imperial obligations, while "the Virginians pretend to have forgotten what was said at Augusta and agreed upon at Hard Labour."[81] Oconostota concluded by hammering Stuart for Hillsborough's policy shift, noting that "when we had a Commissary in the Nation, he governed the Traders and assisted by the Ruling Chiefs, drove away Rogues and Vagabonds, but now they Laugh at us."[82]

To the Cherokees Stuart could only register his unhappiness with colonial behaviour. To parliament and Hillsborough's replacement, Lord Dartmouth, however, he (and others) pressed their conviction that only centralized power could stabilize the West and bring order to the North American Empire. By 1772 they were making headway. At that moment colonial authorities were refusing to establish more unified rules for Indian Trade. William Johnson was fed up, and sincerely hoped that "The King [would take] Indian Affairs & their Expences upon himself."[83] Fortunately for people who shared his perspective, parliament had come to agree: in 1773 Lord Dartmouth decided that "The failure of the colonies to legislate for the Indian trade, the withdrawal of the interior garrisons, and the increased tensions with the tribes in the face of continuous encroachments" had forced the ministry to rethink its Western policy.[84] Centralizing Indian affairs once again was on the table as a means of reducing the flames in the Ohio Valley. It found legal expression in the Quebec Act.

In 1774 Quebec, Governor Guy Carleton observed that the Quebec Act brought to North America the very thing that people like Benjamin Franklin, Stuart, Gage, and Johnson had encouraged for the better part of three decades: a "legal authority [to] enforce order so as to conduct Indian trade."[85] Member of Parliament Alexander Wedderburn had explained it quite well in the House of Commons: the Act was a permanent solution to the impermanence of the 1763 Proclamation because it gave Americans a boundary "beyond which, for the advantage of the whole empire, [they] shall not extend."[86] Individuals could no longer subvert the interests of the whole. William Knox, undersecretary of state for the colonies, reinforced the point, noting that the new boundaries existed "for the avowed purpose of excluding all further settlement" in trans-Appalachia.[87] Although the Act mentioned the Ohio Valley only in Article I, Knox believed that the Quebec legislature had the authority to round out parliament's intent. In addition to stopping encroachment, it would establish "uniform regulations for the Indian trade ... competent to enforce such regulations, [as the] administration is pledged to recommend." Knox was unequivocal: limiting individual and colonial corruption in favour of the general imperial good was one of "the first objects upon which the legislative powers shall be exercised." And should the Quebec legislature falter in its duty, "parliament will not fail to apply an adequate remedy."[88]

Given the chaotic nature of colonial Indian policy, many believed the North Americans would embrace this imperial alteration.[89] They were wrong, of course. The Quebec Act was the victim of poor timing: its centralizing tendency ran exactly counter to the radical arguments gaining steam in the thirteen seaboard colonies. In 1774, parliament had passed its series of "coercive" acts in response to the December 1773 outburst in Boston Harbor, the consequence of which was to put many colonists in a defensive posture and to lend credence to conspiracies of British tyranny. Rather than viewing the Quebec Act as a means by which to stabilize the West, colonists saw it as a loathsome example of legislative despotism: not only did it extend toleration to Catholics and French law codes to the Canadiens, it also closed off valuable land from Americans interested in speculation, sale, and migration. An empire of liberty was developing, as historian Eric Hinderaker has noted, that was rooted in land acquisition and cared little for Indian alliances.[90] In such an environment the Quebec Act was a dead letter. As armed resistance gave way to rebellion on the eastern seaboard, western stability collapsed entirely.[91]

Because of events subsequent to 1774, American historians have had a tendency to overlook the importance of the Quebec Act's boundary regulations. It is worth noting, however, that the impulse to centralize Indian diplomacy did not disappear as the American War of Independence unfolded. Articles VI and IX of the Articles of Confederation specifically placed Indian affairs within the jurisdiction of the central government.[92] If political scientist David Hendrickson is correct that the Articles represent the American leadership's idealized conception of the British empire, then they too saw merit in the powers invoked by the Quebec Act.[93] It was a power with which the republic would struggle for decades thereafter.

NOTES

1 Key historiography on the trans-Appalachian west between 1763 and 1776 include Colin Calloway, *The Scratch of a Pen: 1763 and the Transformation of America* (New York: Oxford University Press, 2006); Gregory

Evans Dowd, *A Spirited Resistance: The North American Indian Struggle for Unity, 1745–1815* (Baltimore: Johns Hopkins University Press, 1992); François Furstenberg, "The Significance of the Trans-Appalachian Frontier in Atlantic History," *American Historical Review* 113, no. 3 (June 2008): 647–77; Kathleen DuVal, *The Native Ground: Indians and Colonists in the Heart of the Continent* (Philadelphia: University of Pennsylvania Press, 2006); Daniel Usner, *Indians, Settlers, and Slaves in a Frontier Exchange Economy: The Lower Mississippi Valley before 1783* (Chapel Hill: University of North Carolina Press, 1992); Eric Hinderaker, *Elusive Empires: Constructing Colonialism in the Ohio Valley, 1670–1800* (New York: Cambridge University Press, 1997); Patrick Griffin, *American Leviathan: Empire, Nation, and Revolutionary Frontier* (New York: Hill and Wang, 2007); Cynthia Cumfer, *Separate Peoples, One Land: The Minds of Cherokees, Blacks, and Whites on the Tennessee Frontier* (Chapel Hill: University of North Carolina Press, 2007); Kristofer Ray, *Cherokees, Europeans, and Empire in the Trans-Appalachian West, 1670–1774* (Norman, OK: University of Oklahoma Press, under contract); Kristofer Ray, ed., *Before the Volunteer State: New Thoughts on Early Tennessee History, 1670–1800* (Knoxville: University of Tennessee Press, December 2014); Michael McDonnell, *Masters of Empire: Great Lakes Indians and the Making of America* (New York: Hill and Wang, 2015); and Michael Witgen, *An Infinity of Nations: How the Native New World Shaped Early America* (Philadelphia: University of Pennsylvania Press, 2012).

2 For more on "Pontiac's War," see Gregory Evans Dowd, *War under Heaven: Pontiac, the Indian Nations, and the British Empire* (Baltimore: Johns Hopkins University Press, 2002).

3 Recent historiography on the *pays des Illinois* includes Robert Morrisey, *Empire by Collaboration: Indians, Colonists, and Governments in Colonial Illinois Country* (Philadelphia: University of Pennsylvania Press, 2015); M.J. Morgan, *Land of Big Rivers: French and Indian Illinois* (Carbondale, IL: Southern Illinois University Press, 2010); Jacob Lee, *Masters of the Middle Waters: Indian Nations and Colonial Ambitions along the Mississippi River* (Cambridge, MA: Harvard University Press, 2019); Karl Ekberg, *French Roots in the Illinois Country: The Mississippi Frontier in Colonial Times* (Urbana: University of Illinois Press, 2000); and Robert Englebert and Guillaume Teasdale, eds, *French and Indians in the Heart of North America, 1630–1815* (Lansing: Michigan State University Press, 2013).

4 Because of the complexity of geographic designations, I have chosen to use the labels that eighteenth-century Indians typically used to explain locations of origin. Westward most commonly referred to Anishnaabeg,

Illinois, Piankeshaws, Kickapoos, Shawnees, and Lenapes. Northward typically meant the Haudenosaunee and Mississaugas. Southward could refer to Cherokees, Catawbas, Chickasaws, Creeks, or Choctaws.

5 John Cartwright's 1774 description of territorial names of Indian groups is standard European fare with a twist – it recognizes Indigenous polities while placing them within strict boundaries created outside their communities. Few Native societies would have recognized the features of this map or acknowledged the limitations on mobility that it suggests. It also is an implicit recognition of Indigenous sovereignty that the British accepted, but over which the American republic would struggle. For more on the issue of independent Indigenous polities, see Kristofer Ray, "'The Indians of every denomination were free, and independent of us': Anglo-American Explorations of Indian Slavery, Freedom, and Society in Virginia, 1772–1830," *American Nineteenth Century History* 17, no. 2 (Summer 2016): 139–59; Kristofer Ray, "Constructing a Discourse of Indigenous Slavery, Freedom, and Sovereignty in Anglo-Virginia, 1600–1750," *Native South* 10 (2017): 19–39; Honor Sachs, "'Freedom by a Judgment': The Legal History of an Afro-Indian Family," *Law and History Review* 30, no. 1 (Feb. 2012); and Gregory Ablavsky, "Making Indians White: The Judicial Abolition of Native Slavery in Revolutionary Virginia and Its Racial Legacy," *University of Pennsylvania Law Review* 159, no. 5 (April 2011): 1457–531.

6 For more on this point, see the writings of men like Benjamin Franklin, Archibald Kennedy, Edmond Atkin, John Stuart, William Johnson, James Glen, and Robert Dinwiddie, to name just a few. See also Timothy Shannon, *Indians and Colonists at the Crossroads of Empire* (Ithaca, NY: Cornell University Press, 2000); and Dowd, *War under Heaven*.

7 Jack Sosin, *Whitehall and Wilderness: The Middle West in British Colonial Policy, 1760–1775* (Lincoln: University of Nebraska Press, 1961), 242.

8 James Glen to Thomas Robinson, 1754, in *Colonial Records of South Carolina: Documents Related to Indian Affairs, 1748–1754*, ed. William McDowell (Columbia, SC: South Carolina Department of Archives and History, 1958), 536 [hereafter cited as *DRIA* 1].

9 *DRIA* 1, 536. For more on the Tennessee River as Long Man, see, for example, James Mooney, "The Cherokee River Cult," *The Journal of American Folklore* 13, no. 48 (Jan.–Mar. 1900): 1–10; and Paul Kelton, *Cherokee Medicine, Colonial Germs: An Indigenous Nation's Fight against Smallpox, 1518–1824* (Norman, OK: University of Oklahoma Press, 2015). See also Gregory D. Smithers, "'Our Hands and Hearts are Joined Together':

Friendship, Colonialism, and the Cherokee People in Early America," *Journal of Social History* 50, no. 4 (2017): 609–29.

10 "Charles Town in America, July 17," *Gentleman's Magazine* 25 (Oct. 1755): 470, American Antiquarian Society Historical Periodicals Collection: Series 1. British officials explicitly connected Cherokee diplomacy with their interactions with the Iroquois Five Nations to the North. For more on this point, see Kristofer Ray, "Cherokees and Trans-Appalachian Empire in the British Imagination, 1670–1730," in *Before the Volunteer State*, ed. Kristofer Ray. See also Ray, "Cherokees and Franco-British Confrontation in the Tennessee Corridor, 1730–1760," *Native South* 7 (2014): 33–67. The British could strengthen their "claim" through the fact that their ally the Chickasaws also made great use of the western end of the corridor.

11 William Anderson and James Lewis, eds, *Guide to Cherokee Documents in Foreign Archives* (Lanham, MD: Scarecrow Press, 1995), 55 [hereafter cited as *GCDFA*].

12 William Ramsey, *The Yamasee War: A Study of Culture, Economy, and Conflict in the Colonial South* (Lincoln: University of Nebraska Press, 2010), 154.

13 *GCDFA*, 51.

14 Charles Town Council Chamber, Jan. 25, 1726/7, CO 5/387 084, British National Archives Online. www.colonialamerica.amdigital.co.uk.dartmouth.idm.oclc.org.

15 Article 15 of the 1713 Treaty of Utrecht. For more on the Six Nations in the Ohio Valley and Illinois, see Hinderaker, *Elusive Empires*; Jon Parmenter, *The Edge of the Woods: Iroquoia, 1534–1701* (Lansing, MI: Michigan State University Press, 2011); and Englebert and Teasdale, eds, *French and Indians in the Heart of North America*.

16 Their efforts culminated in a Cherokee delegation to London in 1730, and the "ratification" of a treaty of alliance. For more on this point, see Tyler Boulware, *Deconstructing the Cherokee Nation: Town, Region, and Nation among Eighteenth-Century Cherokees* (Gainesville: University Press of Florida, 2011); Ray, "Cherokees, Empire, and the Tennessee Corridor in the British Imagination, 1670–1730"; and Ray, "Cherokees and Franco-British Confrontation in the Tennessee Corridor."

17 Neal L. Trubowitz, "Native Americans and French on the Central Wabash," in *Calumet and Fleur-de-Lys: Archaeology of Indian and French Contact in the Midcontinent*, ed. John Walthall and Thomas Emerson (Washington: Smithsonian Institution Press, 1992), 243, 246. According

to Trubowitz, Mascoutens arrived around Ouiatenon in the 1740s. Trubowitz, 254.

18 For more on mobility from other Indigenous perspectives, see Witgen, *An Infinity of Nations*; McDonnell, *Masters of Empire*; and Stephen Warren, *The Worlds the Shawnees Made: Migration and Violence in the Ohio Valley* (Chapel Hill: University of North Carolina Press, 2014). See also Penelope Drooker, "The Ohio Valley, 1550–1750: Patterns of Sociopolitical Coalescence and Dispersal," in *The Transformation of the Southeastern Indians, 1540–1760*, ed. Robbie Ethridge and Charles Hudson, 115–34 (Oxford, MS: University of Mississippi Press, 2002).

19 McDonnell, *Masters of Empire*, 132.

20 Demere to Lyttelton, 2 March 1758, William H. Lyttelton Papers, William L. Clements Library [hereafter WLC].

21 Kerlerec to Berryer, 21 December 1760, in *Mississippi Provincial Archives*, vol. 4, ed. Patricia Galloway, Dunbar Rowland, and A.G. Sanders, 263 (Baton Rouge: Louisiana State University Press, 1984) [hereafter cited as *MPA 4*]; Kerlerec to Beryer, 12 June 1760, *MPA 4*, 252–3; Kerlerec to Berryer, Aug. 4, 1760, *MPA 4*, 260.

22 Kerlerec to the Ministre de la Marine, 24 June 1762, AC C13A/43, General Correspondence, Louisiana: 1762–63, Cherokee Documents in Foreign Archives Collection, Hunter Library, Western Carolina University.

23 Thomas Morris, "Journal of Trip to the Wabash, August 26–September 17, 1764," Papers of Thomas Gage, American Series, Vol. 138, WLC [hereafter cited as Gage Papers].

24 Gavin Cochrane to Thomas Gage, 10 October 1764, Gage Papers, Vol. 25.

25 Gage to John Stuart 19 June 1764, Gage Papers, Vol. 20.

26 Ibid.

27 Ibid. Cochrane explained that "Cherokees cannot be brought to employ their time at present, in cutting off the Supplies sent our enemies; they plead its being the hunting season & the great debts they have contracted with the Indian traders." Gavin Cochrane to Thomas Gage, 10 October 1764, Gage Papers, Vol. 25. Fortunately for Gage, negotiations at Detroit combined with an Ohio invasion by British forces to calm temporarily tensions related to "Pontiac's Rebellion" in 1765.

28 Kelton, *Cherokee Medicine, Colonial Germs*, 11, 109.

29 Ted Gragson and Paul Bolstad, "A Local Analysis of Early-Eighteenth-Century Cherokee Settlement," *Social Science History* 31, no. 3 (Fall 2007): 437–8.

30 Boulware, *Deconstructing the Cherokee Nation*, chap. 7; M. Thomas Hatley, *The Dividing Paths: Cherokees and South Carolinians through the Era of*

the Revolution (New York: Oxford University Press, 1993), 158–9; and John Oliphant, *Peace and War on the Anglo-Cherokee Frontier, 1756–1763* (Baton Rouge: Louisiana State University Press, 2001). Historiographically, Boulware does not focus upon the west, although his exploration of hunting spaces and on western raids anticipates the larger issues afoot. Hatley describes Oconostota as an isolationist, and leaves alone the activity taking place in the Ohio Valley well before the peace between the Cherokees and then Six Nations in 1768. Cherokee mobility from a central region resembles the pattern described by Jon Parmenter regarding Haudenosaunee. See Parmenter, *The Edge of the Woods.*

31 Fraser Report, Gage Papers, Vol. 137, 7–8.

32 Dowd, *War under Heaven*, 226.

33 Lagautrais to Farmar, undated early 1765 from Illinois, enclosed in Farmar to Gage, 13 April 1765, Gage Papers, Vol. 34.

34 Ibid.

35 Ibid.

36 In one notable example Cherokees took Creeks on an offensive campaign, although they had to stop when Creeks attempted to kill English fur trappers instead of Westward Indians. Extract of a Letter from Alex. Cameron Esq. Deputy Agent for Indian Affairs in the Cherokee Nation dated at Fort Prince George 10 May 1766, Great Britain Indian Department Collection, Box 1, WLC.

37 Quoted in John D. Nichols, "Alexander Cameron, British Agent among the Cherokee, 1764–1781," *South Carolina Historical Magazine* 97, no. 2 (April 1996): 97.

38 Kittagusta asked John Stuart to inform Onondaga "that the Cherokees send to ask for a Peace from their Town House in Chote where Peace has been made before, Belts of Whampum & Pipes exchanged & Tobacco smoaked." Proceedings at a Congress at Fort Prince George in the Cherokee Country, 8 May 1766, Great Britain Indian Department Collection, Box 1, WLC.

39 For more on Catawbas, see James Merrell, *The Indians' New World*; and Brooke Bauer, "This 'Inalienable' Land: The World of Sally New River, Catawba Indian, 1746–1840" (PhD Diss., University of North Carolina at Chapel Hill, 2016).

40 Perdue, "Cherokee Relations with the Iroquois in the Eighteenth Century," 135–50.

41 Ibid., 135.

42 Journal of the Superintendent's Proceedings of Congress held at Hard

Labour, South Carolina, 28 September–17 October 1768, Gage Papers, vol. 137, 4. See also Boulware, 143–4; and Hinderaker, *Elusive Empires*.

43 For more on the Fort Stanwix negotiations, see William J. Campbell, *Speculators in Empire: Iroquoia and the 1768 Treaty of Fort Stanwix* (Norman, OK: University of Oklahoma Press, 2012).

44 For more on Shawnee efforts in Cherokee Country, see for example Dowd, *A Spirited Resistance*; and Warren, *The Worlds the Shawnees Made*.

45 Oconostota explained the new alliance to John Stuart at the Congress at Hard Labour in October 1768. With the support of William Johnson, Cherokees had "met the chiefs of the Northern Tribes who were at war with us we buried the Hatchet and cleared the path of every thorn and obstacle that rendered it bad; some of the Northern Warriors are now at Chote sitting upon a White Seat." Speech of Oconostota, Journal of the Superintendent's Proceedings of Congress held at Hard Labour, South Carolina, 28 September–17 October 1768, Gage Papers, Vol. 137, 8.

46 Johnson to Croghan, 16 March 1768, as quoted in Campbell, *Speculators in Empire*, 238n59.

47 Speech of John Stuart, Proceedings of a Congress of the principal Chiefs and Warriors of the Cherokee Nation with John Stuart held at Congarees, South Carolina, 3 April 1770, Gage Papers, Vol. 137, 3.

48 Regarding land, Oconostota informed Stuart that after the boundaries were perfected to the Kanawha River he would "dig a deep ditch" over which whites could not pass. Journal of the Superintendent's Proceedings of Congress held at Hard Labour, South Carolina, 28 September–17 October 1768, Gage Papers, Vol. 137, 6.

49 Speech of Oconostota, Journal of the Superintendent's Proceedings of Congress held at Hard Labour, South Carolina, 28 September–17 October 1768, Gage Papers, Vol. 137, 8.

50 This particular statement, although about 1768, was part of a 1770 speech. Speech of John Stuart, Proceedings of a Congress of the principal Chiefs and Warriors of the Cherokee Nation with John Stuart held at Congarees, South Carolina, 3 April 1770, Gage Papers, Vol. 137, 3.

51 Speech of John Stuart, Journal of the Superintendent's Proceedings of Congress held at Hard Labour, South Carolina. 28 September–17 October 1768, Gage Papers, Vol. 137, 10.

52 Ibid., 16.

53 Wilkins Speech to the Indians at Post Vincent, Wabash, & Ohio Rivers, Great Britain Indian Department Collection, Box 1, WLC.

54 Ibid.

55 Quoted in Ray "The Indians of every denomination were free and independent of us"; Emmerich de Vattel, *The Law of Nations*, ed. by Bela Kapossy and Richard Whatmore (1758; reprint Indianapolis: Liberty Fund, 2008), Book 2, chapter 7, 310. See also Winthrop, "Reasons to be Considered for justifying the Undertakers of the intended Plantation in New England and for Encouraging Such Whose Hearts God Shall Move to Join Them in It (1629)," Massachusetts Historical Society *Proceedings* 8 (1864–65, 420–5); and Locke, *Two Treatises of Government*, ed. Peter Laslett (New York: Cambridge University Press, 1960).

56 Thomas Gage to John Stuart, 21 June 1772, Gage Papers, Vol. 112.

57 Gage to Johnson, 5 February 1775, Gage Papers, Vol. 125.

58 On Dunmore's War, see Woody Holton, *Forced Founders*; and James Corbett David, *Dunmore's New World: The Extraordinary Life of a Royal Governor in Revolutionary America* (Charlottesville, VA: University of Virginia Press, 2015). For more on Henderson and the Transylvania Company, see Stephen Aron, *How the West Was Lost* (Baltimore: Johns Hopkins University Press, 1997); Marjoleine Kars, *Breaking Loose Together: The Regulator Rebellion in Pre-Revolutionary North Carolina* (Chapel Hill: University of North Carolina Press, 2002); Mark Miller, "Richard Henderson: The Making of a Land Speculator" (MA thesis, University of North Carolina at Chapel Hill, 1975); and Natalie Inman, "Military Families: Kinship in the American Revolution," in *Before the Volunteer State*, ed. Kristofer Ray, 131–54.

59 "Talk by Old Tassel," in *American State Papers, Class II, Indian Affairs*, ed. Walter Lowrie and Arthur St Clair Clarke, vol. 1, 42 (Washington, DC: Gales and Seaton, 1932), https://memory.loc.gov/ammem/amlaw/lwsplink.html. See also David Andrew Nichols, "Red Gentlemen and White Savages: Indian Relations and Political Culture after the American Revolution, 1784–1800" (PhD diss., University of Kentucky, 2000), 87.

60 Johnson to Gage, 23 April 1768, Gage Papers, Vol. 76.

61 Albany Plan of Union 1754, Articles 10–12, http://avalon.law.yale.edu/18th_century/albany.asp#1. For more on this point see Timothy Shannon, *Indians and Colonists at the Crossroads of Empire*.

62 Franklin to Collinson, 29 December 1754, in Leonard Labaree et al., eds, *The Papers of Benjamin Franklin*, vol. 5 (New Haven, CT: Yale University Press, 1959): 453–4.

63 Earl of Loudoun to William Denny, 5 May 1757, in the Loudoun Papers, Box 77 #3562, Huntington Library, San Marino, CA. The original Indian Superintendents were Sir William Johnson for the north and

Edmond Atkin for the south. Upon the latter's death in 1761, John Stuart became Southern Indian Superintendent.

64 Wright, Dobbs, Fauquier, Boone, and Stuart to Egremont, 10 November 1763, in the Minutes of the Southern Congress at Augusta Georgia, 1 October 1763–21 November 1763, *Colonial Records of North Carolina*, Vol. 11, 205. Available at http://docsouth.unc.edu/csr/.

65 William Johnson to Gage, 14 April 1764, Gage Papers, Vol. 17.

66 The Royal Proclamation – 7 October 1763, http://avalon.law.yale.edu/18th_century/proc1763.asp.

67 For more on the proclamation, see Calloway, *The Scratch of a Pen*.

68 "Copy Kings Instruction to the Gov[r] No. 109 respecting Indian lands, ca. 1760–1775," British Public Records, ca. 1600–1782 [manuscript], Southern Historical Collection #517, Unit 2, University of North Carolina at Chapel Hill. To drive home the point further, the ministry instructed that neither Tryon nor any other official in North Carolina "do upon any pretence whatever upon pain of Our highest Displeasure, and of being forthwith removed from Your or his Office, pass any Grant or Grants to any Persons whatever of any Lands within or adjacent to the Territories possessed or occupied by the said Indians or the Property or Possession of which has at any Time been reserved to or claimed by them." The colony also would have to proclaim publicly that squatters would be removed from Indian land, and, so that no misunderstandings would arise, North Carolina would have to publicize "amongst the several Tribes of Indians living within the [Province] to the End that Our Royal Will and Pleasure in the Premises may be made known, and that the Indians may be apprized of Our determined Resolution to support them in their just Rights." Subsequent violators would suffer prosecution for their transgressions.

69 By the Hon. Francis Fauquier, Esq., His Majesty's lieutenant-governour, and commander in chief of the said colony and dominion: a proclamation, 17 May 1765, Early American Imprints, Series I, #41593.

70 Abstract of Patrick Tonyn, Gov. of East Florida [to John Stuart], 18 December 1774, enclosed in Stuart to Thomas Gage, 18 January 1775, Gage Papers, Vol. 125, 25 December 1774–10 February 1775. John Wilkins to Gage, 18 February 1768, Gage Papers, Vol. 74.

71 A perfect example comes from the Hard Labour Congress of 1768. Despite Fauquier's proclamation, Virginia did nothing to condole Cherokees for the murders. It so frustrated people from the town of Chilowee that in 1768 they took their own form of retribution by killing a group of Virginians travelling through Cherokee Country on

the way to the Mississippi River. Stuart expressed his dismay, but Oconostota stood firm: if the British would do nothing to provide relief for their deaths, Cherokees would seek their own justice. See Hard Labour Congress, Gage Papers, Vol. 137. For more on Cherokee justice in the eighteenth century, see Boulware, *Deconstructing the Cherokee Nation*; Hatley, *The Dividing Paths*; and John Philip Reid, *A Law of Blood: The Primitive Law of the Cherokee Nation* (New York: New York University Press, 1970).

72 Gage to Johnson, 14 October 1768, Gage Papers, Vol. 125.

73 Guy Johnson to Thomas Gage, 16 June 1768, Gage Papers, Vol. 78.

74 Iroquois-Cherokee Congress, Gage Papers, Vol. 75.

75 Ibid., 19.

76 Ibid.

77 Hard Labour Congress, 9.

78 Speech of John Stuart, Proceedings of a Congress of the principal Chiefs and Warriors of the Cherokee Nation with John Stuart held at Congarees, South Carolina, 3 April 1770, Gage Papers, Vol. 137, 6.

79 Ibid., 6–7.

80 Specifically, he expressed his "desire [that] my Father may get this matter settled for us, and the Line marked agreeable to Treaty."

81 Speech of Oconostota, Proceedings of a Congress of the principal Chiefs and Warriors of the Cherokee Nation with John Stuart held at Congarees, South Carolina, 3 April 1770, Gage Papers Vol. 137, 9–10.

82 Ibid., 11.

83 Johnson to Gage, 20 January 1772, Gage Papers, Vol. 109.

84 Sosin, *Whitehall and the Wilderness*, 238.

85 Ibid., 246. Supporters of the Act believed that Britons at home would benefit from it as well. Prime Minister Lord North, for example, explained to parliament that London merchants supported the Act because they "felt that they could not conduct the Indian trade with safety as long as the interior remained outside the jurisdiction of some civil authority." Ibid., 244.

86 Ibid., 245.

87 Knox, William. *The justice and policy of the late act of Parliament for making more effectual provision for the government of the province of Quebec asserted ...* London, 1774. *Sabin Americana*. Gale, Cengage Learning, 43. http://galenet.galegroup.com.ezproxy.lib.apsu.edu/servlet/Sabin?af=RN&ae=CY105992355&srchtp=a&ste=14.

88 Knox, 44–5, 47.

89 William Johnson insisted, for example, that locals were no longer "very

desirous of meddling" with Indian affairs and would welcome a re-application of crown control. Johnson to Gage, 20 Jan. 1772, Gage Papers, Vol. 109.

90 Eric Hinderaker, *Elusive Empires*. See also Furstenberg, "The Significance of the Trans-Appalachian Frontier in Atlantic History"; and Peter Silver, *Our Savage Neighbors: How Indian War Transformed Early America* (New York: Norton, 2008).

91 In *American Leviathan*, Patrick Griffin describes the west as nearly Hobbesian, and suggests that a strong central power was necessary to stabilize it in the 1790s. See also Kristofer Ray, *Middle Tennessee, 1775–1825: Progress and Popular Democracy on the Southwestern Frontier* (Knoxville: University of Tennessee Press, 2007).

92 Articles of Confederation, Yale Law School Avalon Project, http://avalon.law.yale.edu/18th_century/artconf.asp.

93 David Hendrickson, "The First Union: Nationalism versus Internationalism in the American Revolution," in *Empire and Nation: The American Revolution in the Atlantic World*, ed. Peter Onuf and Eliga Gould, 35–53 (Baltimore: Johns Hopkins University Press, 2005). See also, Hendrickson, *Peace Pact: The Lost World of the American Founding* (Lawrence: University Press of Kansas, 2003).

10

The Quebec Act and the Indigenous Land Issue in Canada

Alain Beaulieu

The beginnings of the British regime occupy a central place in the legal debates of the past years on the rights of the Indigenous peoples of Canada. The decision of the Canadian government to include in the Constitution Act of 1982 special protections for treaty rights and the rights resulting from the Royal Proclamation of 1763 contributed to this phenomenon.[1] Since then, several cases have been heard, especially in Eastern Canada and Quebec, and important decisions have radically changed Canadian jurisprudence relating to the rights of the First Nations.[2] The Royal Proclamation plays a significant role in the legal discussions regarding these rights. Since the nineteenth century, this document has become an essential symbol of British Indian policy, as the mark of their desire to protect the rights of the Indigenous peoples, and even as a sign of their willingness to deal with them as equals.[3]

There is obviously a good deal of idealization in the legal – but also political – discourses on this document, around which a kind of mythology has been created. This probably derives in part from a lack of knowledge of British colonial history, but also from the need for Indigenous nations that were seeking to have their rights recognized to highlight all the historical events that recognized their special status within the colonial empires. In this regard, the Royal Proclamation of 1763, which emanated from the highest political authority, appears as one of the most explicit forms of recognition. Not only did this proclamation create an immense territory reserved for the Indians, but it also acknowledged, at least in its most widespread interpretation, the existence of their territorial rights and fixed the golden rule that must be followed to dispossess them of their land: the establishment of treaties.

In contrast, the Quebec Act of 1774 occupies a marginal position in the debates for the recognition of the rights of the Indigenous peoples of Canada. Unlike the Royal Proclamation, the Quebec Act never stood as a symbol of the British's "generous" Indian policy, instead arousing, since the nineteenth century, a certain unease in this regard. This is firstly due to the fact that this constitutional document, which considerably expands the boundaries of the Province of Quebec, seems to completely abandon the Indigenous issue, never even mentioning the word "Indians." Worse, and this is the main source of embarrassment generated by this document since the nineteenth century, the Quebec Act also repealed the proclamation within the new Province of Quebec.

Given these circumstances, it is easy to understand why the Quebec Act never became essential in the legal and political imagination as a significant landmark in the evolution of Indigenous rights. Rather it figures as an obstacle. It is a document that we would prefer to quickly put aside as a piece of legislation, one that had no great significance or impact in the chain of events that mark the history of Indigenous rights in Canada. Since the end of the nineteenth century, Canadian jurisprudence has indeed developed the thesis that the rights created by the Proclamation of 1763 had survived the abolition of the document that created them in the first place.

Two main arguments have been cited to support this thesis. The first concerns the context and intentions of the British: as the adoption of the Quebec Act had nothing to do with Indigenous issues, the abolition of the Royal Proclamation could not result in the dissolution of rights that would have been created in 1763. The second argument refers to a passage in the Quebec Act, which specifies that nothing in this document could nullify or modify rights to the land, regardless of how these rights had been acquired. Even if Indigenous territorial rights were not mentioned specifically in this passage, it is nevertheless considered sufficiently broad and encompassing to include them.[4]

In recent years, however, a breach opened in the legal reasoning that had been developed since the nineteenth century on this issue. This breach does not affect the rights created by the Royal Proclamation, but the process by which those rights can be extinguished, attacking what is considered to be the only valid rule to achieving this end, namely the signing of a treaty. This position, developed for the first time by the Court of Appeal for Ontario in the decision regarding Bear Island (1989),[5] argues that the Quebec Act did not extinguish the rights created by the proclamation, but removed one of the obligations contained in this document, namely the need to conclude a treaty with Natives before taking possession of their land – and thus opens the door to other methods of eliminating those rights. This idea was reflected in another recent decision of the Court of Appeal for Ontario, but the Supreme Court of Canada has not yet ruled directly on this interpretation, although it did so indirectly by refusing to hear the first case on appeal.

Even if it has not been a fundamental issue in the debates in the past years regarding Indigenous rights to their land, the effects of the Quebec Act are not negligible. Only the future will tell us which legal interpretation will eventually prevail in this regard. However, for now, a possible legal interpretation is that, after the adoption of the Quebec Act, the colonial government was no longer required to conclude treaties with the Indigenous peoples for their land. Rights did not disappear with the Quebec Act, but the means to abolish them would be diversified and their validity would no longer rely on the single mechanism: the treaty system.

This legal background set the stage for this article. However, my intention is not to resolve the issue or to argue whether the Quebec Act did or did not result in loss of rights or in the abolition of the obligation to make treaties with the Native peoples. My approach is essentially historical: it is to grasp the scope of this document in the history of the relations between the British and Indigenous peoples, specifically through the issue of land, one of the most fundamental issues in the second half of the eighteenth century. Does the Quebec Act mark a significant change in British policy towards Indigenous lands? Should we read this document as the expression of the will of British authorities to substantially amend the policy set out in the Royal Proclamation of 1763? Would it be possible that the Quebec Act, despite appearances, is actually an expression of continuity in this respect?

A TURNING POINT IN THE BRITISH INDIAN POLICY

We cannot grasp the historic scope of the Quebec Act in relation to Indigenous peoples without turning to the transformations that marked the Indian policy of the British in the second half of the eighteenth century. Those transformations would lead to the publication of the Royal Proclamation in October 1763, a few months after the signing of the Treaty of Paris.

In the Context of a Rivalry with France

In the aftermath of the War of Austrian Succession (1744–48), the Indigenous issue took on a truly significant role in Great Britain's imperial strategies in North America. The rivalry with France and, above all, the superiority with which the French had established numerous alliances with Indigenous people, played an important role in the process leading to the revision of the British Indian policy.[6] In the eyes of the British, many factors contributed to the superiority of the French Indian policy. The centralized administration of Indian affairs in New France, as opposed to extreme decentralization in the Thirteen Colonies, and the trading practices of the French, who appear less affected by irregularities than the British, were among the key elements contributing to this superiority. But the land was certainly also one of the main issues explaining the failure of the British to develop, as the French did, a huge network of Native allies. The demographic weakness of the French in North America was their main asset in relations with the Indigenous peoples. As they were few and concentrated in the St Lawrence Valley, their colonial policy was not territorially threatening. In contrast, the British, whose colonies had experienced very rapid population growth since the seventeenth century, had a voracious appetite for Indigenous lands.

The Provisions of the Royal Proclamation

After the signing of the Treaty of Paris in February 1763, the issue of relations with the Indigenous nations still appeared as an important element of the program that the British government envisioned for administering the huge territories ceded by France. And the three elements mentioned above – centralization of the administration of Indian Affairs, trade regulation, and control of territorial expansion – continued to structure the way the Indigenous question was approached. At this time, these reflections were part of a plan to manage an empire that had greatly expanded and from which strong autonomist feelings that threatened to undermine British control in North America had begun to emerge.

These concerns are reflected in preliminary reports prepared in the months following the signing of the Treaty of Paris, and their main recommendations concerning the Native peoples would appear in the Royal Proclamation of 7 October 1763.[7] The creation of a huge territory reserved for Indigenous peoples was certainly the most dramatic measure of this proclamation. This territory included all land lying west of the headwaters of the rivers flowing into the Atlantic ocean (in general, beyond the line formed by the Appalachian mountains), outside the boundaries of the three new provinces created by the royal proclamation (Quebec and the two Floridas) and outside the lands belonging to the Hudson's Bay Company (see figure 10.1). Land grants on the reserved territory could not be made without the king's consent.

In the old colonies, the royal proclamation also explicitly prohibited, without the prior permission of the king, the granting of land that, having not been surrendered to the crown, was considered as reserved for Indigenous peoples. Purchases of those lands by individuals were illegal; the only lawful way to acquire them was to reach treaties on behalf of the British crown, and these treaties had to be ratified by the chiefs of the Indigenous nations concerned.

THE QUEBEC ACT

Eleven years after the publication of this proclamation, the British parliament apparently chose to change this policy radically with the adoption of the Quebec Act, which expanded the borders of the Province of Quebec to include much of the Indian territory (see figure 10.2) and abolished the Royal Proclamation.[8] Is this new piece of legislation really a turning point in the British policy regarding indigenous land? I will try to answer this question by considering three things: the silence of the Quebec Act on Indigenous issues; the disappearance of the reserved territory, due to the expansion of the borders of the Province of Quebec; and the question of the methods of acquiring Indigenous land.

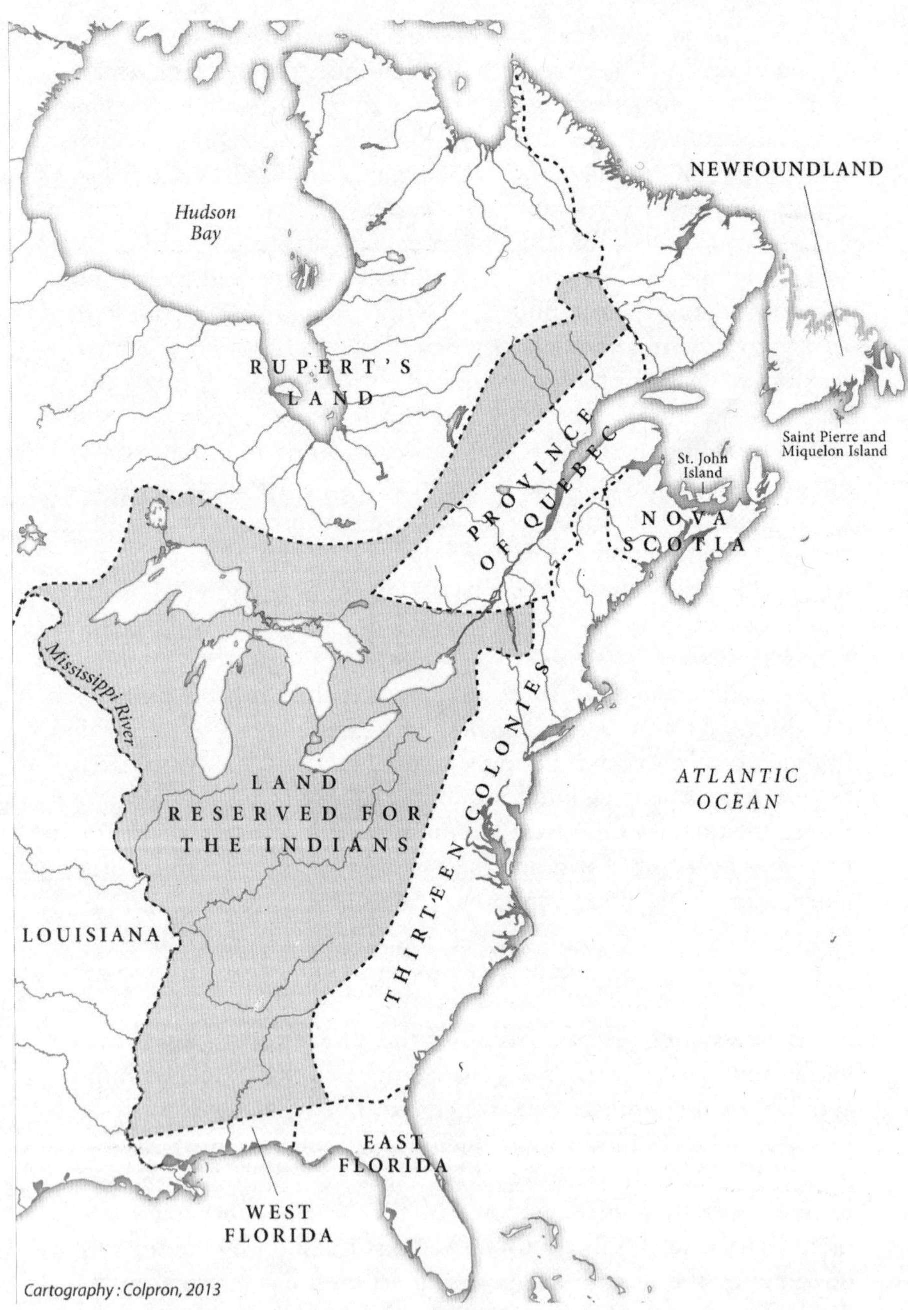

10.1 The Royal Proclamation of 1763

A Telling Silence?

What should we think of the silence on Indigenous issues in the Quebec Act? Should we see it as a sign that the policy of 1763 was abandoned? We know that the decision to expand the boundaries of the colony of Quebec had an Indigenous component. One of the goals behind this border expansion was to establish a system of uniform regulations for trade with Indigenous peoples on the territory of 1763. This problem had remained unsolved since the Conquest, mainly as a result of London's refusal to invest the necessary sums to maintain large garrisons in the hinterland, but also because the colonies refused to help finance these garrisons and were unable – or unwilling – to define uniform rules for this trade, despite the requests from London. By placing this immense territory under the control of a single governor, that of Quebec, London hoped to settle this problem.[9]

Why then the silence of the Quebec Act on Indians? Part of the answer to this question, if not the fundamental one, lies in another question concerning the Royal Proclamation. Why was the Indigenous issue so extensively addressed in this first constitutional document in the history of Canada? The Quebec Act's silence seems amazing only in contrast to the "noisy" nature of the Royal Proclamation on this subject. The other constitutional documents that punctuate the history of Canadian political life before the Constitution Act of 1867, which created Canada, were actually as silent on Indigenous issues as the Quebec Act of 1774.

The circumstances that led to the publication of the Royal Proclamation of 1763 highlight the exceptional nature of the provisions concerning Indigenous peoples in this document. In the first months following the signing of the Treaty of Paris, the British government had no intention of implementing this new Indian policy through such a document, but rather by means of a more modest instrument, namely the Instructions to Governors of the various colonies. It was an unexpected event, a great Indigenous uprising in the Great Lakes region and the Ohio Valley – "Pontiac's War" – which ultimately led the British government to change its strategy and to use a more meaningful public document to appease the nations of the continental interior. Somehow, the proclamation was a historical accident, the emergency response to a problematical situation, not the result of a "normal" political decision or process.[10]

This fortuitous dimension must be kept in mind when comparing the Quebec Act. It certainly puts into perspective the difference between a constitutional document like the Quebec Act – silent on Indigenous issues – and its predecessor. Actually, the silence of the Quebec Act had no particular significance with regard to the Indian policy of the British. At that time they were not using a legislative document to set out the guidelines for their Indian policy, but rather – as planned in 1763 – the Instructions to Governors.

Disappearance of the Reserved Territory

If the silence of the Quebec Act regarding Indians had no particular meaning, can the same be said of the expansion of borders, which apparently led to the abolition of a large part of the territory reserved for the Indians? On a map, the consequences of the Quebec Act seemed indeed to have been important: an immense area, once set aside for the Natives, had apparently become open to colonization (see figure 10.2). This impression, however, does not match reality. The line drawn in 1763 was actually much more flexible than one might think. The formulation of the proclamation reminds us that the creation of this reserve territory was temporary – the line was drawn "for the present" – and that it was designed to be moved and eventually to disappear.

Of course, the intention of the British authorities in the first years following the publication of the Royal Proclamation was to maintain this line, but their will was strongly opposed from the outset. On paper, the 1763 plan looked very consistent: to decrease tensions with Indigenous peoples, a huge area was temporarily closed to colonization and the settlers were encouraged to establish themselves in regions that the British authorities had decided to open to settlement (Quebec, Nova Scotia, and the two Floridas). The main weakness of this plan, however, was the idea that the colonists would comply voluntarily, out of deference, with the royal directives, and that the British government would not have to invest heavily to ensure its implementation.

The idea of closing the West to settlement would not resist very long the many pressures to open these lands for settlement. The Royal Proclamation directly opposed the eastern colonies' drive to continue their expansion towards the interior of the continent. It did not put

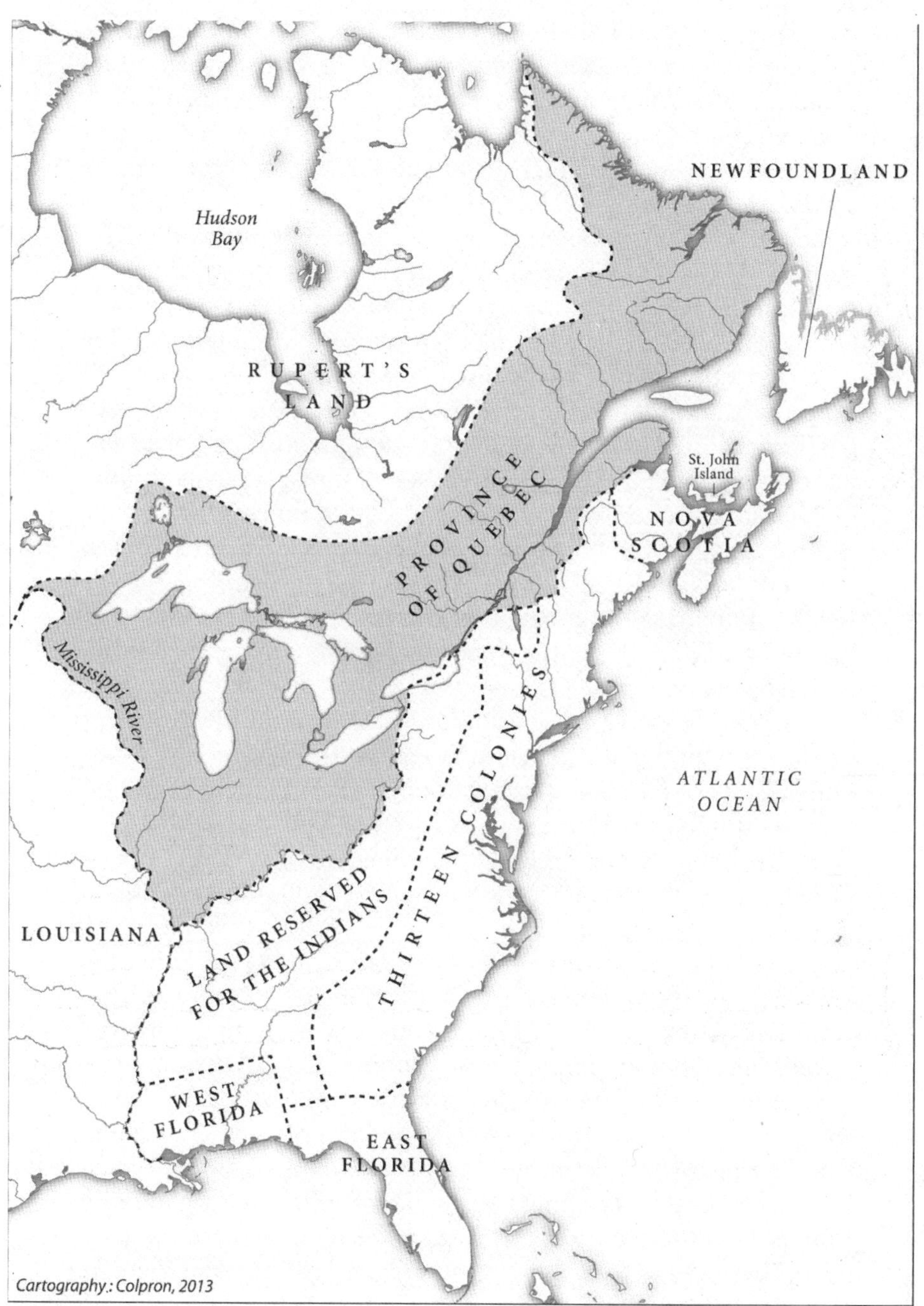

NEWFOUNDLAND
Hudson Bay
RUPERT'S LAND
PROVINCE OF QUEBEC
St. John Island
NOVA SCOTIA
Mississippi River
THIRTEEN COLONIES
ATLANTIC OCEAN
LAND RESERVED FOR THE INDIANS
LOUISIANA
WEST FLORIDA
EAST FLORIDA
Cartography.: Colpron, 2013

10.2 The Quebec Act

an end to westward movement, which continued as if nothing had happened, and the limited interventions of the British troops to dislodge some squatters provided no tangible results.[11] For example, Commander-in-Chief Thomas Gage reported, in 1768, that squatters removed by the soldiers quickly returned to the spot, followed by several hundred more.[12]

Stopping or slowing down this expansionist movement would have meant a considerable financial and military investment, which the British authorities did not want to make. From their perspective, closing the lands of the West to colonization would facilitate the management of the empire. It would reduce administration costs by limiting the sources of tensions with the Natives and thus avoiding conflicts that would have to be suppressed by force. The line of 1763 was therefore not an end in itself, but a tool for improving the governance of the interior, without incurring significant costs.

What followed was predictable: unable to block access to the western lands and to suppress illegal installations, the British authorities finally approved the negotiation of treaties to open a portion of the land reserved in 1763, thereby standardizing a movement that became impossible to suppress.[13] The opening of these new territories made it possible to preserve the illusion of British control by formalizing previously prohibited settlements. To the north, this led to the signing of the Treaty of Fort Stanwix in 1768, by which the British obtained from the Iroquois the surrender of a huge territory stretching up to Ohio. This river became the new line that separated the territories open to colonization from those reserved for Indigenous peoples.[14]

In the years preceding the Quebec Act, the British government had therefore not given up the idea of a boundary dividing the Indigenous peoples from the colonial world, but had begun to move the line, placing it in areas where this project was not as strongly contested, rather than engaging in a process to enforce what had been charted in 1763. And somehow, the line drawn in 1763 no longer existed at the end of the 1760s – or existed only in the form of fragments in areas that were not yet really threatened by colonial expansion. Elsewhere, it had been largely redesigned by a series of treaties with Indigenous nations. It was also no coincidence that the new southern boundary of the Province of Quebec of 1774 was located in Ohio, the new limit negotiated at the Treaty of Fort Stanwix.

The disappearance of the territory that had been reserved under the Royal Proclamation was therefore widely achieved at the time of the adoption of the Quebec Act, but the idea of a line of demarcation between two worlds – the Indigenous and the colonial – was still alive in 1774. The instructions given the following year to the governor of the enlarged Province of Quebec were a good indication of this: Carleton was told not to allow settlers to establish themselves in areas that the British authorities had not yet decided to open to colonization.[15] In a less dramatic form, the Quebec Act continued, by means of instructions to the governor of the colony, the policy that had given rise to the Royal Proclamation, a policy which sought to contain and control colonial expansion by delineating areas open to colonization and others reserved for Indigenous peoples. The use of the Instructions to the Governors was, it should be remembered, the measure that had been scheduled in 1763, before the news of the great Indian uprising – "Pontiac's War" – arrived in London.

An Obligation That Disappears?

From the preceding, we can conclude that the silence of the Quebec Act regarding Indigenous issues was not of particular significance and that the extension of the boundaries of the province of Quebec was not intended to introduce a break in British Indian policy. It would be surprising, in the circumstances, if the abolition of the Royal Proclamation by the Quebec Act indicated a desire to get rid of the treaty system used since the seventeenth century to acquire Indigenous lands.

To my knowledge, there is no indication in the documents of this period of a desire on the part of the British authorities to use the Quebec Act to eliminate the treaty system. In the discussions leading to the adoption of this law, emphasis was never placed on that provision of the Royal Proclamation relating to the obligation to make treaties with the Native peoples. There again, the instructions given in 1775 to Governor Carleton showed instead the continuity in British designs on this subject. In his relations with Indigenous peoples, Carleton indeed had to be guided by a plan prepared in 1764 for the administration of Indian Affairs, a plan which, although it had never been officially adopted, contained a series of directives that directly prolonged the guidelines set out in the Royal Proclamation, including those concerning the acquisition of Indian lands.[16]

It should also be kept in mind that, in the second half of the eighteenth century, the treaty system had an important role to play in the assertion of British sovereignty. The "treaty provisions" of the Royal Proclamation were part of a prohibition on individuals directly purchasing Indian lands, a point that we do not always stress enough. The treaties with the Indians, negotiated only by the crown agents, also served to defend the king's prerogative to purchase Indigenous lands. It was an important issue at the time and the subject of protests by some land speculators who sometimes tried to justify their attempts to purchase Indian land by invoking the political status of the Indigenous peoples. As independent nations, they argued, Indigenous peoples had the right to sell their land without government intervention. The obligation imposed by the crown to acquire land by treaties, then, was not only the result of a willingness to respect the Indigenous peoples' rights, but also the necessary means, in certain regions, to assert the king's sovereignty.

On this point, therefore, the Quebec Act cannot be interpreted as a change in British policy to break free from a binding rule that the king had imposed on himself in 1763. That being said, an important question remains: if the Quebec Act does not alter the policy on the acquisition of Indian lands, does that mean that the British were then necessarily faced with only one system, that of the treaties, which was established by the Royal Proclamation?

The easiest (and the most typical) way to consider this question is to see the proclamation as the result of a decision to institute a general and uniform policy regarding the acquisition of Indigenous lands. From this perspective, after 1763, all the Indigenous peoples of the North American British Empire had the same rights over their lands, and it was imperative, before opening them to colonization, to get the surrender of those Indigenous rights through a treaty. This view, widespread in legal circles, conceals some ambivalence in British politics. I would like to point out here very quickly a few of the particularly significant examples.

The first example of the ambiguity of British policy towards Indigenous lands is the case of Nova Scotia. In 1763, this "province" would have been considered an "old colony," since its takeover dates back to the Treaty of Utrecht of 1713, by which France ceded Acadia to England. If the logic set out in the Royal Proclamation of 1763 was followed, all Indigenous lands in Nova Scotia would have fallen into the category of land that, never having been ceded to the British crown, should have been purchased by a treaty before being made available for settlement. Yet the guidelines of the Royal Proclamation were never adopted there, and no land-cession treaties have ever been negotiated with the Mi'kmaq. The British decision not to move in this direction, then, dates back to the first half of the eighteenth century and was based mainly on the idea that, by the Treaty of Utrecht, the King of Great Britain had acquired all rights to this land, making it unnecessary to negotiate with Indigenous peoples. Here, in the spirit of the British authorities, the Royal Proclamation did not apply, as the Indigenous lands did not fall within the category of reserved lands.[17]

The second example is provided by the Royal Proclamation itself, which suggests an ambiguity regarding the policy to be followed with respect to Indigenous lands. It placed, or seemed to place, the former British colonies – that is, those existing prior to 1763 – on different footing than those created in 1763, including the Province of Quebec. While the proclamation specified that there should not be any concessions on the lands reserved for Indigenous peoples in the former colonies – which seems to correspond to all the land that had not yet been subjected to a formal cession by the Indians – the same document made no such provision for the new colonies (Quebec and the Floridas), as if they were not covered by this rule and there was no land reserved for Indigenous peoples within these colonies.

There is a long legal-historical controversy about this passage of the proclamation, some seeing the ambiguity as essentially a drafting problem and not the result of a desire to establish a very clear distinction between the old and the new colonies.[18] I have no intention or pretention to decide the issue here, but I would seriously consider the possibility of such a distinction, which may well reflect the continuation of the logic at work in Nova Scotia. Indeed, the terms of the Treaty of Paris regarding the surrender of territory between France and Great Britain are not fundamentally different from those of the Treaty of Utrecht, and it is possible that the same ideas came to play in the organization of new possessions acquired in 1763. In this perspective, it is conceivable that the British considered the lands ceded by Louis XV as lands belonging by right of conquest to the king of Great Britain and that, as in Nova Scotia, they did not need to be formally surrendered by the Native inhabitants before they were opened to settlement. Although it is not possible to formally demonstrate this hypothesis, it would give meaning to the distinction made in the proclamation between former British colonies – where Indigenous rights were to be extinguished – and the new provinces – where all rights to the land would have been obtained from another European power.

To underscore the ambivalence of British policy, I will briefly mention a last example, that of the 1768 Treaty of Fort Stanwix, which was mentioned above. In principle, this treaty seemed to fit perfectly into the logic of the Royal Proclamation, recognizing the rights of Indigenous peoples on their lands, rights that had to be surrendered before their settlement. But this treaty was also based on a fiction, since it was the Iroquois who ceded the lands to the British, lands that they did not occupy – they were actually owned by other nations – but that they had "conquered" in the seventeenth century. In this example, the fiction that legitimized the sale, even if the actors were also Indigenous, is not fundamentally different from that which was at work in the Treaty of Utrecht or the Treaty of Paris. The British negotiated not with those who actually owned the land, but with those who claimed to have rights on the land, validating by a treaty of cession a legal fiction that was very useful.

These examples illustrate well the ambivalence of the British territorial policy. They confirm that the historical analysis of this policy must also be informed by other legal concepts than those contained in the Royal Proclamation. In particular, these examples help to avoid the crystallization of an image of uniformity in Great Britain's legal conceptions concerning Indigenous land rights in the eighteenth century, when diversity was indeed well represented, both before and after the Royal Proclamation, as well as before and after the Quebec Act.

CONCLUSION

In short, the Quebec Act fit into a continuity and was not at odds with the Royal Proclamation, but it was also in continuity with the ambivalence of British policy towards Indigenous land. This ambivalence would manifest itself in two different acquisition policies around Indigenous lands in Canada: one built on the treaty system in what became the province of Ontario; the other built on unilateral appropriation, without land surrenders, in Quebec and the Maritime provinces. At Canadian Confederation in 1867, the treaty system did not yet figure as the standard, but rather as the exception, since it had been implemented in a single province, Ontario. It is only with the opening of the West that this system would be generalized and become the model to follow (or that should have been followed).

The ambivalence of British policy is particularly revealing of the colonial logic at work in this process. In other circumstances and for other subjects, historians would undoubtedly prefer to stress this logic, because it is an integral part of their critical approach. However, in the Canadian legal and political context, this ambivalence raises some discomfort. Indeed, by a strange paradox, highlighting the colonial character of British politics is also to attack some of the basics of jurisprudence relating to the rights of Indigenous peoples and to question specific certainties that are the basis of the recognition of specific rights for the First Nations.

NOTES

1 Article 25 provides that the Charter of Rights and Freedoms does not infringe on treaty rights or on those recognized by the Royal Proclamation; Article 35 protects the existing and treaty rights. Renée Dupuis, *Le statut juridique des peuples autochtones en droit canadien* (Scarborough, ON: Carswell, 1999), 107–9; Sébastien Grammond, *Terms of Coexistence: Indigenous Peoples and Canadian Law* (Scarborough, ON: Carswell, 2013), 128 – 31.

2 On the evolution of Canadian jurisprudence on Indigenous rights, see in particular: Grammond, *Terms of Coexistence*, and, in a larger perspective, extended to all of the former British colonies, Paul G. McHugh, *Aboriginal Title: The Modern Jurisprudence of Tribal Land Rights* (Oxford: Oxford University Press, 2011).

3 In the first half of the nineteenth century, a commission of inquiry created to investigate the administration of Indian Affairs in the United-Canada found that Indigenous people saw "this piece as their Charter" ("Rapport sur les Affaires des Sauvages en Canada, section[s] I et II, mis devant l'Assemblée legislative," 20 March 1845, in Canada, *Appendice du 4e volume des Journaux de l'Assemblée législative de la Province du Canada du 28 novembre 1844, au 29 mars 1845*. Sect. I: *Histoire des relations entre le gouvernement et les Sauvages* (Montréal, L. Perrault, 1845), np. In 1887, in St Catharine's Milling & Lumber Co. v. R (1887) 13 SCR 577, a judge of the Supreme Court of Canada described the proclamation as the "Indian Bill of Rights," a phrase that was repeated in 1973 by another judge of the Supreme Court in the Calder case (Dupuis, *Le statut juridique des peuples autochtones*, 112). The symbolic power of this docu-

ment has not diminished over the years, as evidenced by the proposal of the Royal Commission on Aboriginal Peoples in its final report in 1996 to publish a new Royal Proclamation to establish relations with Indigenous nations on new, stronger, and more respectful bases (*Rapport de la Commission royale sur les peuples autochtones*, Ottawa, Commission royale sur les peuples autochtones, 1996, vol. 5:5).

4 Dupuis, *Le statut juridique des peuples autochtones*, 15, 26; Michel Morin, *L'usurpation de la souveraineté autochtone: Le cas des peuples de la Nouvelle-France et des colonies anglaises de l'Amérique du Nord* (Montreal, Boréal, 1997), 330, n240.

5 *Ontario (Attorney-General) vs. Bear Island Foundation* (1989) 58 DLR (4th) 117, 133–4. For a critical perspective, see Kent McNeil, "The High Cost of Accepting Benefits from the Crown: A Comment on the Temagami Indian Land Case," *Canadian Native Law Reporter* 1 (1992): 40–69; Tony Hall, "Where Justice Lies: Aboriginal Rights and Wrongs in Temagami," in *Temagami: A Debate on Wilderness*, ed. Matthew Bray and Ashley Thomson, 223–55 (Toronto, Dundurn Group, 1996).

6 For the context of this revision of the British Indian policy, see John R. Alden, "The Albany Congress and the Creation of the Indian Superintendencies," *Mississippi Valley Historical Review* 27 (1940): 193–210; Jack M. Sosin, *Whitehall and the Wilderness: The Middle West in British Colonial Policy, 1760–1775* (Lincoln: University of Nebraska Press, 1961), 3–78; Timothy J. Shannon, *Indians and Colonists at the Crossroads of Empire. The Albany Congress of 1754* (Ithaca: Cornell University Press, 2000), 67–76.

7 Some of the preliminary reports are published in Adam Shortt and Arthur G. Doughty, eds, *Documents Relating to the Constitutional History of Canada, 1759–1791* (Ottawa: J. de L. Taché, 1918) ("Papers Relating to the Establishment of Civil Government in the Territories Ceded to Britain by the Treaty of 1763," Part I, 127–63; the Royal Proclamation is also published in this book [163–8]).

8 The *Quebec Act* is also published by Shortt and Doughty (ibid., 570–6)

9 On the role played by the Indigenous issue in the factors leading to the extension of the borders of the colony of Quebec, see: Sosin, *Whitehall and the Wilderness*, 211–50; Thomas Elliot Norton, *The Fur Trade in Colonial New York, 1686–1776* (Madison: University of Wisconsin Press, 1974), 209–20; Murray G. Lawson, *Fur: A Study in English Mercantilism, 1700–1775* (Toronto: University of Toronto Press, 1943), 42–64.

10 On the original intentions of the British authorities and their decision to publicize their Indian policy in a Royal Proclamation, see The Lords

of the Board of Trade to Egremont, Whitehall, 5 August 1763; Shortt and Doughty, eds, *Documents Relating*, Part I, 125–6; Halifax to the Lords of the Board of Trade, 19 September 1763, ibid., 154. There are many studies on the "War of Pontiac." The most interesting is certainly that by Gregory Evans Dowd, *War under Heaven: Pontiac, the Indian Nations, and the British Empire* (Baltimore: Johns Hopkins University Press, 2002).

11 On westward expansion and the failure of the British to stop it, see notably: Patrick Griffin, *American Leviathan: Empire, Nation, and Revolutionary Frontier* (New York: Hill and Wang, 2007), 46–71.

12 Ibid., 81–2.

13 On the evolution of British policy on this matter, see Peter Marshall, "Colonial Protest and Imperial Retrenchment: Indian Policy, 1764–1768," *Journal of American Studies* 5, no 1 (1971): 1–17; Dorothy V. Jones, *License for Empire: Colonialism by Treaty in Early America* (Chicago, University of Chicago Press, 1982), 92–100.

14 On the negotiation that led to the Fort Stanwix Treaty, see Jones, *License for Empire*; Peter Marshall, "Sir William Johnson and the Treaty of Fort Stanwix, 1768," *Journal of American Studies* 1, no. 2 (Oct. 1967): 149–79.

15 Instructions to Governor Carleton, 1775, in Shortt and Doughty, eds, *Documents Relating to the Constitutional History of Canada*, Part II, 607.

16 "Plan for Imperial Control of Indian Affairs, July 10, 1764," *Collections of the Illinois State Historical Library*, vol. 10, 273–9 (articles 41, 42, and 43).

17 I develop this point in another article: "The Acquisition of Aboriginal Land in Canada: The Genealogy of an Ambivalent System (1600–1867)," in *Empire by Treaty: The History of Treaty-making in the Appropriation of Indigenous Lands*, ed. Saliha Belmessous, 101–31 (London: Oxford University Press, 2014).

18 For an overview of the different points of view on this issue, see: Brian Slattery, *The Land Rights of Indigenous Canadian Peoples as Affected by the Crown's Acquisition of the Territories* (PhD diss., Oxford University, 1979); Jacqueline Beaulieu, Christiane Cantin, and Maurice Ratelle, "La Proclamation royale de 1763: le droit refait l'histoire," *La revue du Barreau* 49, no. 3 (May–June 1989): 317–40; Paul Dionne, "Les postulats de la Commission Dorion et le titre aborigène au Québec: vingt ans après," *La revue du Barreau* 51, no. 1 (1991): 128–71; Richard Boivin, "Pour en finir avec la Proclamation royale : la décision *Côté*," *Revue générale de droit* 25, no. 1 (1994): 136–42; David Schulze, "The Privy Council Decision Concerning George Allsopp's Petition, 1767: An Imperial Precedent on the

Application of the Royal Proclamation to the Old Province of Quebec," *Canadian Native Law Reporter* 2 (1995): 1–46. For the land policy followed in the Province of Quebec after the Conquest, see also: Alain Beaulieu, "'An equitable right to be compensated': The Dispossession of the Aboriginal Peoples of Quebec and the Emergence of a New Legal Rationale, 1760–1860)," *Canadian Historical Review* 94, no. 1 (March 2013): 1–27.

Contributors

ALAIN BEAULIEU is professor of history at the Université du Québec at Montréal. His recent work has focused on the history of the relationship between Europeans and Indigenous peoples and the processes by which the latter were progressively dispossessed of their lands and placed under the tutelage of colonial governments.

CHRISTIAN BURSET is associate professor of law at the University of Notre Dame. His research focuses on the development of English and American legal institutions. His current book project, under contract with Yale University Press, explores debates in the eighteenth-century British Empire about what kinds of cases and litigants belonged in common-law courts.

LUCA CODIGNOLA, FRSC, is senior fellow of the Cushwa Center for the Study of American Catholicism of the University of Notre Dame and adjunct professor at the Department of History of Saint Mary's University. He is best known for his work on the Roman Catholic Church in the early-modern North Atlantic and has also written on the history of early European expansion in the Atlantic region. Among his latest books are *Le Saint-Siège, le Canada et le Québec* (2011), *Little Do We Know: History and Historians of the North Atlantic, 1492–2010* (2011), and *Blurred Nationalities Across the North Atlantic: Traders, Priests, and Their Kin Travelling Between North America and the Italian Peninsula, 1763–1846* (2019).

FRANÇOIS FURSTENBERG is professor of history at Johns Hopkins University, where he has taught since 2014. He previously taught at the Université de Montréal. His research focuses on early US history and the early-modern Atlantic World. He is the author of *In the Name of the Father: Washington's Legacy, Slavery, and the Making of a Nation* (2006) and *When the United States Spoke French: Five Refugees Who Shaped a Nation* (2014).

DONALD FYSON is professor of history at Université Laval (Quebec City). He specializes in the history of eighteenth-, nineteenth- and twentieth-century Quebec, notably its social, socio-legal, and socio-political aspects. He is particularly interested in the relationship between law, state, and society, notably as seen through the everyday operation of the criminal and civil justice systems. He has published extensively on the legal and social effects of the British Conquest of Quebec.

OLLIVIER HUBERT is professor of history at the Université de Montréal, specializing in Quebec and Canadian colonial history. He is also a researcher at the Centre interuniversitaire d'études québécoises and the Centre d'histoire des régulations sociales and a member of the French Atlantic History Group. Over the past twenty-five years, he has published research on religious history and the history of education. He now works on colonial violence and imperialist ideology in Canada.

BRAD A. JONES is professor of history at California State University, Fresno. His research interests centre on the impact of the American Revolution on the broader Atlantic world. His forthcoming book, *Resisting Independence: Popular Loyalism in the Revolutionary British Atlantic*, examines how the revolution forced a reimagining of British loyalism in communities across the North Atlantic. He has begun work on a new project that looks at American privateer attacks on the Caribbean slave trade during the War for Independence.

JEFFERS LENNOX is associate professor of history at Wesleyan University. His research and teaching focuses on Indigenous-settler relations in early North America, the American Revolution, and early Canada. He is the author of *Homelands and Empires: Indigenous Spaces,*

Imperial Fictions, and Competition for Territory in Northeastern North America, 1690–1763.

MICHEL MORIN is professor at the Faculty of Law of the Université de Montréal. His research focuses on the comparative legal history of public or private law and the evolution of the rights of Indigenous peoples. In 1998, the Humanities and Social Sciences Federation awarded him the Jean-Charles Falardeau Prize for his book *L'Usurpation de la souveraineté autochtone* (*The Usurpation of Aboriginal Sovereignty*) (1997). He has published, in French, an *Historical Introduction to Roman, French, and English Law* (2004) and, with Arnaud Decroix and David Gilles, *Courts and Arbitration in New France and Quebec, 1740–1784* (2012, Rodolphe-Fournier Prize, 2013).

HANNAH WEISS MULLER is associate professor of history at Brandeis University. Among her publications is *Subjects and Sovereign: Bonds of Belonging in the Eighteenth-Century British Empire* (2017). She is currently working on a comparative history of alien acts passed during the 1790s.

KRISTOFER RAY is Leverhulme Trust Lecturer in Indigenous America at the University of Hull and an affiliate of the Centre for Indigenous and Settler Colonial Studies, University of Kent. He is a student of the early-modern American Indian experience broadly, Indigenous-European interaction in trans-Appalachia specifically, and the European construction of Indigenous slave law. He is the author of *Cherokees, Europeans, and Empire in the Trans-Appalachian West, 1670–1774* (forthcoming), *Middle Tennessee, 1775–1825: Progress and Popular Democracy on the Southwestern Frontier* (2007), and "Constructing a Discourse of Indigenous Slavery, Freedom, and Sovereignty in Anglo-Virginia, 1600–1750," *Native South* 10 (2017).

AARON WILLIS is director of the Bannan Forum in the Ignatian Center for Jesuit Education at Santa Clara University. His research is focused on the history of ideas, politics, and religion, especially in the context of the British Atlantic world.

Index

Note: "The Act" refers to the Quebec Act (1774); and "the Proclamation" refers to the Royal Proclamation (1763). Page numbers with (f) refer to maps and illustrations, and pages with (t) refer to tables.